You may be reading the wrong way!

This book reads right to left to maintain the original presentation and art of the Japanese edition, so action, sound effects and word balloons are reversed. The diagram below shows how to follow the panels. Turn to the other side of the book to begin.

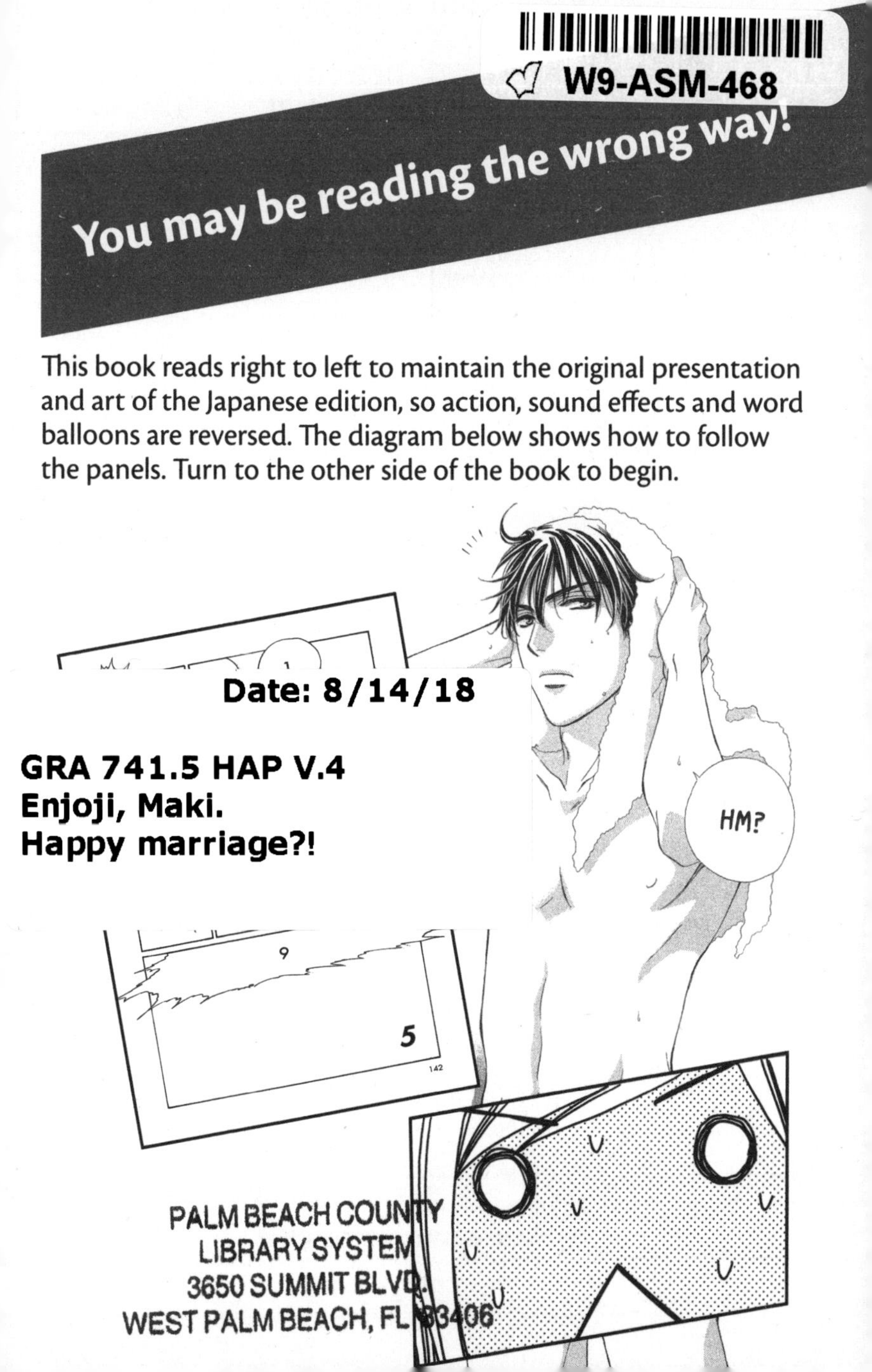
HM?
1
9
5
142

Happy Marriage?!

Volume 4
Shojo Beat Edition

Story and Art by
Maki Enjoji

HAPIMARI - HAPPY MARRIAGE!? - Vol. 4
by Maki ENJOJI
© 2009 Maki ENJOJI
All rights reserved.
Original Japanese edition published by SHOGAKUKAN.
English translation rights in the United States of America, Canada,
the United Kingdom and Ireland arranged with SHOGAKUKAN.

Translation/Tetsuichiro Miyaki
Adaptation/Nancy Thistlethwaite
Touch-up Art & Lettering/Inori Fukuda Trant
Design/Izumi Evers
Editor/Nancy Thistlethwaite

The stories, characters and incidents mentioned in this publication
are entirely fictional.

Printed in the U.S.A.

Published by VIZ Media, LLC
P.O. Box 77010
San Francisco, CA 94107

10 9 8 7 6 5 4 3 2 1
First printing, February 2014

www.viz.com   www.shojobeat.com

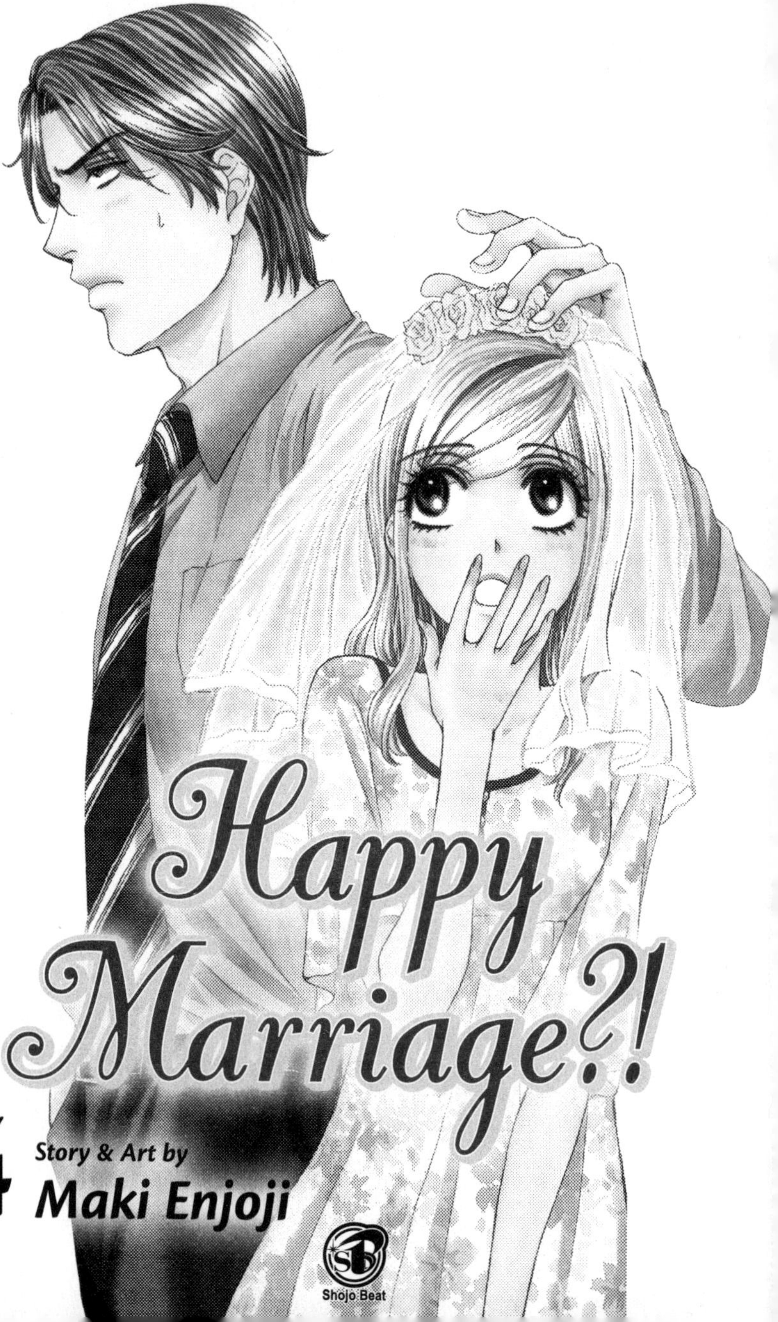

Happy Marriage?!

4

Story & Art by
Maki Enjoji

Shojo Beat

Happy Marriage?!

Characters

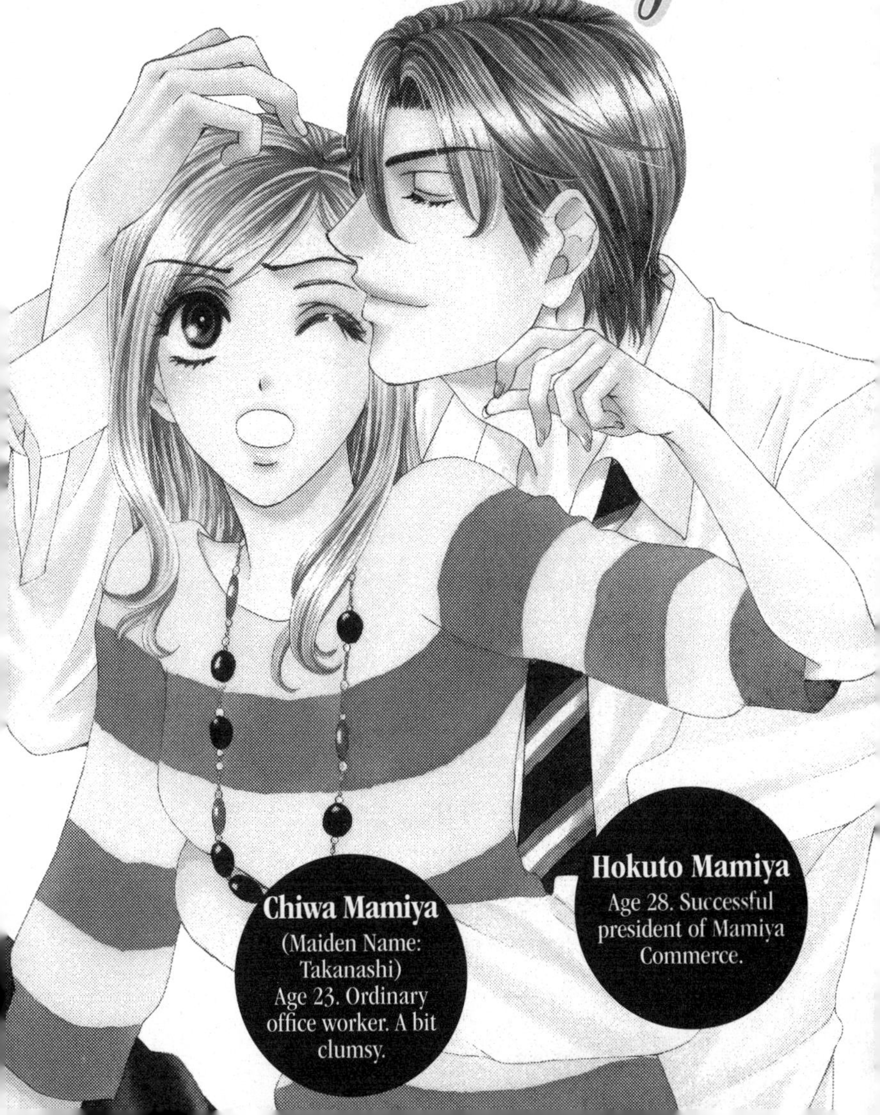
Hokuto Mamiya
Age 28. Successful president of Mamiya Commerce.
Chiwa Mamiya
(Maiden Name: Takanashi) Age 23. Ordinary office worker. A bit clumsy.

Taeko Soma

The president's personal assistant.
She looks young, but she's 55 years old.

Story

Chiwa Takanashi has no girlish fantasies about finding Prince Charming, and she wanted nothing but to lead a normal life until she found herself marrying company president Hokuto to pay off her father's debts. Though the marriage is in name only, Chiwa has fallen in love with her husband. Then she meets the other Mamiya family members. Hokuto warns her that they all hate him because he's an illegitimate child. Without thinking, Chiwa declares her love for Hokuto in front of them all...

Happy Marriage?!

Contents

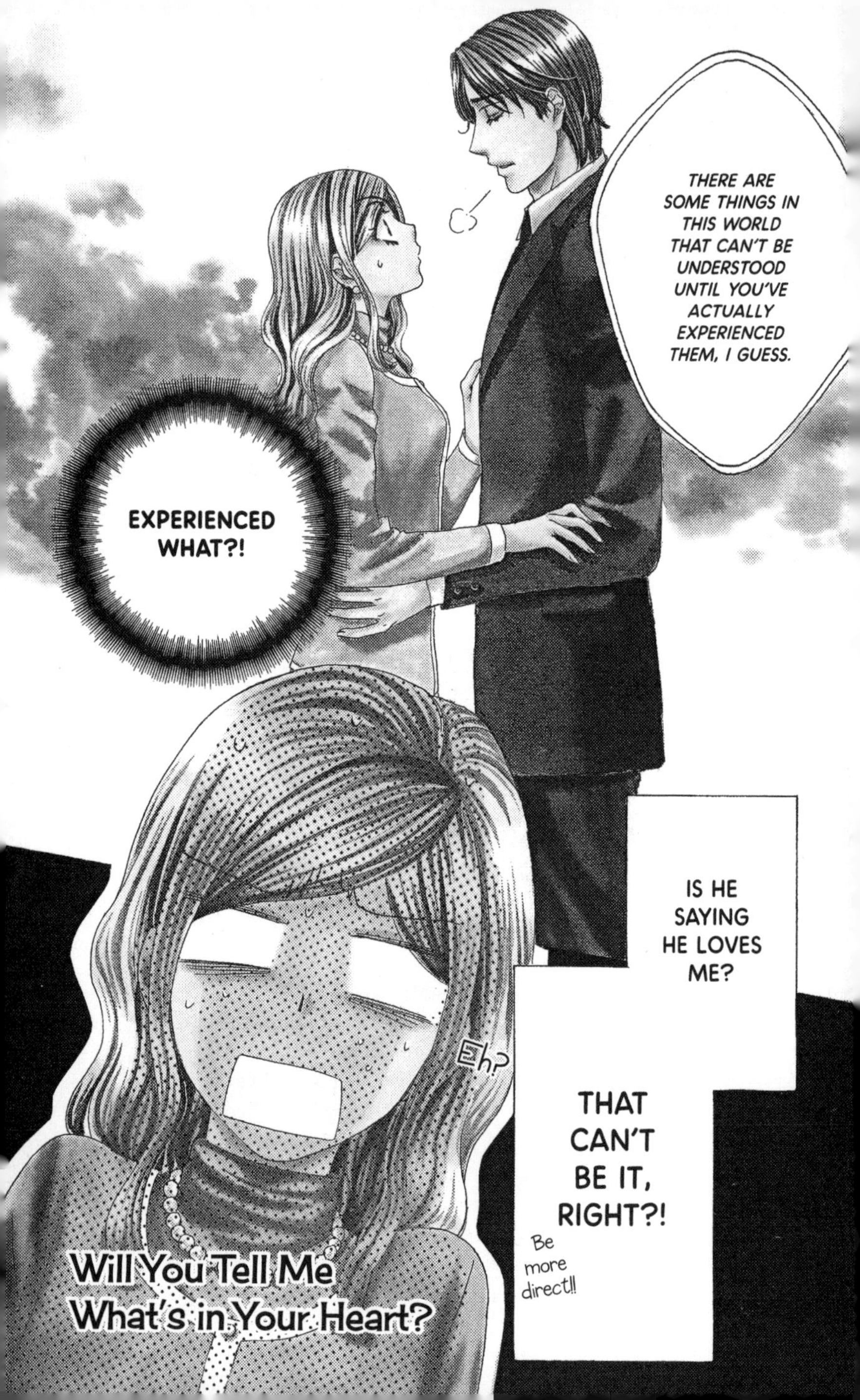
THERE ARE SOME THINGS IN THIS WORLD THAT CAN'T BE UNDERSTOOD UNTIL YOU'VE ACTUALLY EXPERIENCED THEM, I GUESS.
EXPERIENCED WHAT?!
IS HE SAYING HE LOVES ME?
Eh?
THAT CAN'T BE IT, RIGHT?!
Be more direct!!
Will You Tell Me What's in Your Heart?

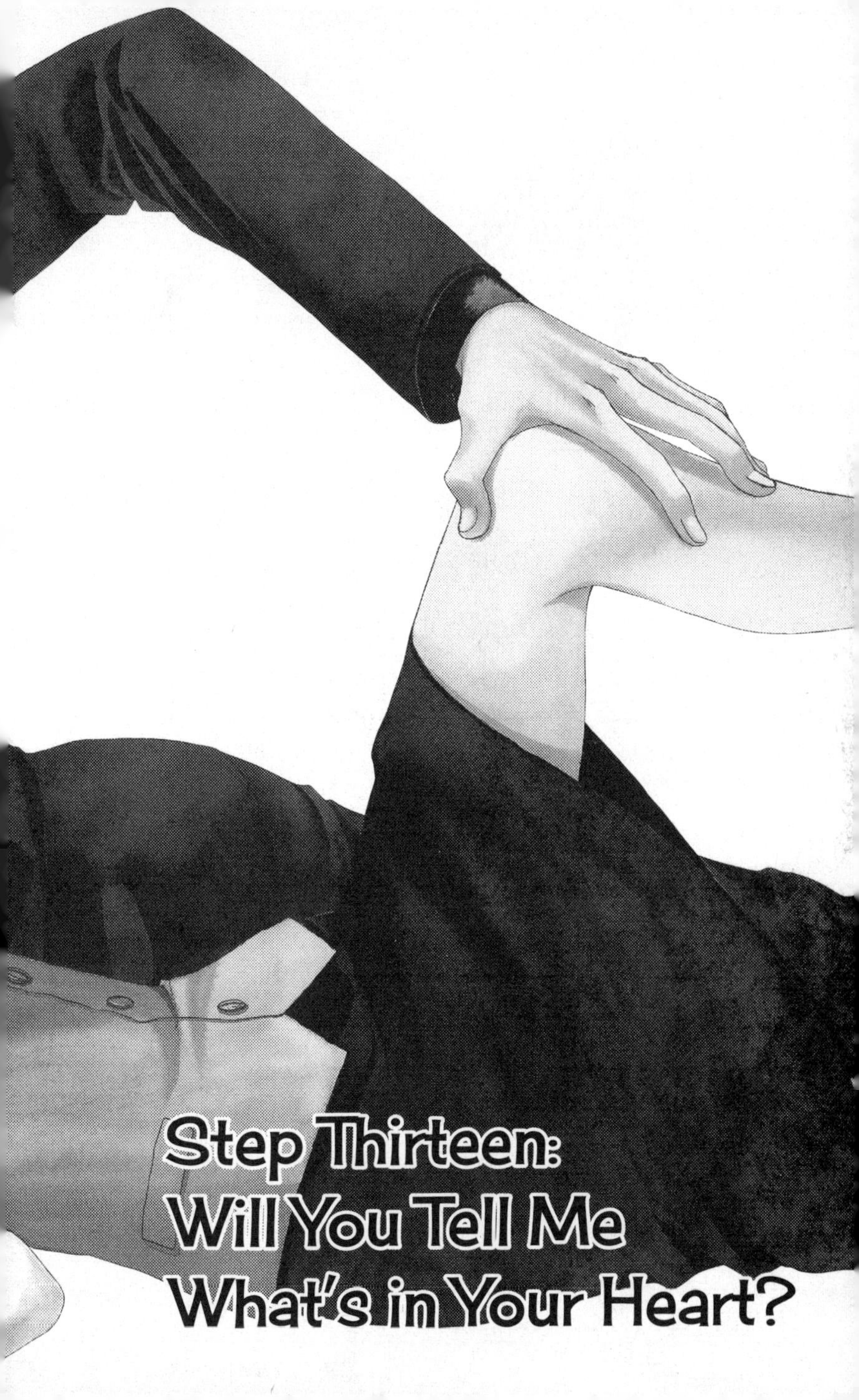
Step Thirteen:
Will You Tell Me
What's in Your Heart?

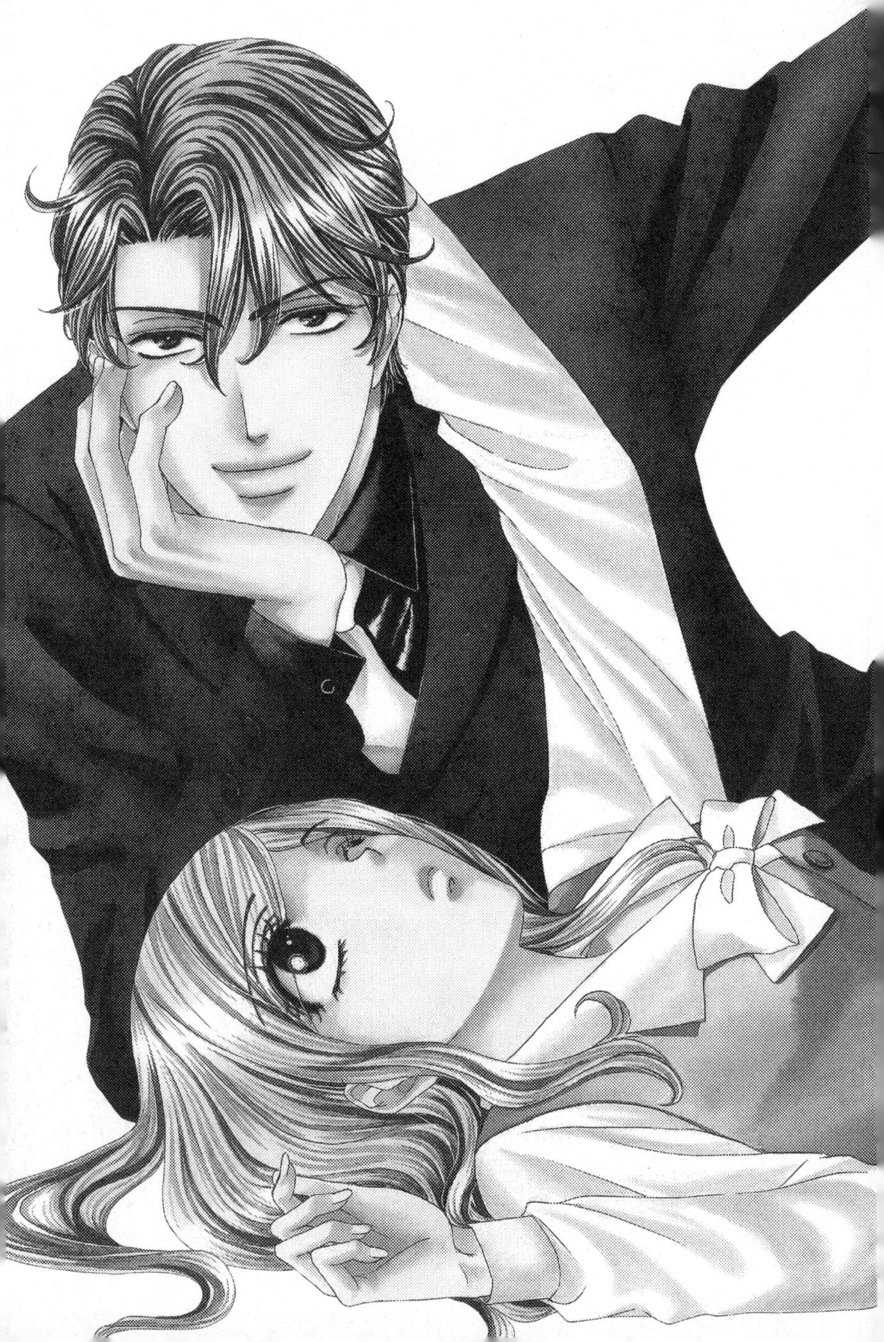

Hello!
We've finally reached volume 4! It's been a while since volume 3 came out, but it's not because I wasn't working... (sweat) By the way, this illustration ↓ was used to announce the first chapter of the series. It looks slightly different than the manga now, doesn't it? Chiwa and Hokuto haven't worn wedding attire in the story so far. I wonder if they'll ever get the chance to wear it?

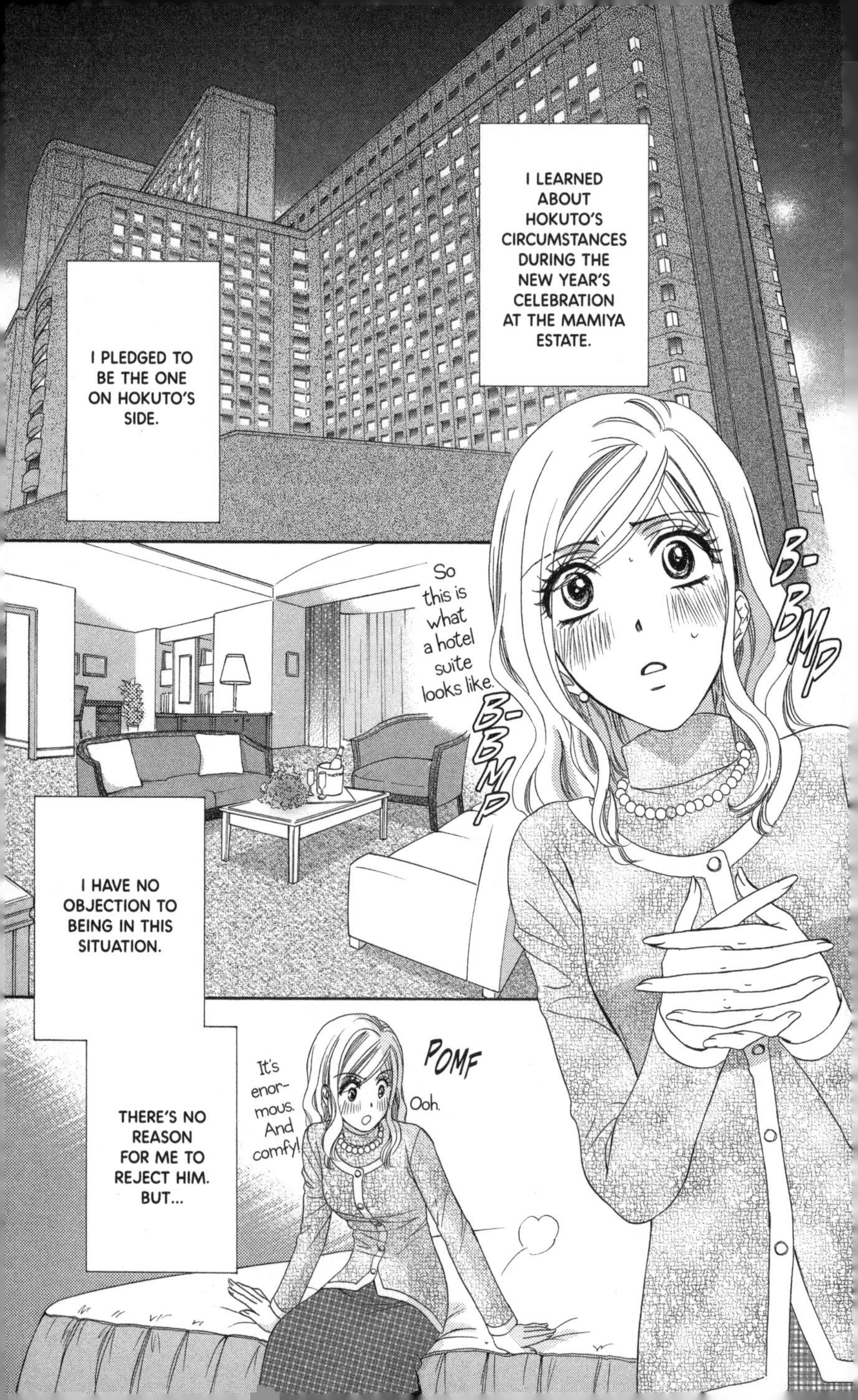
I LEARNED ABOUT HOKUTO'S CIRCUMSTANCES DURING THE NEW YEAR'S CELEBRATION AT THE MAMIYA ESTATE.
I PLEDGED TO BE THE ONE ON HOKUTO'S SIDE.
B-BMP
So this is what a hotel suite looks like.
B-BMP
I HAVE NO OBJECTION TO BEING IN THIS SITUATION.
POMF
Ooh.
It's enormous. And comfy!
THERE'S NO REASON FOR ME TO REJECT HIM. BUT...

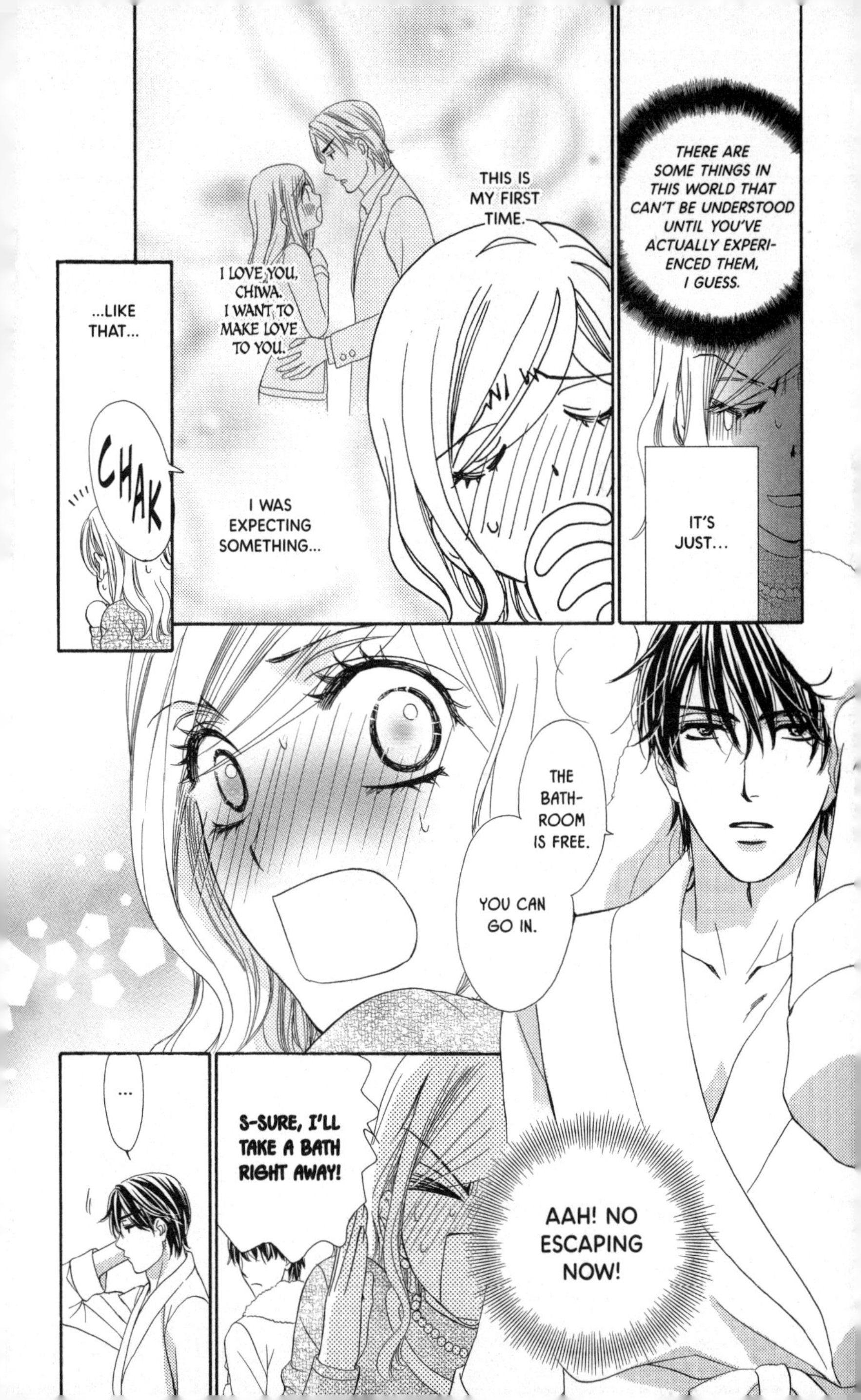
THERE ARE SOME THINGS IN THIS WORLD THAT CAN'T BE UNDERSTOOD UNTIL YOU'VE ACTUALLY EXPERI-ENCED THEM, I GUESS.
IT'S JUST...
THIS IS MY FIRST TIME.
I LOVE YOU, CHIWA. I WANT TO MAKE LOVE TO YOU.
I WAS EXPECTING SOMETHING...
...LIKE THAT...
CHAK
THE BATH-ROOM IS FREE.
YOU CAN GO IN.
AAH! NO ESCAPING NOW!
S-SURE, I'LL TAKE A BATH RIGHT AWAY!
...

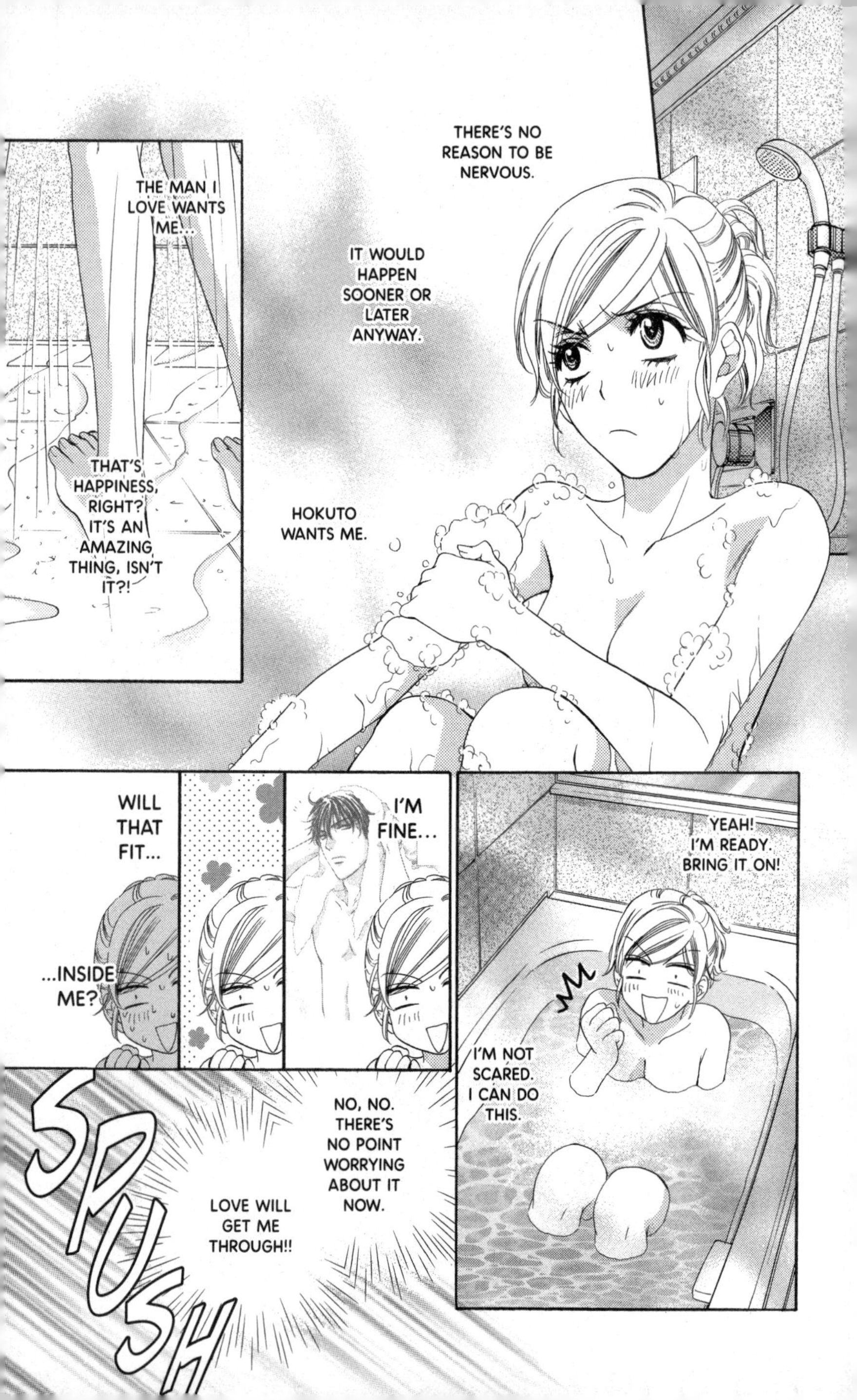
THERE'S NO REASON TO BE NERVOUS.
IT WOULD HAPPEN SOONER OR LATER ANYWAY.
HOKUTO WANTS ME.
THE MAN I LOVE WANTS ME...
THAT'S HAPPINESS, RIGHT? IT'S AN AMAZING THING, ISN'T IT?!
YEAH! I'M READY. BRING IT ON!
I'M NOT SCARED. I CAN DO THIS.
I'M FINE...
WILL THAT FIT...
...INSIDE ME?
NO, NO. THERE'S NO POINT WORRYING ABOUT IT NOW.
LOVE WILL GET ME THROUGH!!
SPUSH

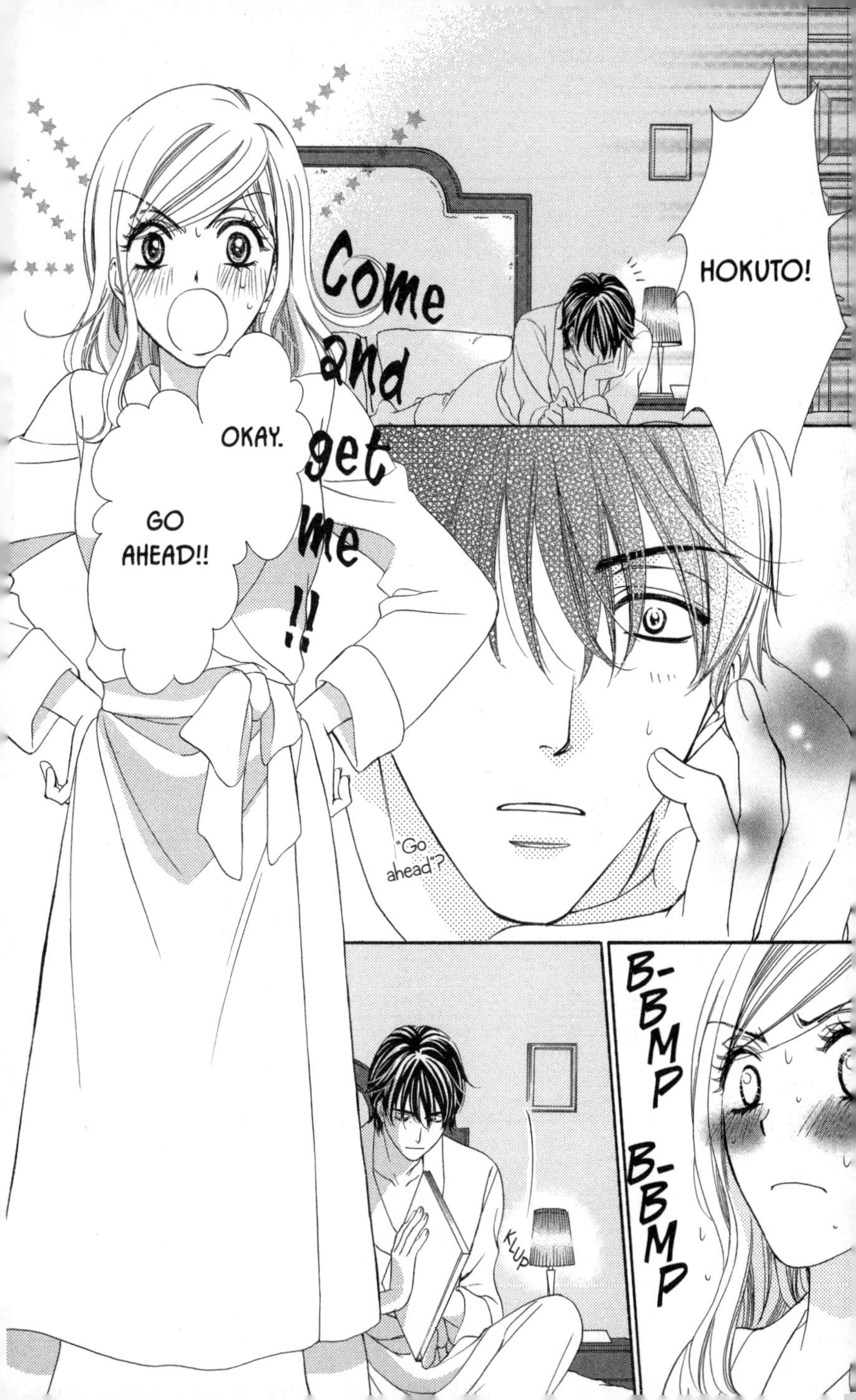
HOKUTO!
Come and get me!!
OKAY.
GO AHEAD!!
"Go ahead"?
B-BMP B-BMP
KLUP

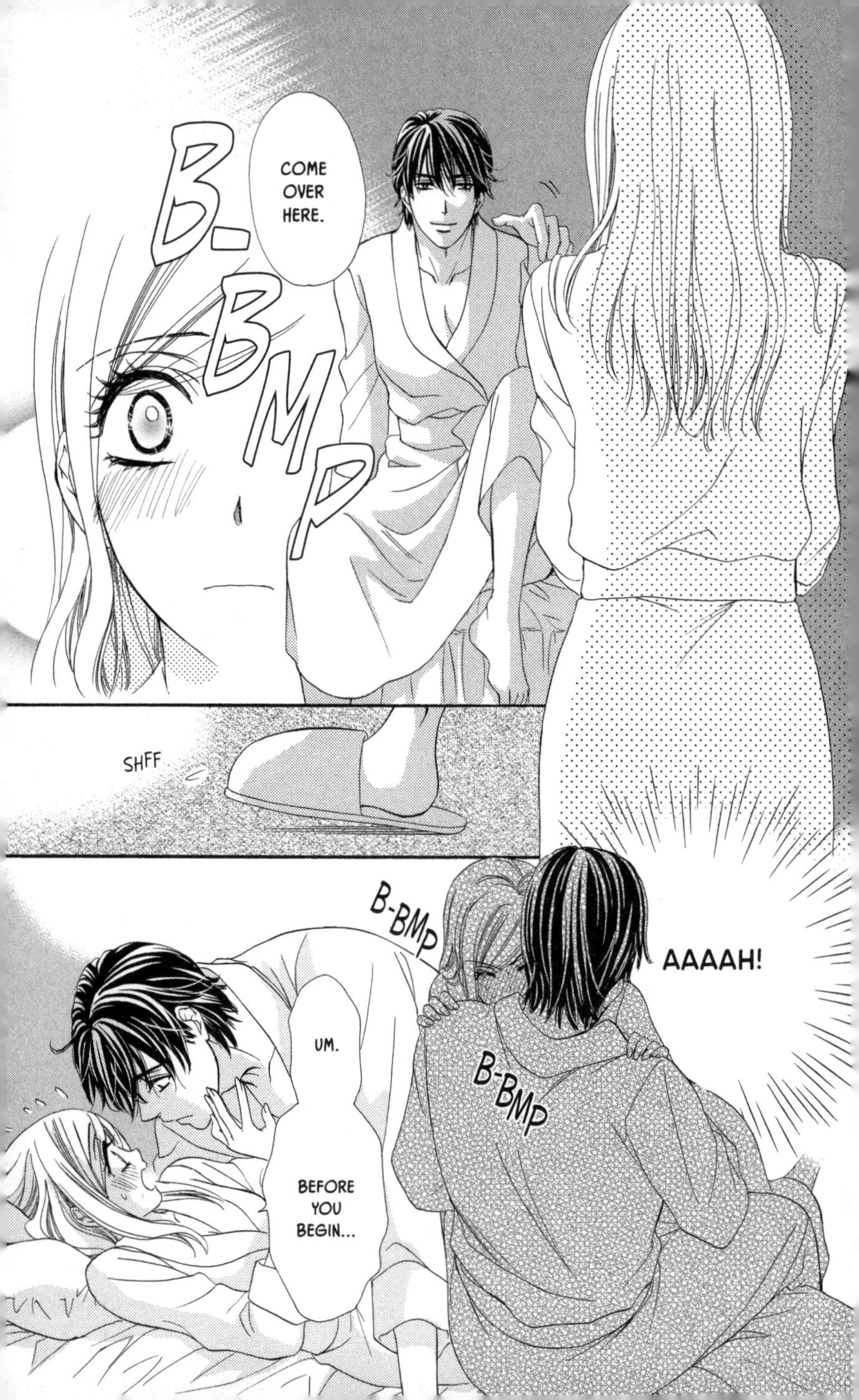
COME OVER HERE.
B-BMP
SHFF
AAAAH!
B-BMP
B-BMP
UM.
BEFORE YOU BEGIN...

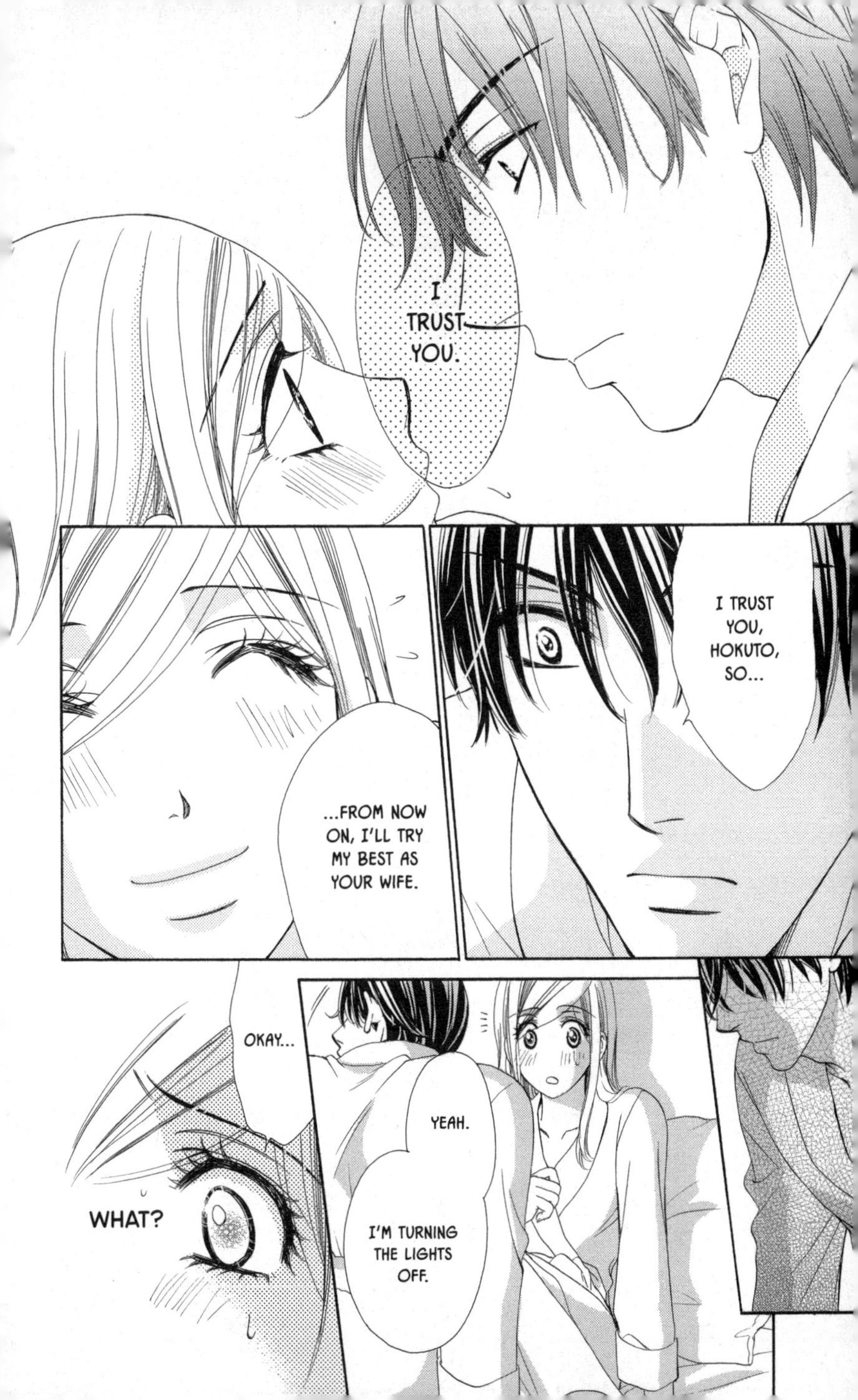
I TRUST YOU.
I TRUST YOU, HOKUTO, SO...
...FROM NOW ON, I'LL TRY MY BEST AS YOUR WIFE.
OKAY...
YEAH.
I'M TURNING THE LIGHTS OFF.
WHAT?

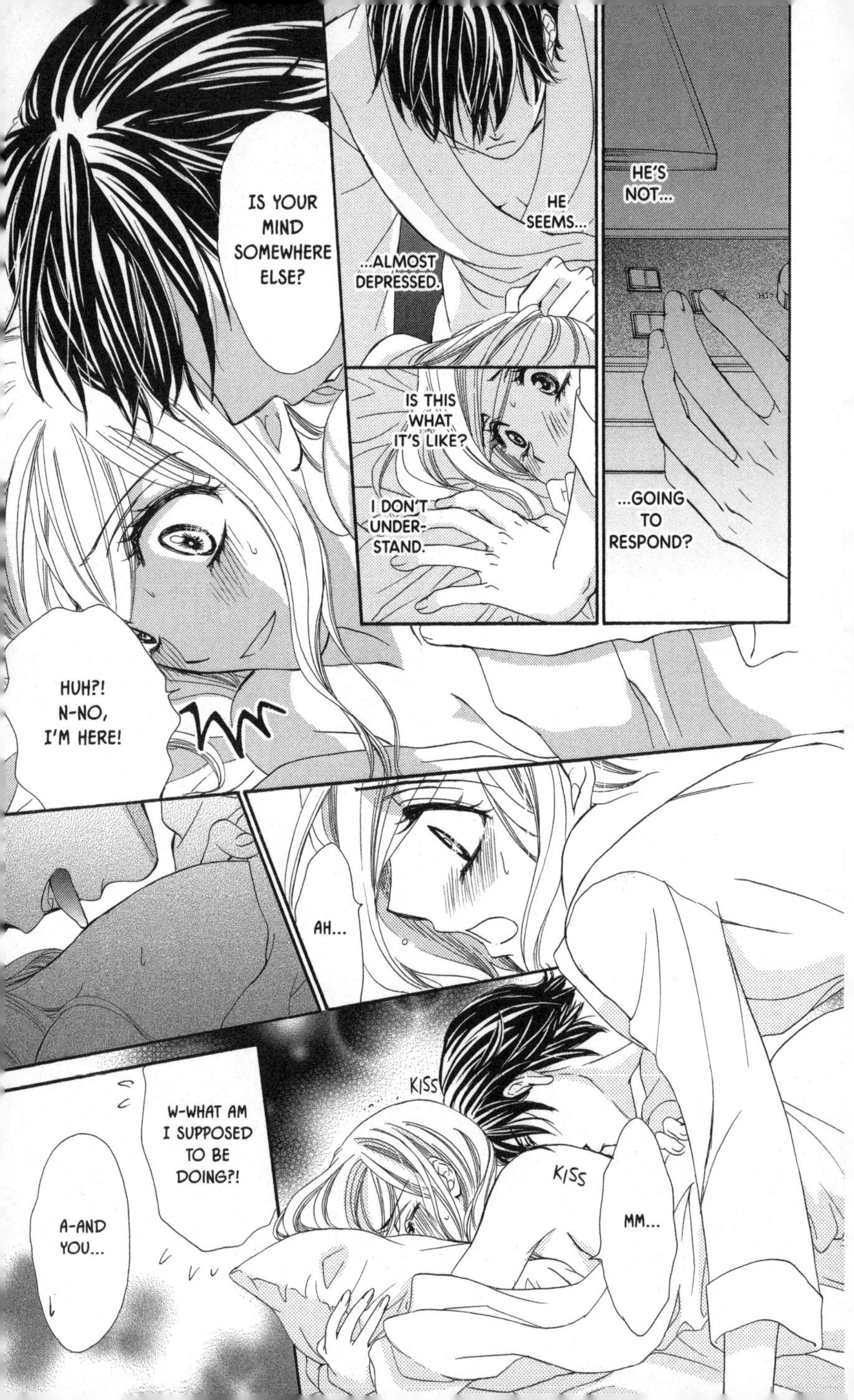
HE'S NOT...
...GOING TO RESPOND?
HE SEEMS...
...ALMOST DEPRESSED.
IS THIS WHAT IT'S LIKE?
I DON'T UNDER-STAND.
IS YOUR MIND SOMEWHERE ELSE?
HUH?! N-NO, I'M HERE!
AH...
KISS
KISS
MM...
W-WHAT AM I SUPPOSED TO BE DOING?!
A-AND YOU...

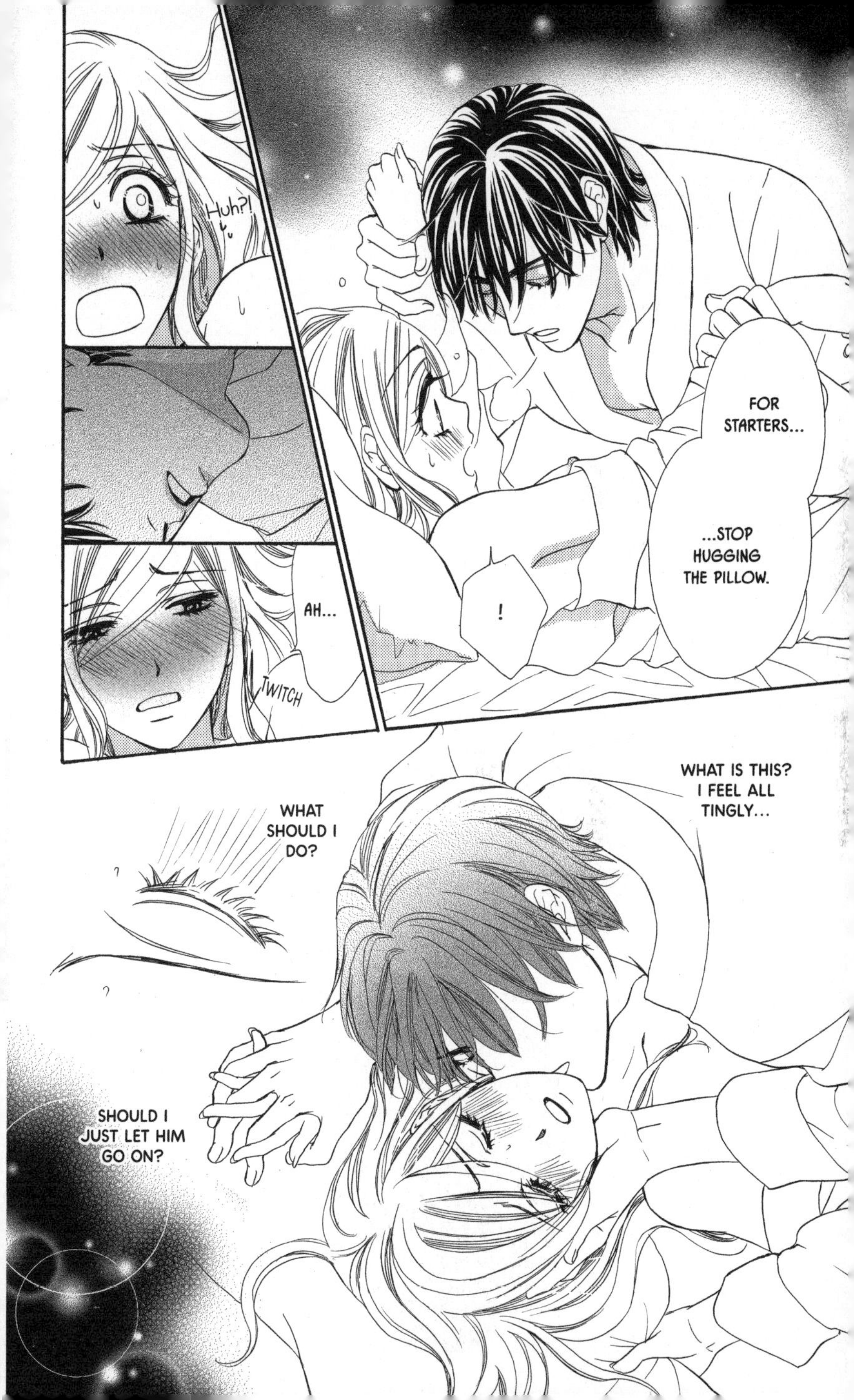
FOR STARTERS...
...STOP HUGGING THE PILLOW.
!
Huh?!
AH...
TWITCH
WHAT IS THIS? I FEEL ALL TINGLY...
WHAT SHOULD I DO?
SHOULD I JUST LET HIM GO ON?

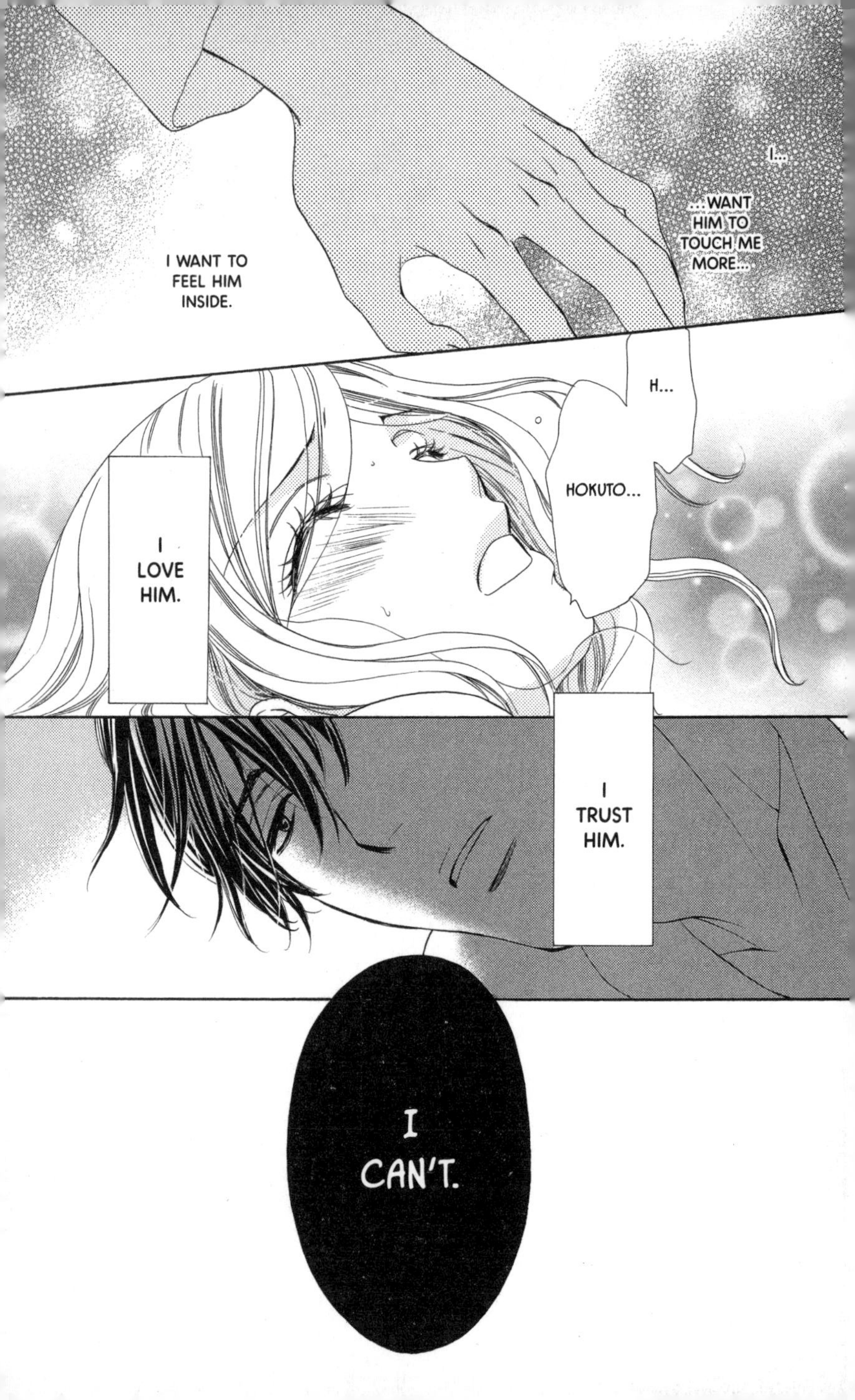
I...
...WANT HIM TO TOUCH ME MORE...
I WANT TO FEEL HIM INSIDE.
H...
HOKUTO...
I LOVE HIM.
I TRUST HIM.
I CAN'T.

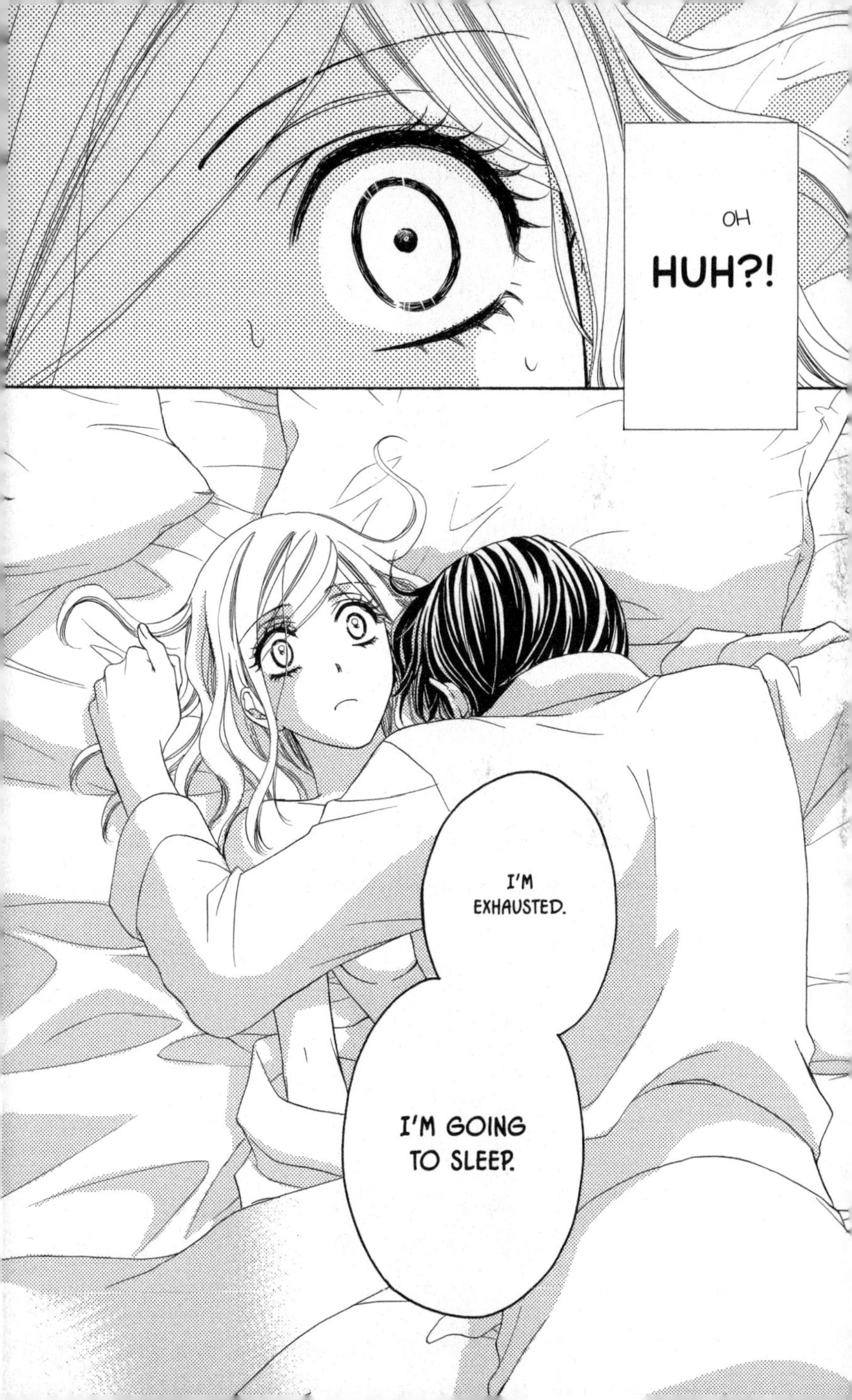
OH
HUH?!
I'M EXHAUSTED.
I'M GOING TO SLEEP.

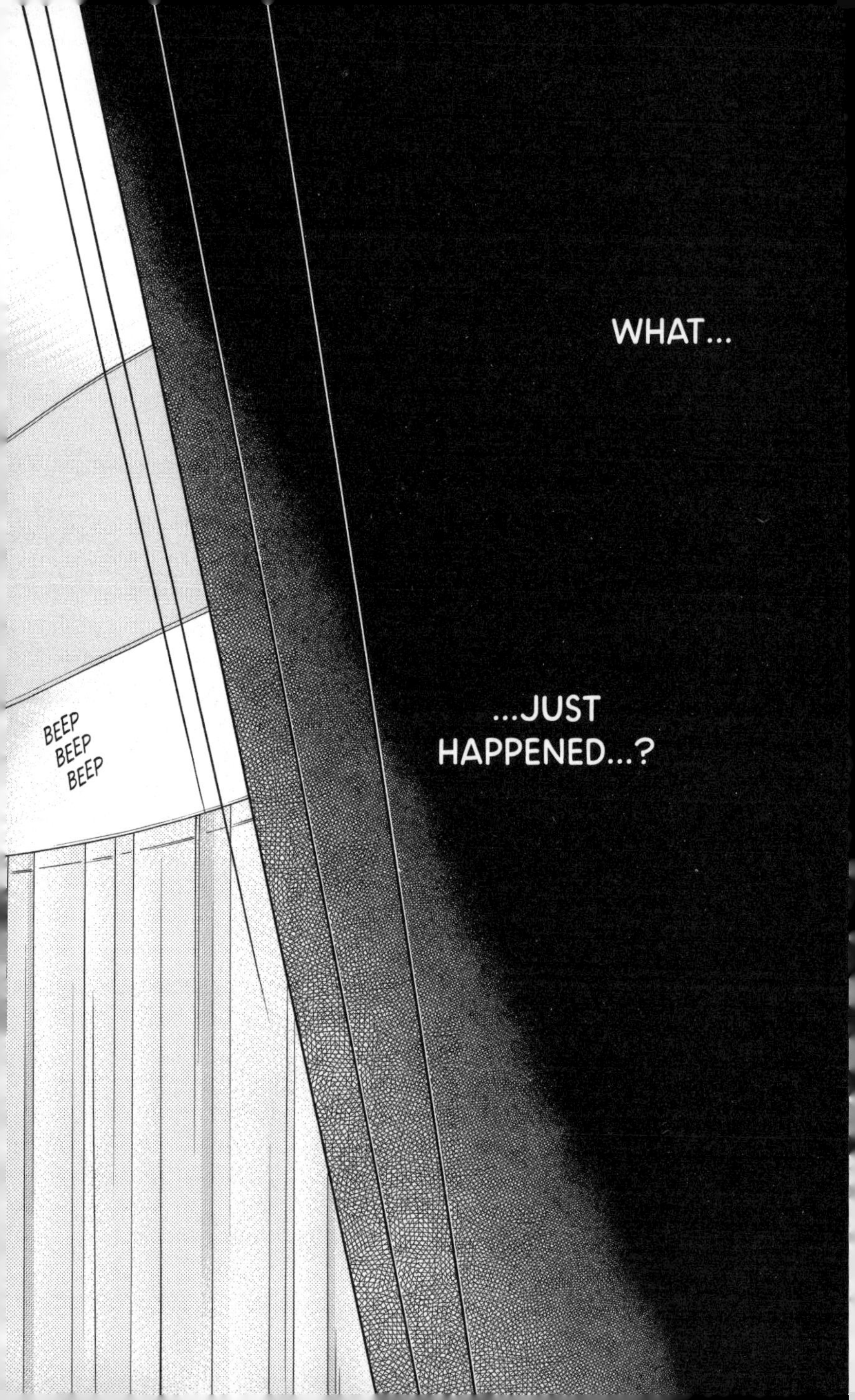
WHAT...
...JUST HAPPENED...?
BEEP BEEP BEEP

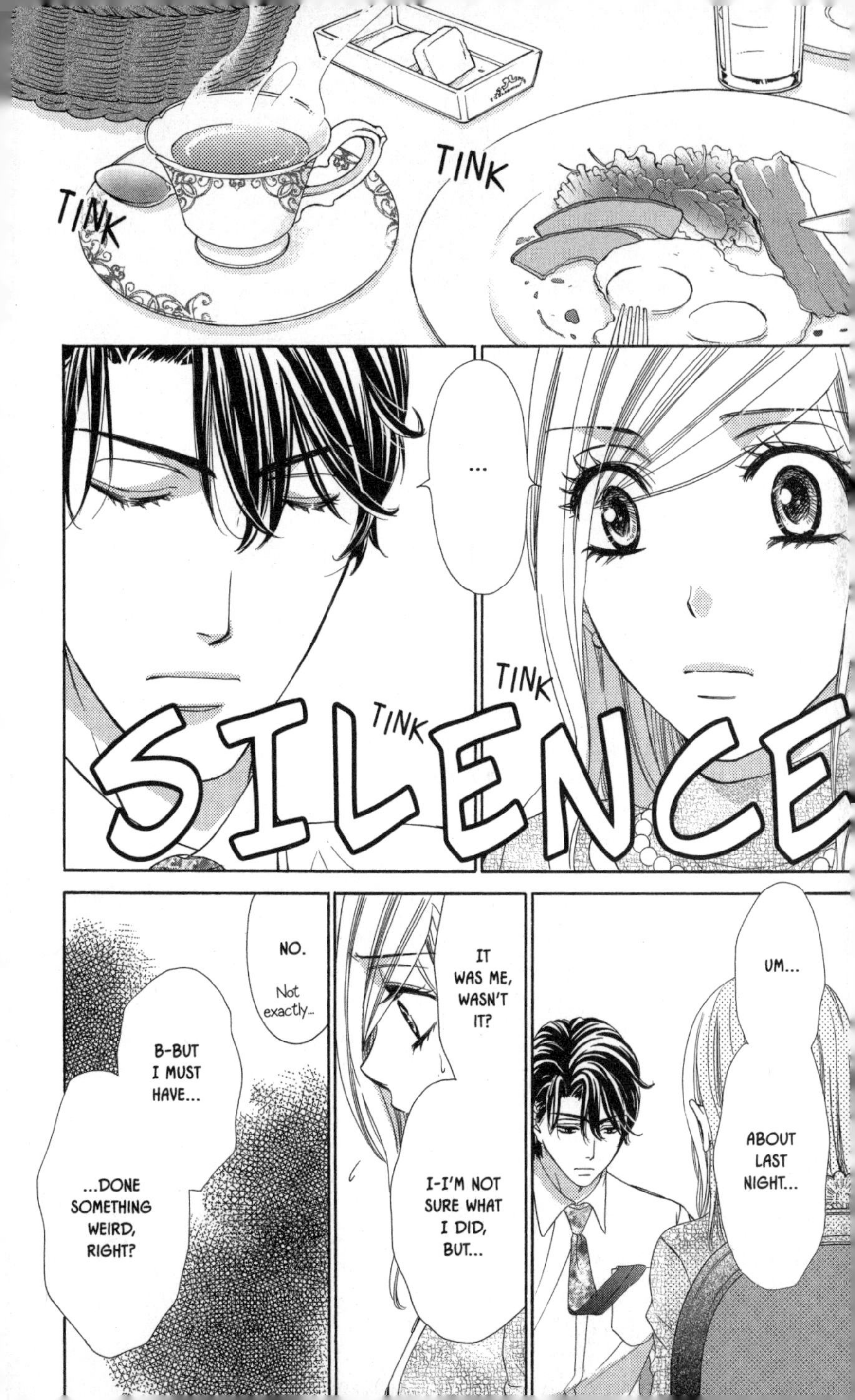
TINK
TINK
TINK
...
TINK
SILENCE
UM...
ABOUT LAST NIGHT...
IT WAS ME, WASN'T IT?
I-I'M NOT SURE WHAT I DID, BUT...
NO.
Not exactly...
B-BUT I MUST HAVE...
...DONE SOMETHING WEIRD, RIGHT?

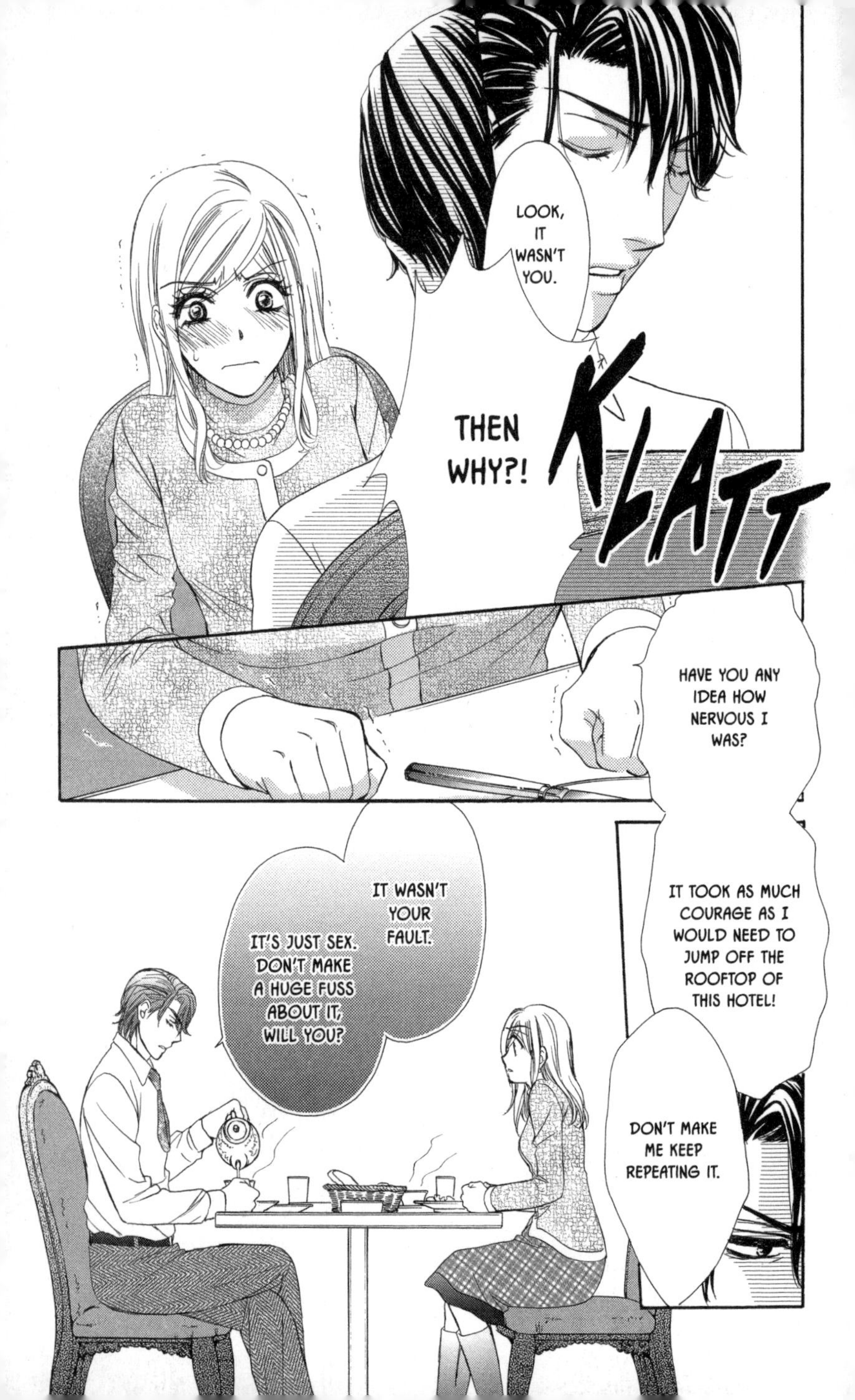
LOOK, IT WASN'T YOU.
KLATT
THEN WHY?!
HAVE YOU ANY IDEA HOW NERVOUS I WAS?
IT TOOK AS MUCH COURAGE AS I WOULD NEED TO JUMP OFF THE ROOFTOP OF THIS HOTEL!
DON'T MAKE ME KEEP REPEATING IT.
IT WASN'T YOUR FAULT.
IT'S JUST SEX. DON'T MAKE A HUGE FUSS ABOUT IT, WILL YOU?

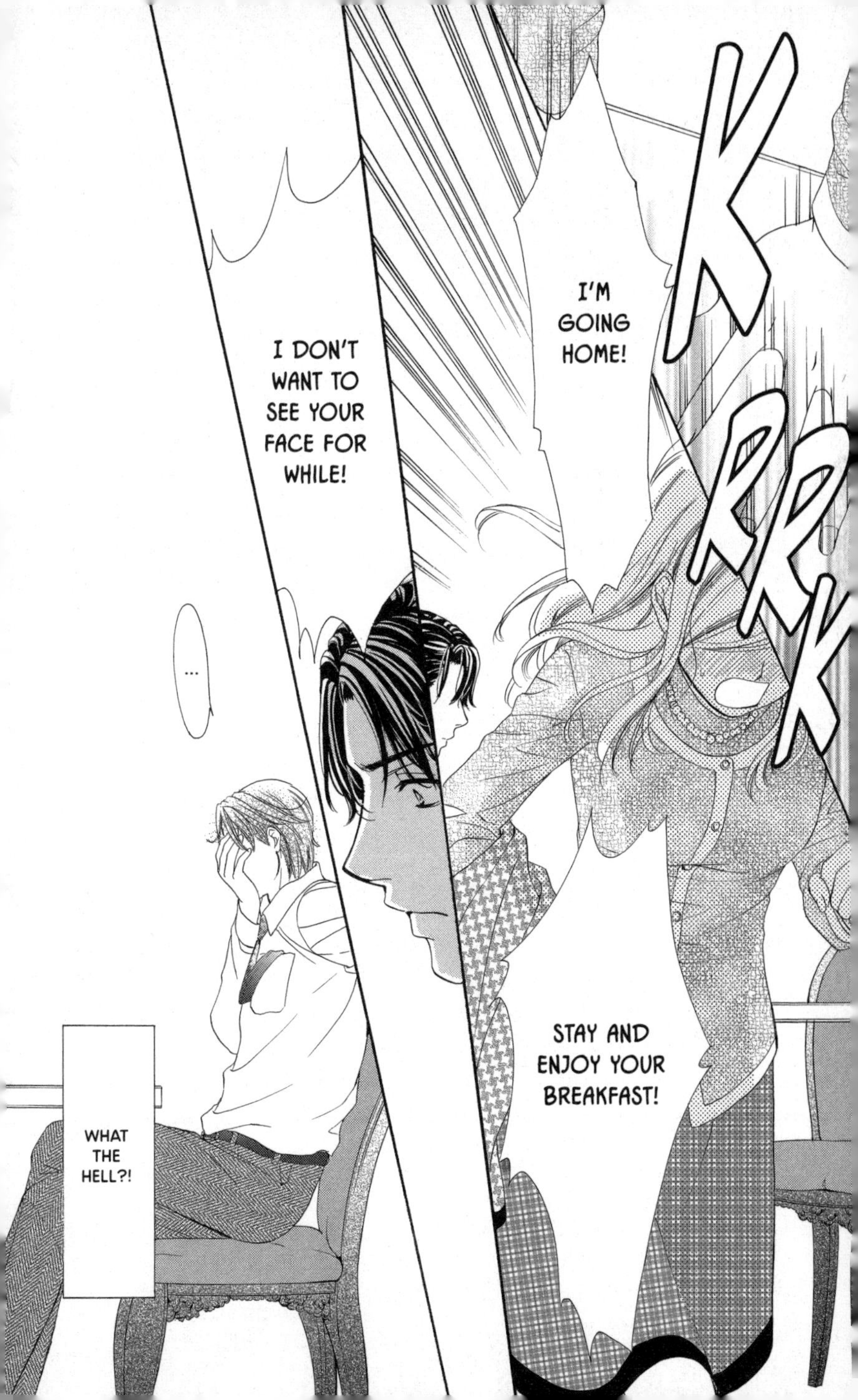
KRRKK
I'M GOING HOME!
STAY AND ENJOY YOUR BREAKFAST!
I DON'T WANT TO SEE YOUR FACE FOR WHILE!
...
WHAT THE HELL?!

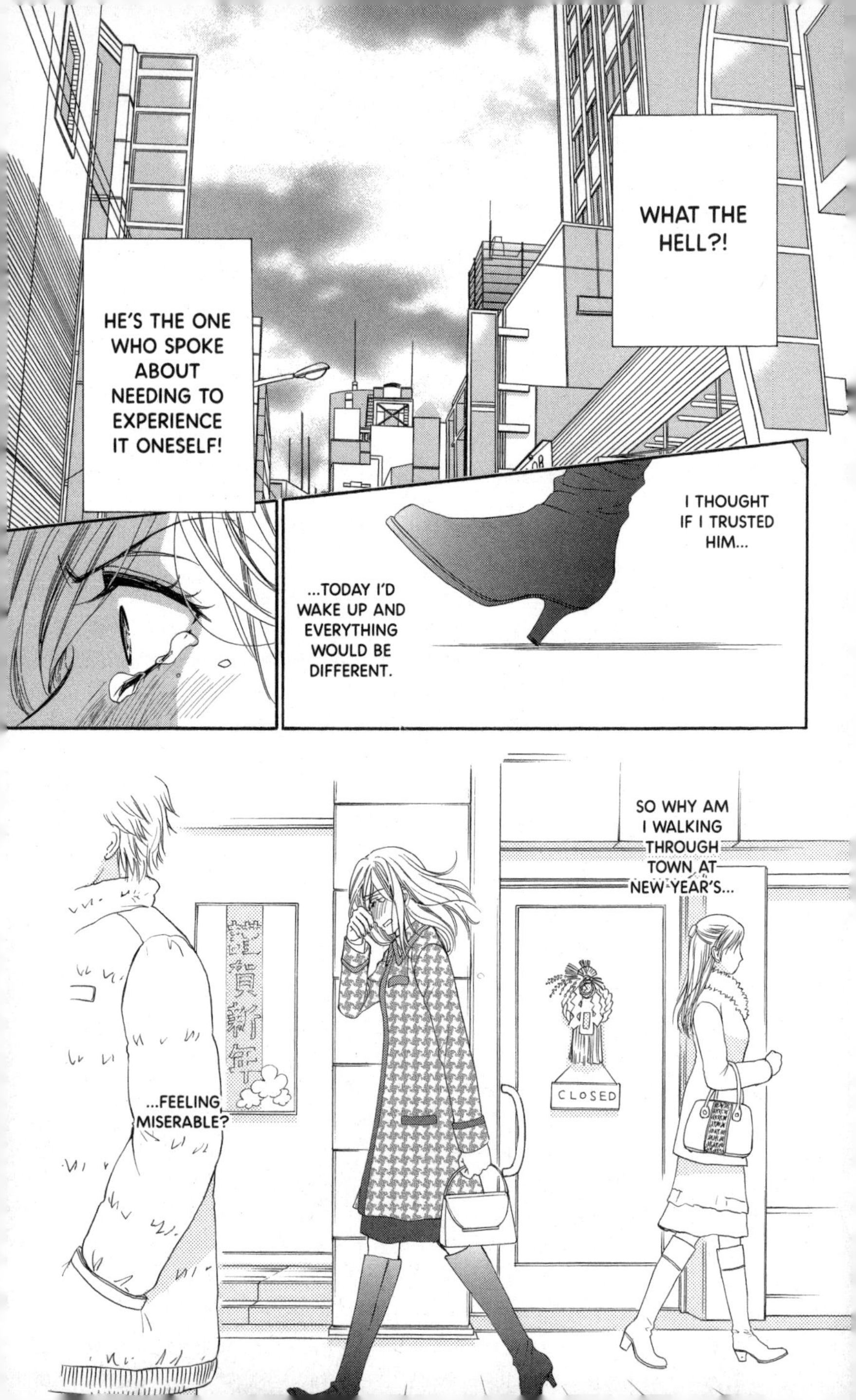
WHAT THE HELL?!
HE'S THE ONE WHO SPOKE ABOUT NEEDING TO EXPERIENCE IT ONESELF!
I THOUGHT IF I TRUSTED HIM...
...TODAY I'D WAKE UP AND EVERYTHING WOULD BE DIFFERENT.
SO WHY AM I WALKING THROUGH TOWN AT NEW YEAR'S...
CLOSED
...FEELING MISERABLE?

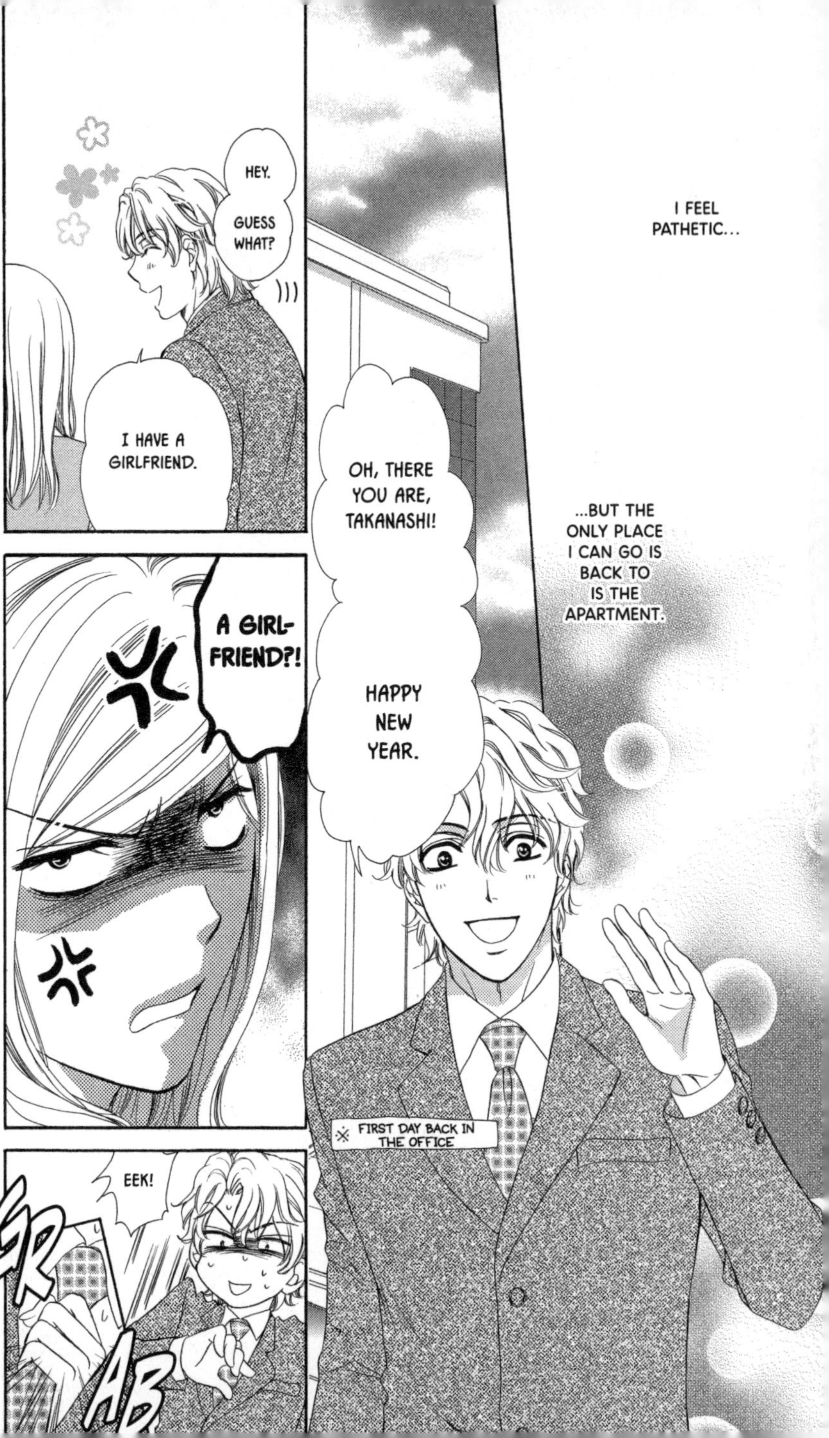
I FEEL PATHETIC...
...BUT THE ONLY PLACE I CAN GO IS BACK TO IS THE APARTMENT.
OH, THERE YOU ARE, TAKANASHI!
HAPPY NEW YEAR.
※ FIRST DAY BACK IN THE OFFICE
HEY.
GUESS WHAT?
I HAVE A GIRLFRIEND.
A GIRL-FRIEND?!
EEK!
GRAB

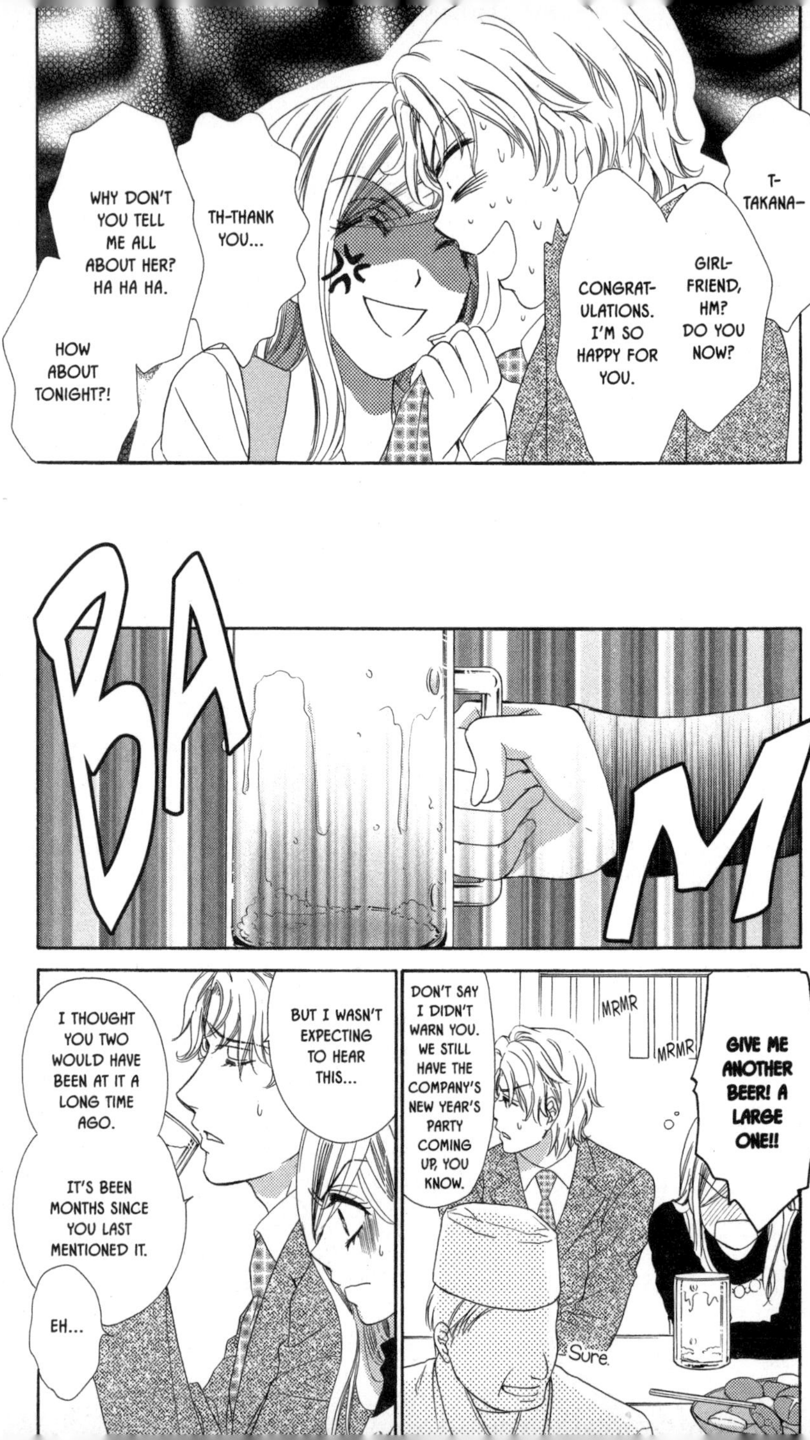
T-TAKANA-
GIRLFRIEND, HM? DO YOU NOW?
CONGRATULATIONS. I'M SO HAPPY FOR YOU.
TH-THANK YOU...
WHY DON'T YOU TELL ME ALL ABOUT HER? HA HA HA.
HOW ABOUT TONIGHT?!
BAM
MRMR
MRMR
GIVE ME ANOTHER BEER! A LARGE ONE!!
DON'T SAY I DIDN'T WARN YOU. WE STILL HAVE THE COMPANY'S NEW YEAR'S PARTY COMING UP, YOU KNOW.
Sure.
BUT I WASN'T EXPECTING TO HEAR THIS...
I THOUGHT YOU TWO WOULD HAVE BEEN AT IT A LONG TIME AGO.
IT'S BEEN MONTHS SINCE YOU LAST MENTIONED IT.
EH...

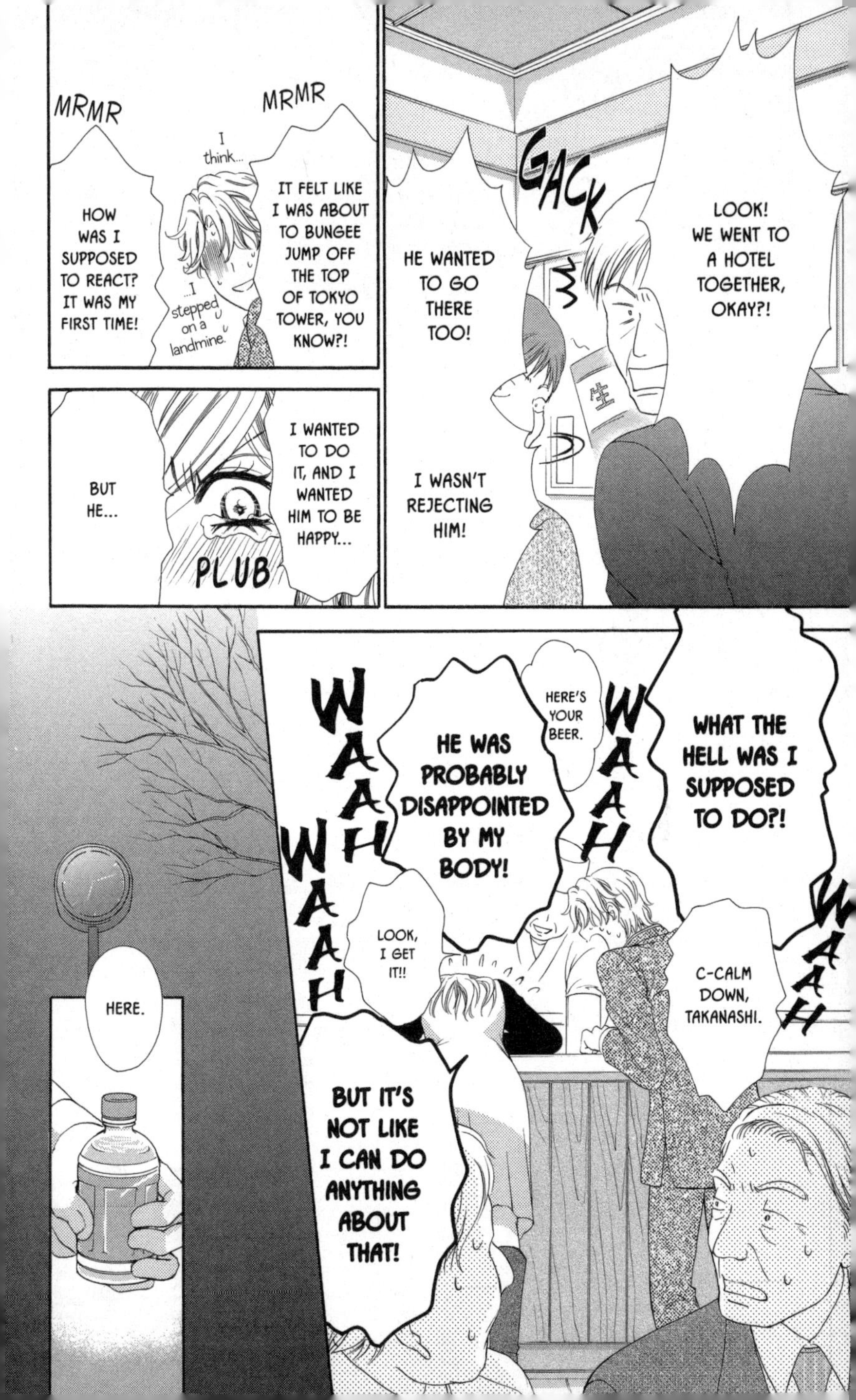
LOOK! WE WENT TO A HOTEL TOGETHER, OKAY?!
GACK
HE WANTED TO GO THERE TOO!
I WASN'T REJECTING HIM!
MRMR
IT FELT LIKE I WAS ABOUT TO BUNGEE JUMP OFF THE TOP OF TOKYO TOWER, YOU KNOW?!
I think...
...I stepped on a landmine.
MRMR
HOW WAS I SUPPOSED TO REACT? IT WAS MY FIRST TIME!
I WANTED TO DO IT, AND I WANTED HIM TO BE HAPPY...
PLUB
BUT HE...
WHAT THE HELL WAS I SUPPOSED TO DO?!
WAAH
HERE'S YOUR BEER.
HE WAS PROBABLY DISAPPOINTED BY MY BODY!
WAAH
WAAH
WAAH
C-CALM DOWN, TAKANASHI.
LOOK, I GET IT!!
BUT IT'S NOT LIKE I CAN DO ANYTHING ABOUT THAT!
HERE.

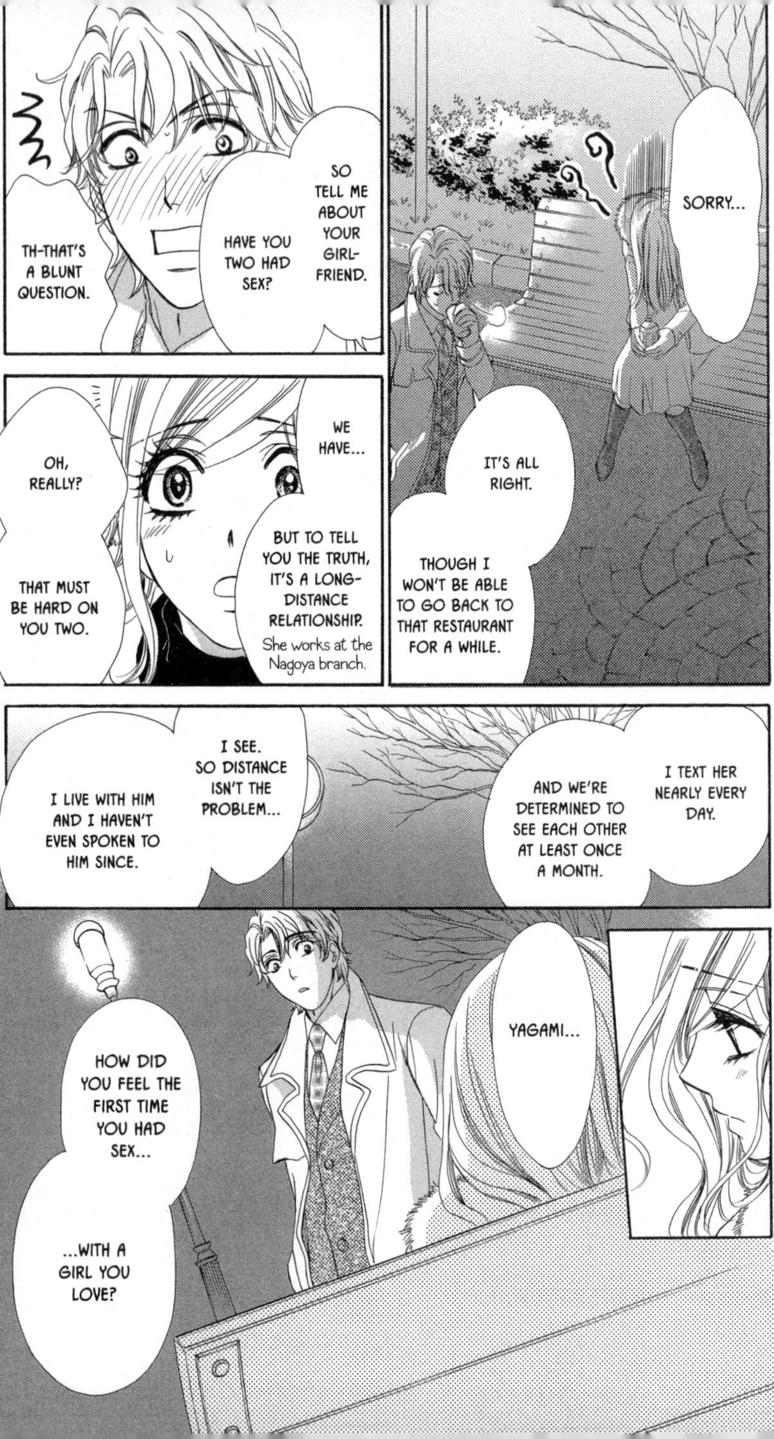
SORRY...
IT'S ALL RIGHT.
THOUGH I WON'T BE ABLE TO GO BACK TO THAT RESTAURANT FOR A WHILE.
SO TELL ME ABOUT YOUR GIRL-FRIEND.
HAVE YOU TWO HAD SEX?
TH-THAT'S A BLUNT QUESTION.
WE HAVE...
BUT TO TELL YOU THE TRUTH, IT'S A LONG-DISTANCE RELATIONSHIP.
She works at the Nagoya branch.
OH, REALLY?
THAT MUST BE HARD ON YOU TWO.
I TEXT HER NEARLY EVERY DAY.
AND WE'RE DETERMINED TO SEE EACH OTHER AT LEAST ONCE A MONTH.
I SEE. SO DISTANCE ISN'T THE PROBLEM...
I LIVE WITH HIM AND I HAVEN'T EVEN SPOKEN TO HIM SINCE.
YAGAMI...
HOW DID YOU FEEL THE FIRST TIME YOU HAD SEX...
...WITH A GIRL YOU LOVE?

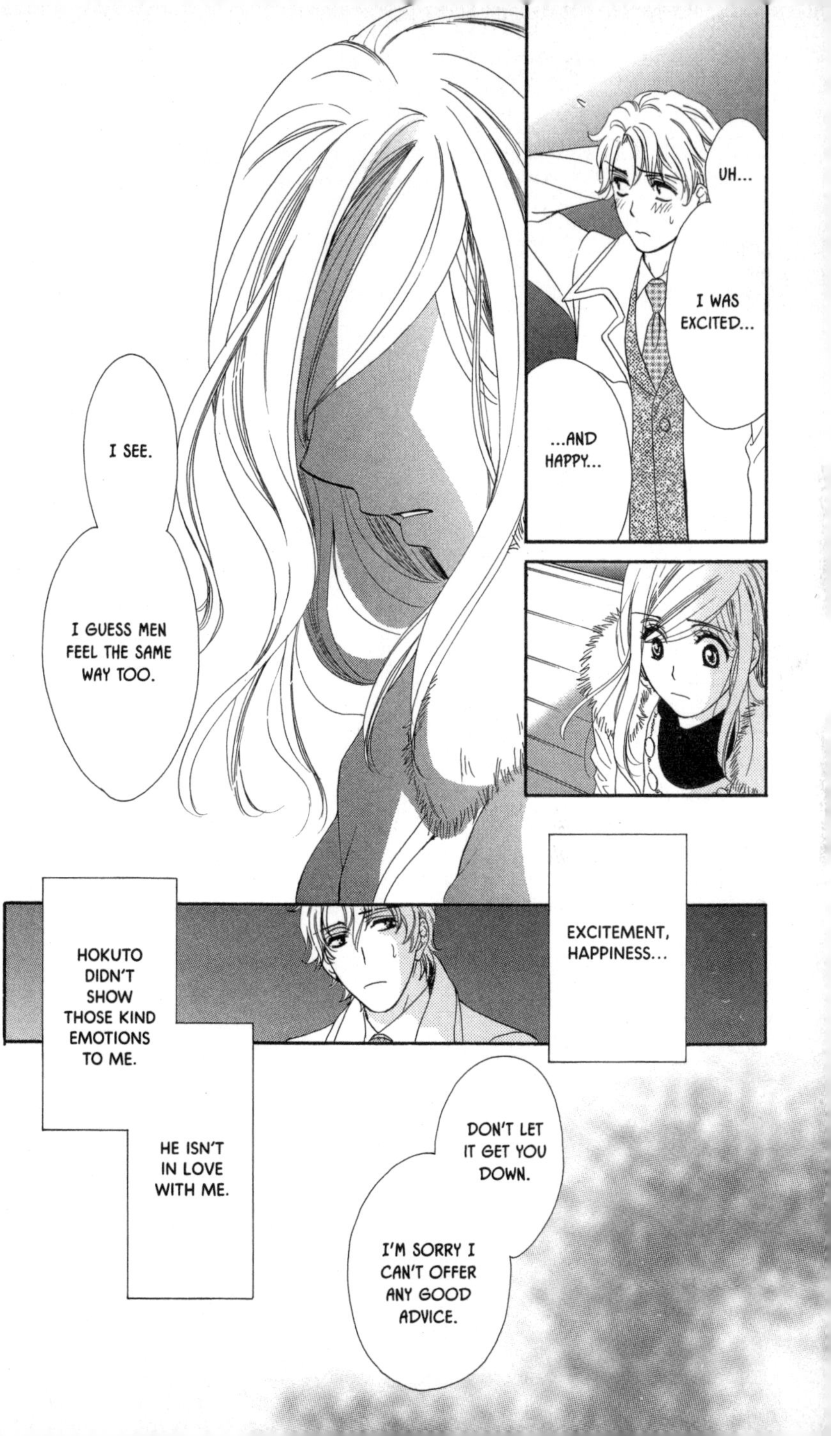
UH...
I WAS EXCITED...
...AND HAPPY...
I SEE.
I GUESS MEN FEEL THE SAME WAY TOO.
EXCITEMENT, HAPPINESS...
HOKUTO DIDN'T SHOW THOSE KIND EMOTIONS TO ME.
HE ISN'T IN LOVE WITH ME.
DON'T LET IT GET YOU DOWN.
I'M SORRY I CAN'T OFFER ANY GOOD ADVICE.

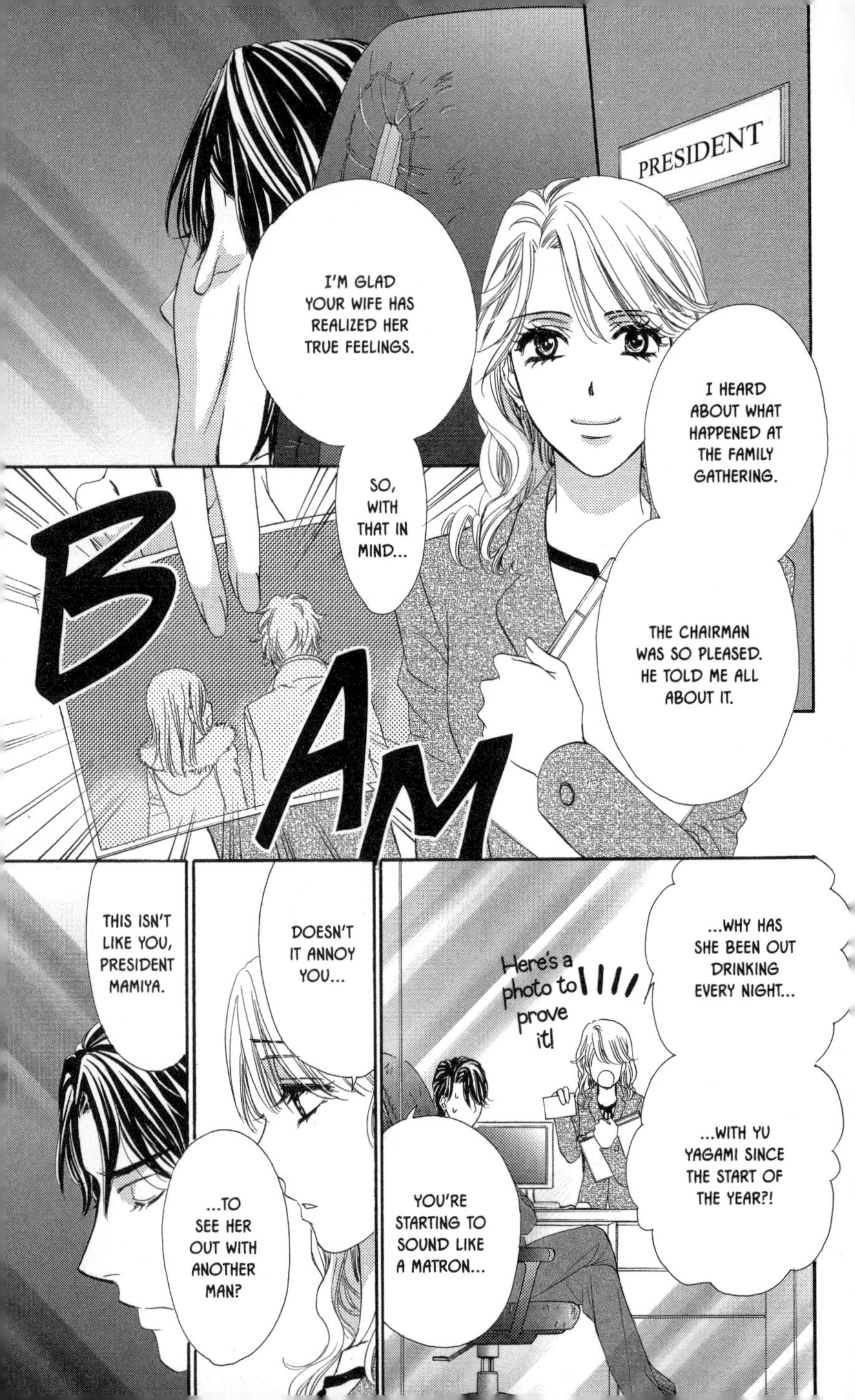
PRESIDENT
I HEARD ABOUT WHAT HAPPENED AT THE FAMILY GATHERING.
THE CHAIRMAN WAS SO PLEASED. HE TOLD ME ALL ABOUT IT.
I'M GLAD YOUR WIFE HAS REALIZED HER TRUE FEELINGS.
SO, WITH THAT IN MIND...
BAM
...WHY HAS SHE BEEN OUT DRINKING EVERY NIGHT...
...WITH YU YAGAMI SINCE THE START OF THE YEAR?!
Here's a photo to prove it!
YOU'RE STARTING TO SOUND LIKE A MATRON...
DOESN'T IT ANNOY YOU...
...TO SEE HER OUT WITH ANOTHER MAN?
THIS ISN'T LIKE YOU, PRESIDENT MAMIYA.

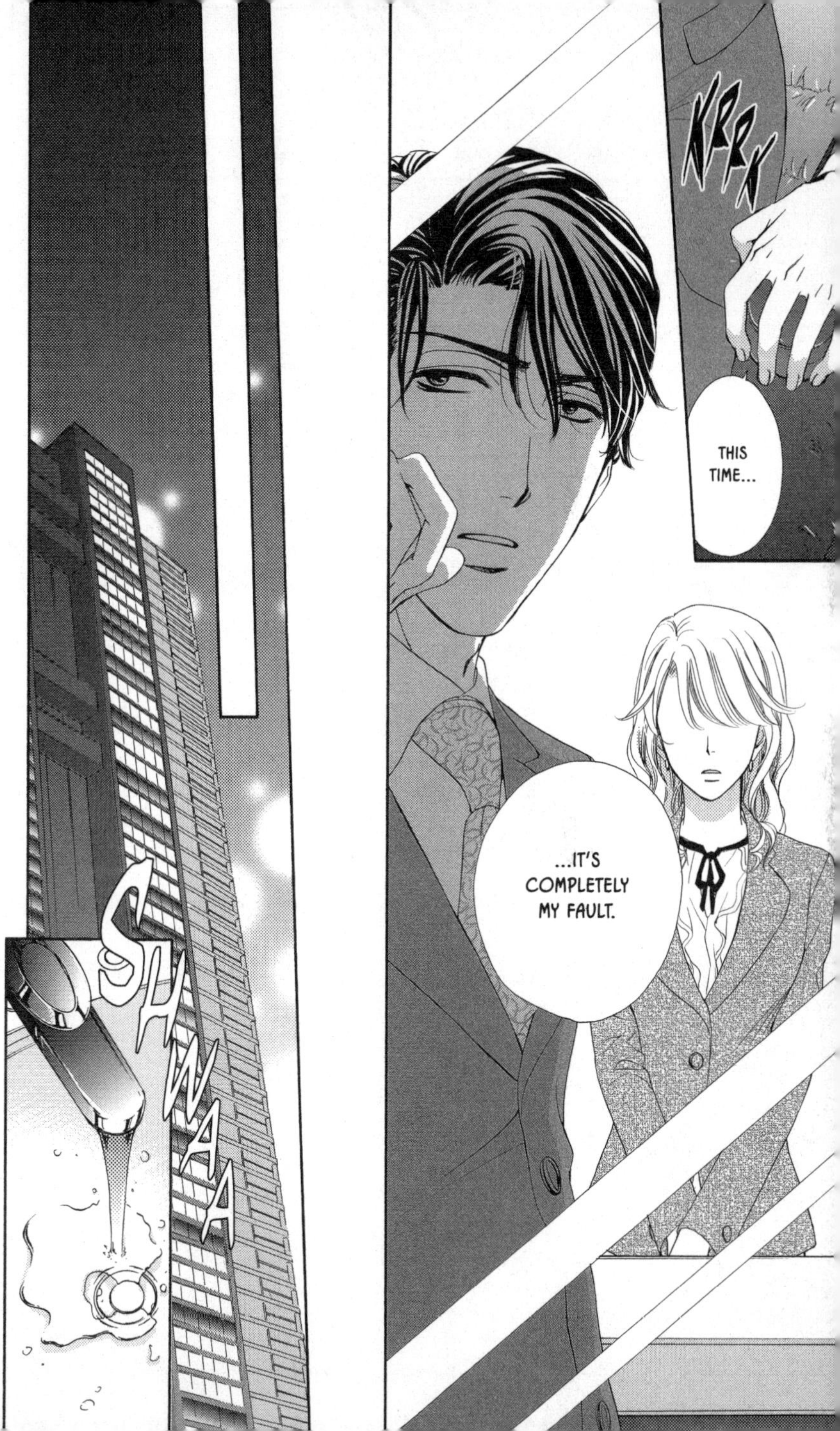
KRRK
THIS TIME...
...IT'S COMPLETELY MY FAULT.
SHWAA

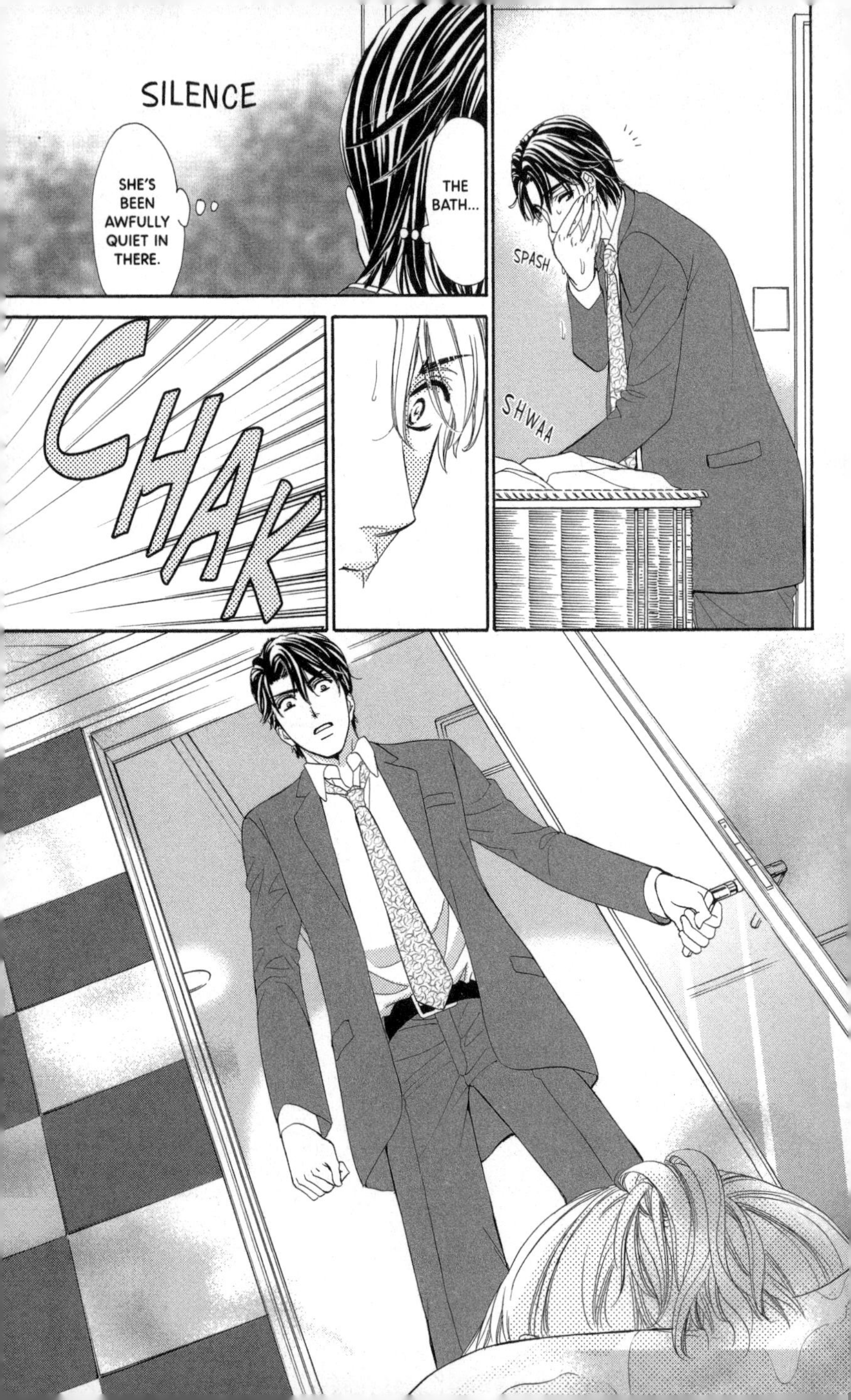

SPASH
SHWAA
THE BATH...
SILENCE
SHE'S BEEN AWFULLY QUIET IN THERE.
CHAK

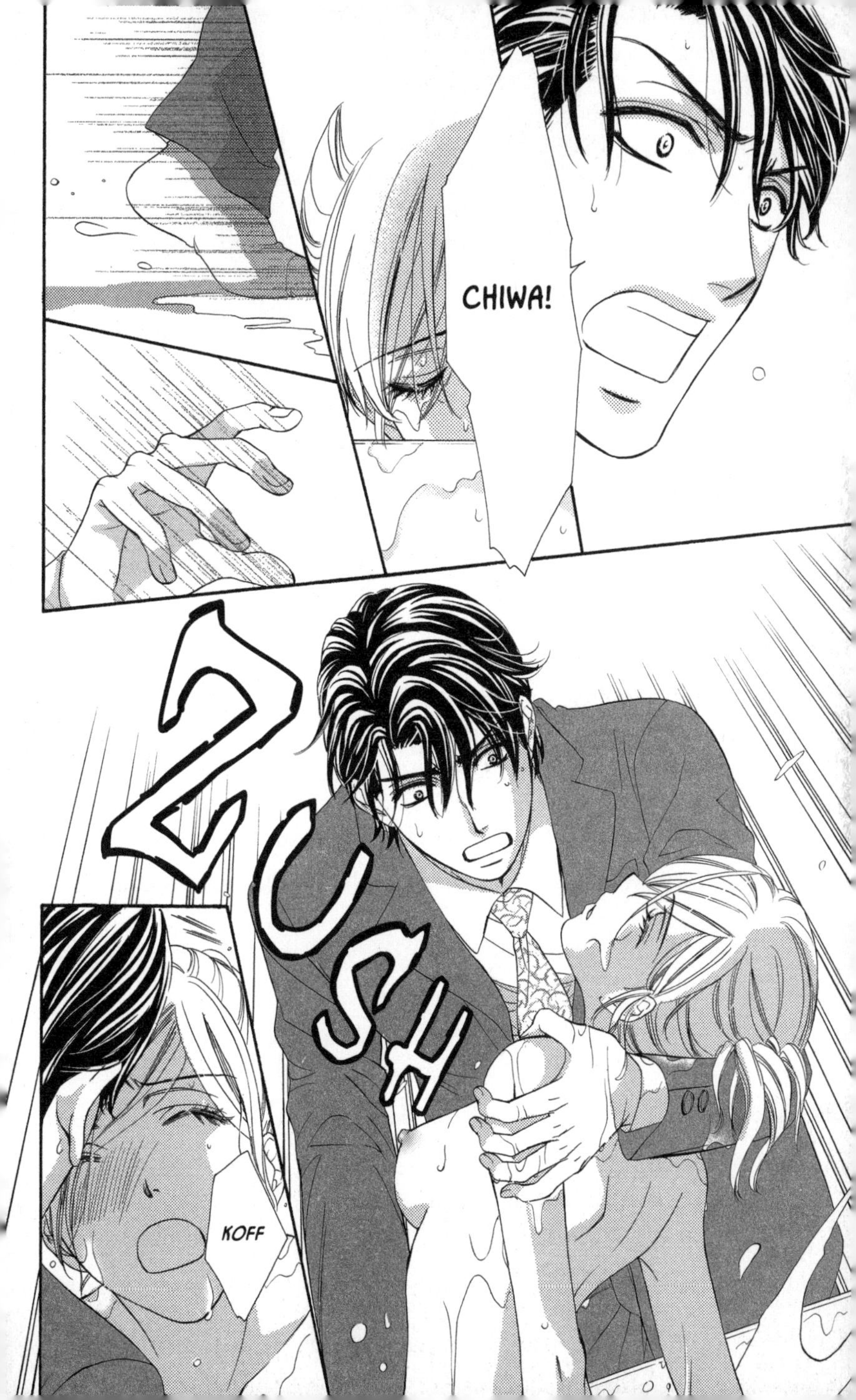
CHIWA!
ZUSH
KOFF

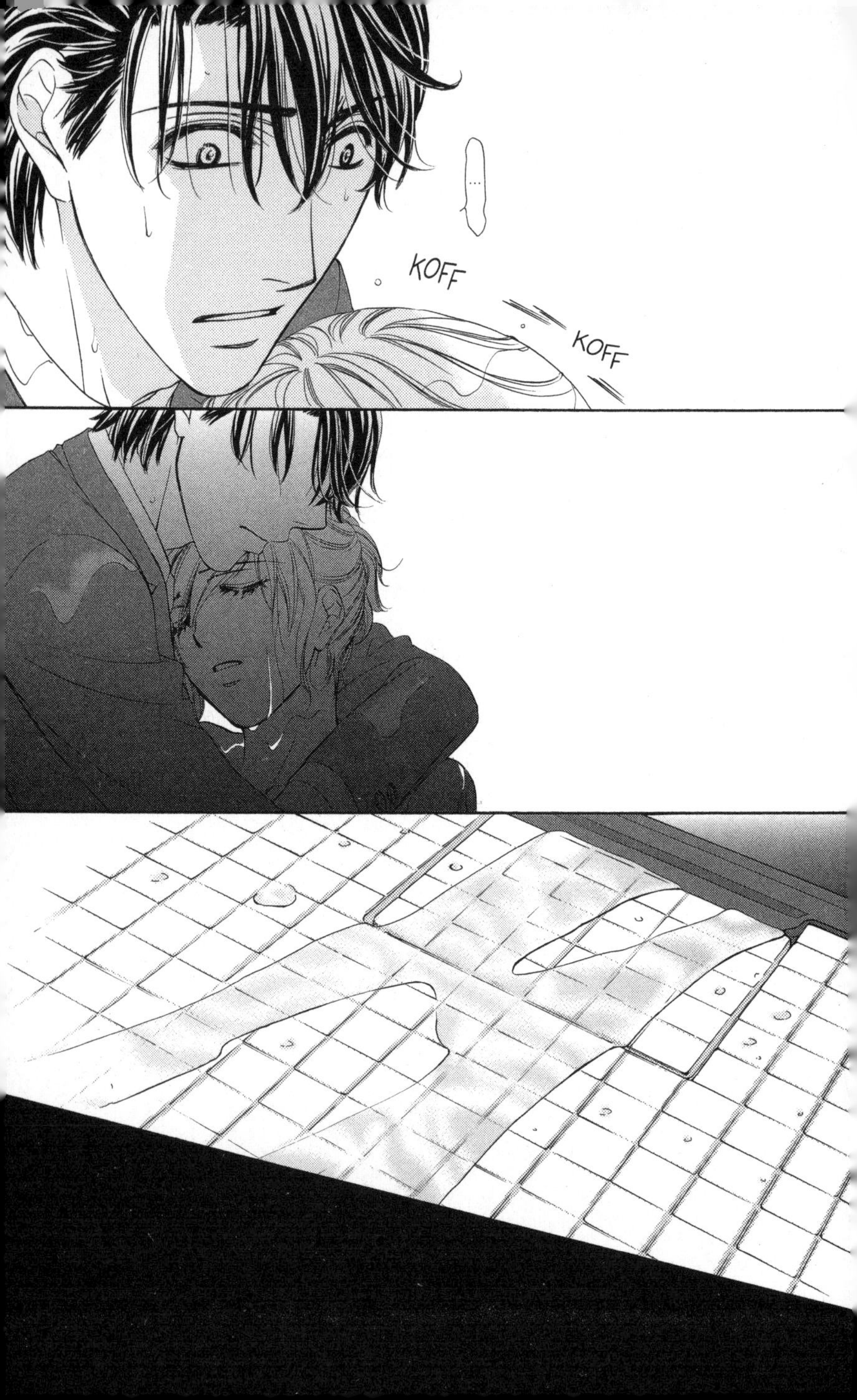
...
KOFF
KOFF

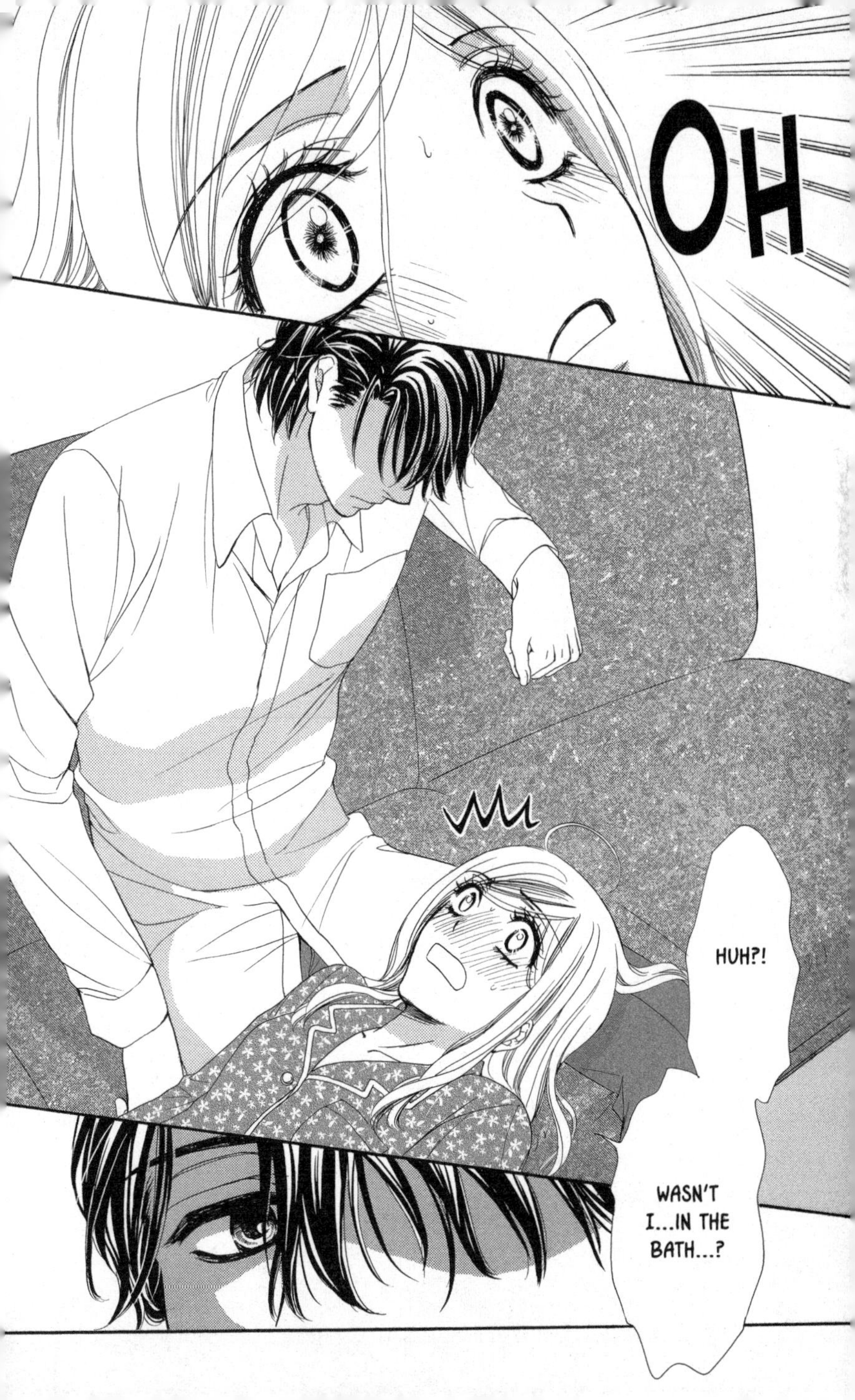
OH
HUH?!
WASN'T I...IN THE BATH...?

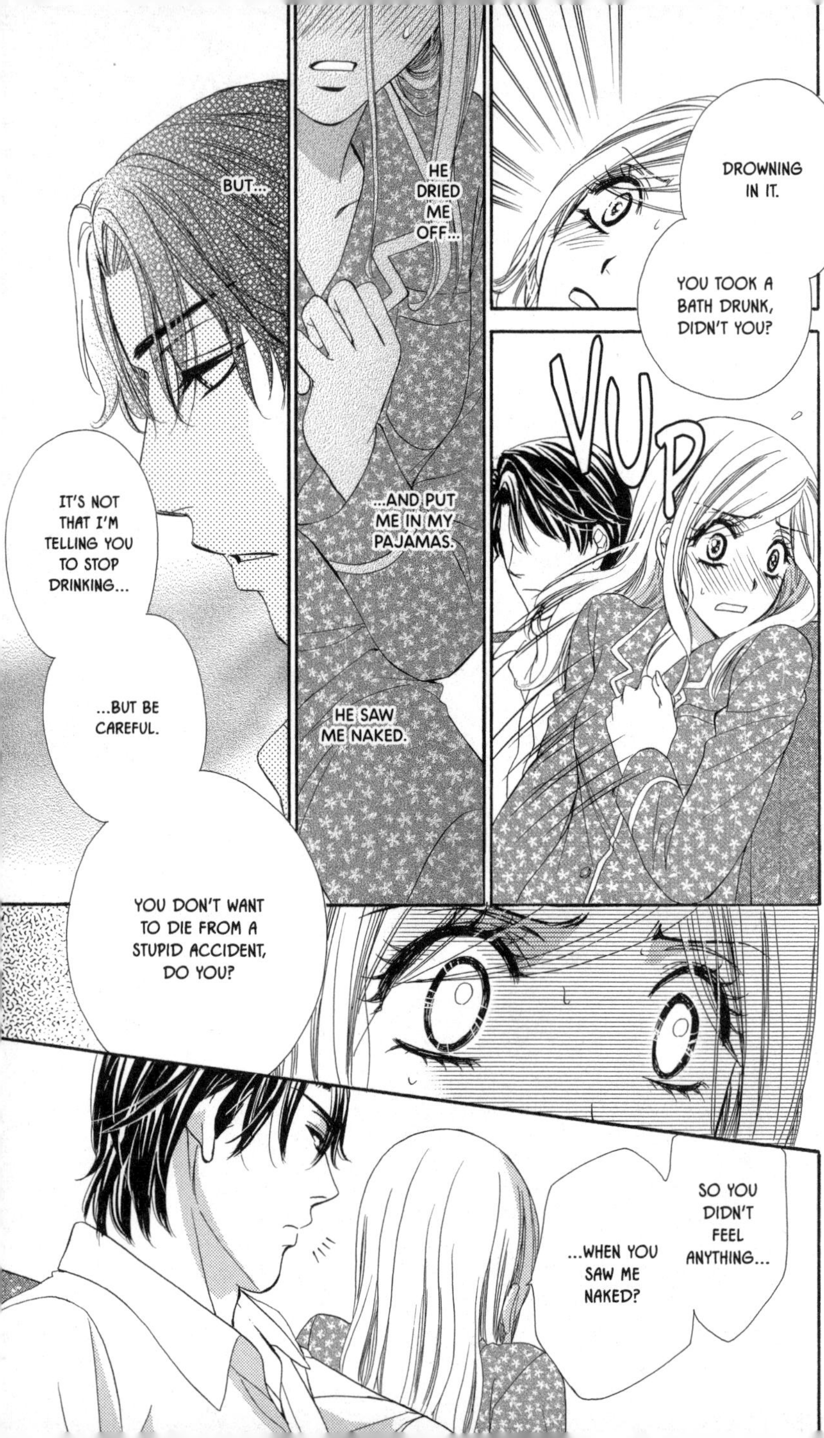
DROWNING IN IT.
YOU TOOK A BATH DRUNK, DIDN'T YOU?
VUP
HE DRIED ME OFF...
...AND PUT ME IN MY PAJAMAS.
HE SAW ME NAKED.
BUT...
IT'S NOT THAT I'M TELLING YOU TO STOP DRINKING...
...BUT BE CAREFUL.
YOU DON'T WANT TO DIE FROM A STUPID ACCIDENT, DO YOU?
SO YOU DIDN'T FEEL ANYTHING...
...WHEN YOU SAW ME NAKED?

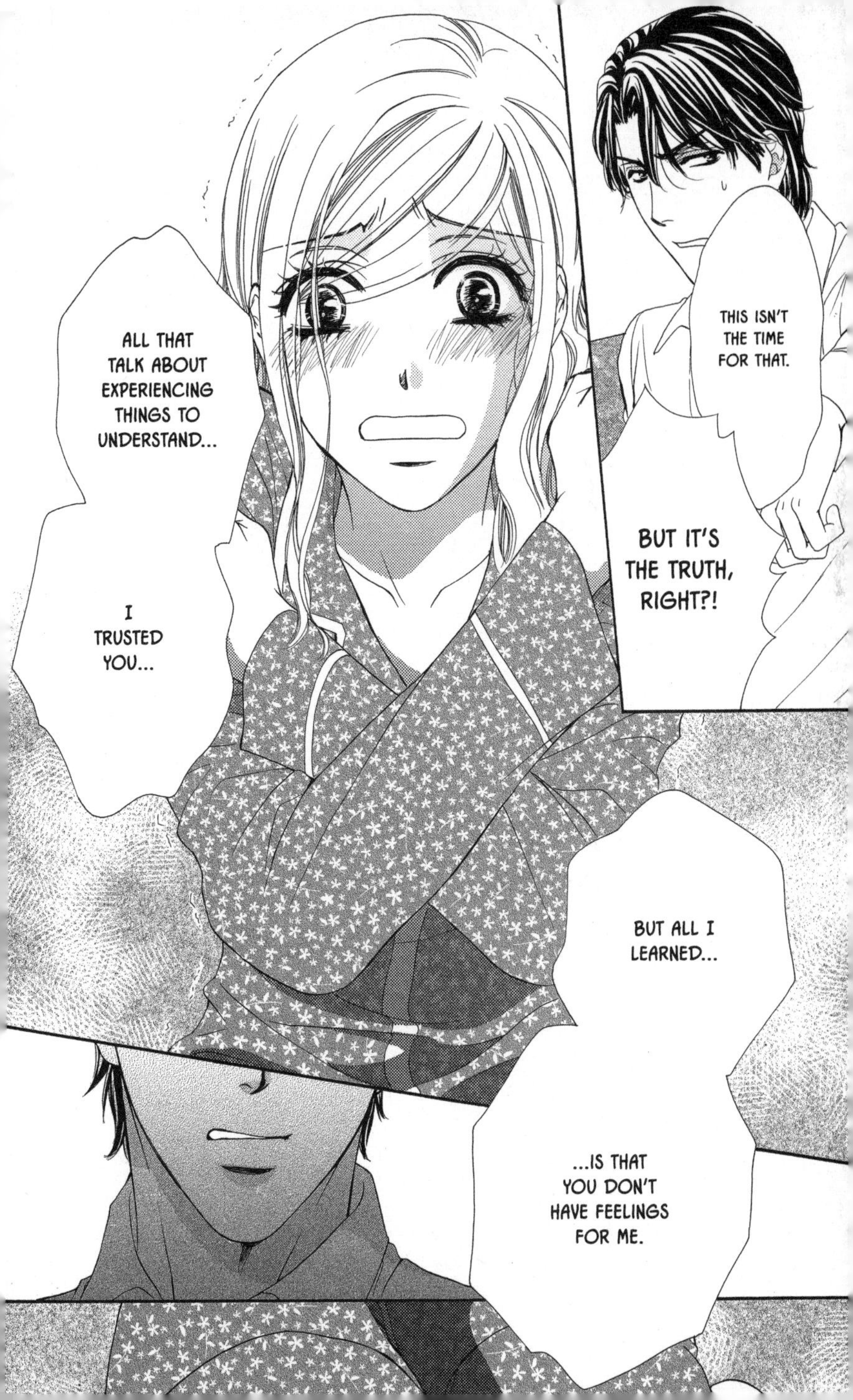
THIS ISN'T THE TIME FOR THAT.
BUT IT'S THE TRUTH, RIGHT?!
ALL THAT TALK ABOUT EXPERIENCING THINGS TO UNDERSTAND...
I TRUSTED YOU...
BUT ALL I LEARNED...
...IS THAT YOU DON'T HAVE FEELINGS FOR ME.

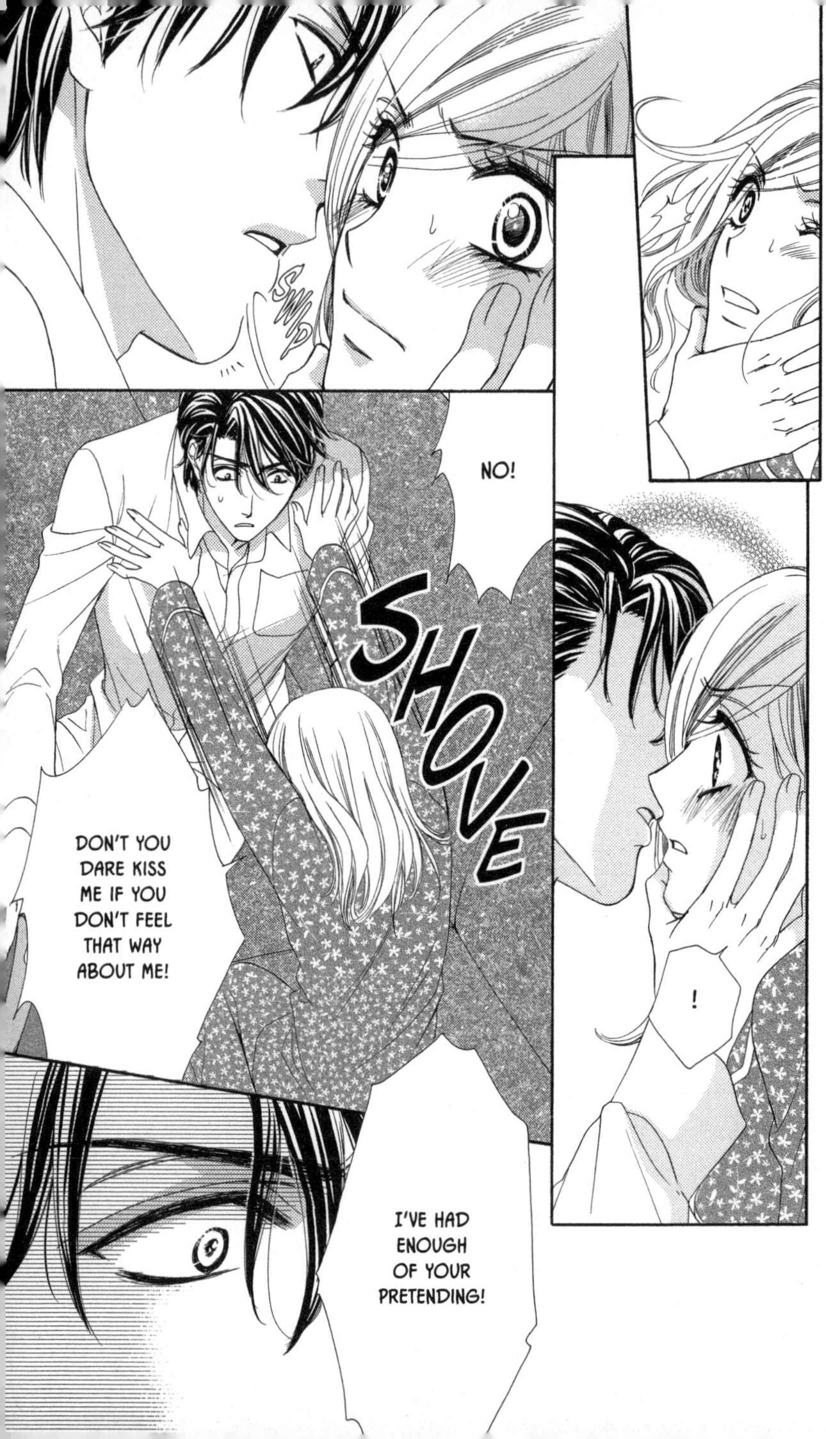
!
NO!
SHOVE
DON'T YOU DARE KISS ME IF YOU DON'T FEEL THAT WAY ABOUT ME!
I'VE HAD ENOUGH OF YOUR PRETENDING!

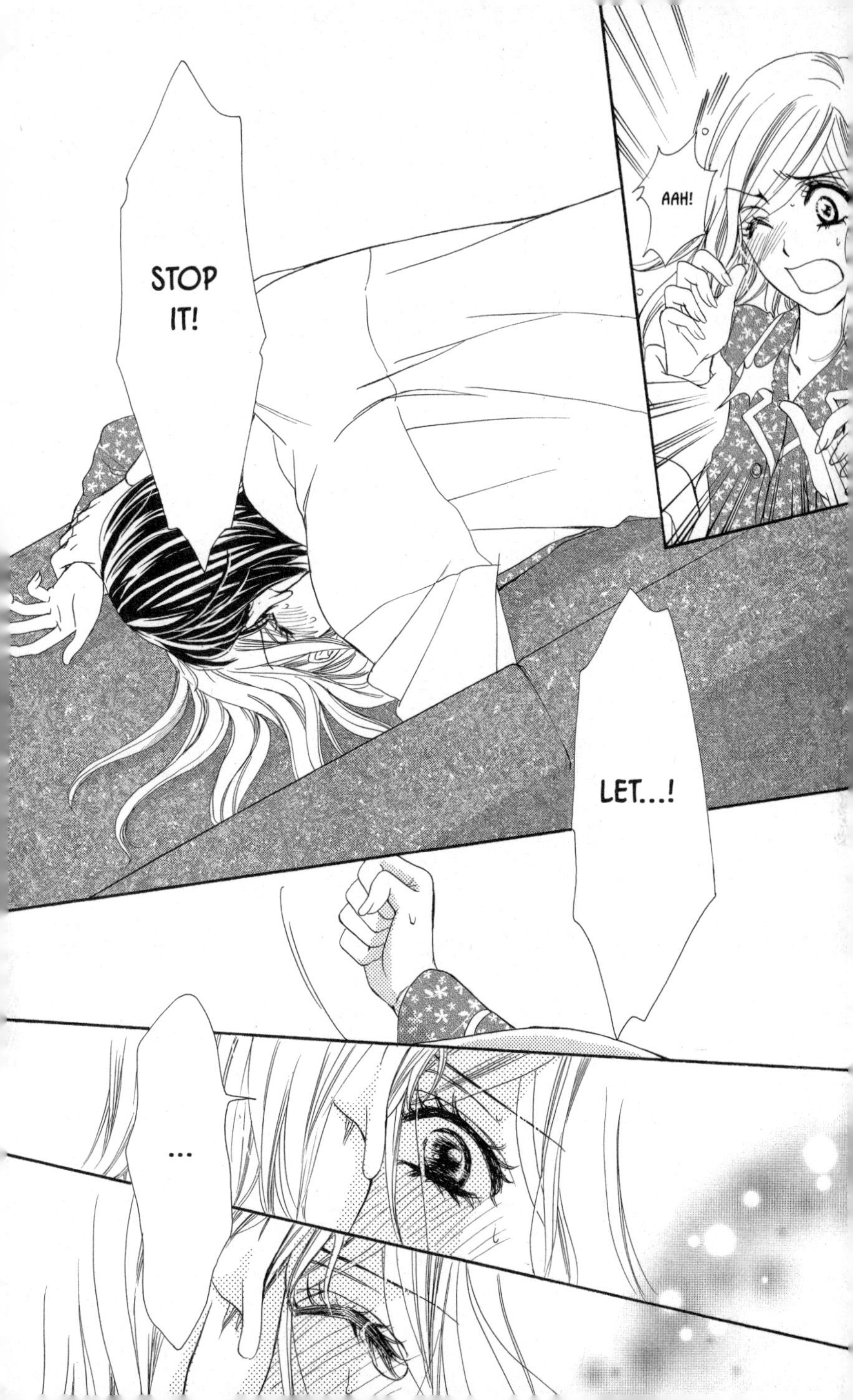
AAH!
STOP IT!
LET...!
...

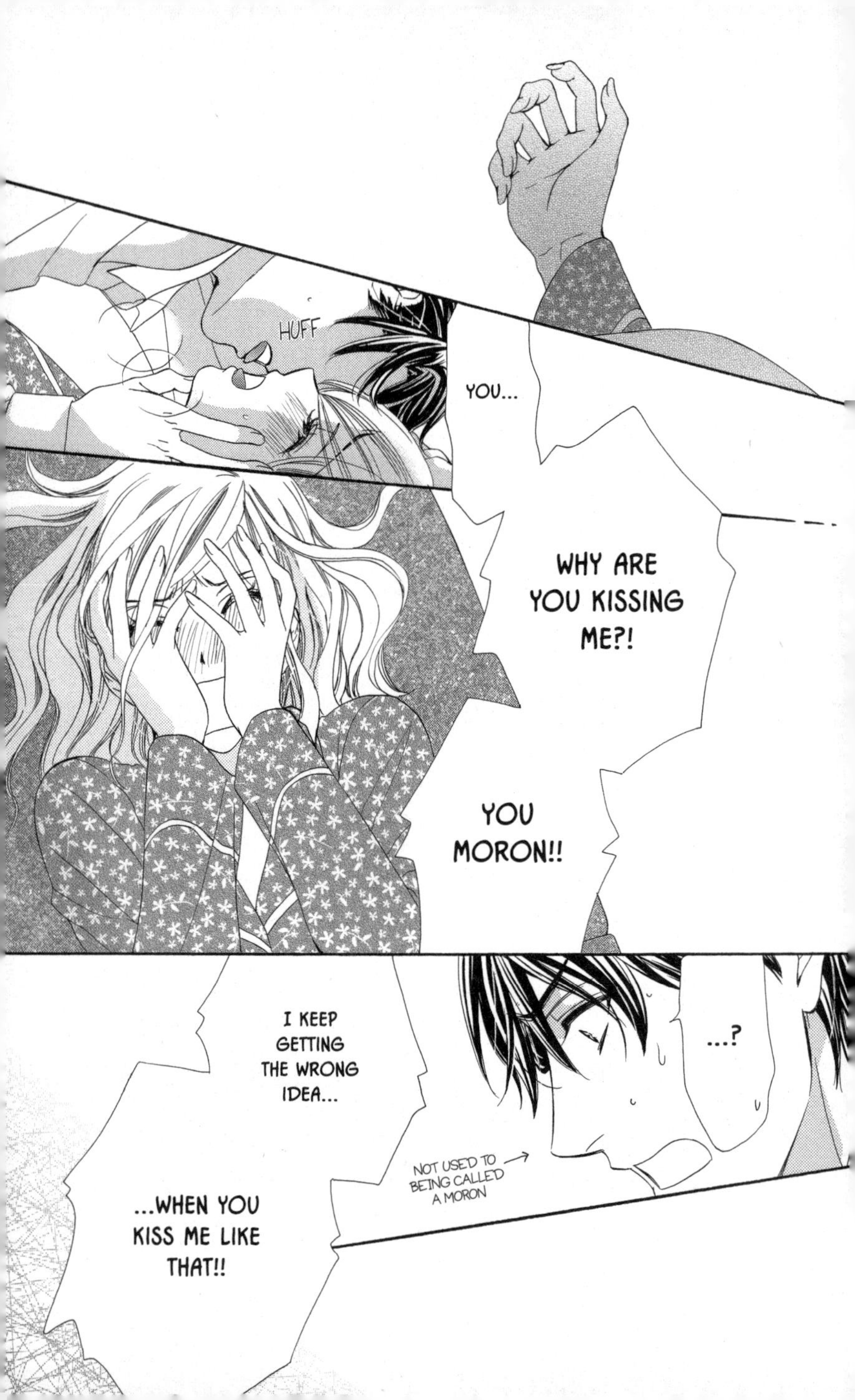
YOU...
WHY ARE YOU KISSING ME?!
YOU MORON!!
HUFF
...?
NOT USED TO BEING CALLED A MORON
I KEEP GETTING THE WRONG IDEA...
...WHEN YOU KISS ME LIKE THAT!!

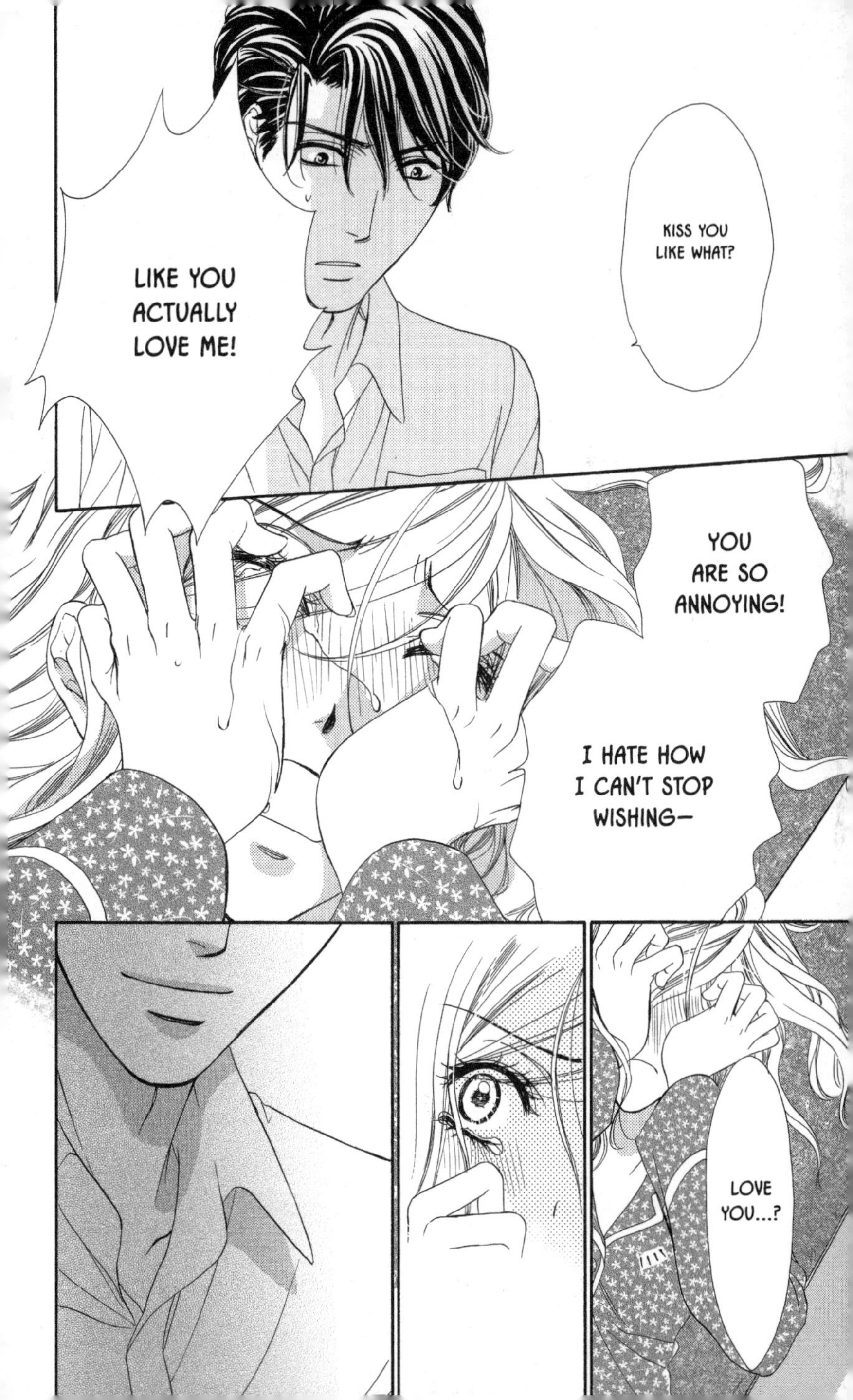
KISS YOU LIKE WHAT?
LIKE YOU ACTUALLY LOVE ME!
YOU ARE SO ANNOYING!
I HATE HOW I CAN'T STOP WISHING—
LOVE YOU...?

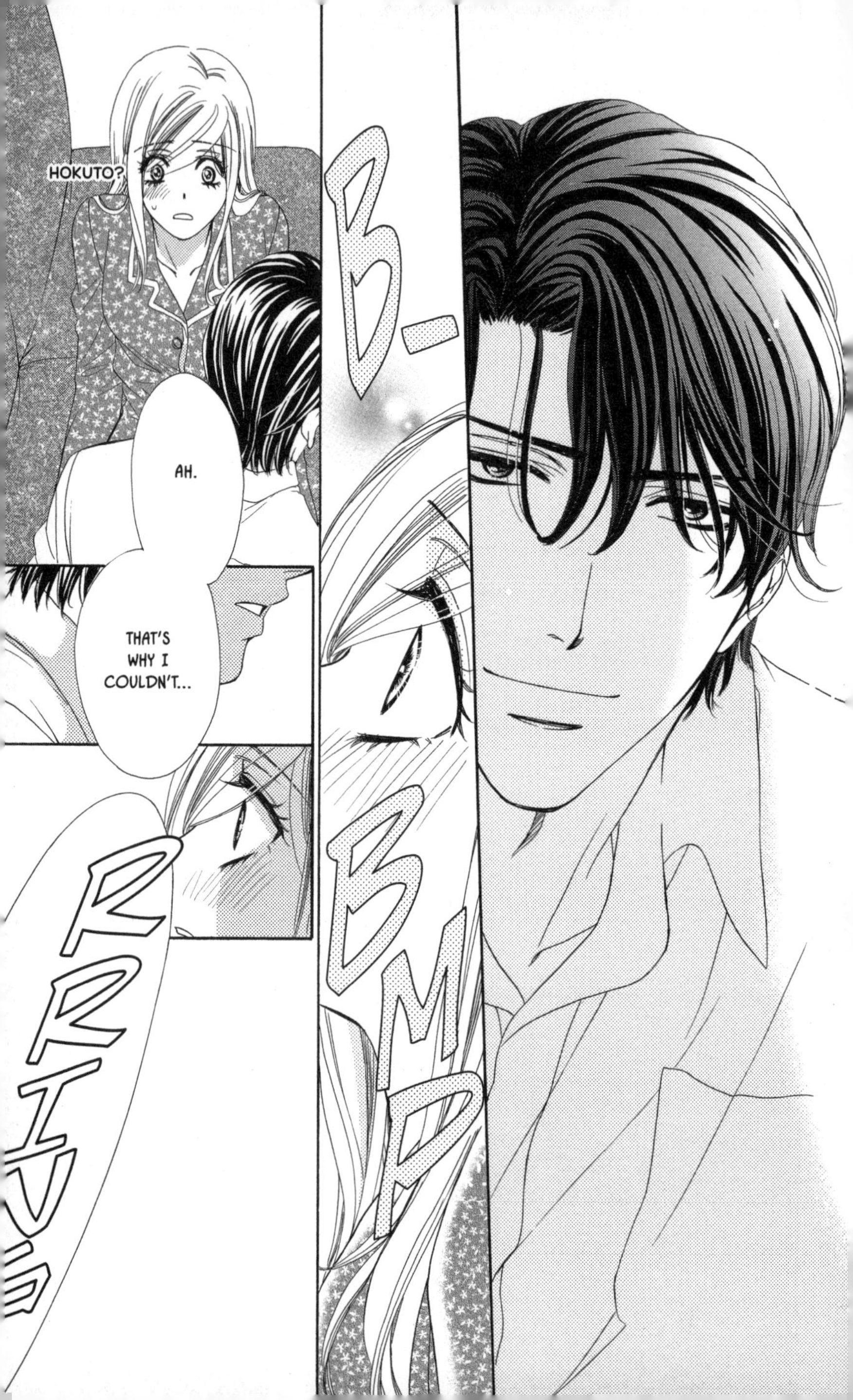
B-
BMP
HOKUTO?
AH.
THAT'S WHY I COULDN'T...
RRING

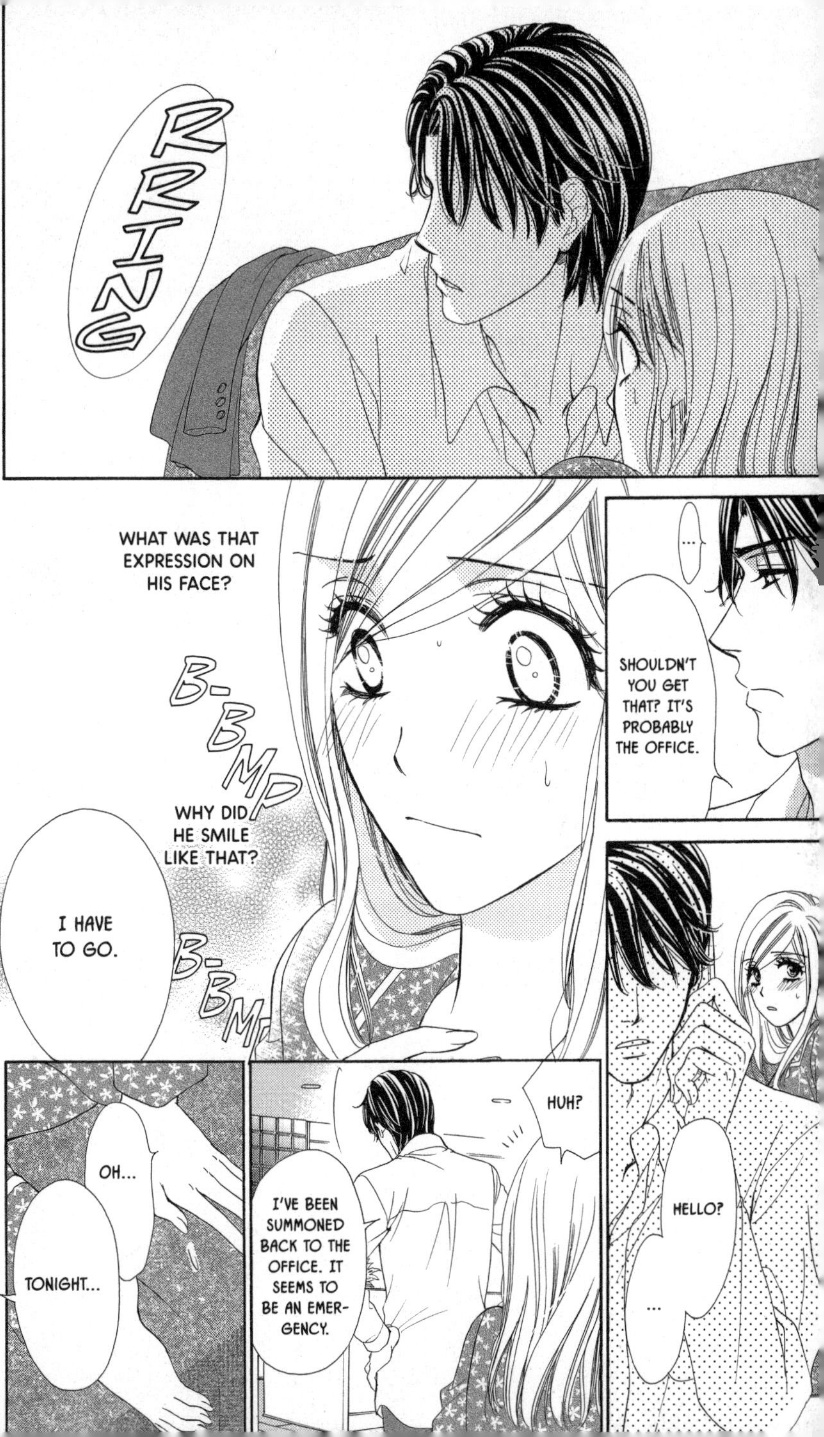
RRING
...
SHOULDN'T YOU GET THAT? IT'S PROBABLY THE OFFICE.
HELLO?
...
WHAT WAS THAT EXPRESSION ON HIS FACE?
B-BMP
WHY DID HE SMILE LIKE THAT?
I HAVE TO GO.
B-BMP
HUH?
I'VE BEEN SUMMONED BACK TO THE OFFICE. IT SEEMS TO BE AN EMERGENCY.
OH...
TONIGHT...

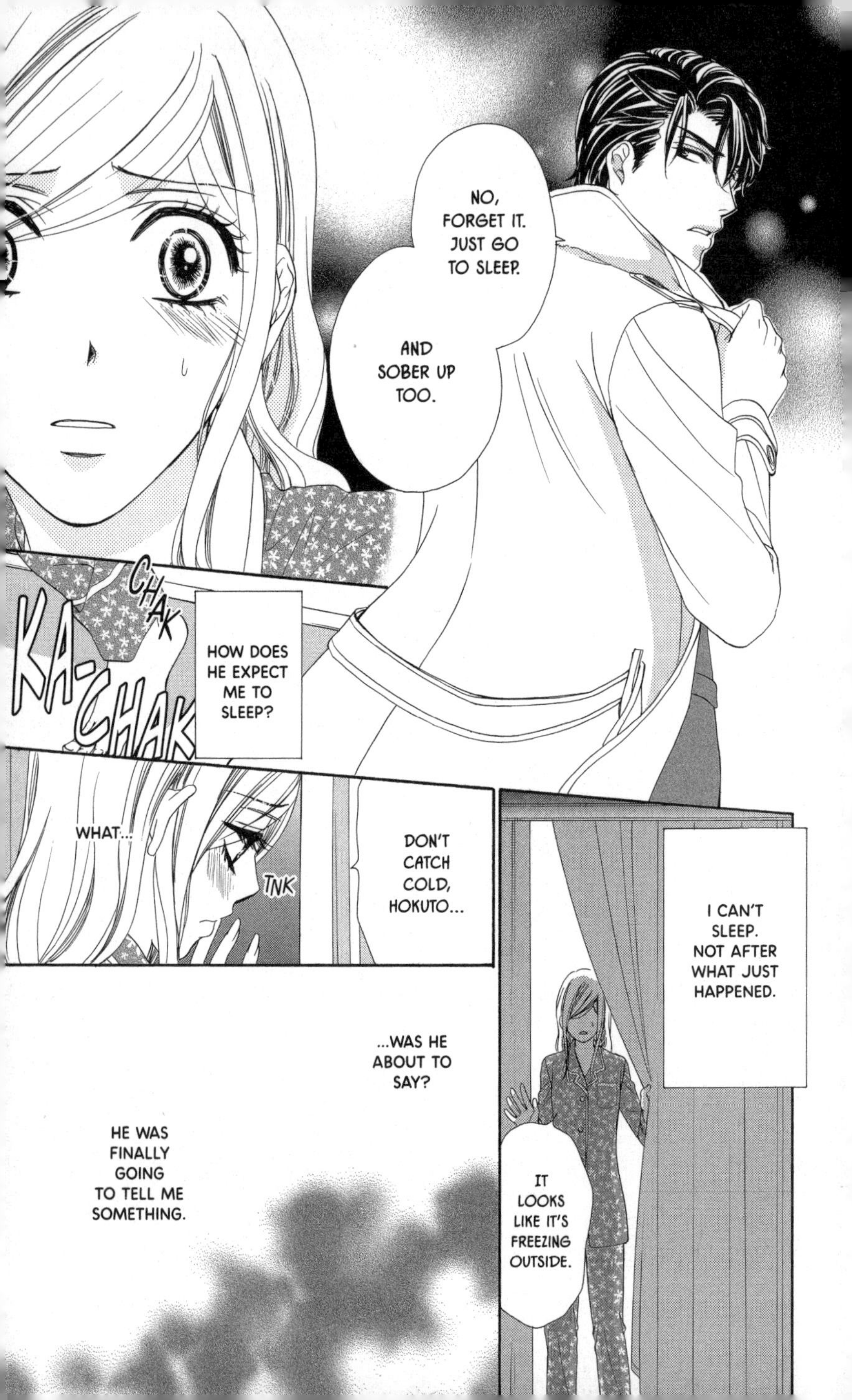
NO, FORGET IT. JUST GO TO SLEEP.
AND SOBER UP TOO.
HOW DOES HE EXPECT ME TO SLEEP?
CHAK
KA-CHAK
DON'T CATCH COLD, HOKUTO...
WHAT...
TNK
I CAN'T SLEEP. NOT AFTER WHAT JUST HAPPENED.
IT LOOKS LIKE IT'S FREEZING OUTSIDE.
...WAS HE ABOUT TO SAY?
HE WAS FINALLY GOING TO TELL ME SOMETHING.

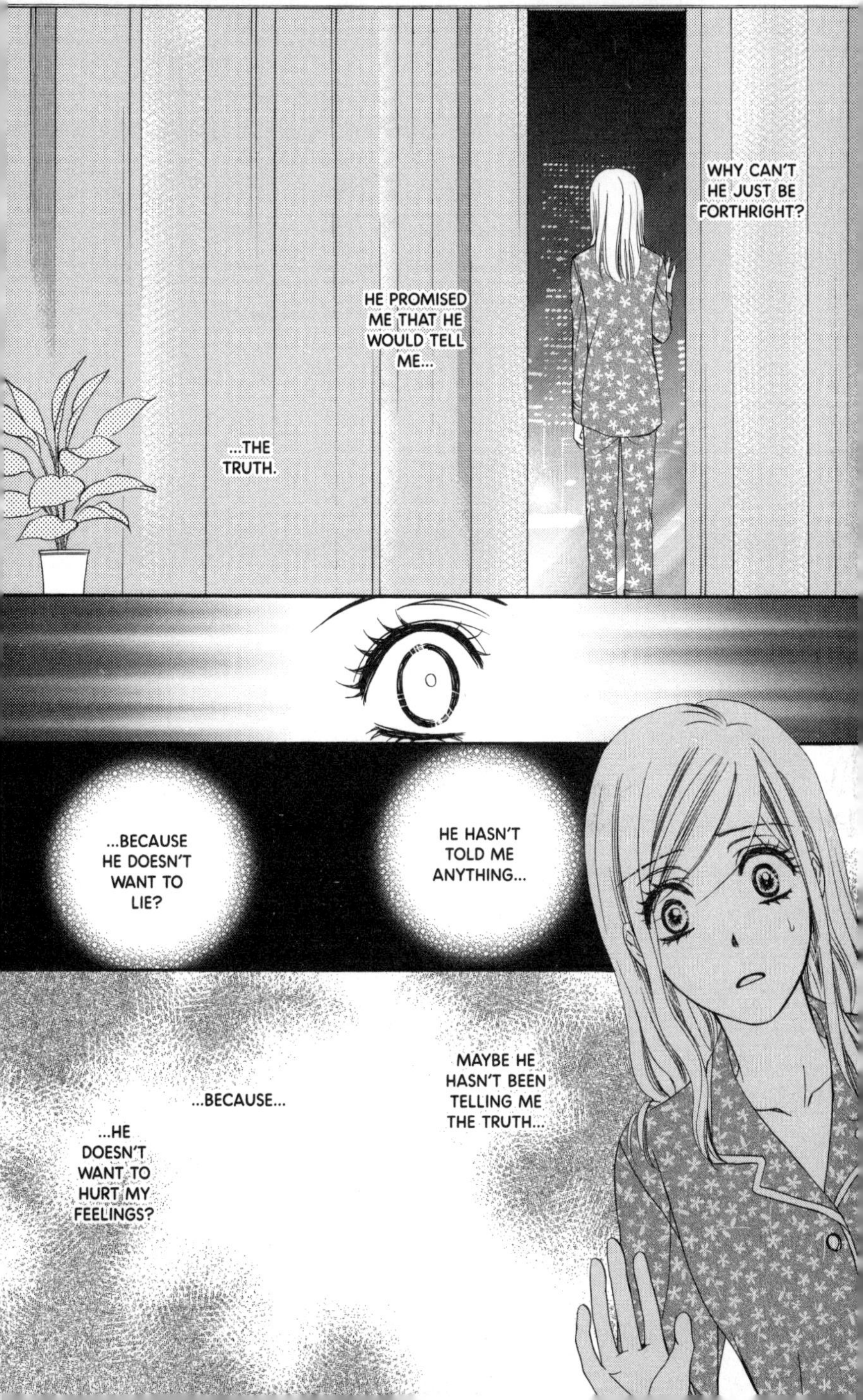
WHY CAN'T HE JUST BE FORTHRIGHT?
HE PROMISED ME THAT HE WOULD TELL ME...
...THE TRUTH.
HE HASN'T TOLD ME ANYTHING...
...BECAUSE HE DOESN'T WANT TO LIE?
MAYBE HE HASN'T BEEN TELLING ME THE TRUTH...
...BECAUSE...
...HE DOESN'T WANT TO HURT MY FEELINGS?

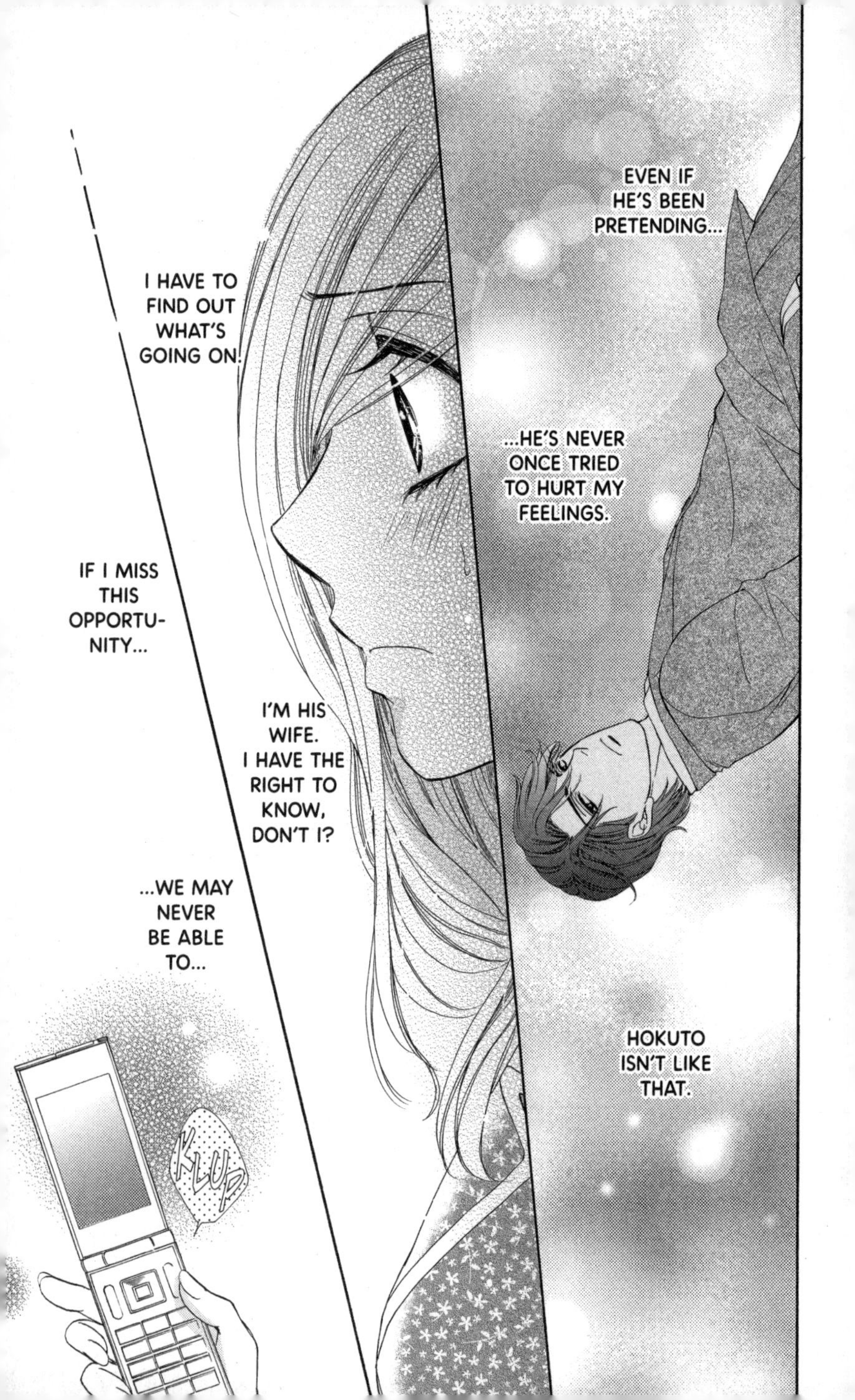
EVEN IF HE'S BEEN PRETENDING...
...HE'S NEVER ONCE TRIED TO HURT MY FEELINGS.
HOKUTO ISN'T LIKE THAT.
I HAVE TO FIND OUT WHAT'S GOING ON!
I'M HIS WIFE. I HAVE THE RIGHT TO KNOW, DON'T I?
IF I MISS THIS OPPORTU-NITY...
...WE MAY NEVER BE ABLE TO...
KLUP

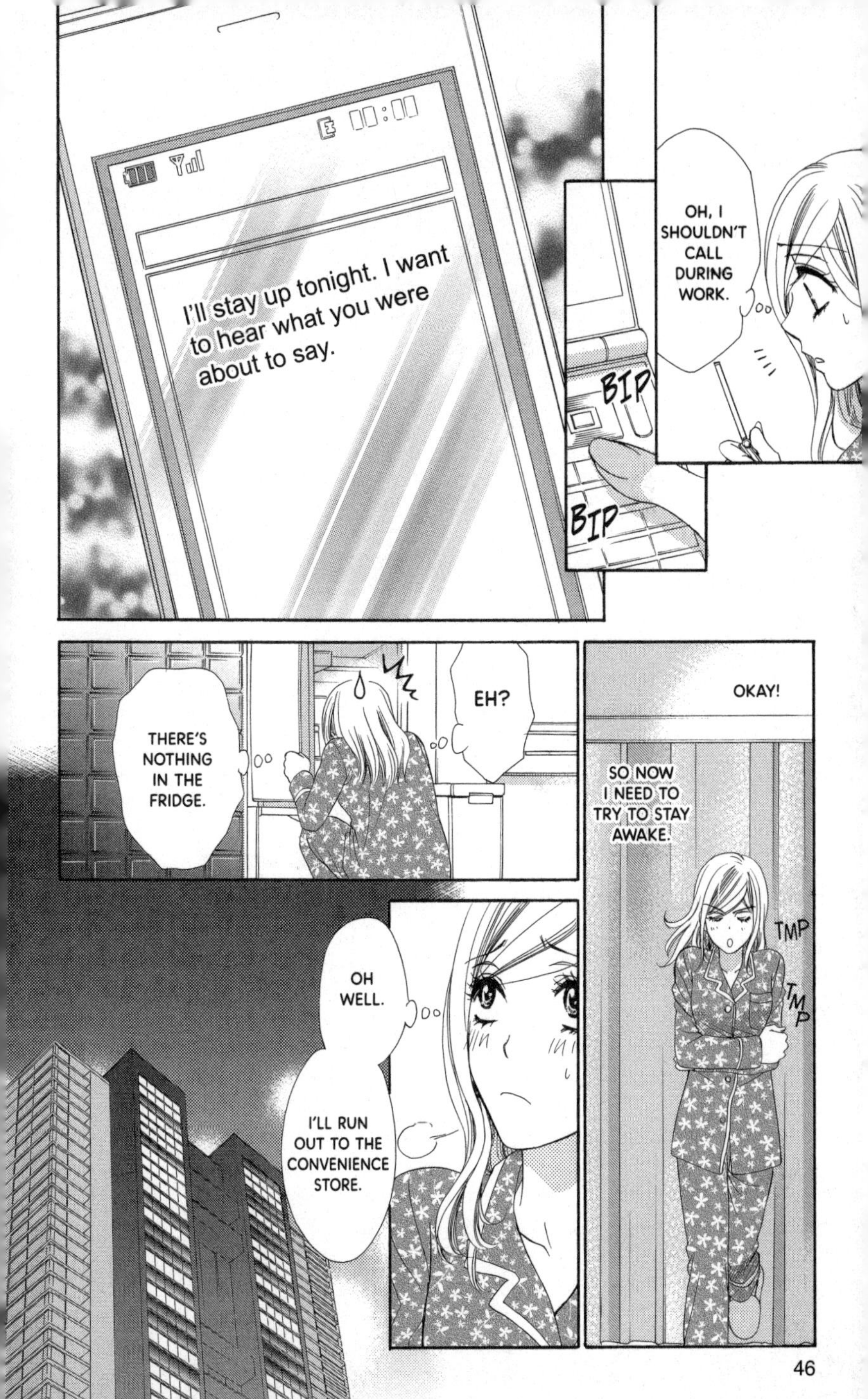
OH, I SHOULDN'T CALL DURING WORK.
BIP
BIP
I'll stay up tonight. I want to hear what you were about to say.
OKAY!
SO NOW I NEED TO TRY TO STAY AWAKE.
TMP
TMP
EH?
THERE'S NOTHING IN THE FRIDGE.
OH WELL.
I'LL RUN OUT TO THE CONVENIENCE STORE.

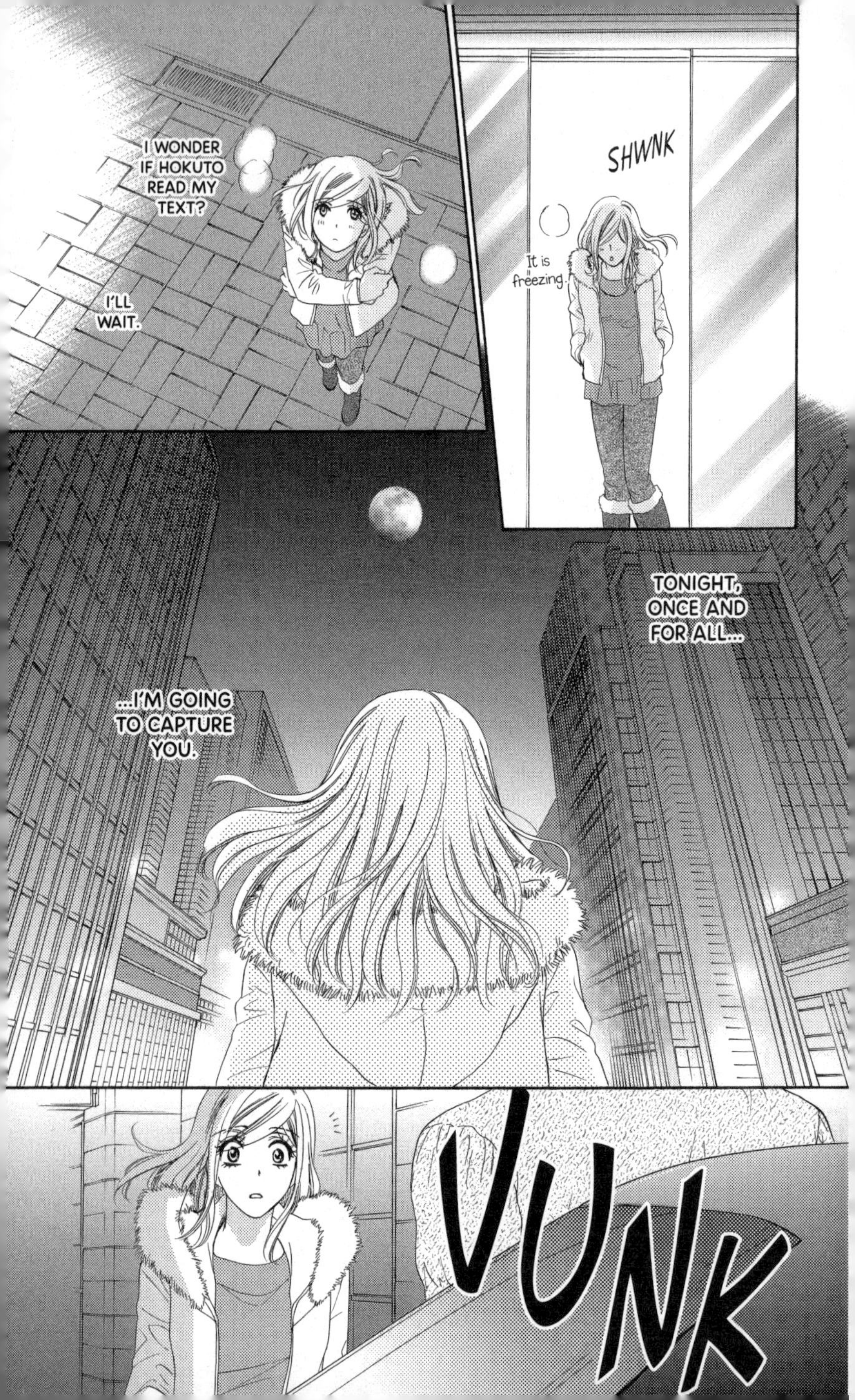
SHWNK
It is freezing.
I WONDER IF HOKUTO READ MY TEXT?
I'LL WAIT.
TONIGHT, ONCE AND FOR ALL...
...I'M GOING TO CAPTURE YOU.
VUNK

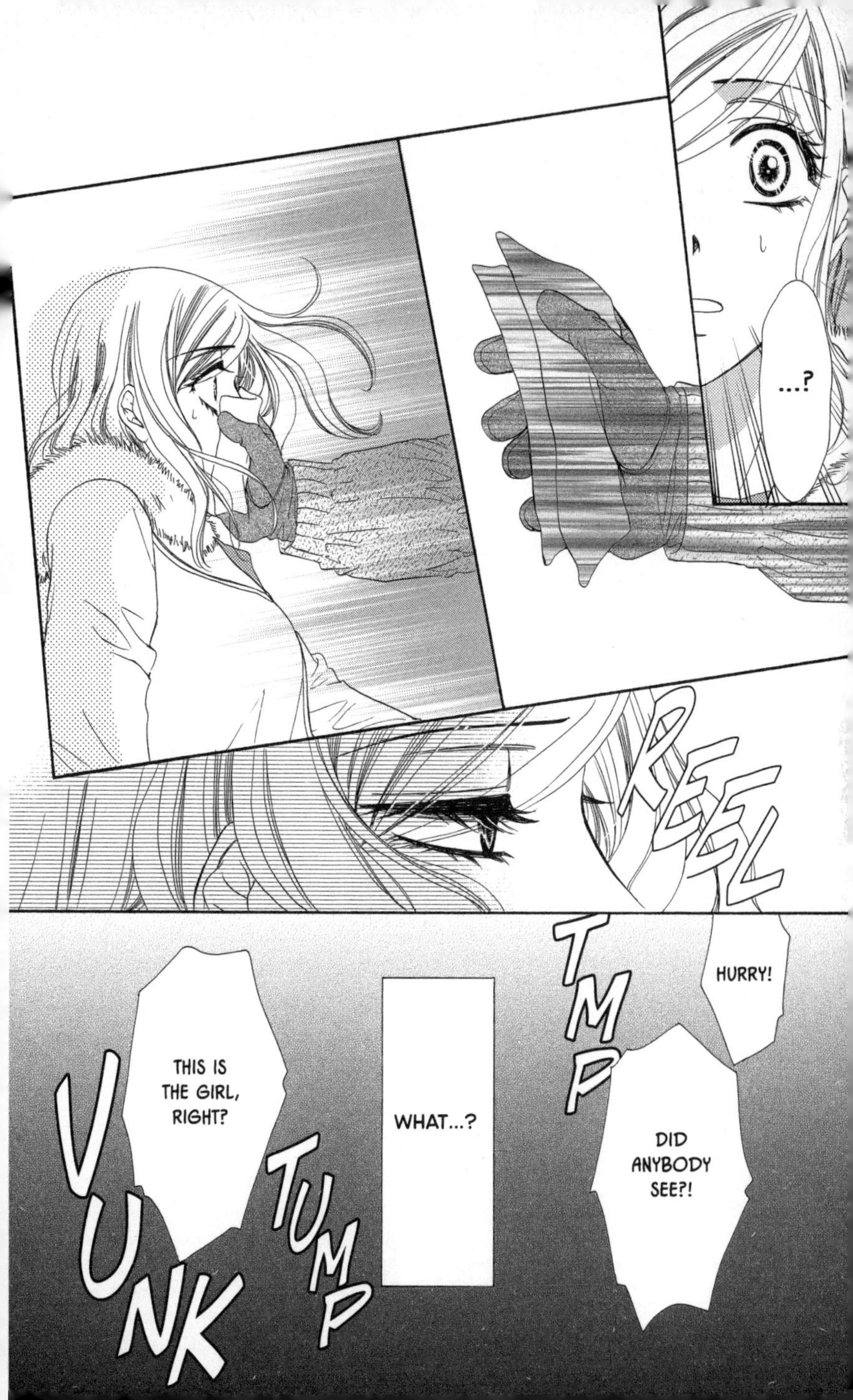

...?
REEL
HURRY!
TMP
DID ANYBODY SEE?!
WHAT...?
THIS IS THE GIRL, RIGHT?
TUMP
VUNK

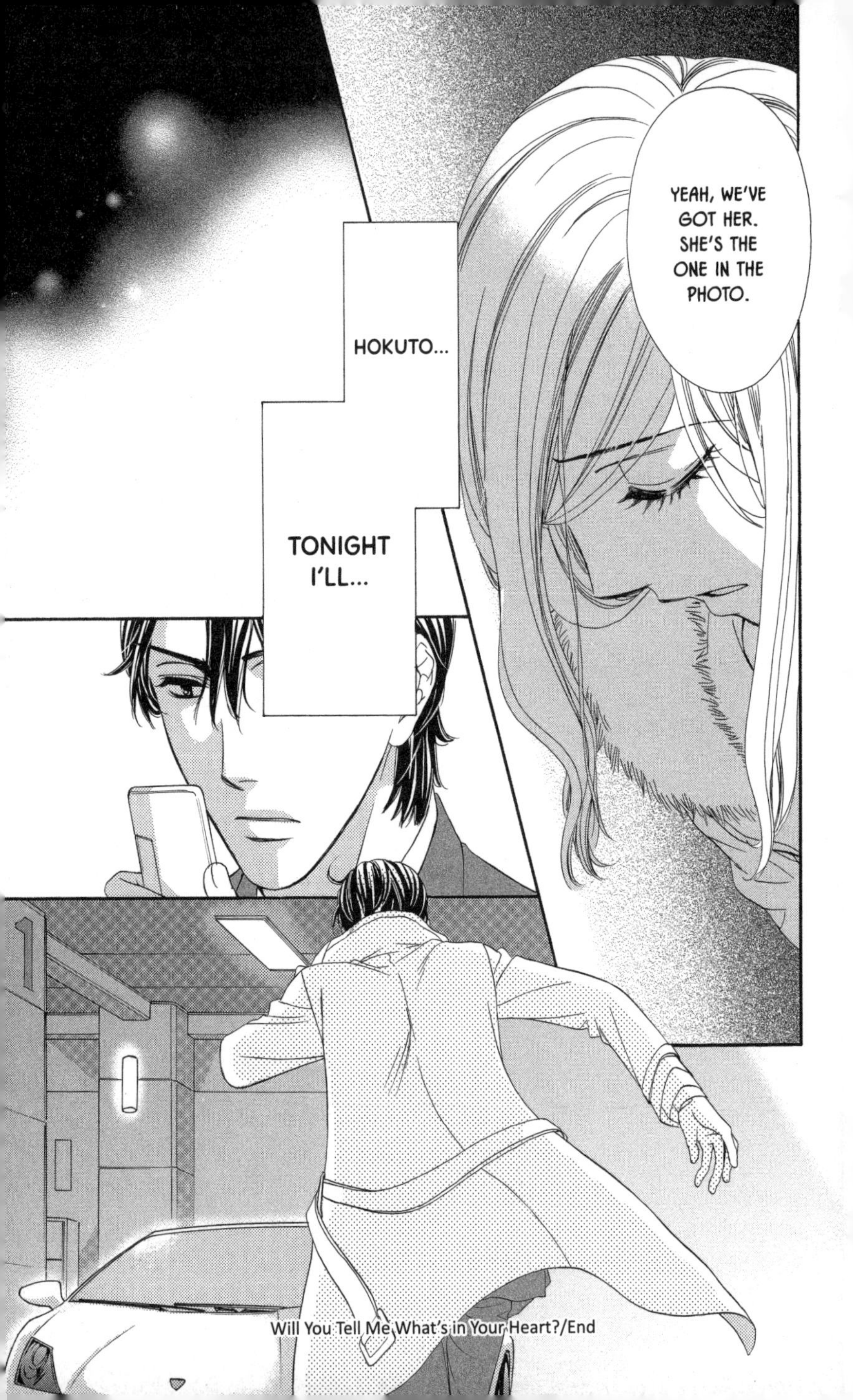
YEAH, WE'VE GOT HER. SHE'S THE ONE IN THE PHOTO.
HOKUTO...
TONIGHT I'LL...
Will You Tell Me What's in Your Heart?/End

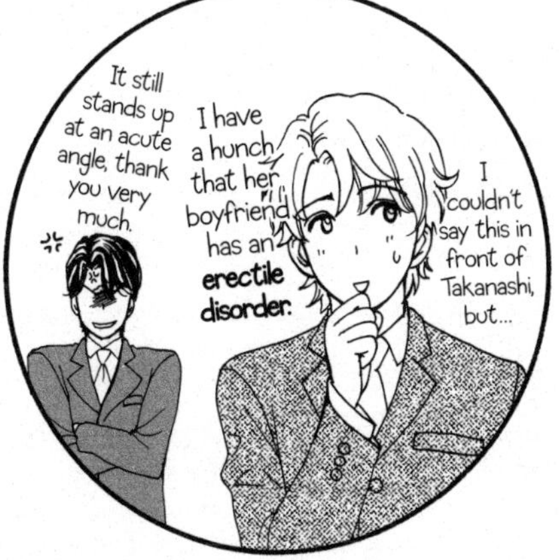
I couldn't say this in front of Takanashi, but...
I have a hunch that her boyfriend has an **erectile disorder.**
It still stands up at an acute angle, thank you very much.

Step Fourteen: Repeat What You Just Said

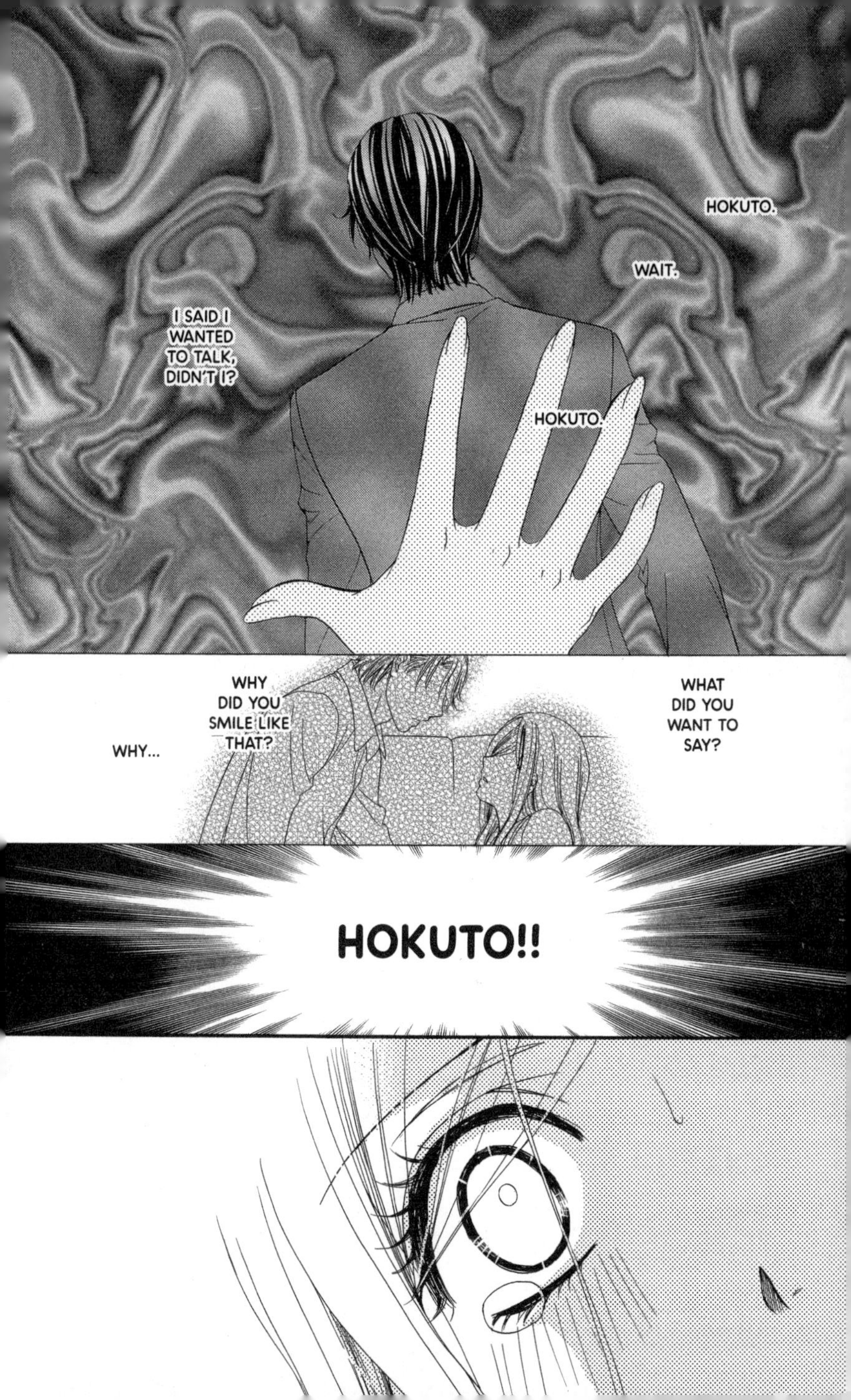
HOKUTO.
WAIT.
HOKUTO.
I SAID I WANTED TO TALK, DIDN'T I?
WHAT DID YOU WANT TO SAY?
WHY DID YOU SMILE LIKE THAT?
WHY...
HOKUTO!!

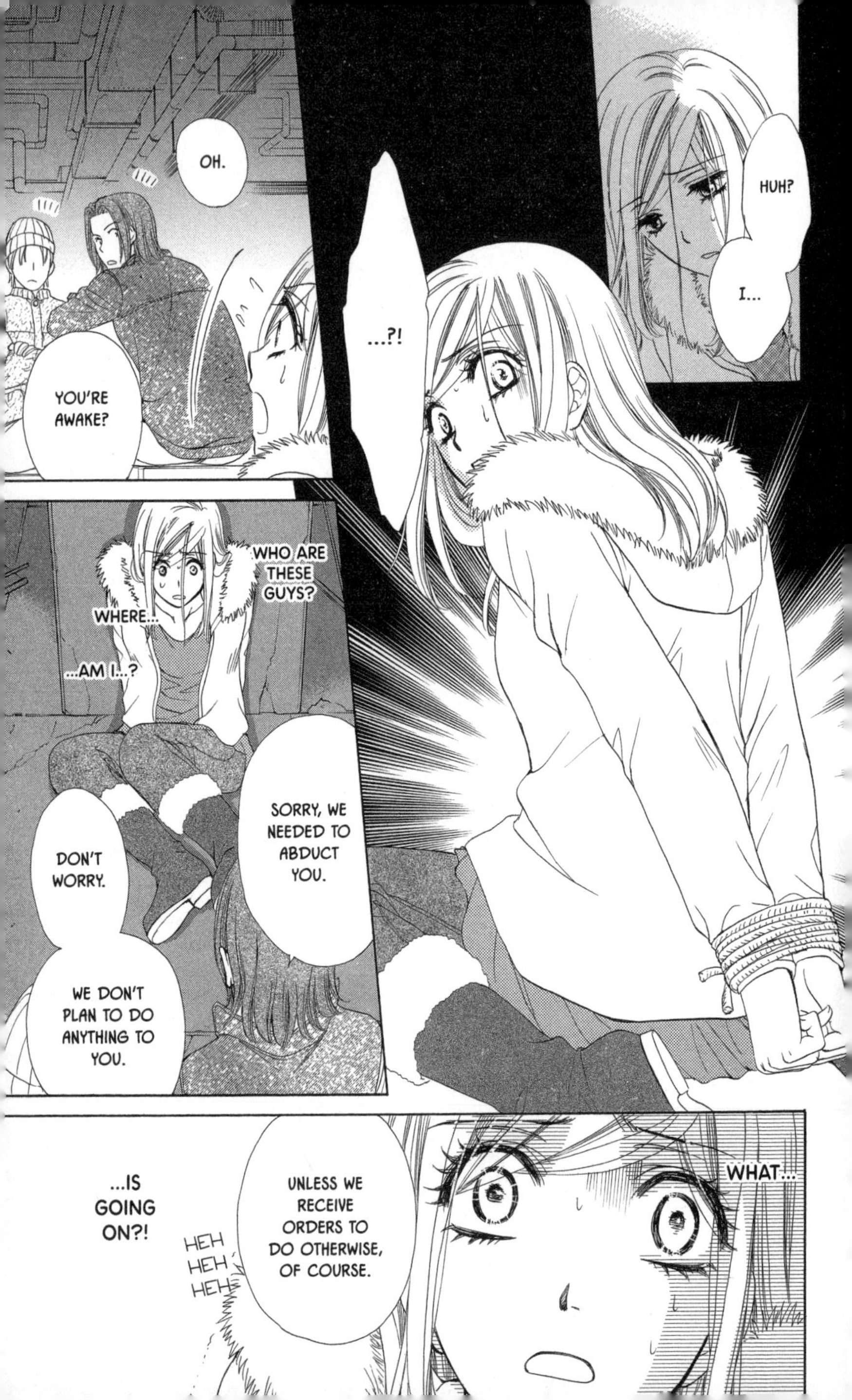
HUH?
I...
OH.
YOU'RE AWAKE?
...?!
WHO ARE THESE GUYS?
WHERE...
...AM I...?
SORRY, WE NEEDED TO ABDUCT YOU.
DON'T WORRY.
WE DON'T PLAN TO DO ANYTHING TO YOU.
WHAT...
UNLESS WE RECEIVE ORDERS TO DO OTHERWISE, OF COURSE.
HEH HEH HEH
...IS GOING ON?!

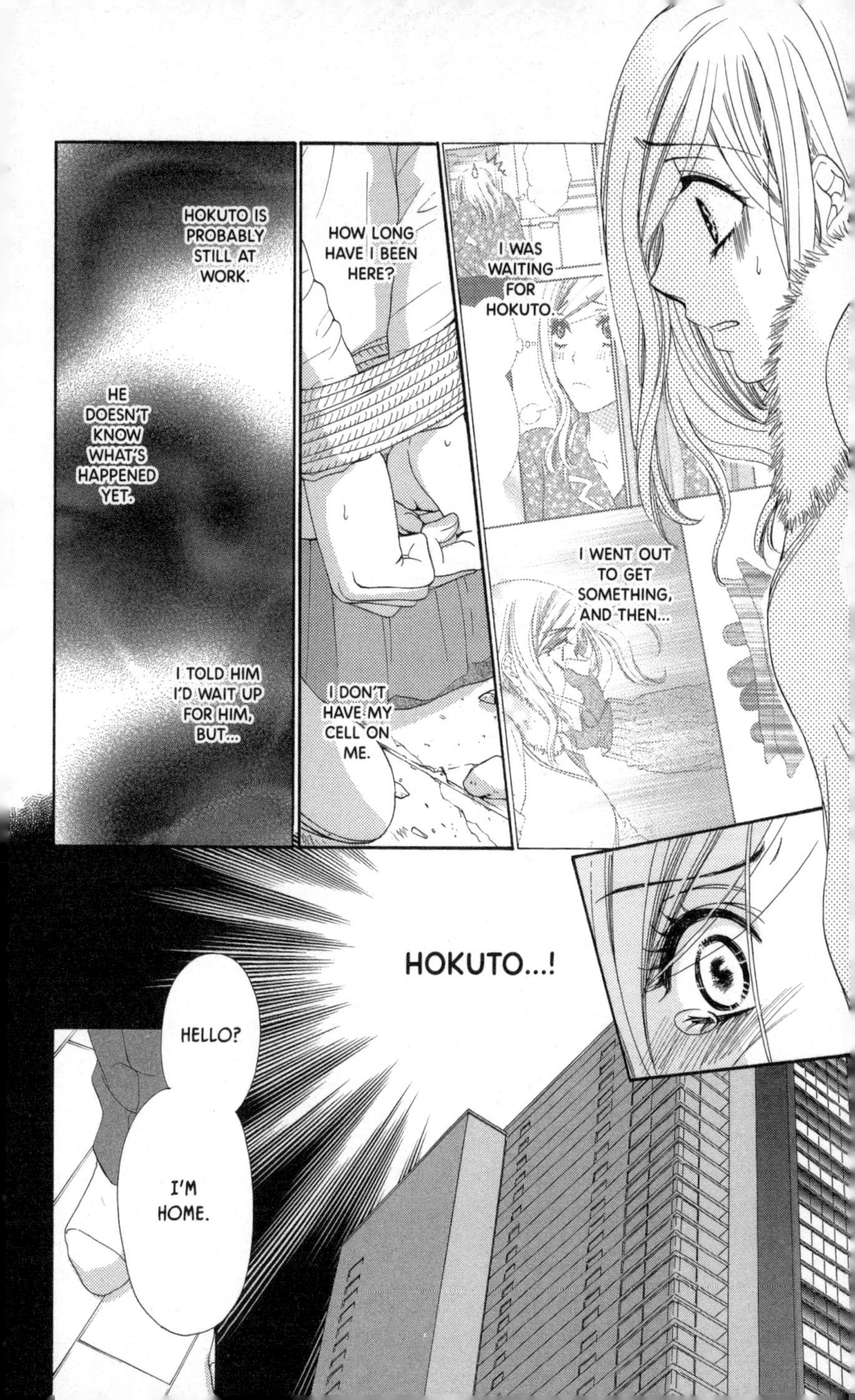
I WAS WAITING FOR HOKUTO.
I WENT OUT TO GET SOMETHING, AND THEN...
HOW LONG HAVE I BEEN HERE?
I DON'T HAVE MY CELL ON ME.
HOKUTO IS PROBABLY STILL AT WORK.
HE DOESN'T KNOW WHAT'S HAPPENED YET.
I TOLD HIM I'D WAIT UP FOR HIM, BUT...
HOKUTO...!
HELLO?
I'M HOME.

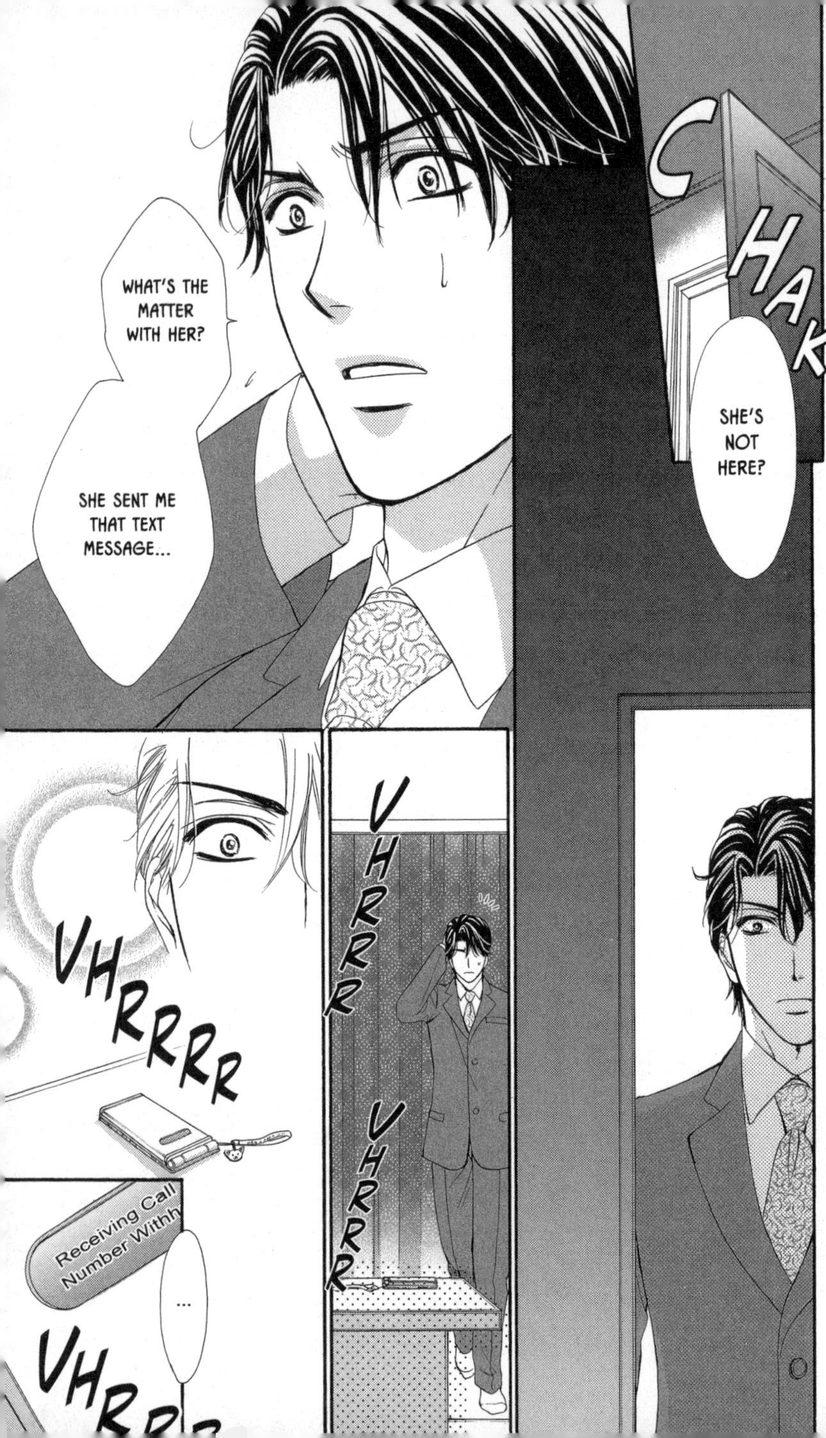
CHAK
SHE'S NOT HERE?
WHAT'S THE MATTER WITH HER?
SHE SENT ME THAT TEXT MESSAGE...
VHRRRR
VHRRRR
VHRRRRR
Receiving Call
Number Withh
...
VHRR

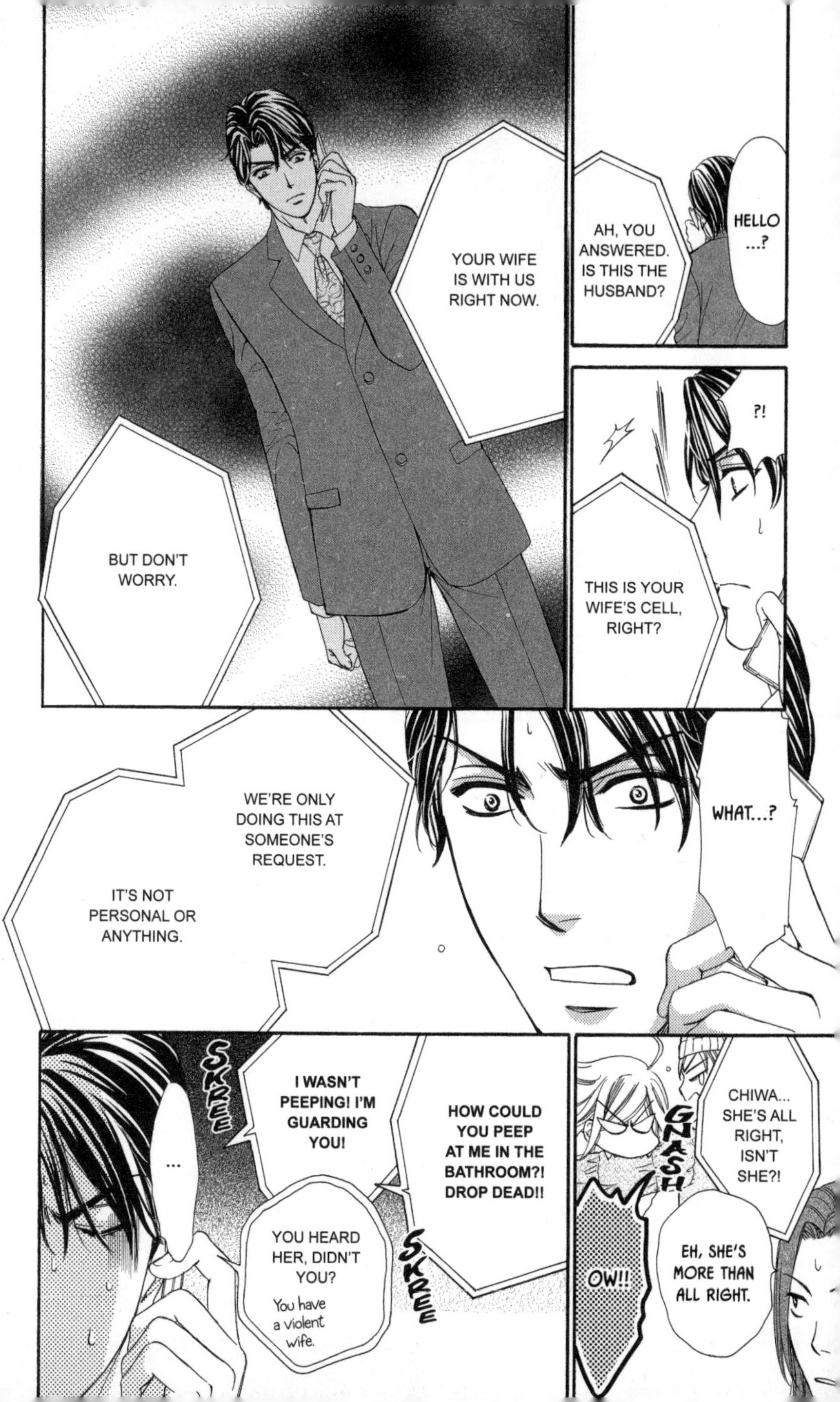
HELLO ...?
AH, YOU ANSWERED. IS THIS THE HUSBAND?
?!
THIS IS YOUR WIFE'S CELL, RIGHT?
YOUR WIFE IS WITH US RIGHT NOW.
BUT DON'T WORRY.
WHAT...?
WE'RE ONLY DOING THIS AT SOMEONE'S REQUEST.
IT'S NOT PERSONAL OR ANYTHING.
CHIWA... SHE'S ALL RIGHT, ISN'T SHE?!
GNASH
EH, SHE'S MORE THAN ALL RIGHT.
OW!!
HOW COULD YOU PEEP AT ME IN THE BATHROOM?! DROP DEAD!!
SKREE
I WASN'T PEEPING! I'M GUARDING YOU!
SKREE
...
YOU HEARD HER, DIDN'T YOU?
You have a violent wife.

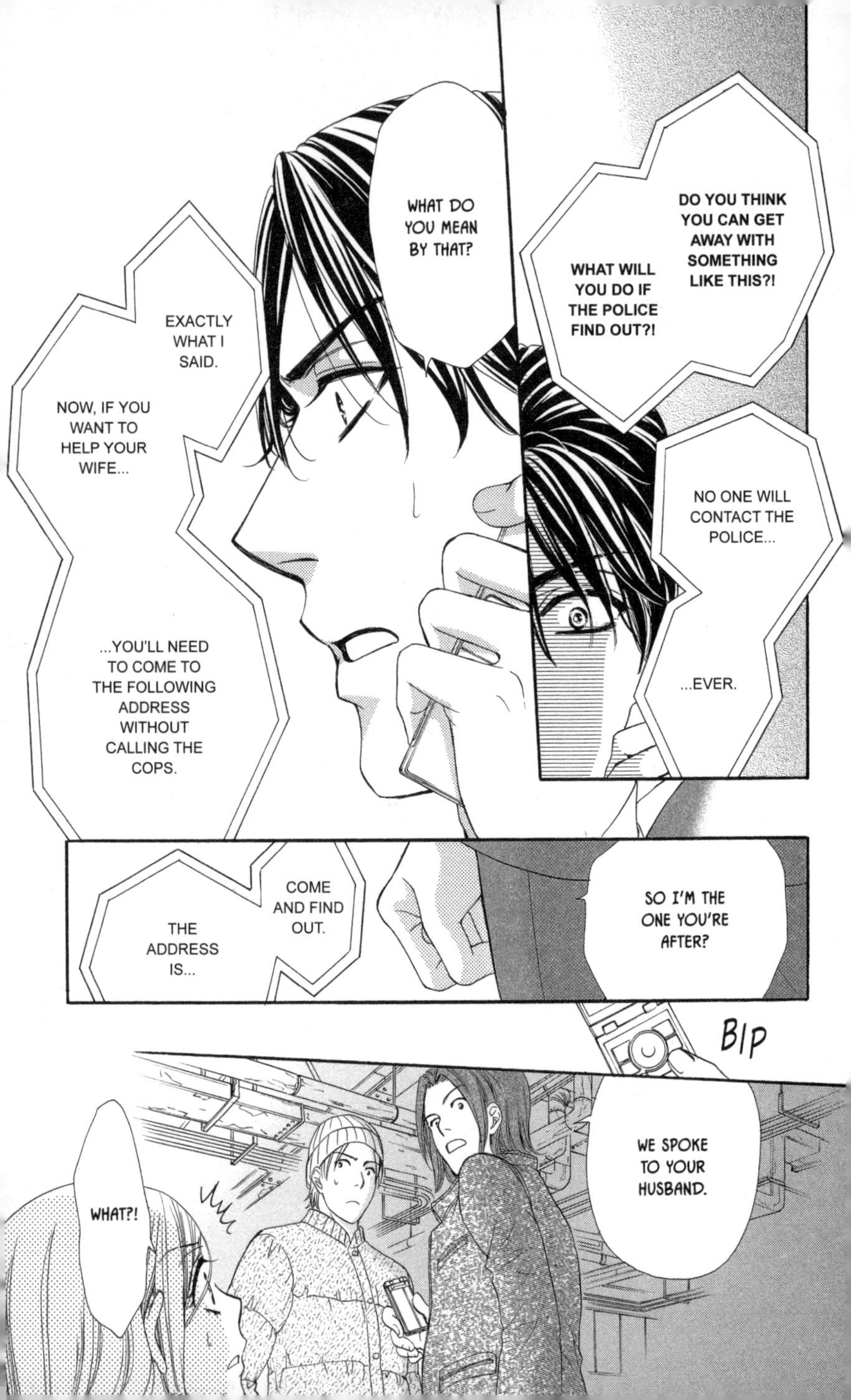
DO YOU THINK YOU CAN GET AWAY WITH SOMETHING LIKE THIS?!
WHAT WILL YOU DO IF THE POLICE FIND OUT?!
NO ONE WILL CONTACT THE POLICE...
...EVER.
WHAT DO YOU MEAN BY THAT?
EXACTLY WHAT I SAID.
NOW, IF YOU WANT TO HELP YOUR WIFE...
...YOU'LL NEED TO COME TO THE FOLLOWING ADDRESS WITHOUT CALLING THE COPS.
SO I'M THE ONE YOU'RE AFTER?
COME AND FIND OUT.
THE ADDRESS IS...
BIP
WE SPOKE TO YOUR HUSBAND.
WHAT?!

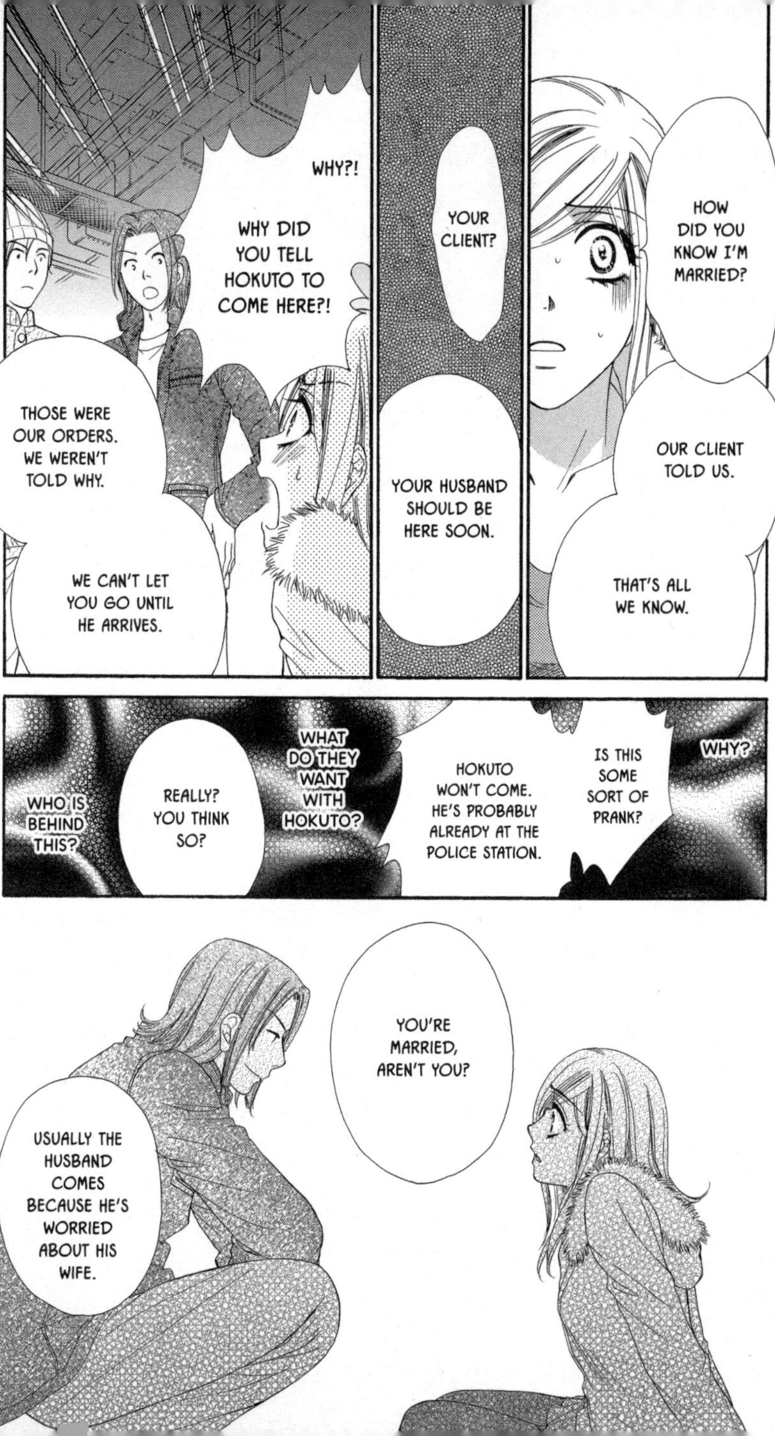
HOW DID YOU KNOW I'M MARRIED?
OUR CLIENT TOLD US.
THAT'S ALL WE KNOW.
YOUR CLIENT?
YOUR HUSBAND SHOULD BE HERE SOON.
WHY?!
WHY DID YOU TELL HOKUTO TO COME HERE?!
THOSE WERE OUR ORDERS. WE WEREN'T TOLD WHY.
WE CAN'T LET YOU GO UNTIL HE ARRIVES.
WHY?
IS THIS SOME SORT OF PRANK?
HOKUTO WON'T COME. HE'S PROBABLY ALREADY AT THE POLICE STATION.
WHAT DO THEY WANT WITH HOKUTO?
REALLY? YOU THINK SO?
WHO IS BEHIND THIS?
YOU'RE MARRIED, AREN'T YOU?
USUALLY THE HUSBAND COMES BECAUSE HE'S WORRIED ABOUT HIS WIFE.

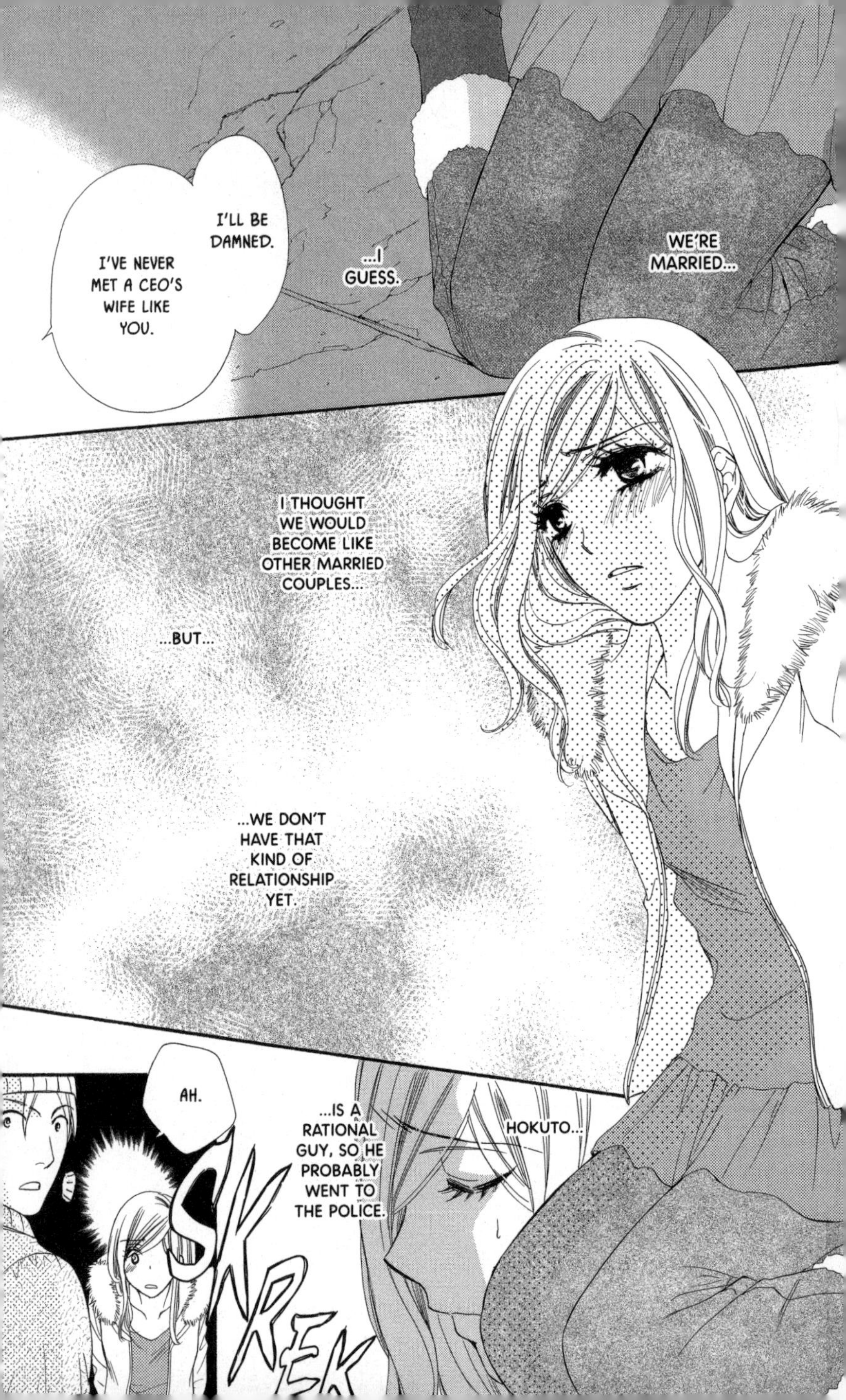
WE'RE MARRIED...
...I GUESS.
I'LL BE DAMNED. I'VE NEVER MET A CEO'S WIFE LIKE YOU.
I THOUGHT WE WOULD BECOME LIKE OTHER MARRIED COUPLES...
...BUT...
...WE DON'T HAVE THAT KIND OF RELATIONSHIP YET.
HOKUTO...
...IS A RATIONAL GUY, SO HE PROBABLY WENT TO THE POLICE.
AH.
SKREK

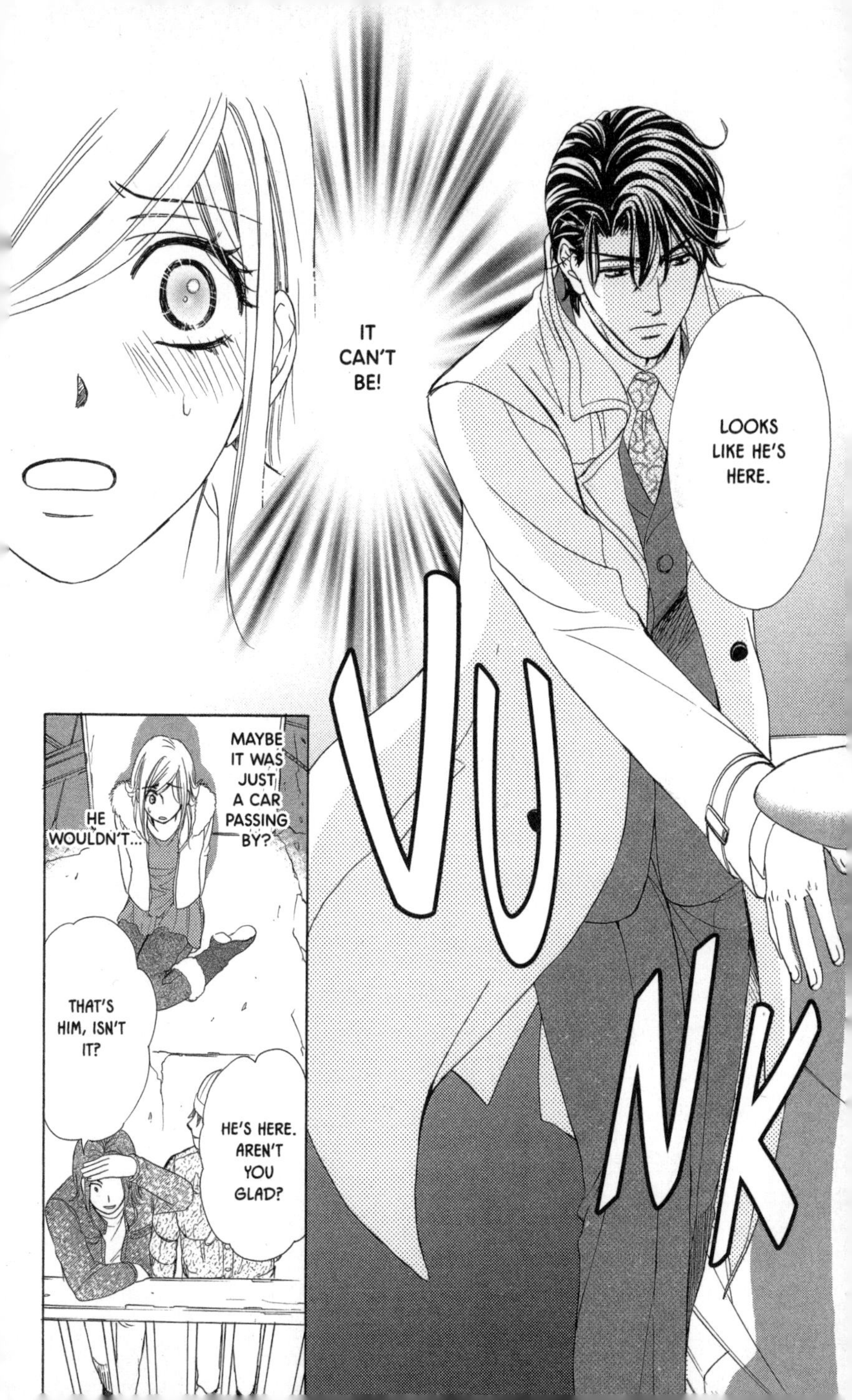
LOOKS LIKE HE'S HERE.
VUNK
IT CAN'T BE!
MAYBE IT WAS JUST A CAR PASSING BY?
HE WOULDN'T...
THAT'S HIM, ISN'T IT?
HE'S HERE. AREN'T YOU GLAD?

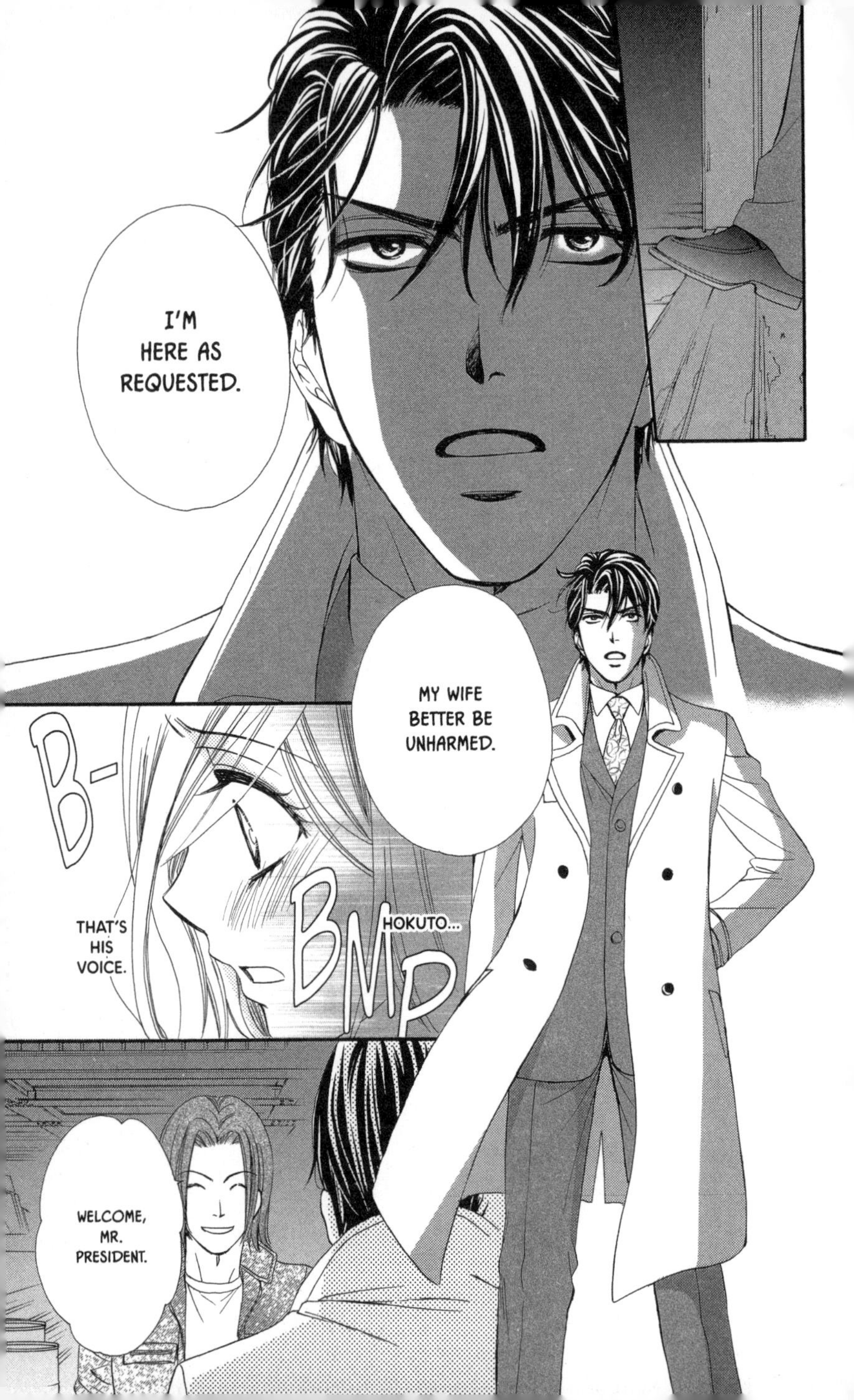
I'M HERE AS REQUESTED.
MY WIFE BETTER BE UNHARMED.
B-
BMP
HOKUTO...
THAT'S HIS VOICE.
WELCOME, MR. PRESIDENT.

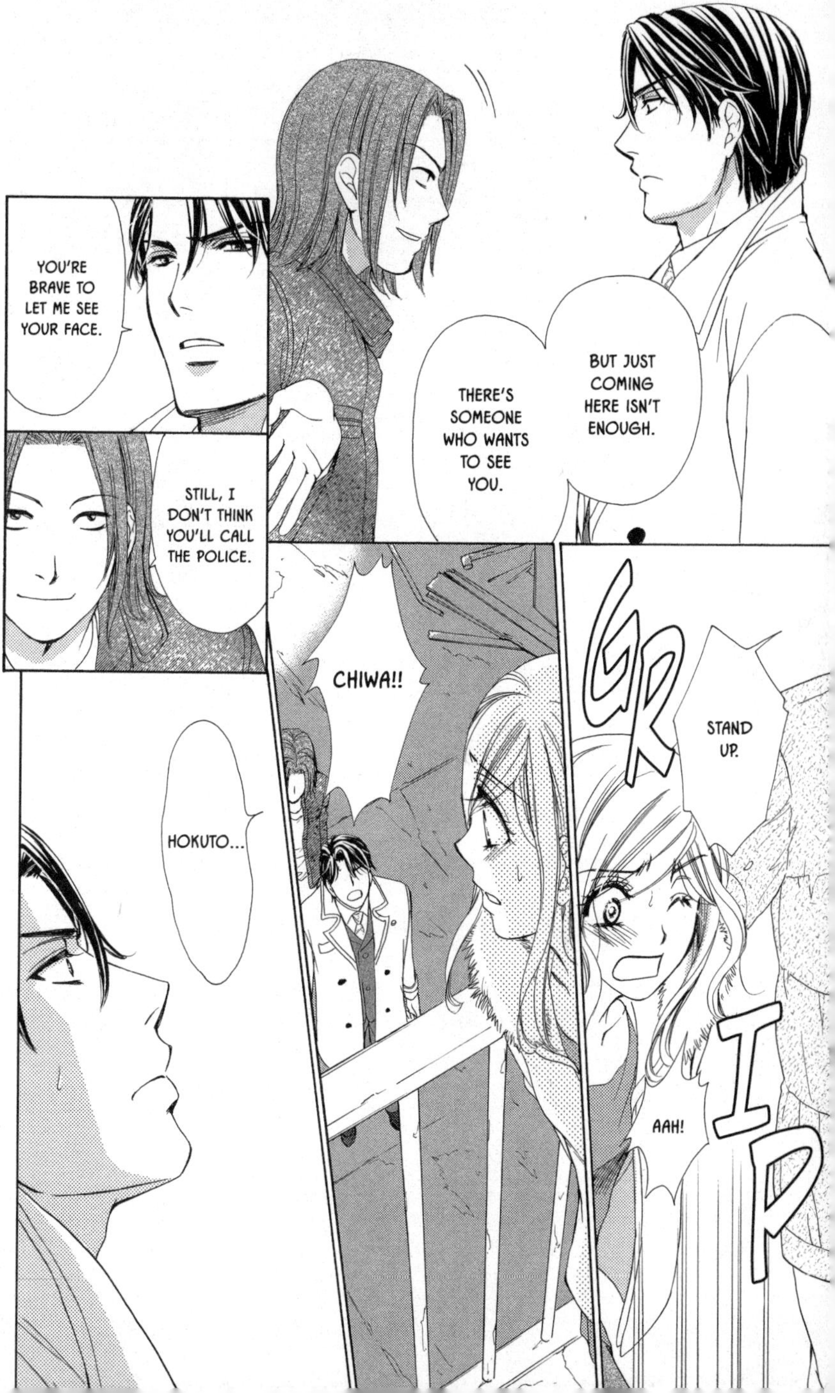
BUT JUST COMING HERE ISN'T ENOUGH.
THERE'S SOMEONE WHO WANTS TO SEE YOU.
YOU'RE BRAVE TO LET ME SEE YOUR FACE.
STILL, I DON'T THINK YOU'LL CALL THE POLICE.
GRIP
STAND UP.
AAH!
CHIWA!!
HOKUTO...

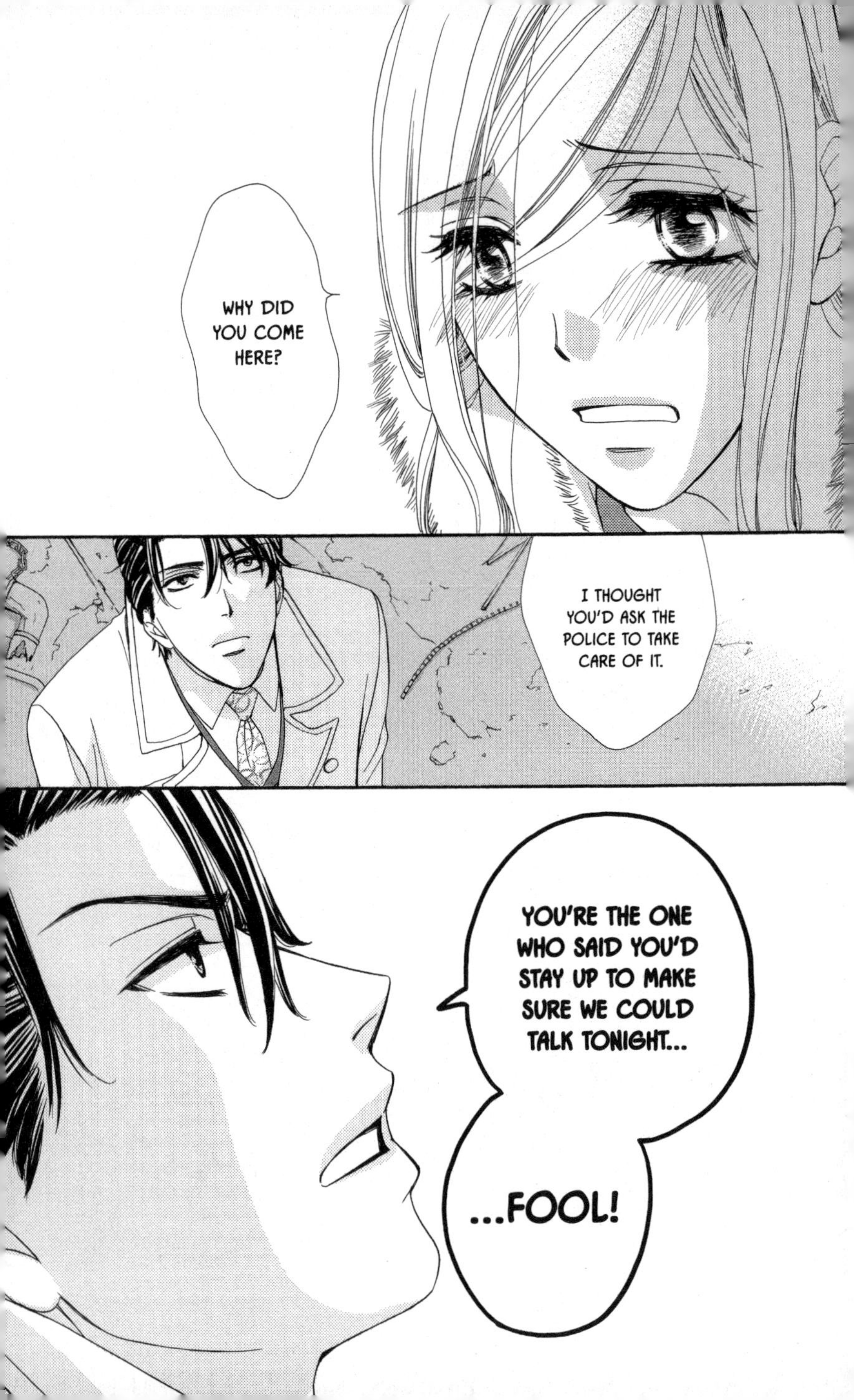
WHY DID YOU COME HERE?
I THOUGHT YOU'D ASK THE POLICE TO TAKE CARE OF IT.
YOU'RE THE ONE WHO SAID YOU'D STAY UP TO MAKE SURE WE COULD TALK TONIGHT...
...FOOL!

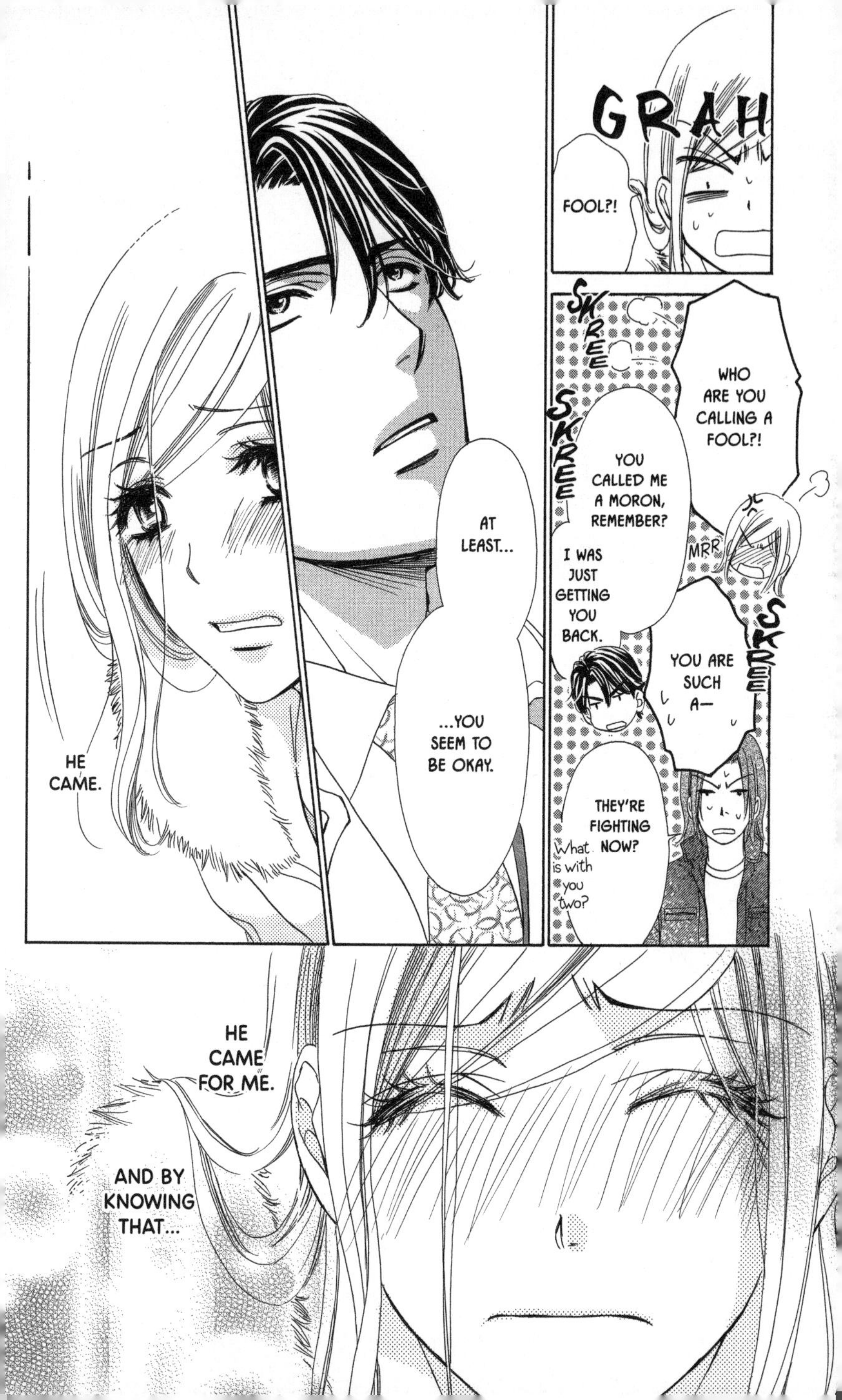
GRAH
FOOL?!
SKREE
SKREE
WHO ARE YOU CALLING A FOOL?!
YOU CALLED ME A MORON, REMEMBER?
I WAS JUST GETTING YOU BACK.
MRR
YOU ARE SUCH A—
SKREE
THEY'RE FIGHTING NOW?
What is with you two?
AT LEAST...
...YOU SEEM TO BE OKAY.
HE CAME.
HE CAME FOR ME.
AND BY KNOWING THAT...

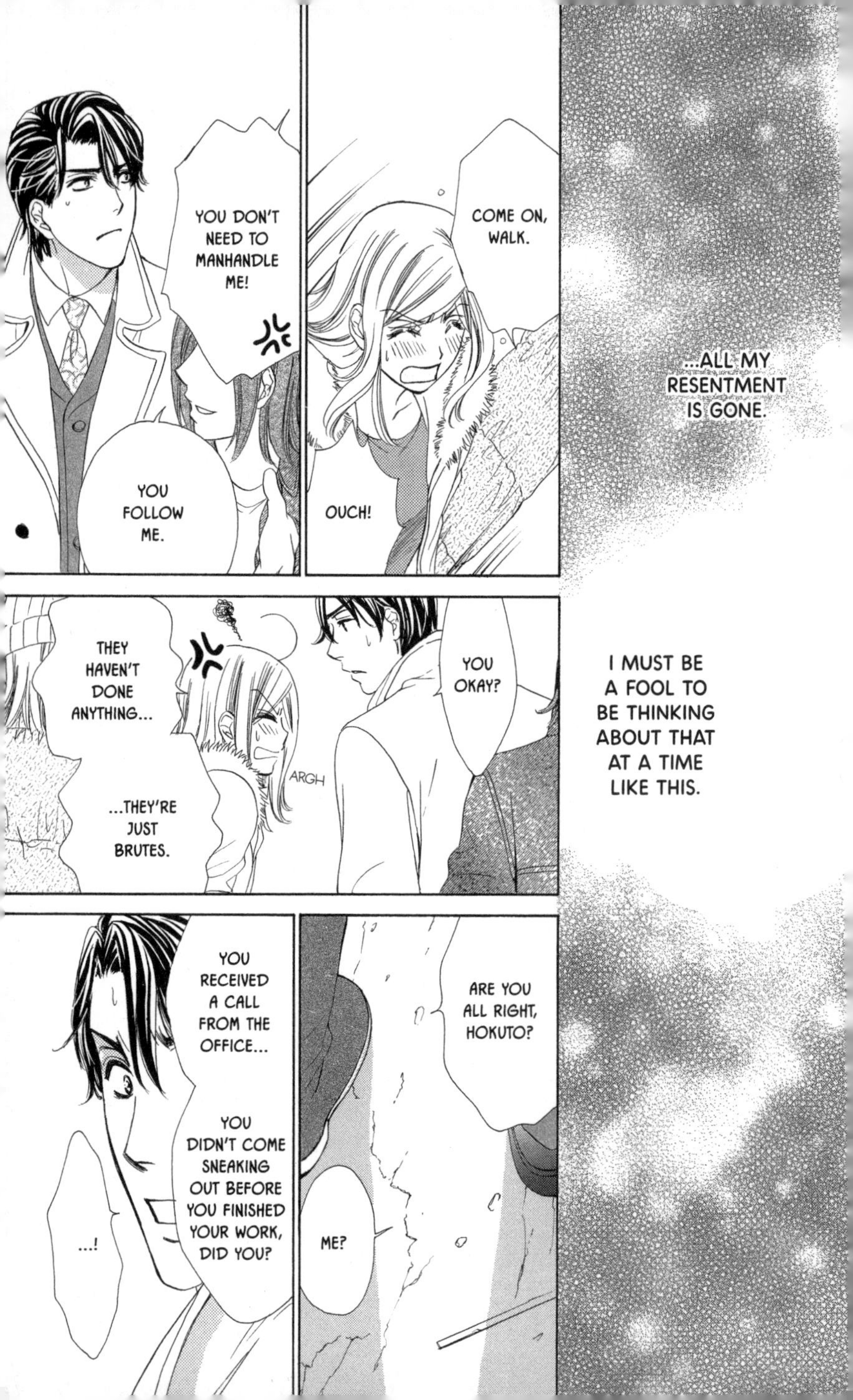
...ALL MY RESENTMENT IS GONE.
I MUST BE A FOOL TO BE THINKING ABOUT THAT AT A TIME LIKE THIS.
COME ON, WALK.
OUCH!
YOU DON'T NEED TO MANHANDLE ME!
YOU FOLLOW ME.
YOU OKAY?
ARGH
THEY HAVEN'T DONE ANYTHING...
...THEY'RE JUST BRUTES.
ARE YOU ALL RIGHT, HOKUTO?
ME?
YOU RECEIVED A CALL FROM THE OFFICE...
YOU DIDN'T COME SNEAKING OUT BEFORE YOU FINISHED YOUR WORK, DID YOU?
...!

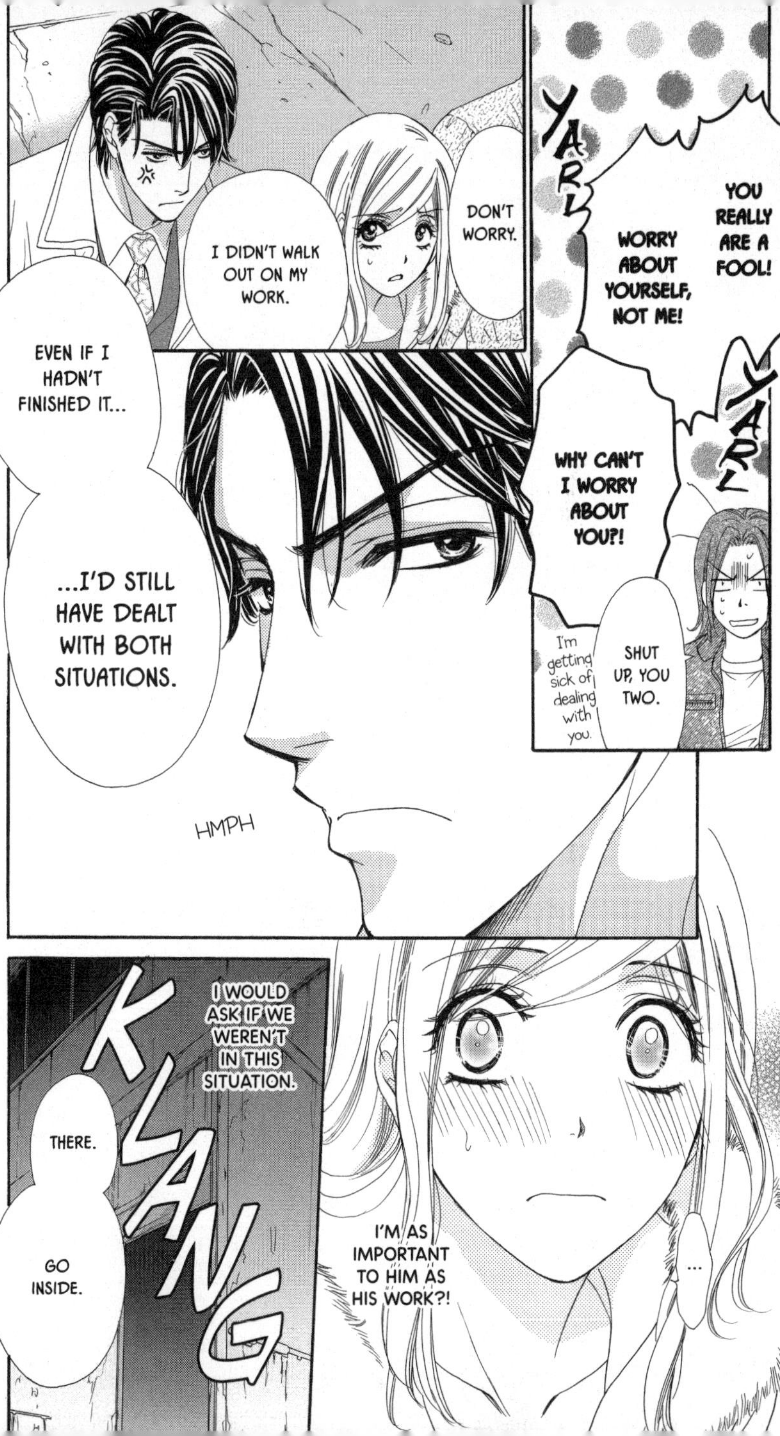
YARI
YOU REALLY ARE A FOOL!
WORRY ABOUT YOURSELF, NOT ME!
YARI
WHY CAN'T I WORRY ABOUT YOU?!
SHUT UP, YOU TWO.
I'm getting sick of dealing with you.
DON'T WORRY.
I DIDN'T WALK OUT ON MY WORK.
EVEN IF I HADN'T FINISHED IT...
...I'D STILL HAVE DEALT WITH BOTH SITUATIONS.
HMPH
...
I'M AS IMPORTANT TO HIM AS HIS WORK?!
I WOULD ASK IF WE WEREN'T IN THIS SITUATION.
KLANG
THERE.
GO INSIDE.

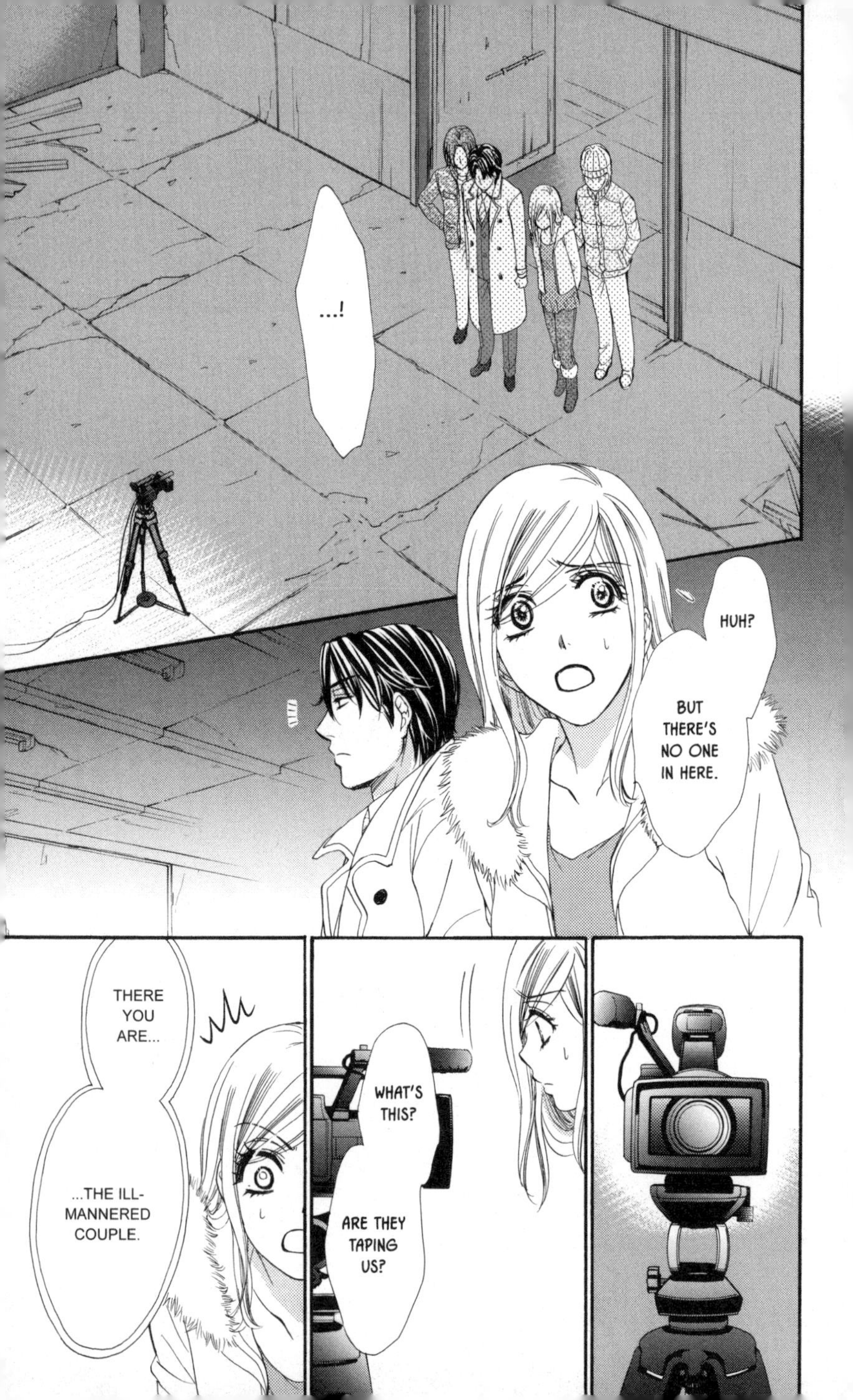
...!
HUH?
BUT THERE'S NO ONE IN HERE.
WHAT'S THIS?
ARE THEY TAPING US?
THERE YOU ARE...
...THE ILL-MANNERED COUPLE.

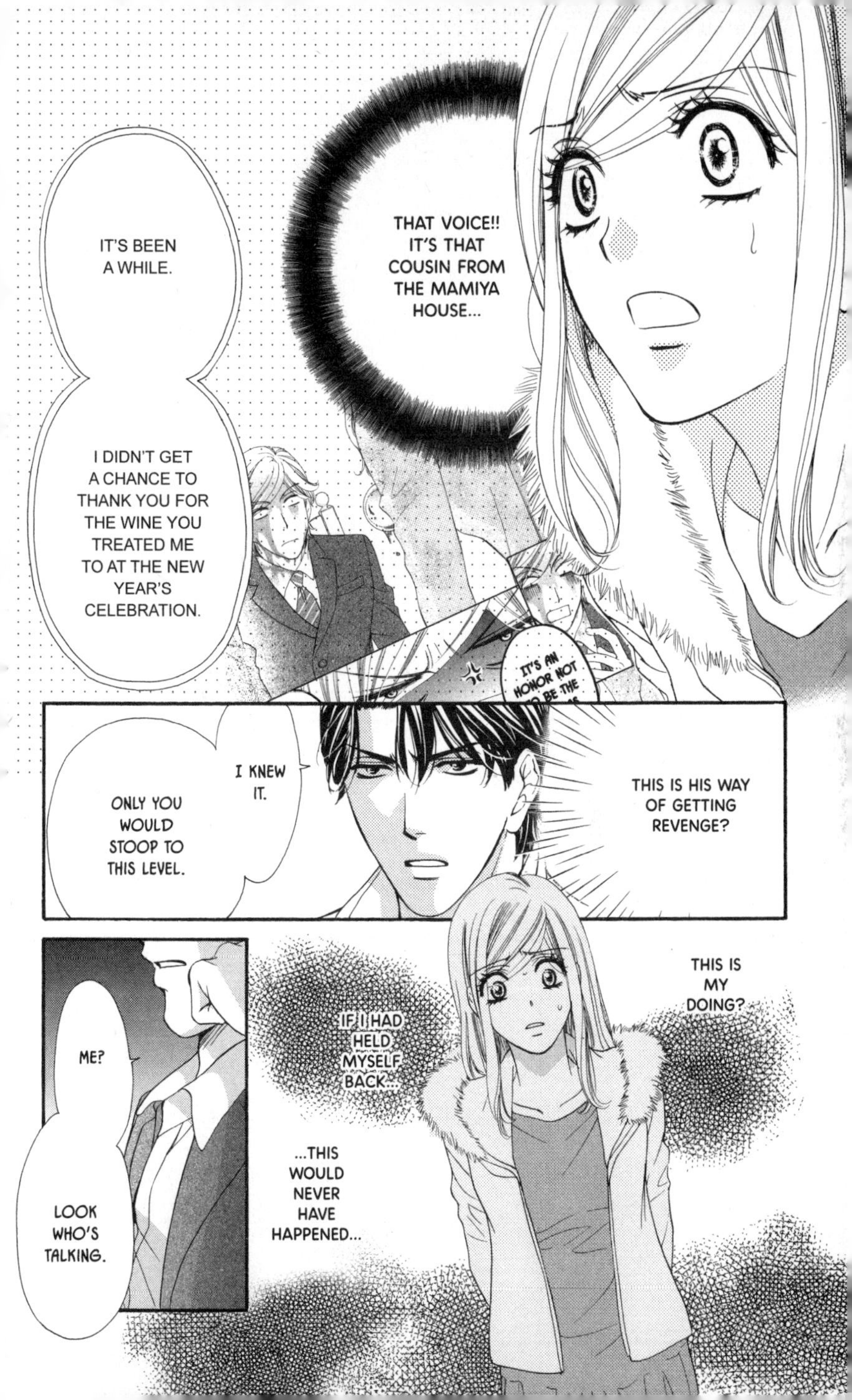
THAT VOICE!! IT'S THAT COUSIN FROM THE MAMIYA HOUSE...
IT'S BEEN A WHILE.
I DIDN'T GET A CHANCE TO THANK YOU FOR THE WINE YOU TREATED ME TO AT THE NEW YEAR'S CELEBRATION.
IT'S AN HONOR NOT
THIS IS HIS WAY OF GETTING REVENGE?
I KNEW IT.
ONLY YOU WOULD STOOP TO THIS LEVEL.
THIS IS MY DOING?
IF I HAD HELD MYSELF BACK...
...THIS WOULD NEVER HAVE HAPPENED...
ME?
LOOK WHO'S TALKING.

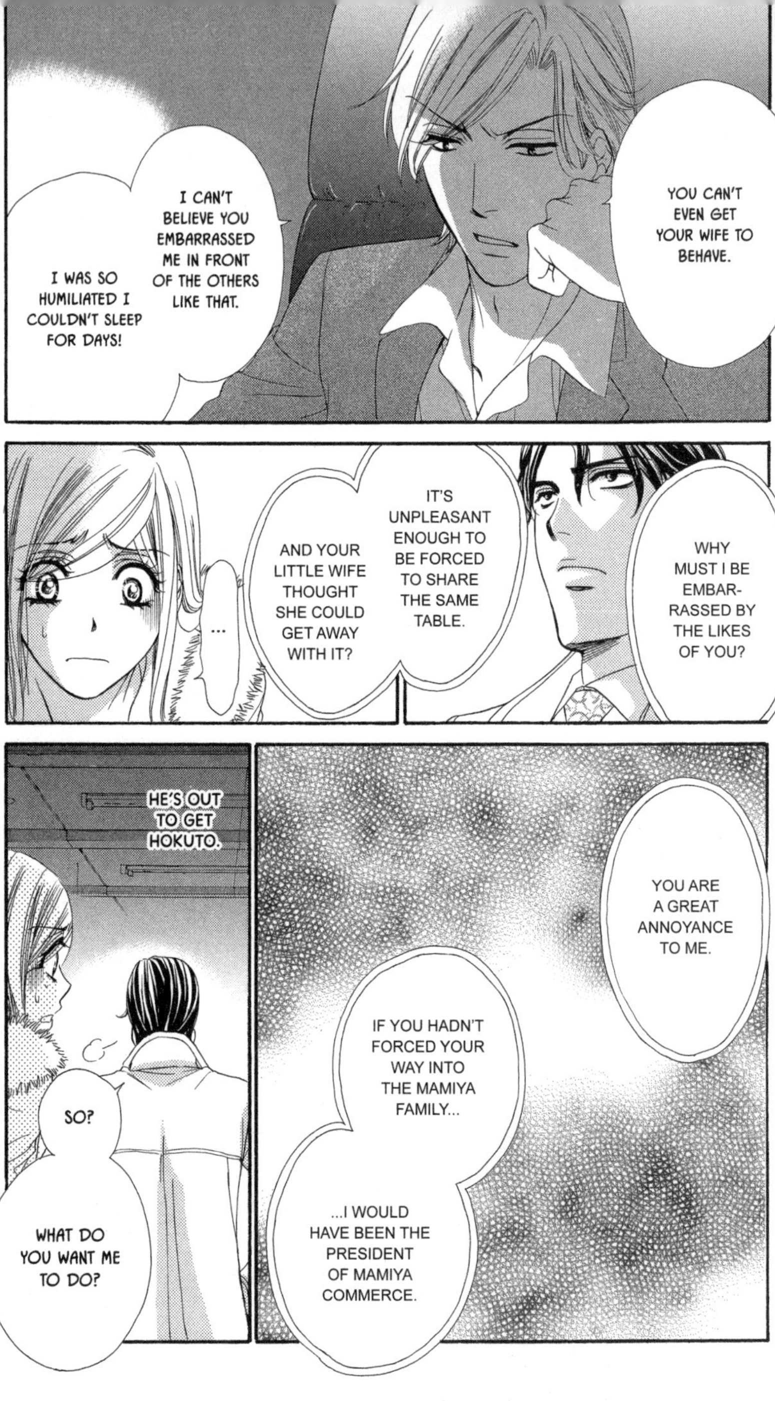
YOU CAN'T EVEN GET YOUR WIFE TO BEHAVE.
I CAN'T BELIEVE YOU EMBARRASSED ME IN FRONT OF THE OTHERS LIKE THAT.
I WAS SO HUMILIATED I COULDN'T SLEEP FOR DAYS!
WHY MUST I BE EMBAR-RASSED BY THE LIKES OF YOU?
IT'S UNPLEASANT ENOUGH TO BE FORCED TO SHARE THE SAME TABLE.
AND YOUR LITTLE WIFE THOUGHT SHE COULD GET AWAY WITH IT?
...
YOU ARE A GREAT ANNOYANCE TO ME.
IF YOU HADN'T FORCED YOUR WAY INTO THE MAMIYA FAMILY...
...I WOULD HAVE BEEN THE PRESIDENT OF MAMIYA COMMERCE.
HE'S OUT TO GET HOKUTO.
SO?
WHAT DO YOU WANT ME TO DO?

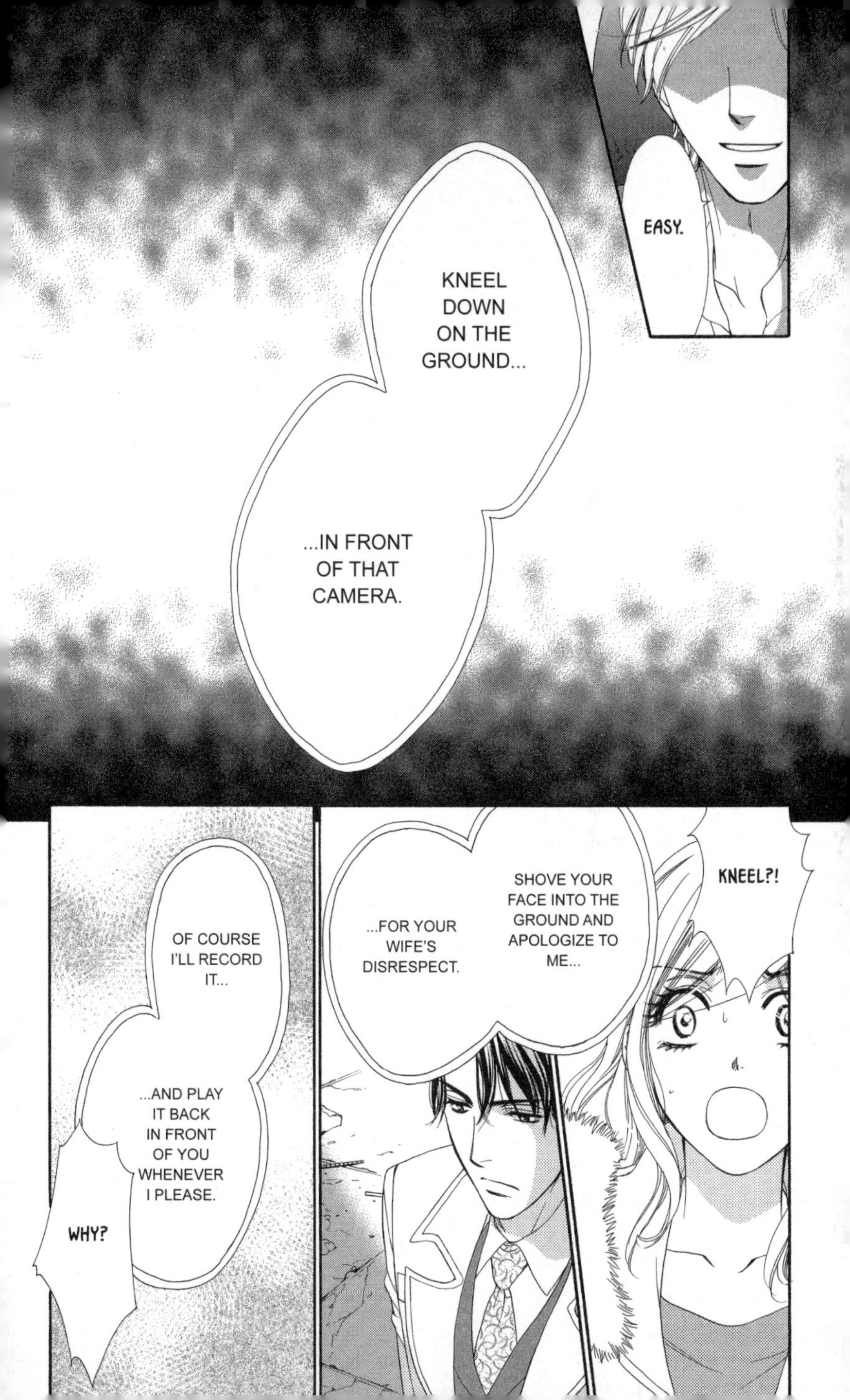
EASY.
KNEEL DOWN ON THE GROUND...
...IN FRONT OF THAT CAMERA.
KNEEL?!
SHOVE YOUR FACE INTO THE GROUND AND APOLOGIZE TO ME...
...FOR YOUR WIFE'S DISRESPECT.
OF COURSE I'LL RECORD IT...
...AND PLAY IT BACK IN FRONT OF YOU WHENEVER I PLEASE.
WHY?

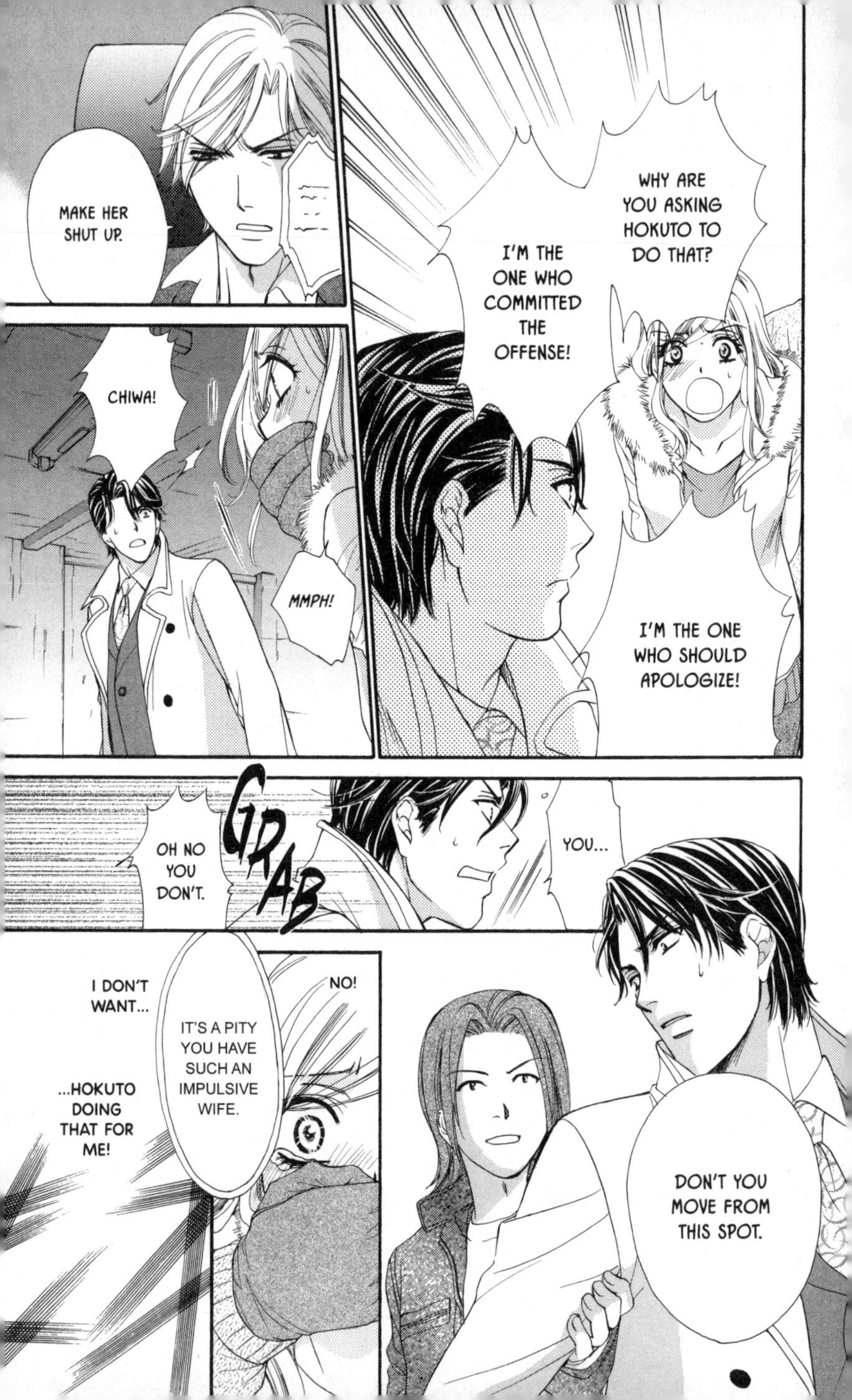
WHY ARE YOU ASKING HOKUTO TO DO THAT?
I'M THE ONE WHO COMMITTED THE OFFENSE!
I'M THE ONE WHO SHOULD APOLOGIZE!
MAKE HER SHUT UP.
CHIWA!
MMPH!
YOU...
GRAB
OH NO YOU DON'T.
DON'T YOU MOVE FROM THIS SPOT.
IT'S A PITY YOU HAVE SUCH AN IMPULSIVE WIFE.
NO!
I DON'T WANT...
...HOKUTO DOING THAT FOR ME!

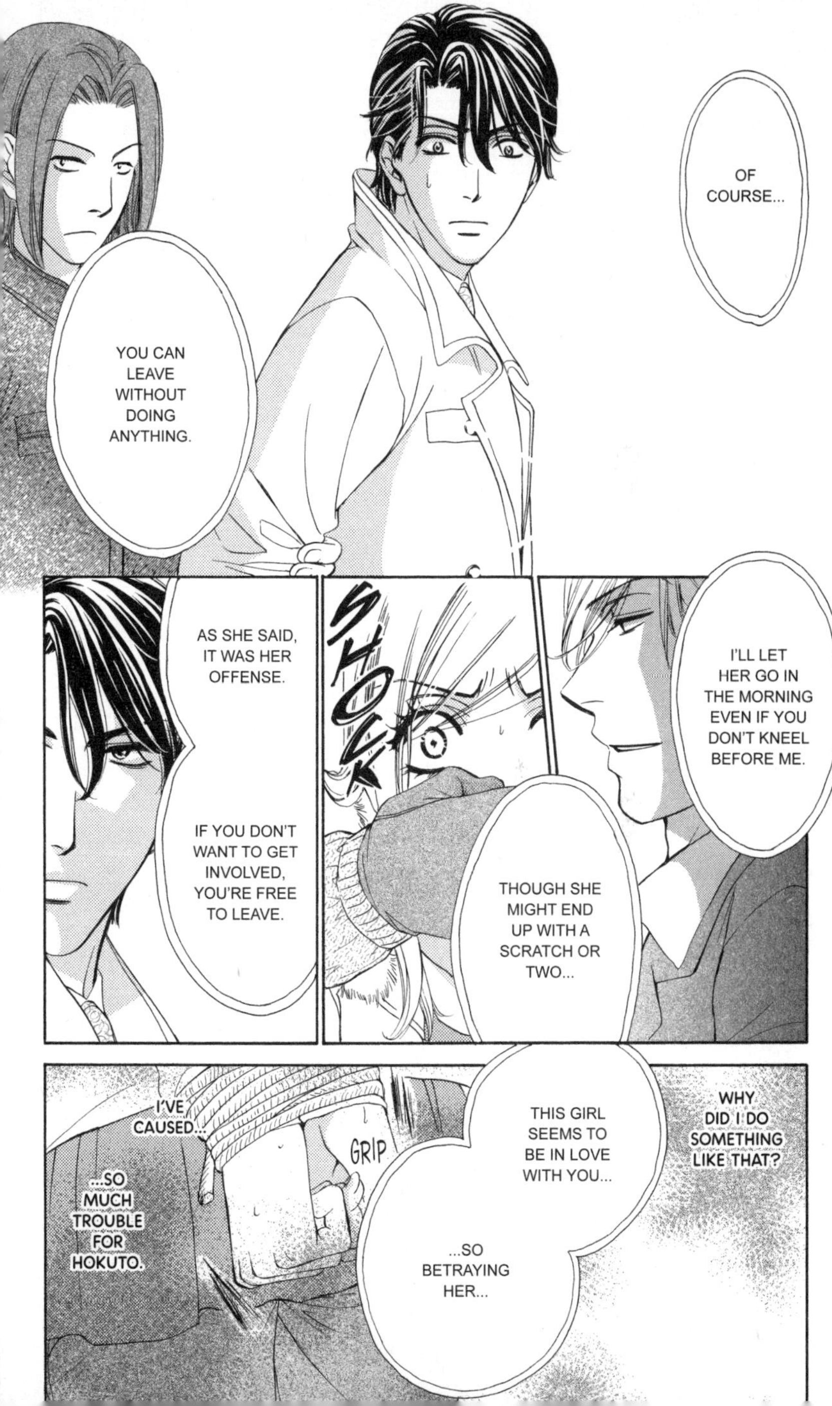
OF COURSE...
YOU CAN LEAVE WITHOUT DOING ANYTHING.
I'LL LET HER GO IN THE MORNING EVEN IF YOU DON'T KNEEL BEFORE ME.
SHOCK
THOUGH SHE MIGHT END UP WITH A SCRATCH OR TWO...
AS SHE SAID, IT WAS HER OFFENSE.
IF YOU DON'T WANT TO GET INVOLVED, YOU'RE FREE TO LEAVE.
WHY DID I DO SOMETHING LIKE THAT?
THIS GIRL SEEMS TO BE IN LOVE WITH YOU...
...SO BETRAYING HER...
GRIP
I'VE CAUSED...
...SO MUCH TROUBLE FOR HOKUTO.

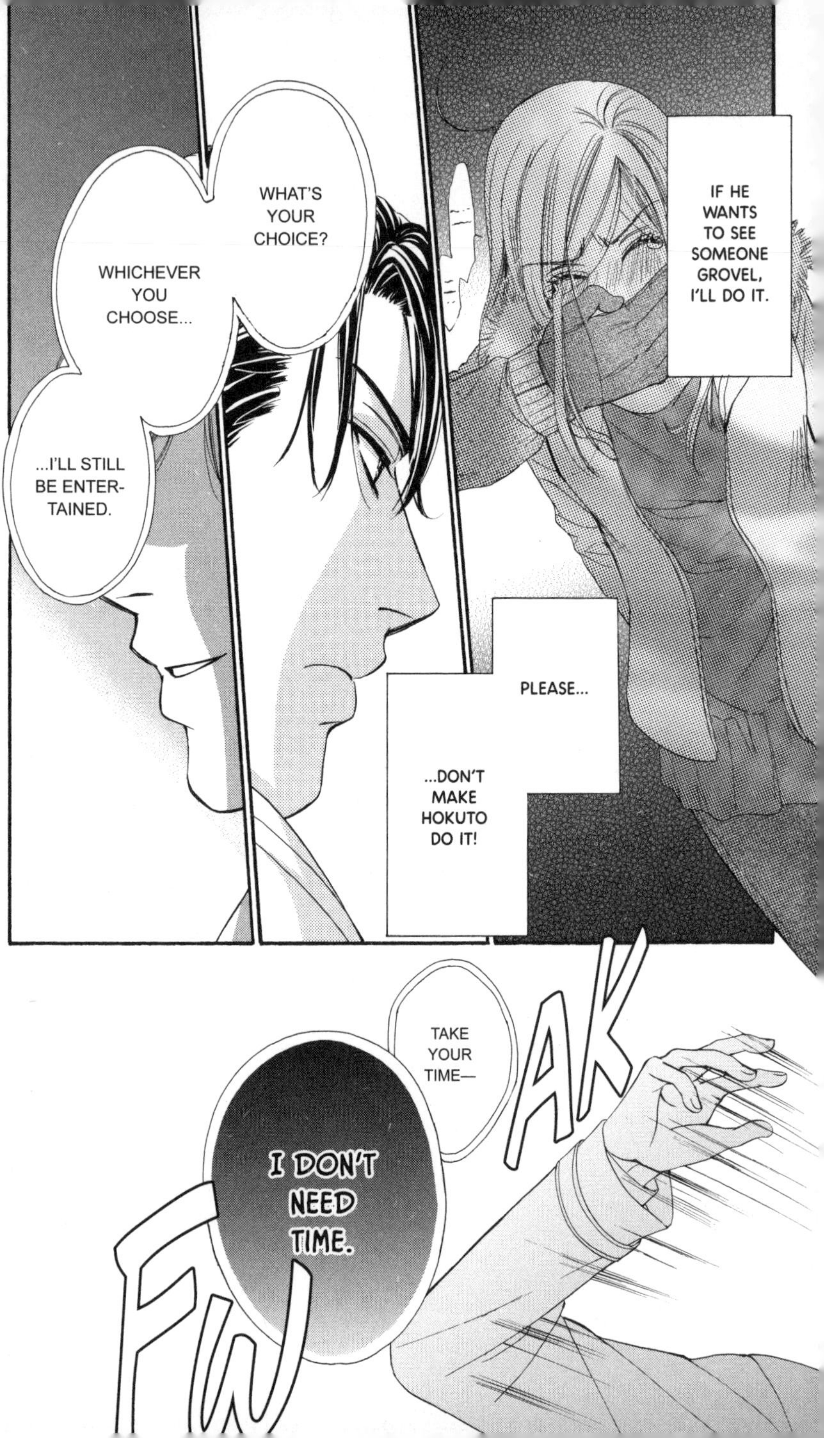
IF HE WANTS TO SEE SOMEONE GROVEL, I'LL DO IT.
PLEASE...
...DON'T MAKE HOKUTO DO IT!
WHAT'S YOUR CHOICE?
WHICHEVER YOU CHOOSE...
...I'LL STILL BE ENTERTAINED.
TAKE YOUR TIME—
I DON'T NEED TIME.
FWAK

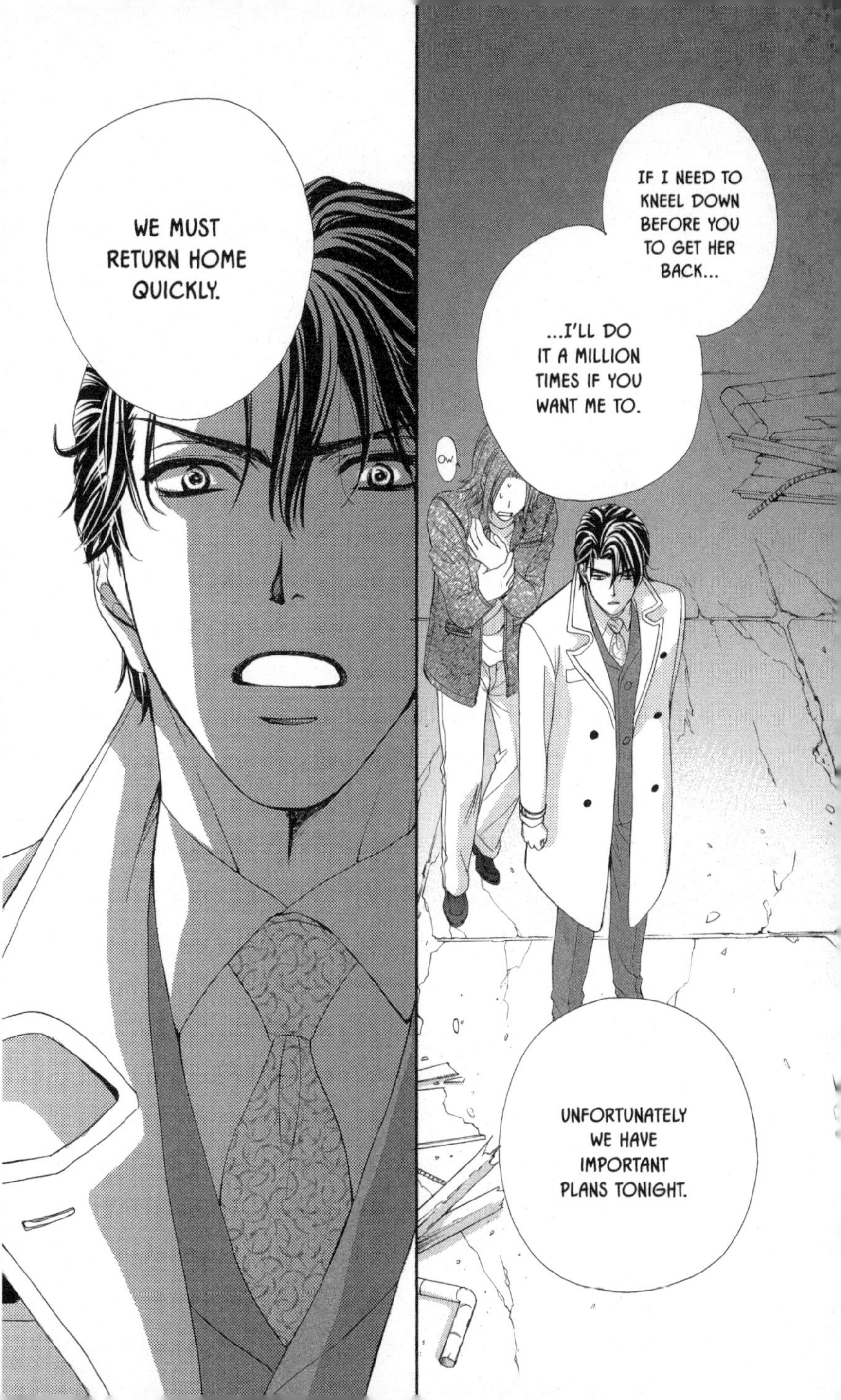
IF I NEED TO KNEEL DOWN BEFORE YOU TO GET HER BACK...
...I'LL DO IT A MILLION TIMES IF YOU WANT ME TO.
OW.
UNFORTUNATELY WE HAVE IMPORTANT PLANS TONIGHT.
WE MUST RETURN HOME QUICKLY.

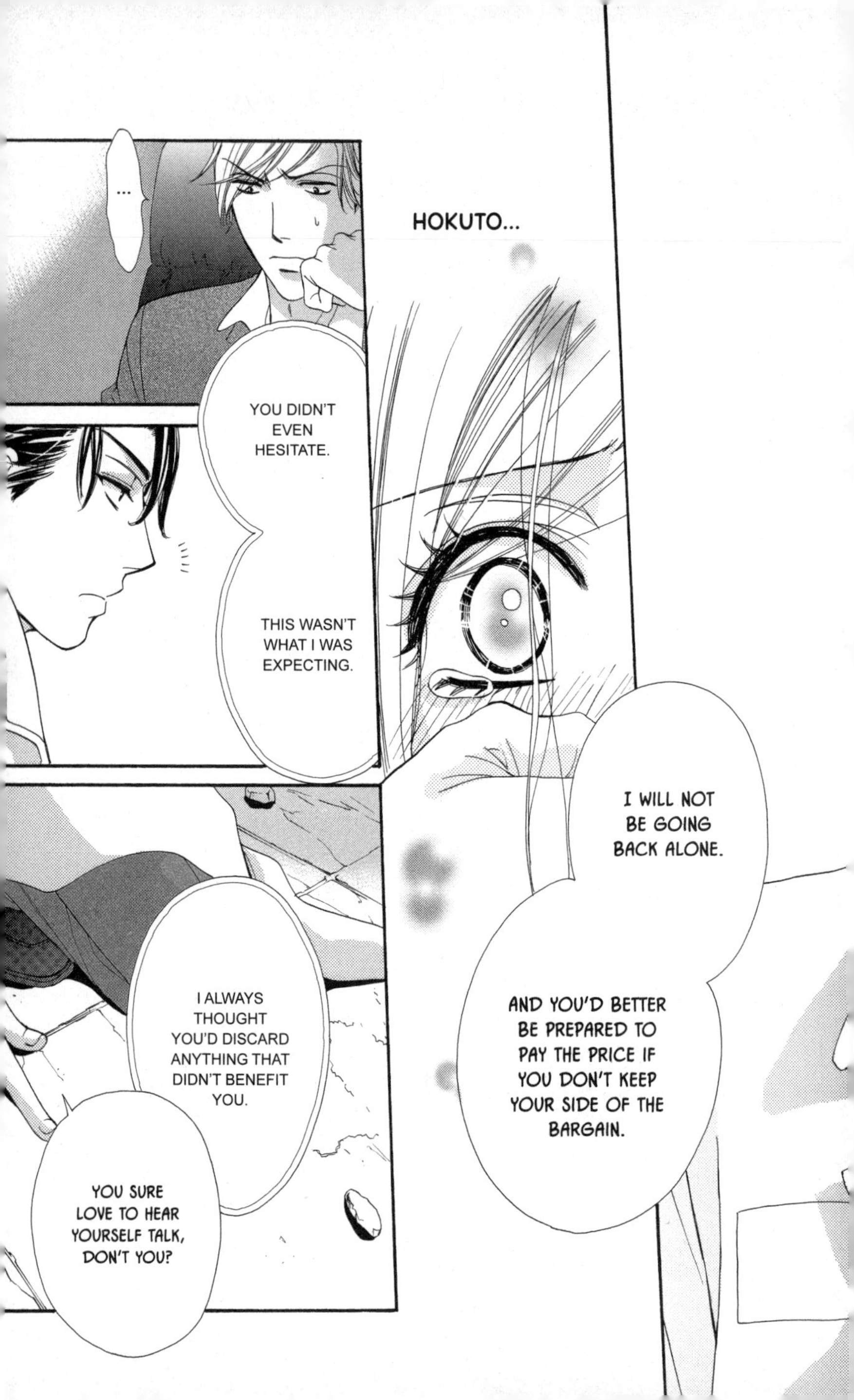
HOKUTO...
...
YOU DIDN'T EVEN HESITATE.
THIS WASN'T WHAT I WAS EXPECTING.
I WILL NOT BE GOING BACK ALONE.
AND YOU'D BETTER BE PREPARED TO PAY THE PRICE IF YOU DON'T KEEP YOUR SIDE OF THE BARGAIN.
I ALWAYS THOUGHT YOU'D DISCARD ANYTHING THAT DIDN'T BENEFIT YOU.
YOU SURE LOVE TO HEAR YOURSELF TALK, DON'T YOU?

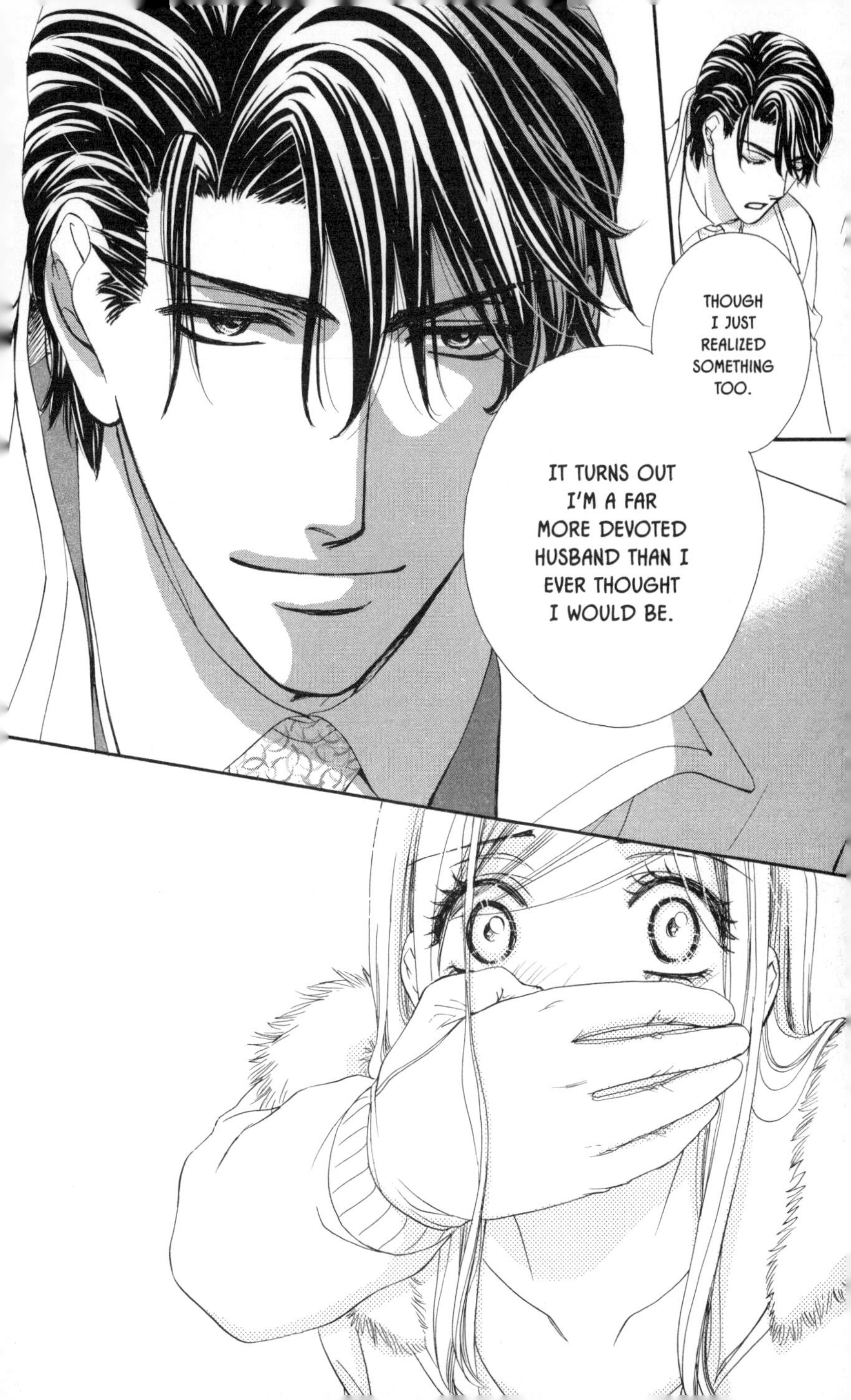
THOUGH I JUST REALIZED SOMETHING TOO.
IT TURNS OUT I'M A FAR MORE DEVOTED HUSBAND THAN I EVER THOUGHT I WOULD BE.

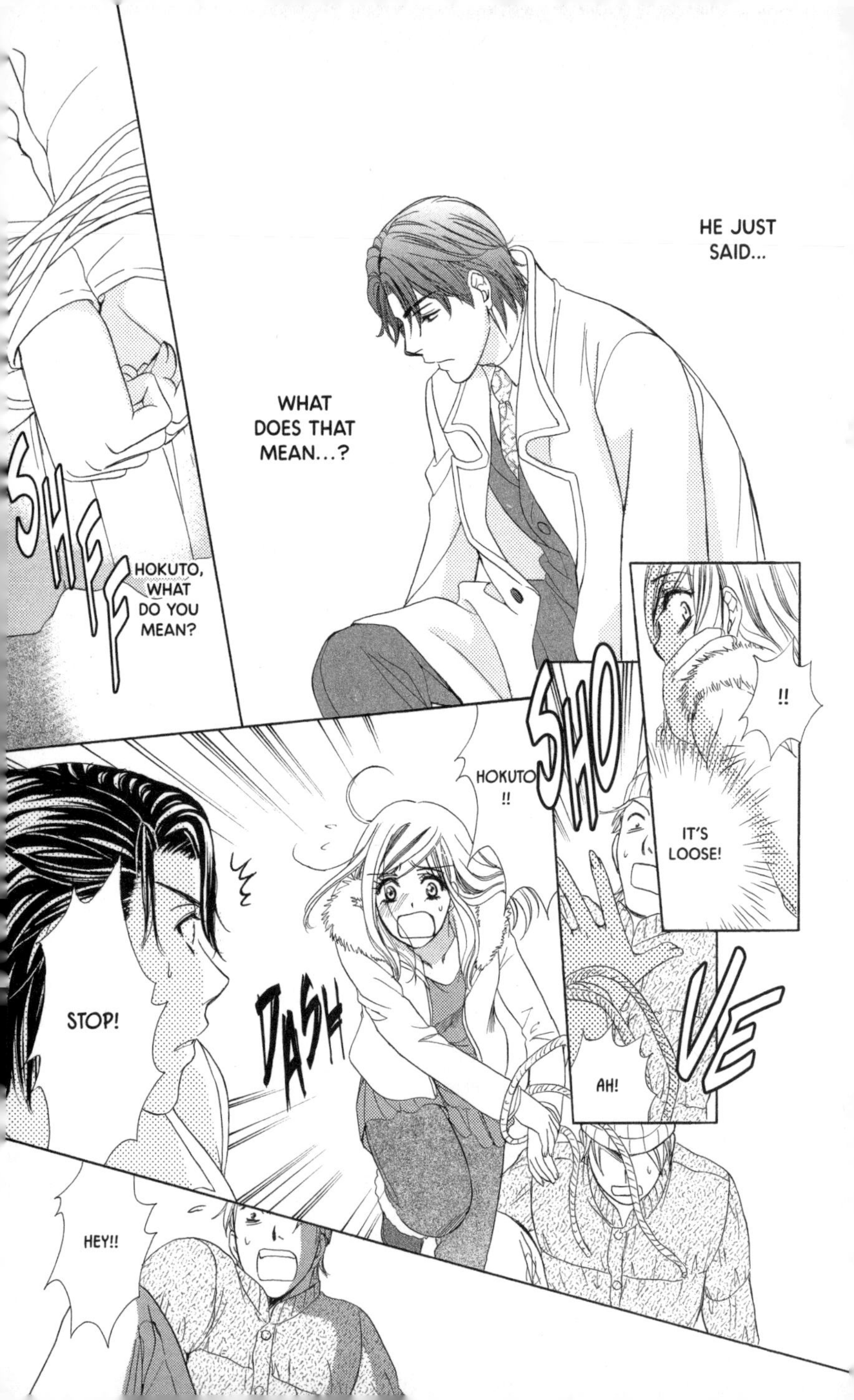
HE JUST SAID...
WHAT DOES THAT MEAN...?
SHFF
HOKUTO, WHAT DO YOU MEAN?
!!
IT'S LOOSE!
SHOVE
AH!
HOKUTO !!
DASH
STOP!
HEY!!

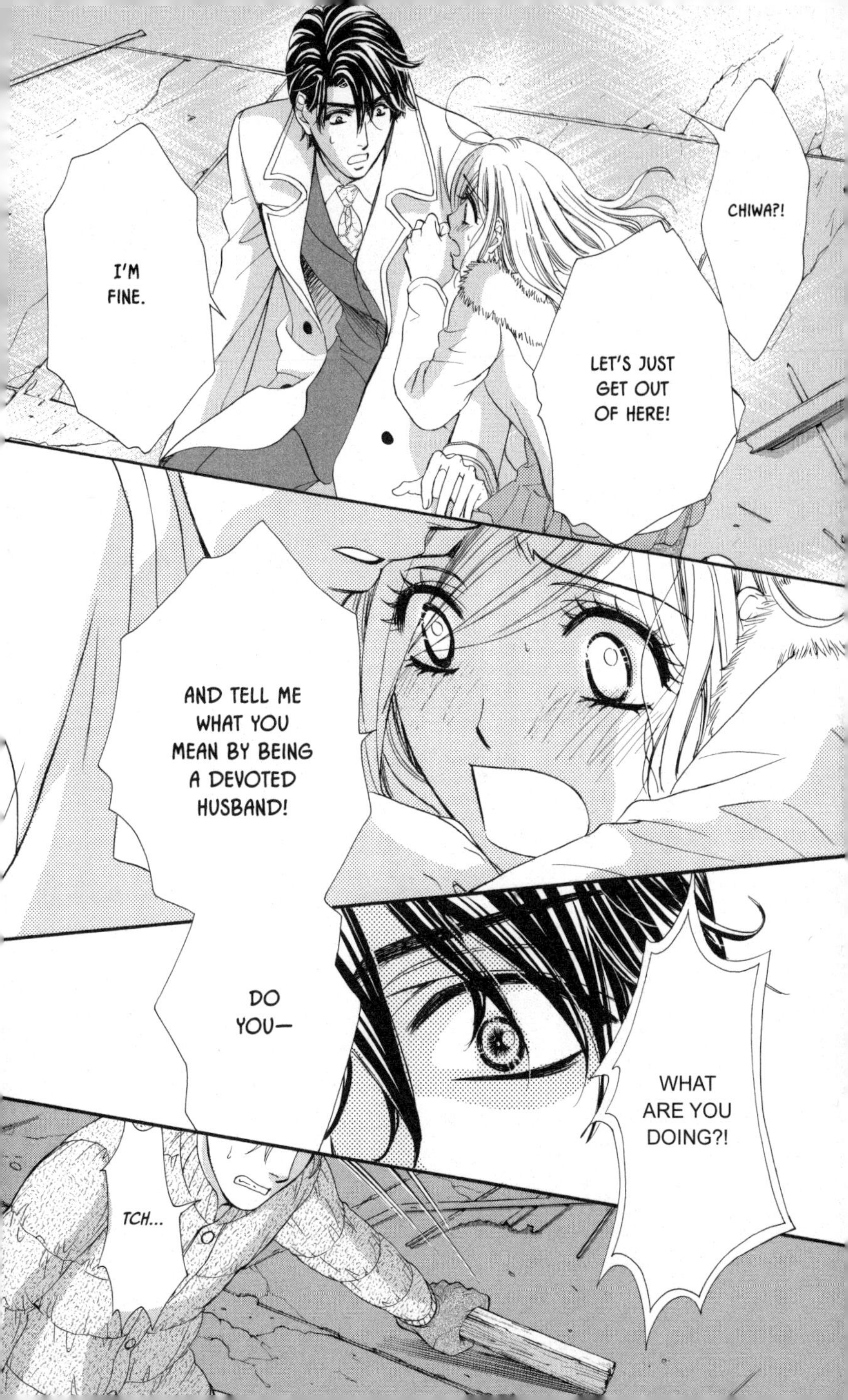
CHIWA?!
I'M FINE.
LET'S JUST GET OUT OF HERE!
AND TELL ME WHAT YOU MEAN BY BEING A DEVOTED HUSBAND!
DO YOU—
WHAT ARE YOU DOING?!
TCH...

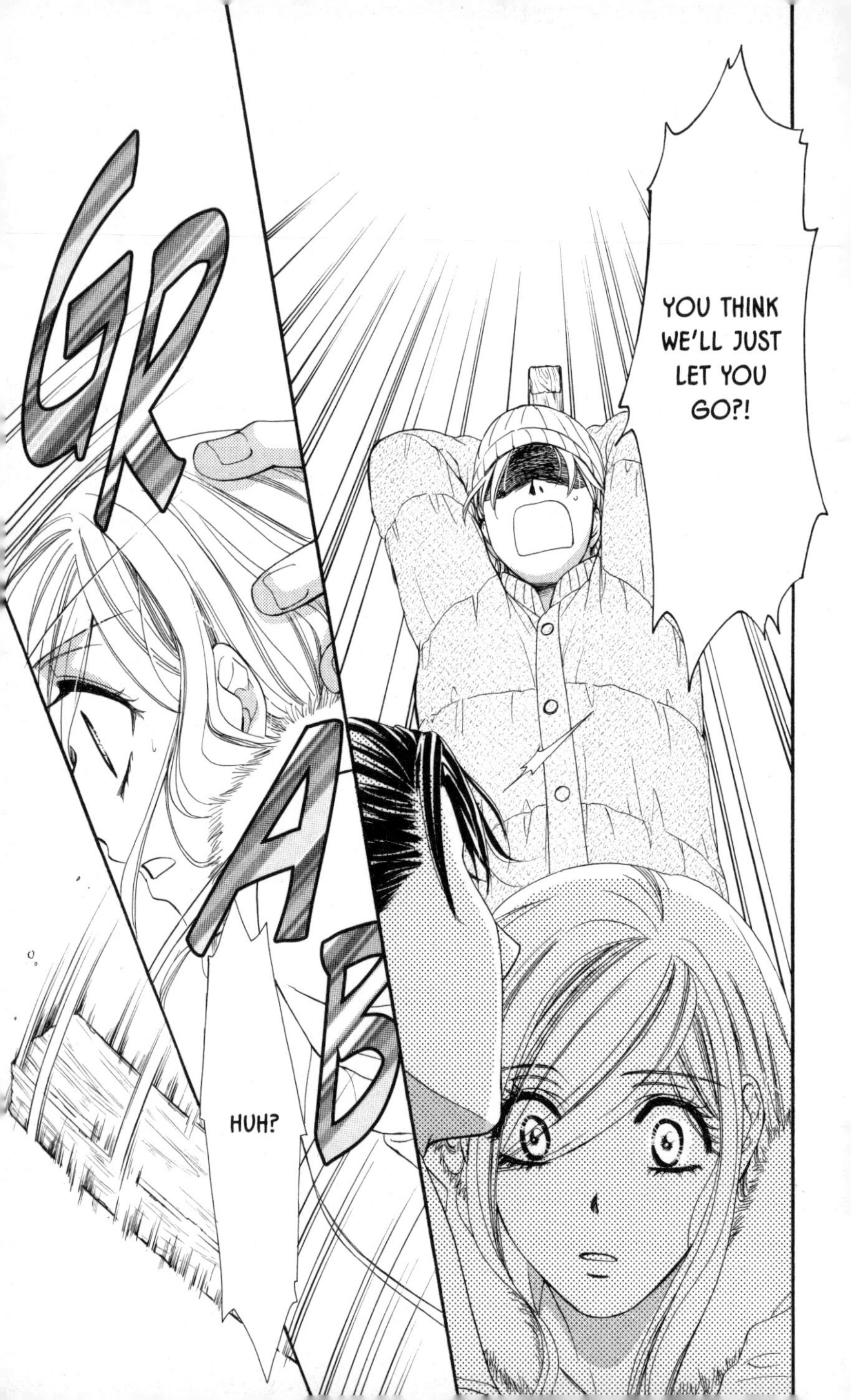
YOU THINK WE'LL JUST LET YOU GO?!
GRAB
HUH?

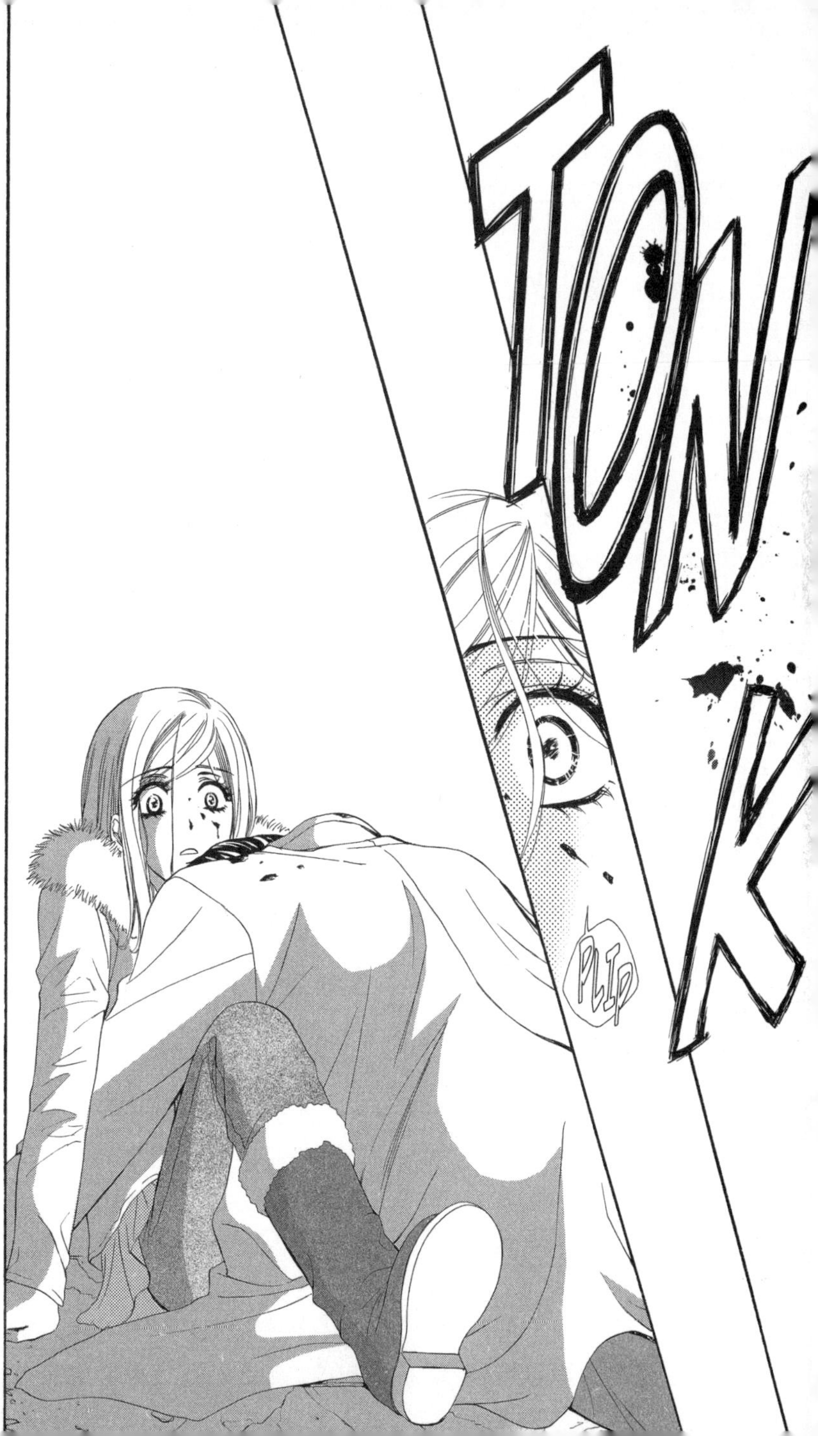
TONK
PLIP

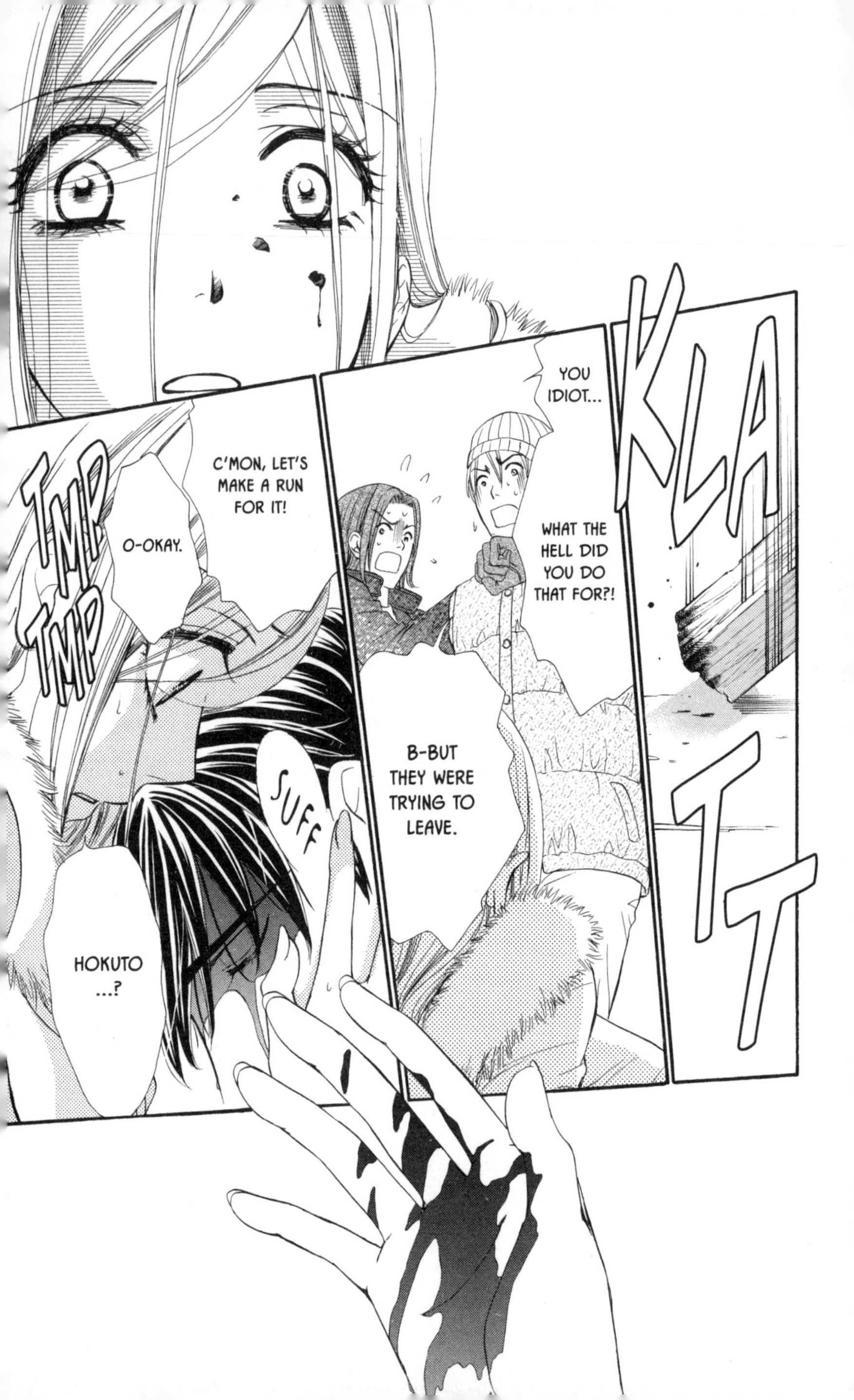
KLATTT
YOU IDIOT...
WHAT THE HELL DID YOU DO THAT FOR?!
B-BUT THEY WERE TRYING TO LEAVE.
C'MON, LET'S MAKE A RUN FOR IT!
O-OKAY.
TMP TMP
SUFF
HOKUTO ...?

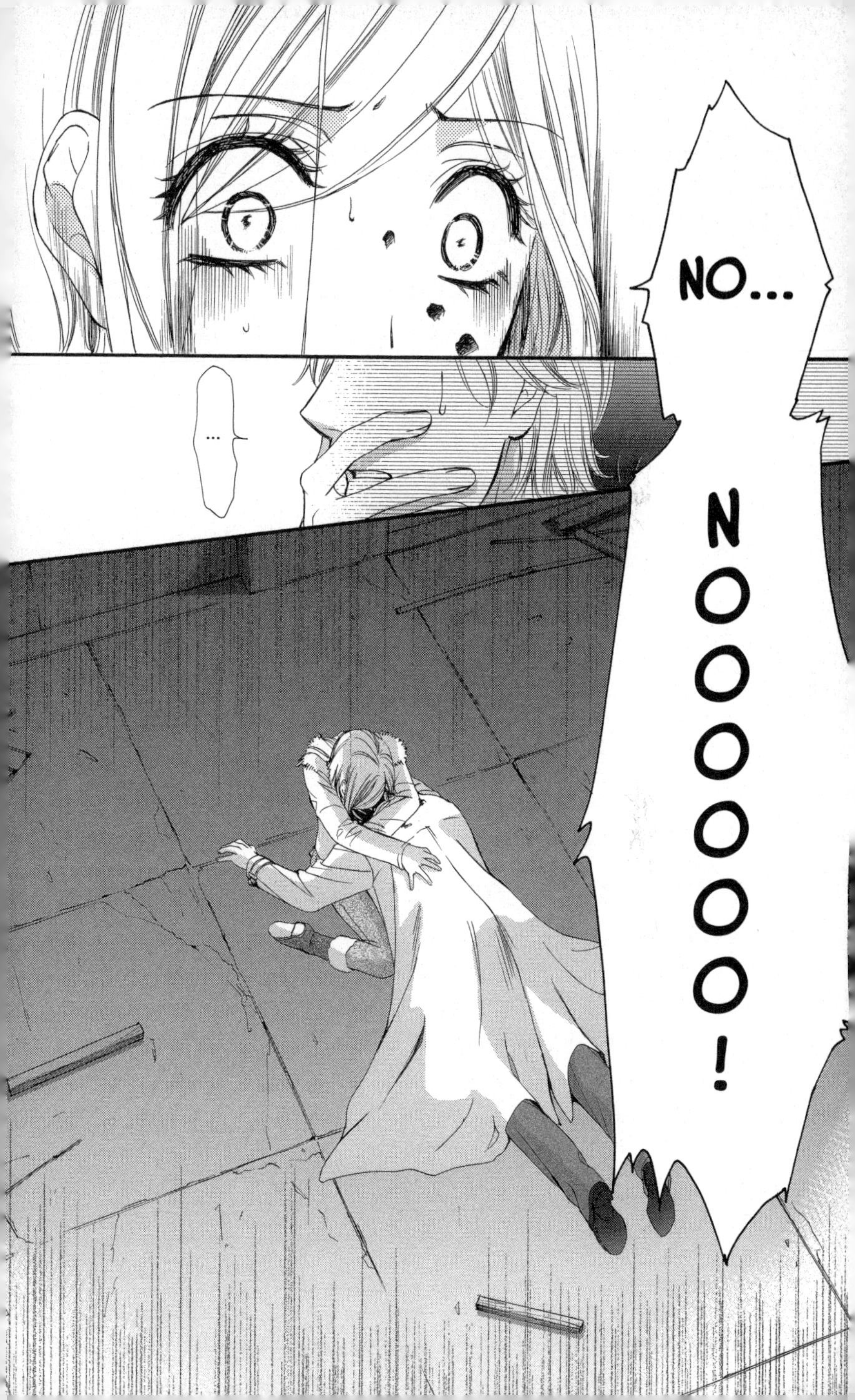
NO...
NOOOOOOOO!
...

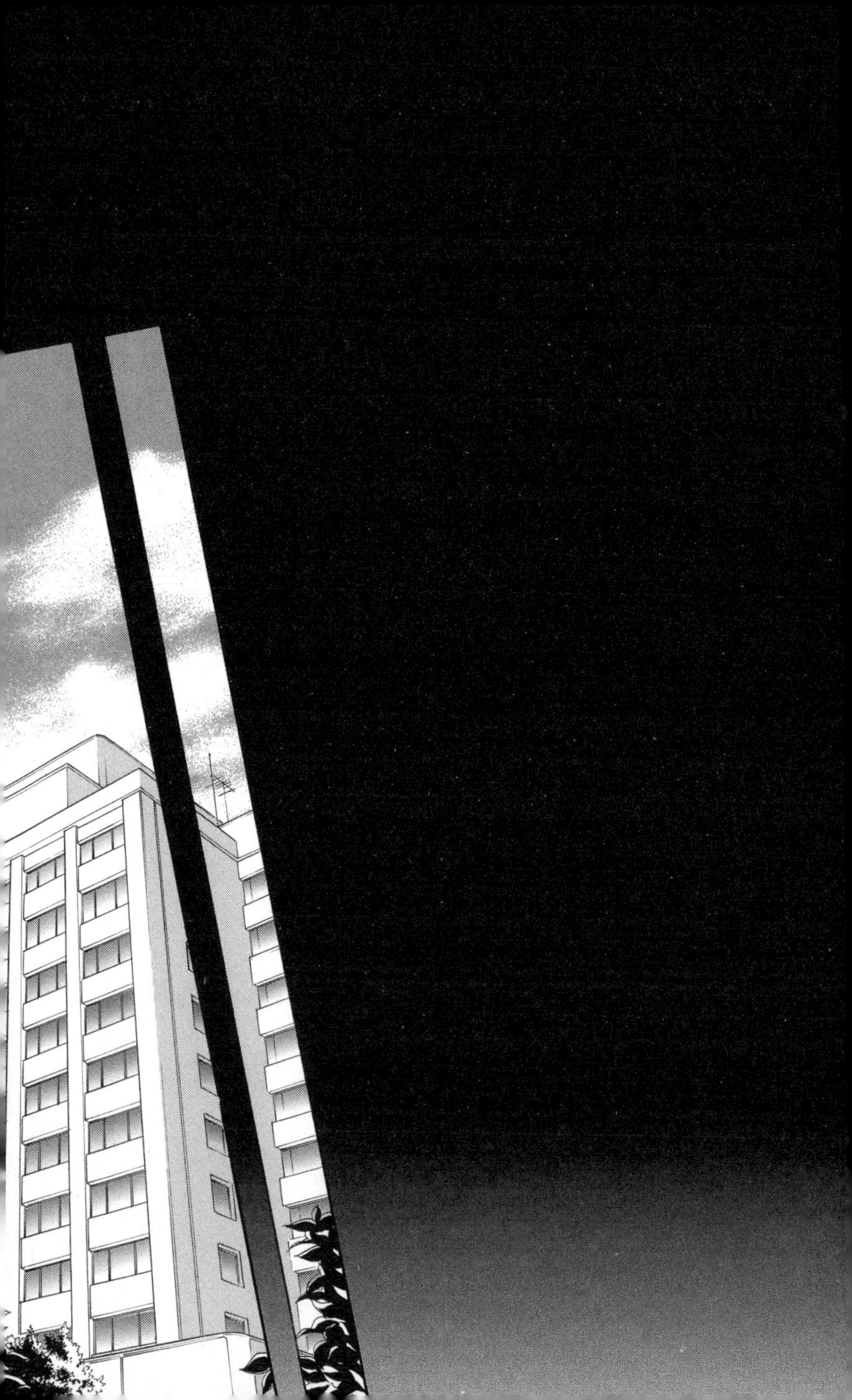

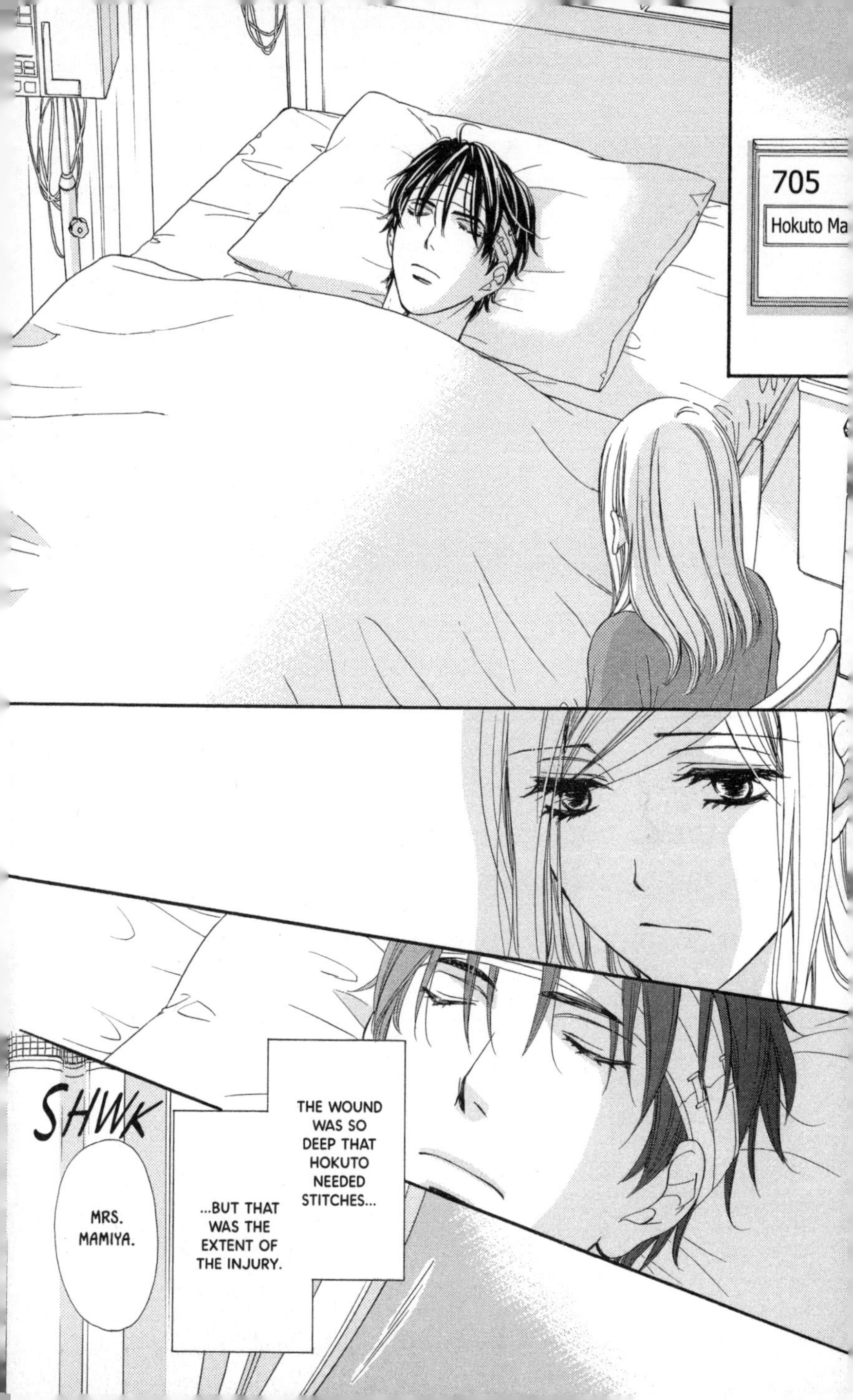
705
Hokuto Ma
THE WOUND WAS SO DEEP THAT HOKUTO NEEDED STITCHES...
...BUT THAT WAS THE EXTENT OF THE INJURY.
SHWK
MRS. MAMIYA.

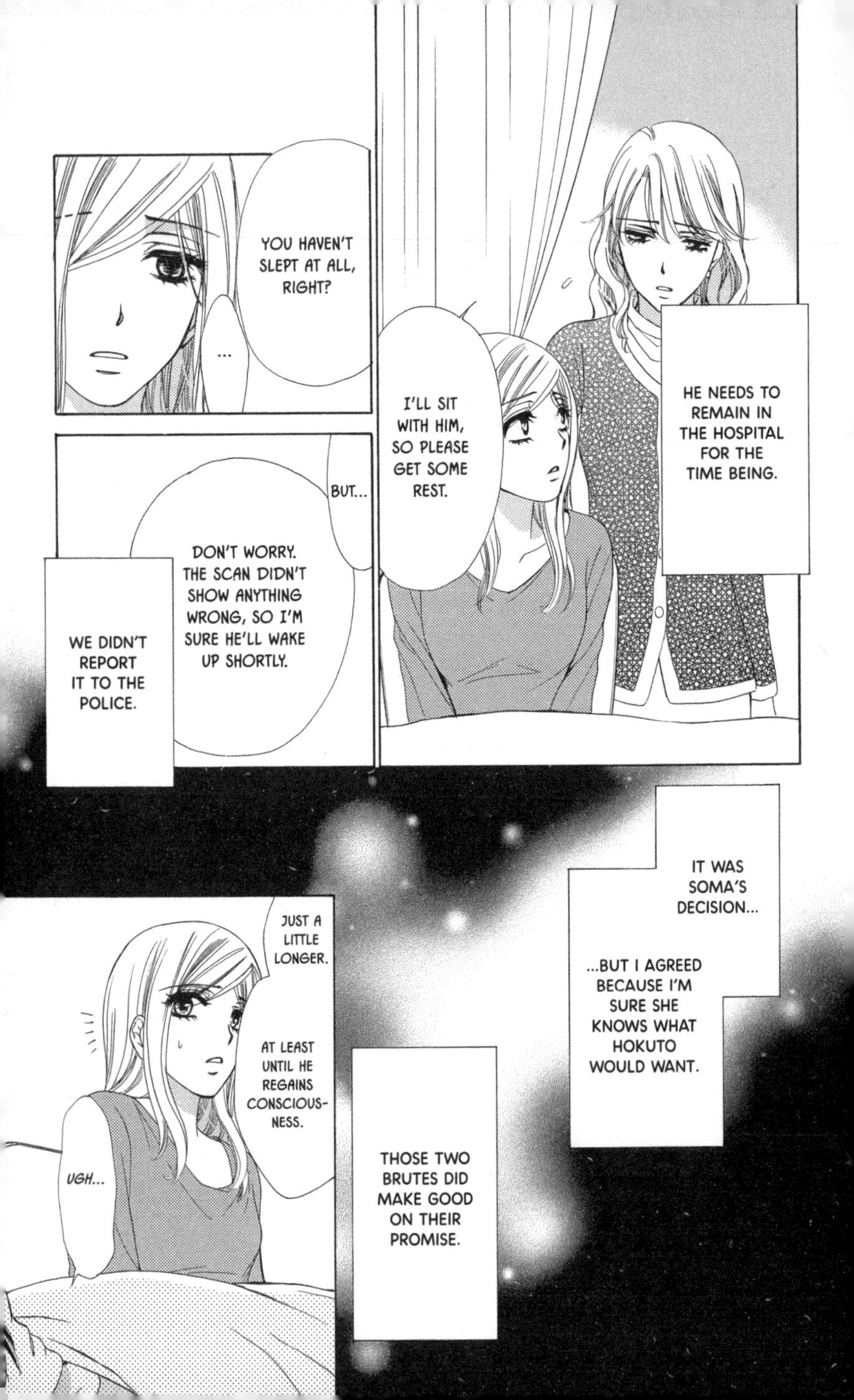
HE NEEDS TO REMAIN IN THE HOSPITAL FOR THE TIME BEING.
I'LL SIT WITH HIM, SO PLEASE GET SOME REST.
YOU HAVEN'T SLEPT AT ALL, RIGHT?
...
BUT...
DON'T WORRY. THE SCAN DIDN'T SHOW ANYTHING WRONG, SO I'M SURE HE'LL WAKE UP SHORTLY.
WE DIDN'T REPORT IT TO THE POLICE.
IT WAS SOMA'S DECISION...
...BUT I AGREED BECAUSE I'M SURE SHE KNOWS WHAT HOKUTO WOULD WANT.
THOSE TWO BRUTES DID MAKE GOOD ON THEIR PROMISE.
JUST A LITTLE LONGER.
AT LEAST UNTIL HE REGAINS CONSCIOUS-NESS.
UGH...

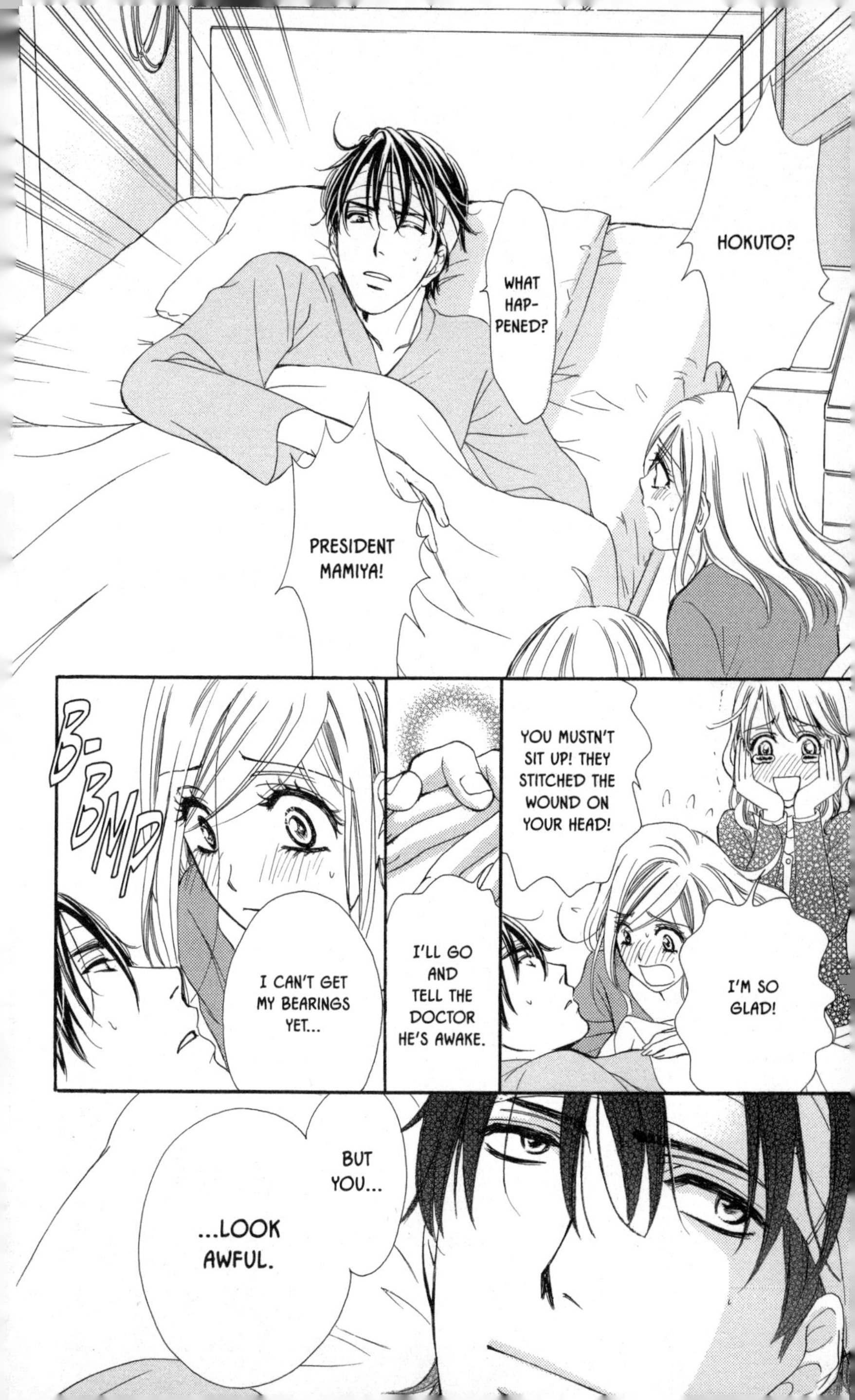

HOKUTO?
WHAT HAP-PENED?
PRESIDENT MAMIYA!
YOU MUSTN'T SIT UP! THEY STITCHED THE WOUND ON YOUR HEAD!
I'M SO GLAD!
I'LL GO AND TELL THE DOCTOR HE'S AWAKE.
B-BMP
I CAN'T GET MY BEARINGS YET...
BUT YOU...
...LOOK AWFUL.

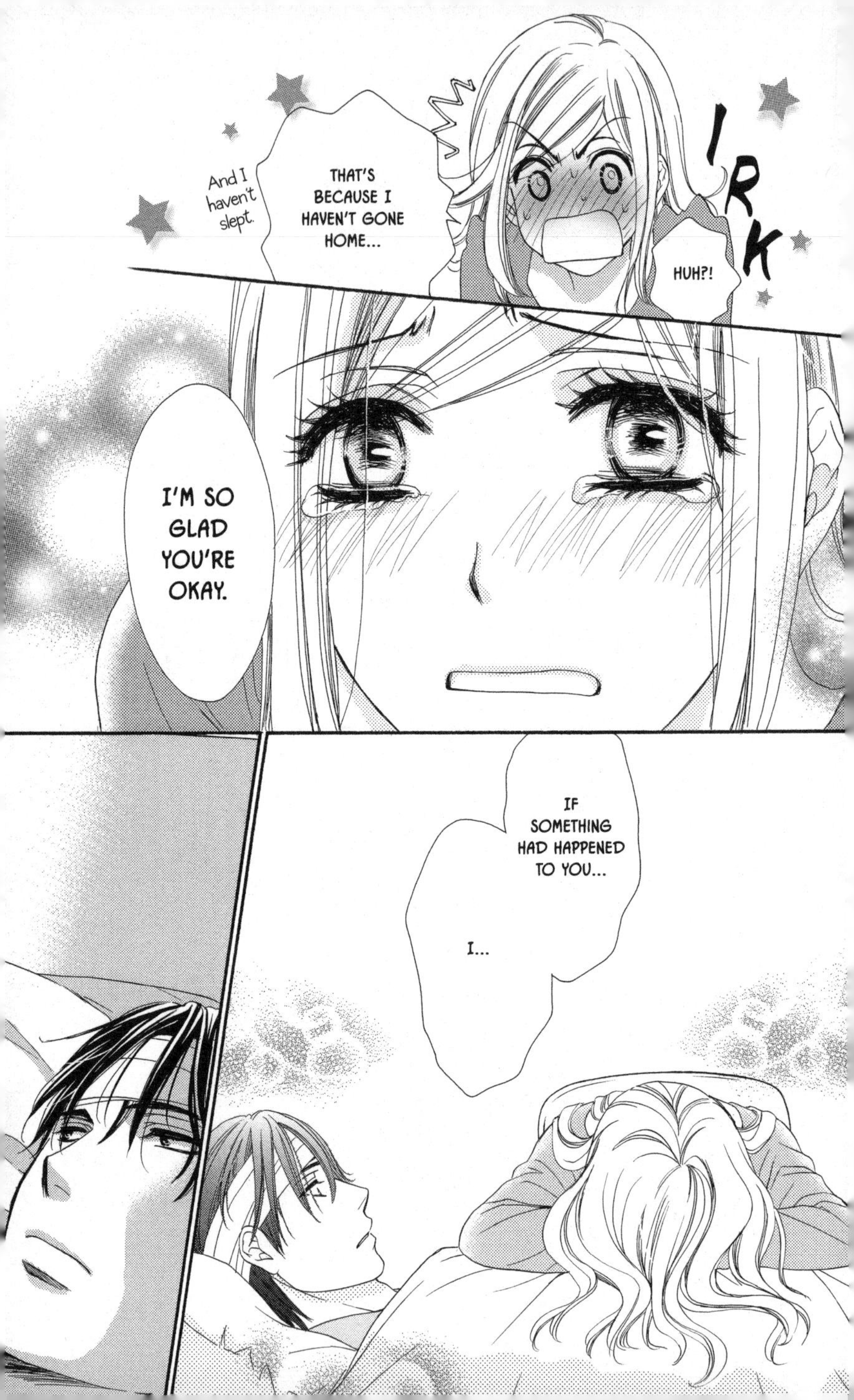
IRK
HUH?!
THAT'S BECAUSE I HAVEN'T GONE HOME...
And I haven't slept.
I'M SO GLAD YOU'RE OKAY.
IF SOMETHING HAD HAPPENED TO YOU...
I...

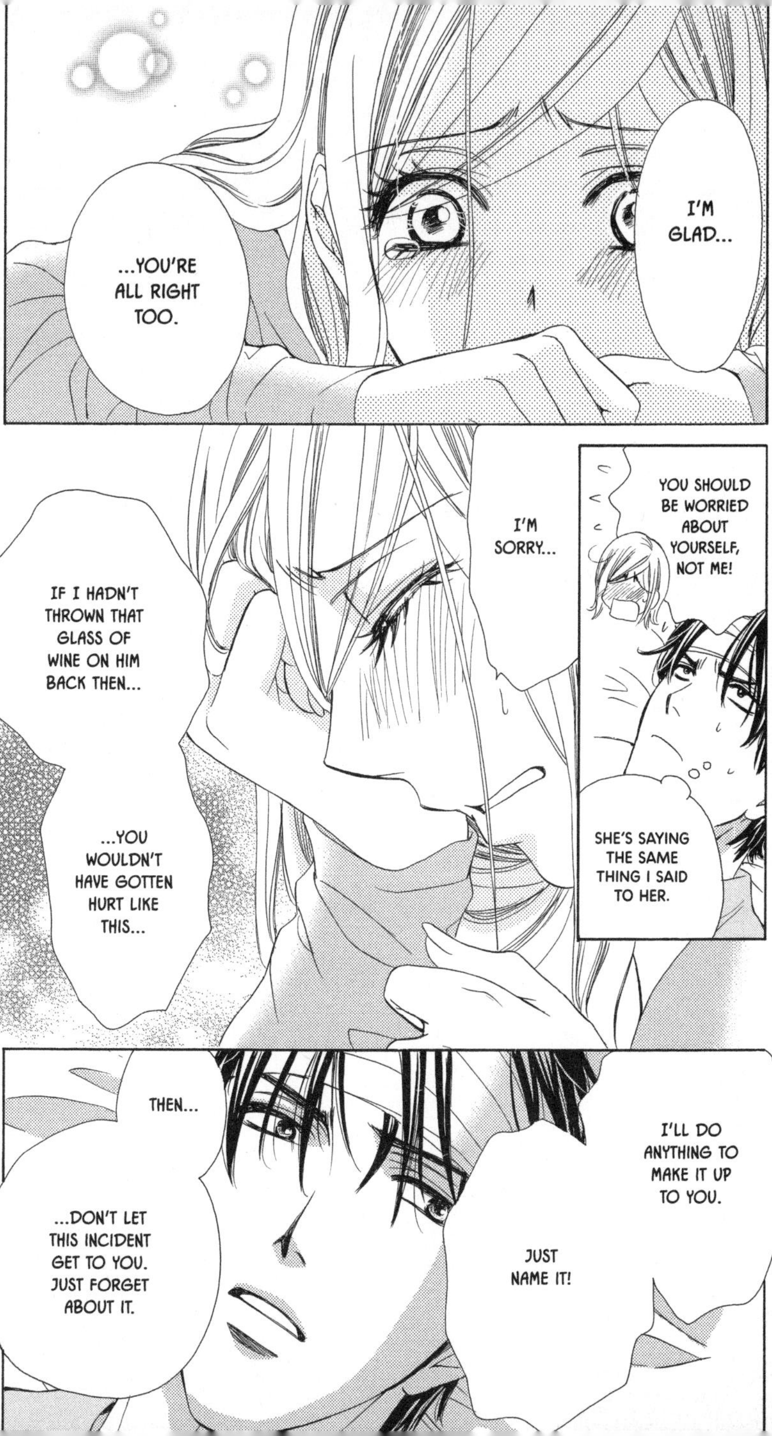

I'M GLAD...
...YOU'RE ALL RIGHT TOO.
YOU SHOULD BE WORRIED ABOUT YOURSELF, NOT ME!
SHE'S SAYING THE SAME THING I SAID TO HER.
I'M SORRY...
IF I HADN'T THROWN THAT GLASS OF WINE ON HIM BACK THEN...
...YOU WOULDN'T HAVE GOTTEN HURT LIKE THIS...
I'LL DO ANYTHING TO MAKE IT UP TO YOU.
JUST NAME IT!
THEN...
...DON'T LET THIS INCIDENT GET TO YOU. JUST FORGET ABOUT IT.

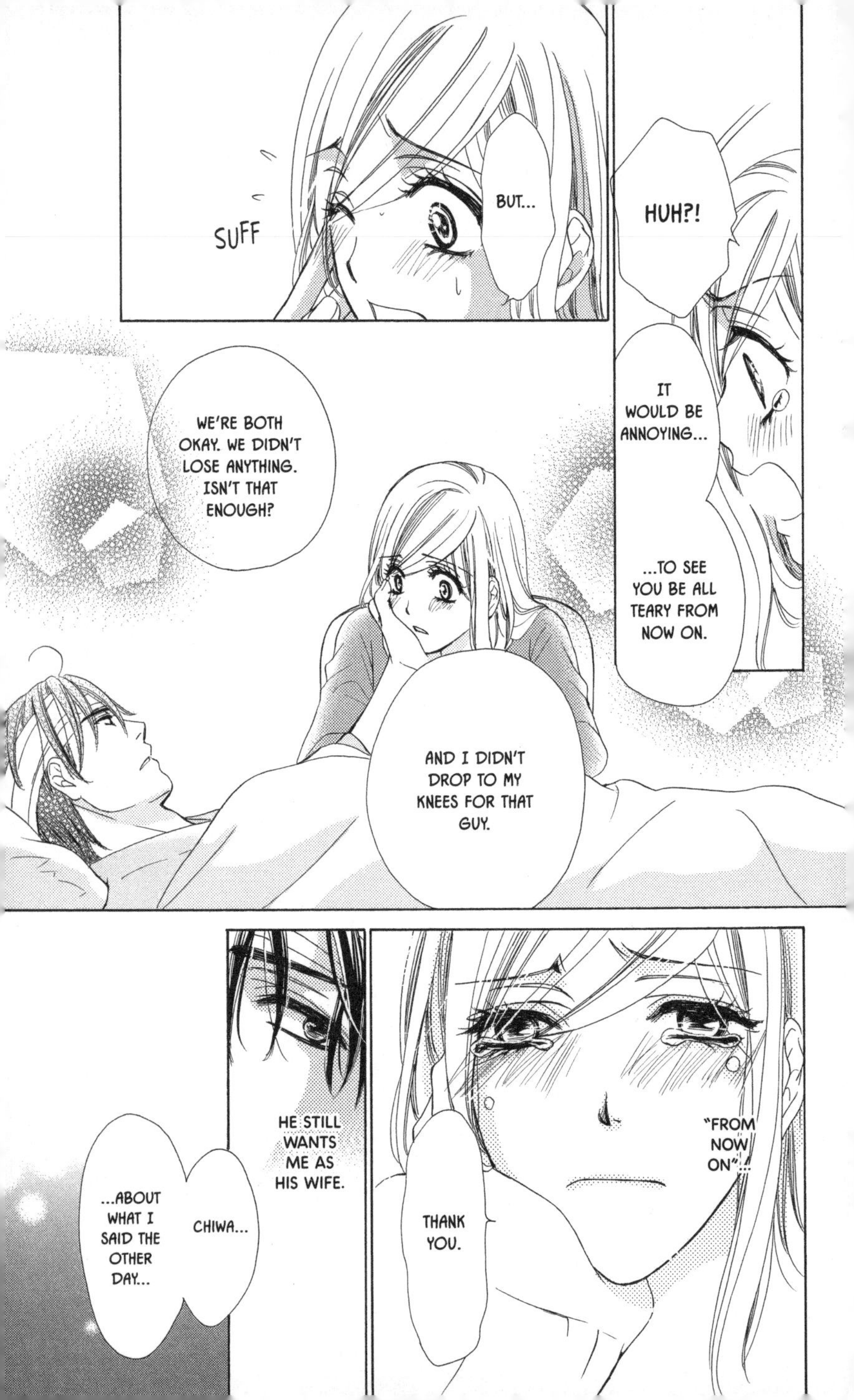
HUH?!
IT WOULD BE ANNOYING...
...TO SEE YOU BE ALL TEARY FROM NOW ON.
SUFF
BUT...
WE'RE BOTH OKAY. WE DIDN'T LOSE ANYTHING. ISN'T THAT ENOUGH?
AND I DIDN'T DROP TO MY KNEES FOR THAT GUY.
"FROM NOW ON"...
THANK YOU.
HE STILL WANTS ME AS HIS WIFE.
CHIWA...
...ABOUT WHAT I SAID THE OTHER DAY...

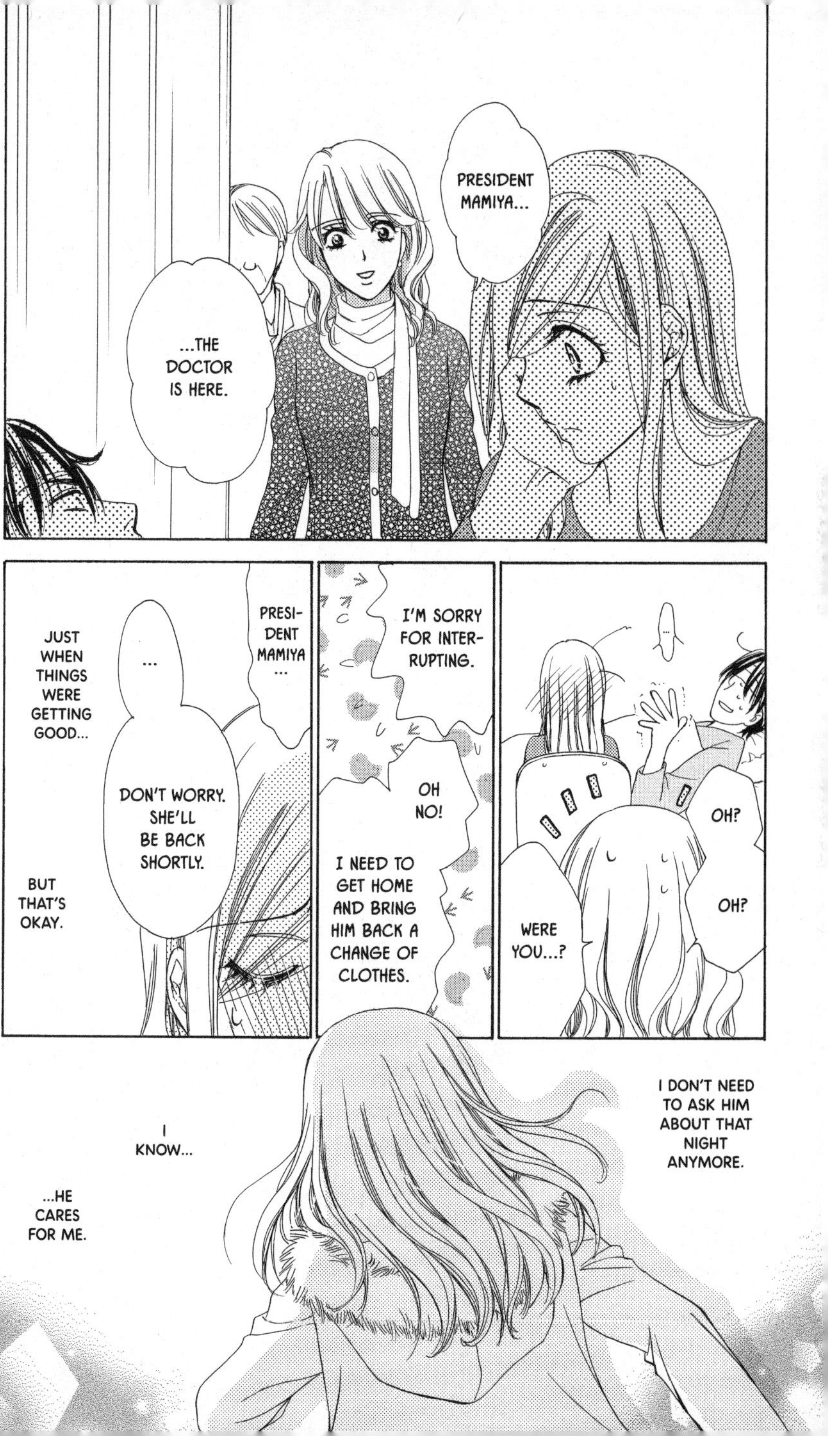
PRESIDENT MAMIYA...
...THE DOCTOR IS HERE.
...
OH?
OH?
WERE YOU...?
I'M SORRY FOR INTERRUPTING.
OH NO!
I NEED TO GET HOME AND BRING HIM BACK A CHANGE OF CLOTHES.
PRESIDENT MAMIYA...
...
JUST WHEN THINGS WERE GETTING GOOD...
DON'T WORRY. SHE'LL BE BACK SHORTLY.
BUT THAT'S OKAY.
I DON'T NEED TO ASK HIM ABOUT THAT NIGHT ANYMORE.
I KNOW...
...HE CARES FOR ME.

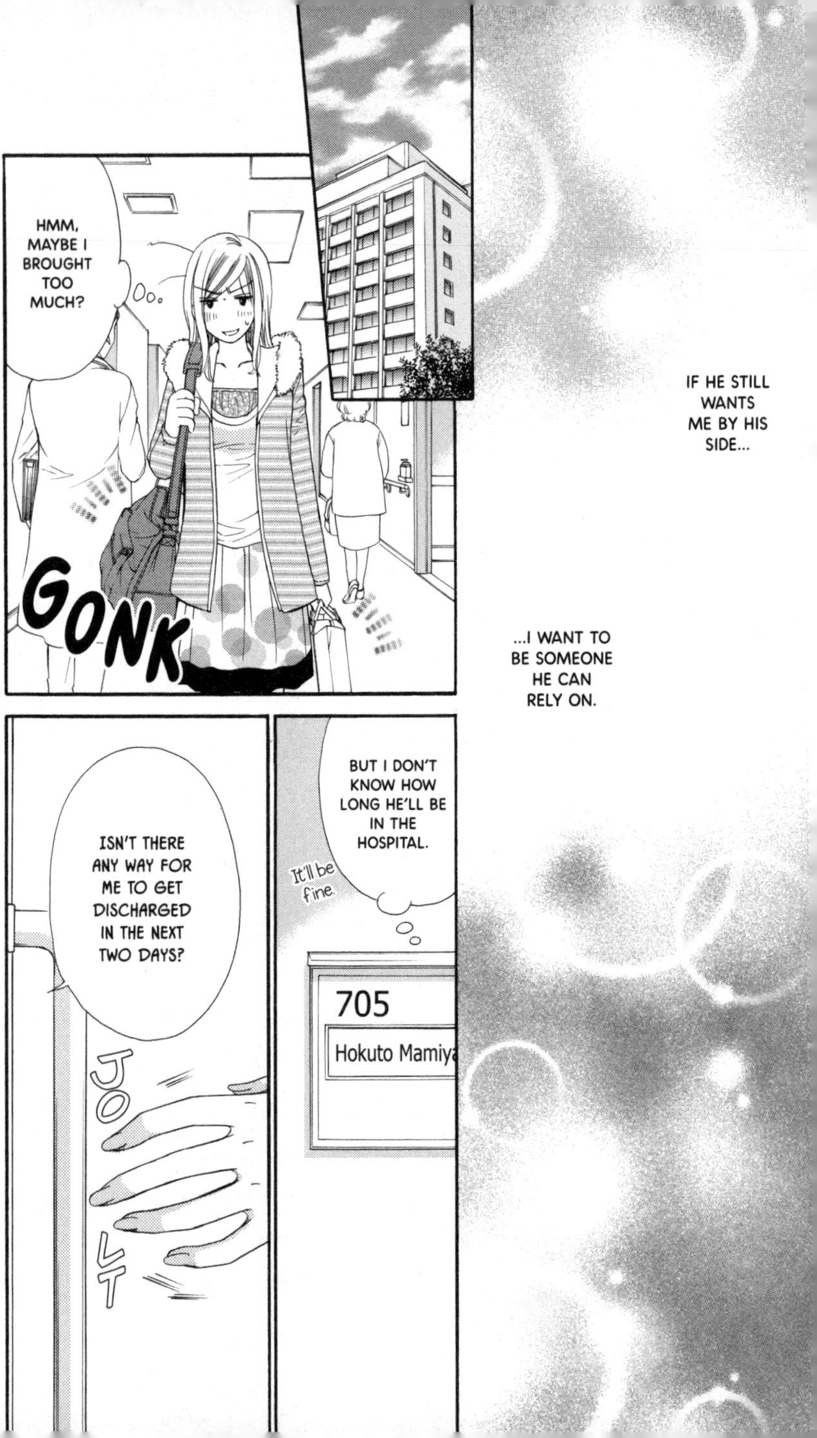
IF HE STILL WANTS ME BY HIS SIDE...
...I WANT TO BE SOMEONE HE CAN RELY ON.
HMM, MAYBE I BROUGHT TOO MUCH?
Oo.
GONK
BUT I DON'T KNOW HOW LONG HE'LL BE IN THE HOSPITAL.
It'll be fine.
705
Hokuto Mamiya
ISN'T THERE ANY WAY FOR ME TO GET DISCHARGED IN THE NEXT TWO DAYS?
JOLT

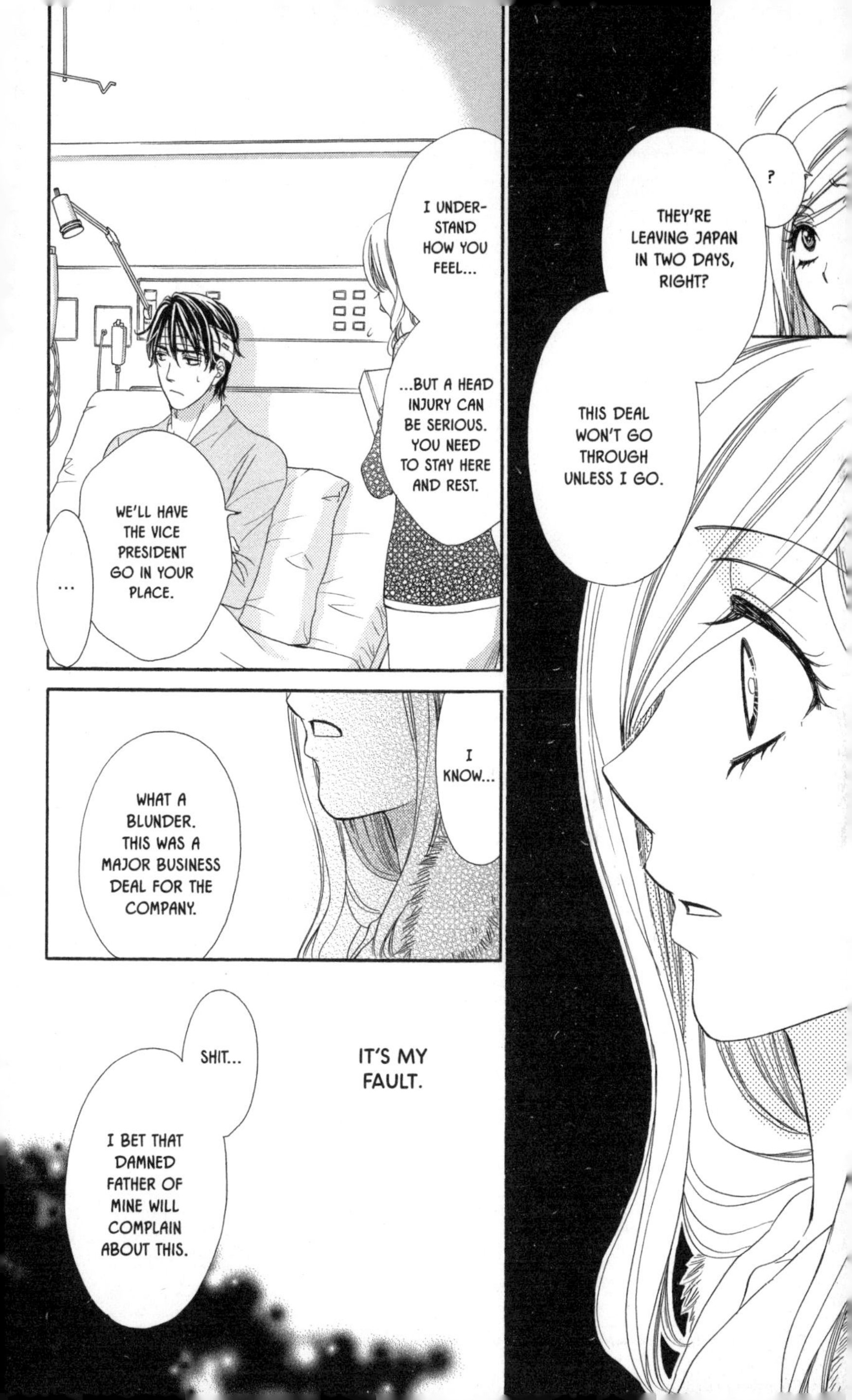
?
THEY'RE LEAVING JAPAN IN TWO DAYS, RIGHT?
THIS DEAL WON'T GO THROUGH UNLESS I GO.
I UNDER-STAND HOW YOU FEEL...
...BUT A HEAD INJURY CAN BE SERIOUS. YOU NEED TO STAY HERE AND REST.
WE'LL HAVE THE VICE PRESIDENT GO IN YOUR PLACE.
...
I KNOW...
WHAT A BLUNDER. THIS WAS A MAJOR BUSINESS DEAL FOR THE COMPANY.
IT'S MY FAULT.
SHIT...
I BET THAT DAMNED FATHER OF MINE WILL COMPLAIN ABOUT THIS.

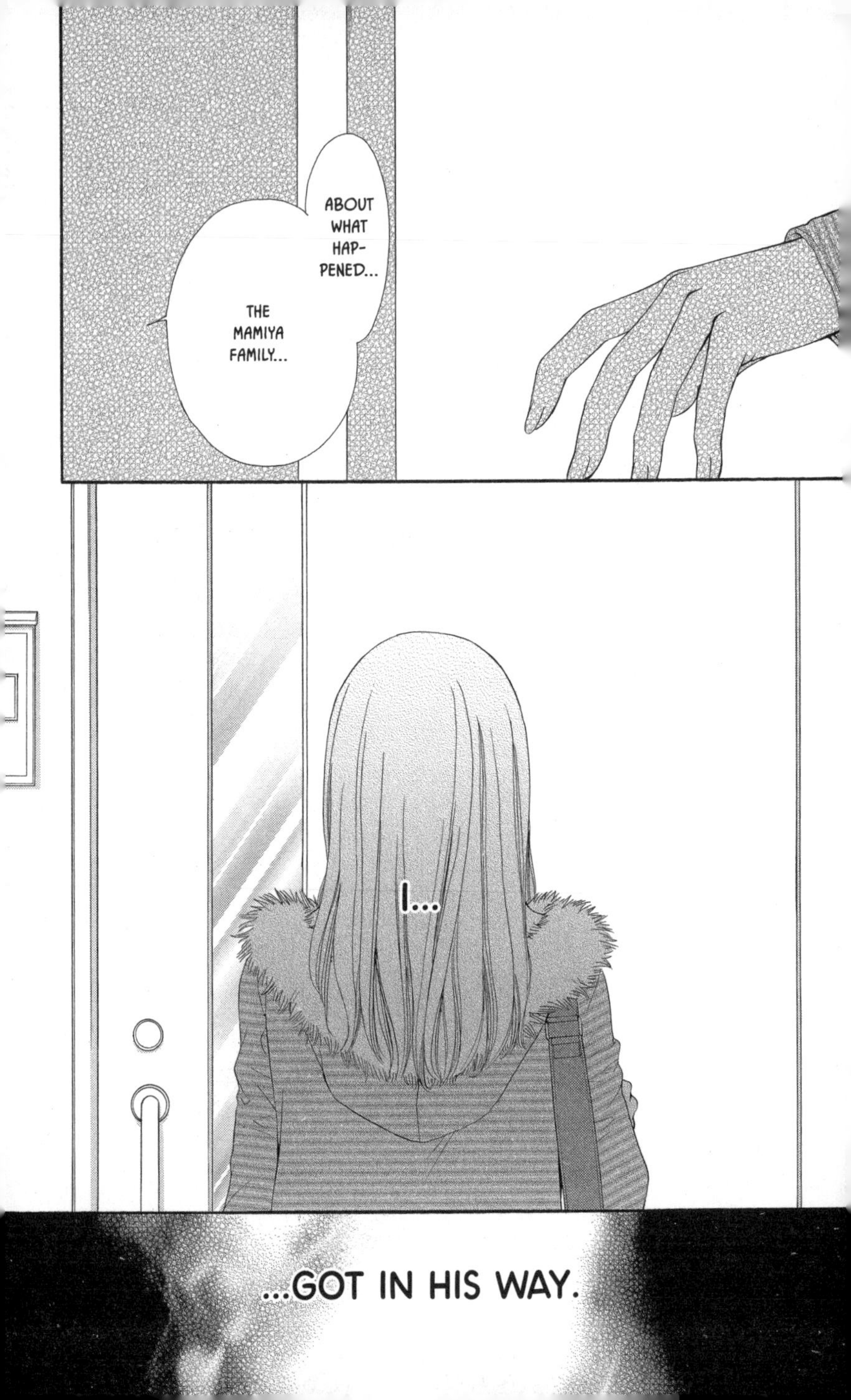
ABOUT WHAT HAP-PENED...
THE MAMIYA FAMILY...
I...
...GOT IN HIS WAY.

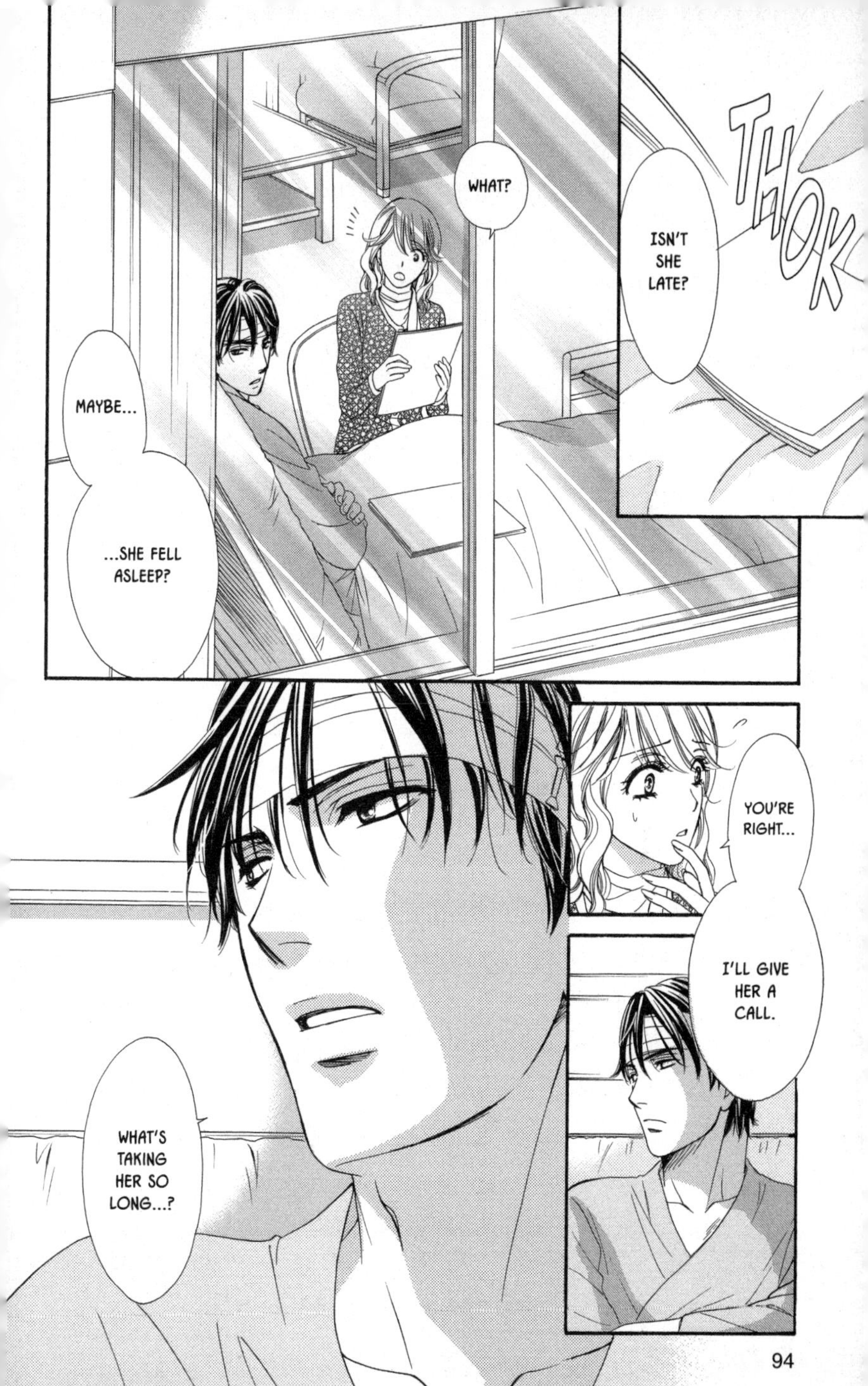
THOK
ISN'T SHE LATE?
WHAT?
MAYBE...
...SHE FELL ASLEEP?
YOU'RE RIGHT...
I'LL GIVE HER A CALL.
WHAT'S TAKING HER SO LONG...?

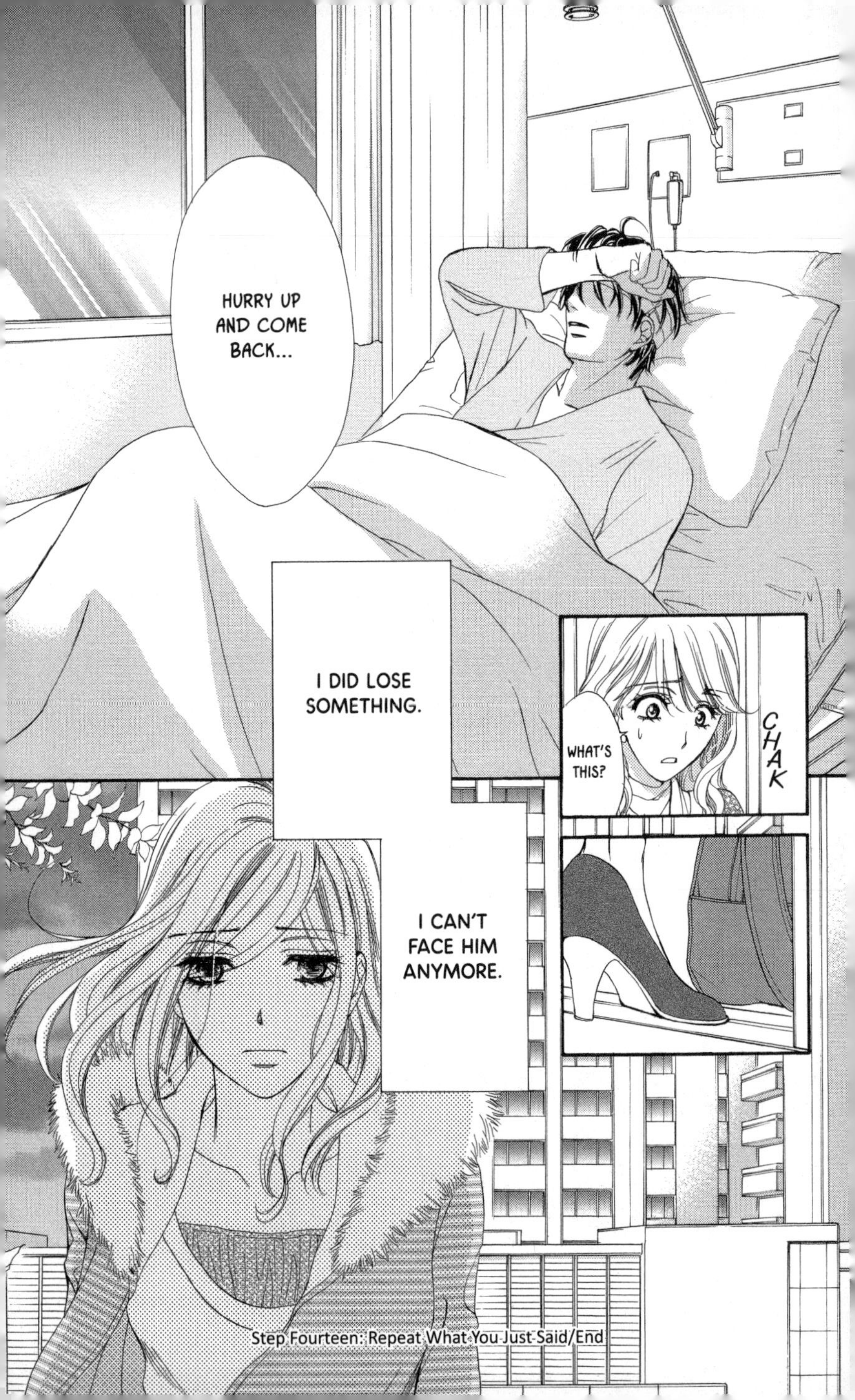
HURRY UP AND COME BACK...
WHAT'S THIS?
CHAK
I DID LOSE SOMETHING.
I CAN'T FACE HIM ANYMORE.
Step Fourteen: Repeat What You Just Said/End

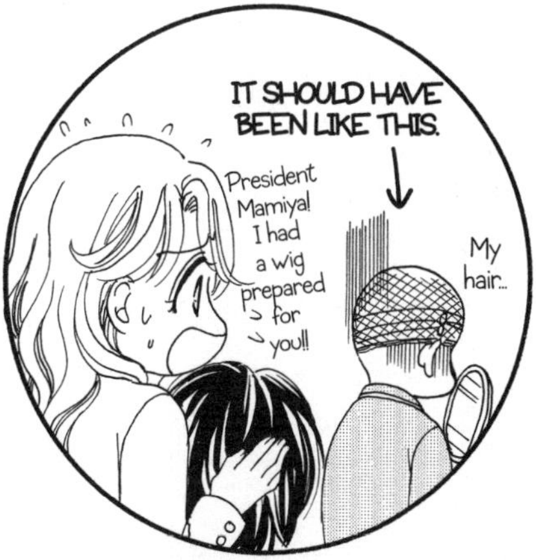
IT SHOULD HAVE BEEN LIKE THIS.
President Mamiya! I had a wig prepared for you!!
My hair...

BUT I COULDN'T DO IT FOR OBVIOUS REASONS.

Step Fifteen: Is This Your True Heart?

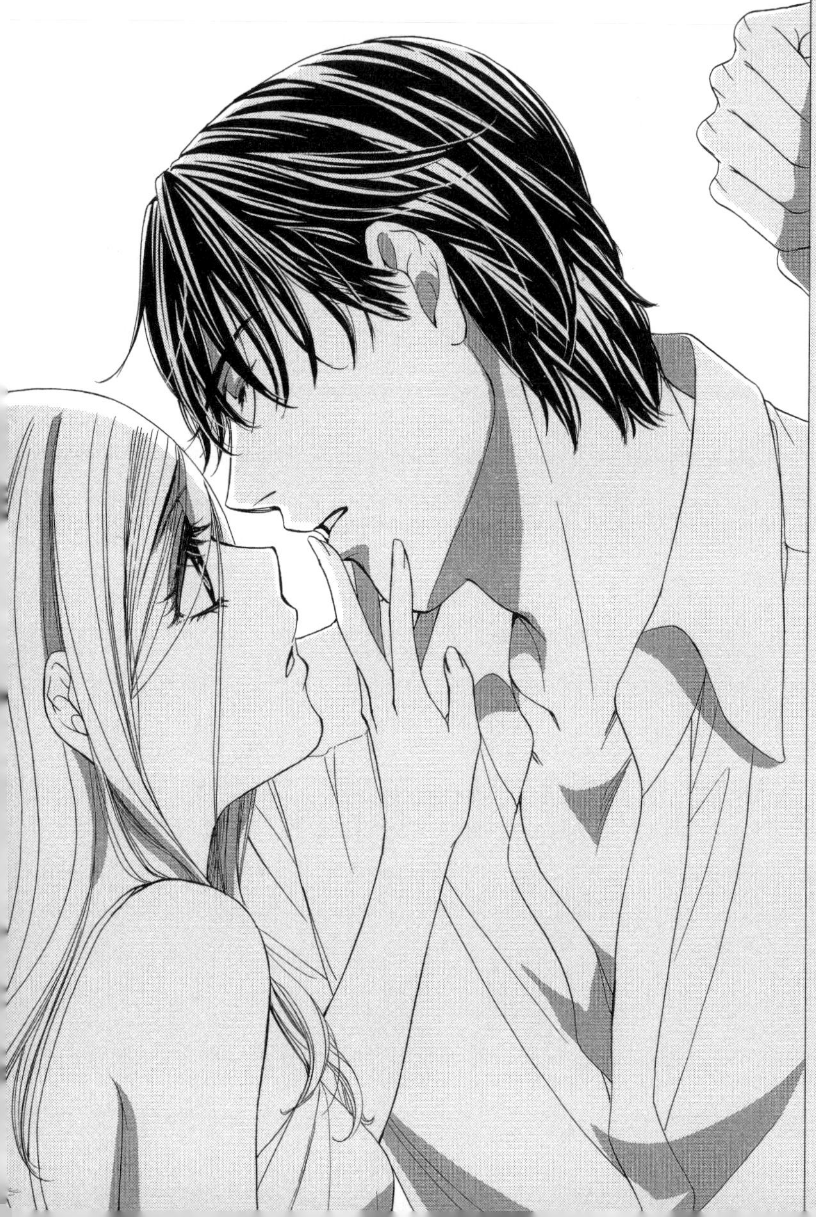

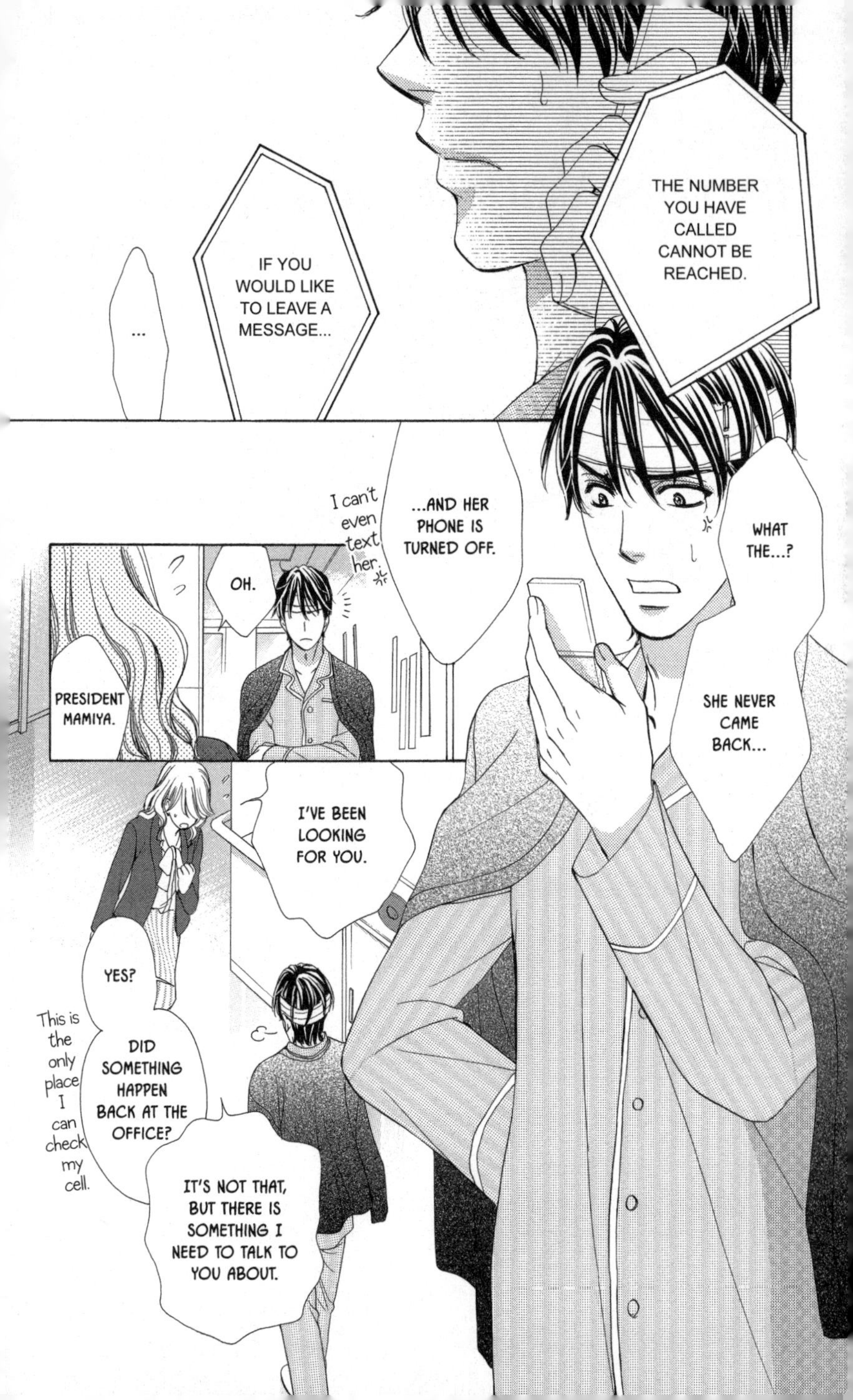
THE NUMBER YOU HAVE CALLED CANNOT BE REACHED.
IF YOU WOULD LIKE TO LEAVE A MESSAGE...
...
WHAT THE...?
...AND HER PHONE IS TURNED OFF.
I can't even text her.
SHE NEVER CAME BACK...
OH.
PRESIDENT MAMIYA.
I'VE BEEN LOOKING FOR YOU.
YES?
DID SOMETHING HAPPEN BACK AT THE OFFICE?
This is the only place I can check my cell.
IT'S NOT THAT, BUT THERE IS SOMETHING I NEED TO TALK TO YOU ABOUT.

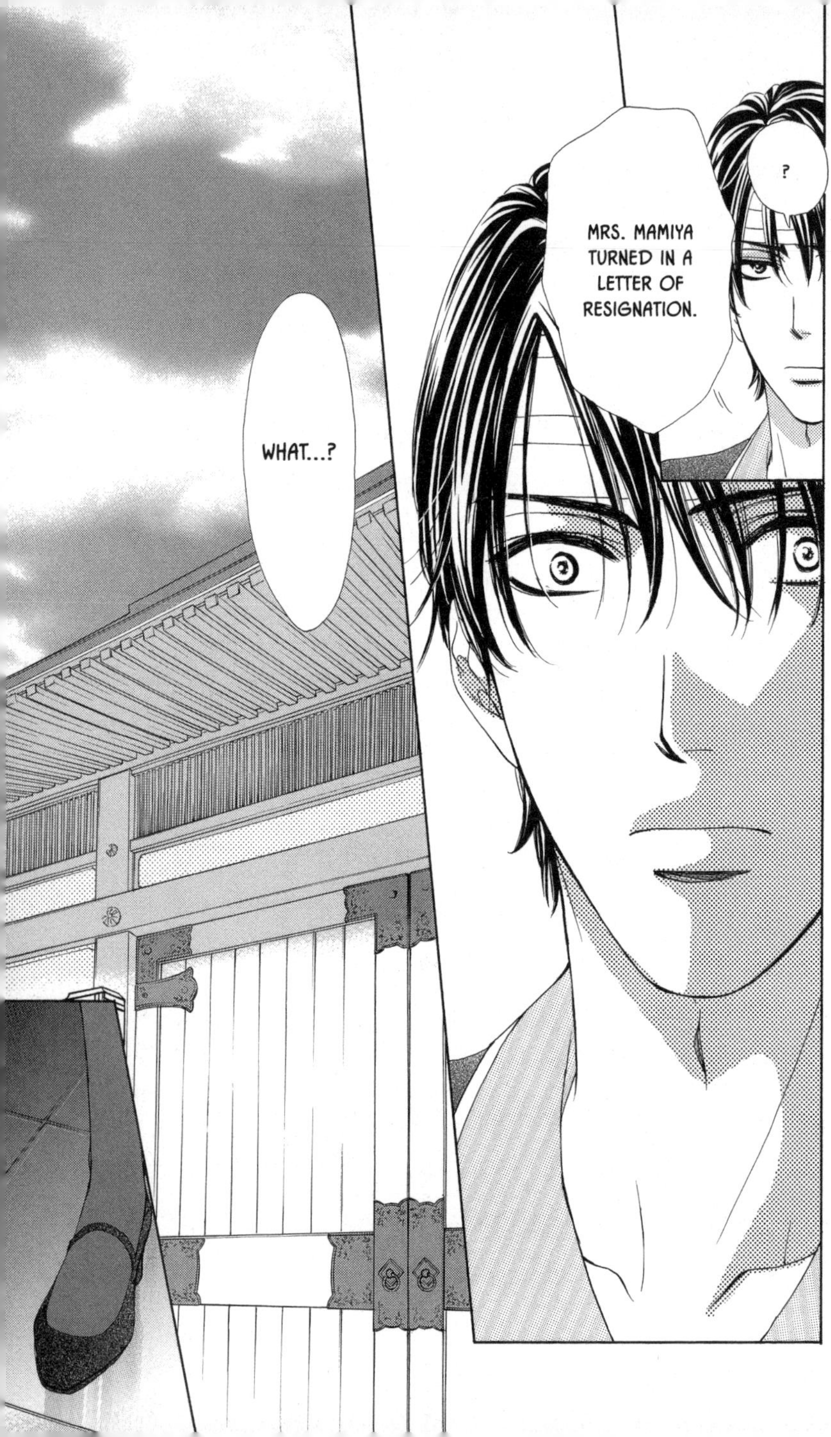
?
MRS. MAMIYA TURNED IN A LETTER OF RESIGNATION.
WHAT...?

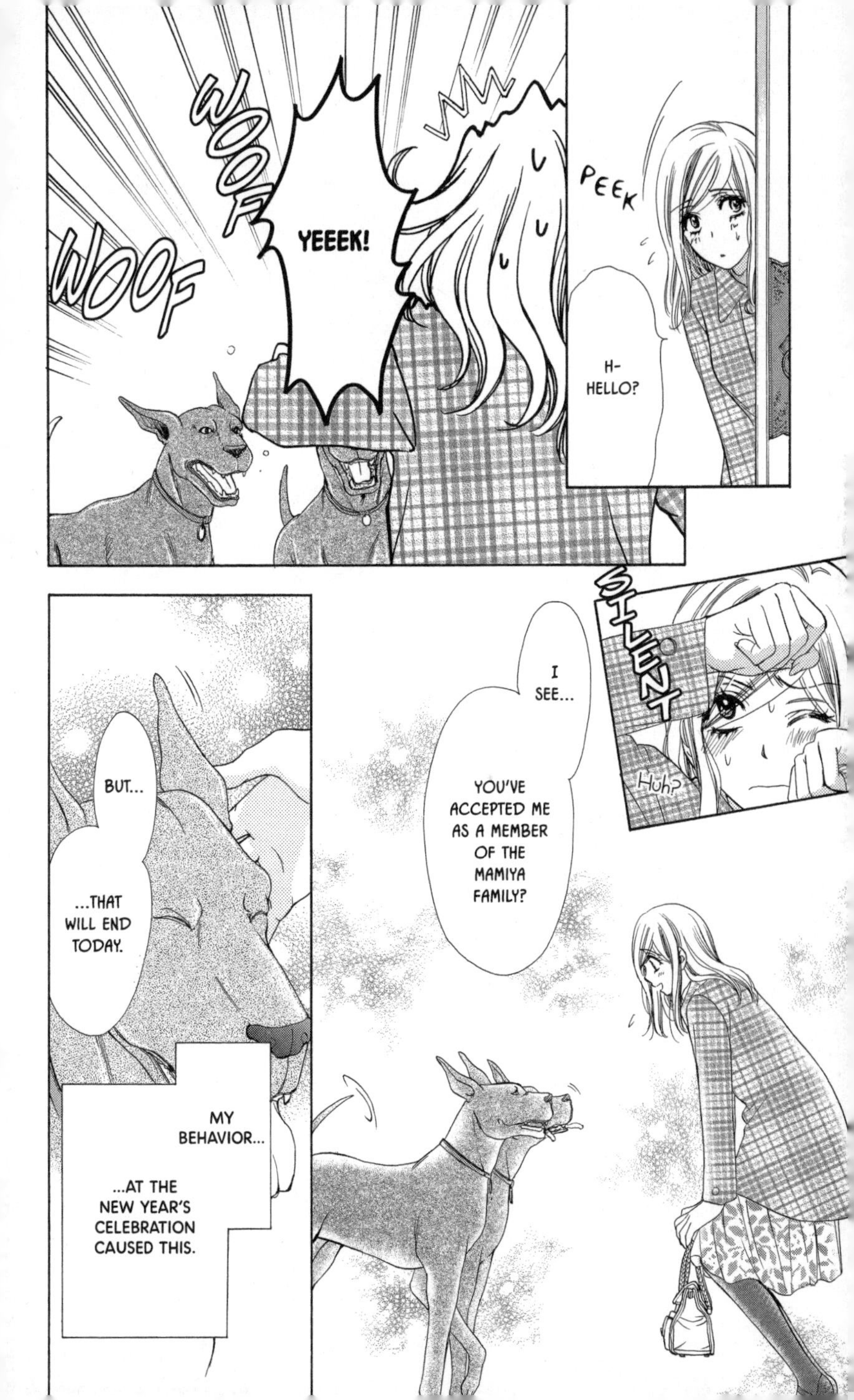
PEEK
H-HELLO?
YEEEK!
WOOF
WOOF
SILENT
Huh?
I SEE...
YOU'VE ACCEPTED ME AS A MEMBER OF THE MAMIYA FAMILY?
BUT...
...THAT WILL END TODAY.
MY BEHAVIOR...
...AT THE NEW YEAR'S CELEBRATION CAUSED THIS.

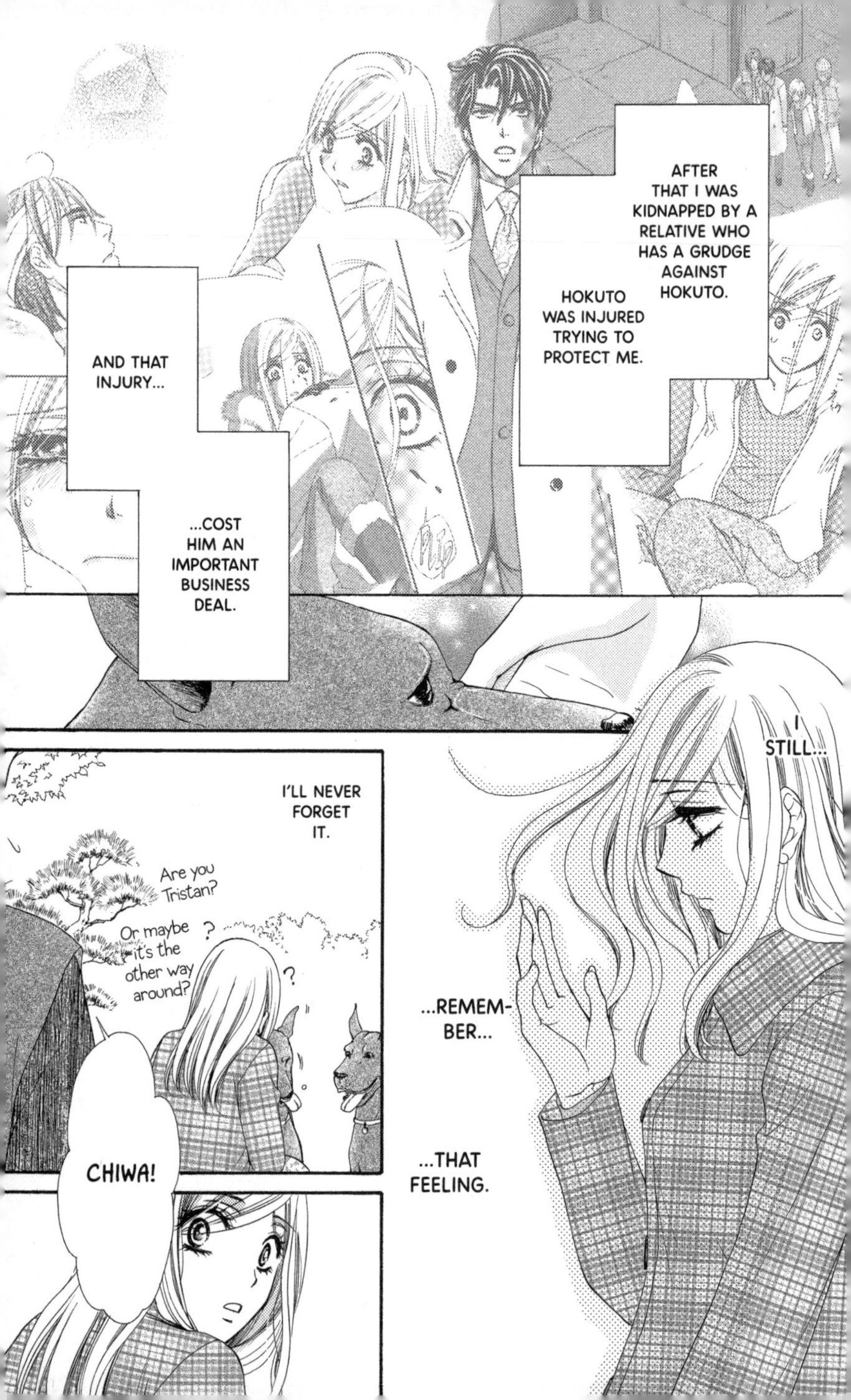
AFTER THAT I WAS KIDNAPPED BY A RELATIVE WHO HAS A GRUDGE AGAINST HOKUTO.
HOKUTO WAS INJURED TRYING TO PROTECT ME.
AND THAT INJURY...
...COST HIM AN IMPORTANT BUSINESS DEAL.
I STILL...
...REMEM-BER...
...THAT FEELING.
I'LL NEVER FORGET IT.
Are you Tristan?
Or maybe it's the other way around?
CHIWA!

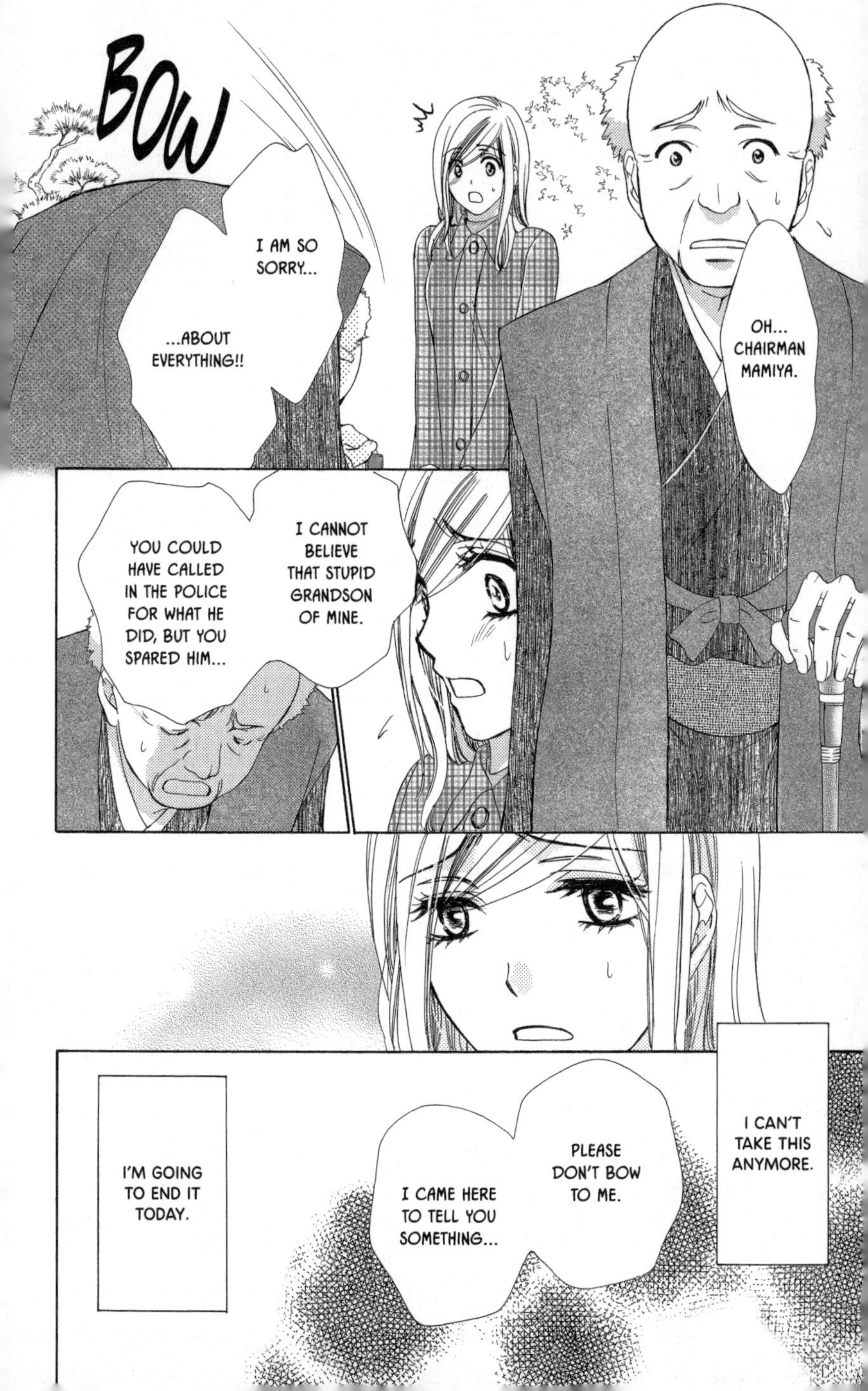
OH... CHAIRMAN MAMIYA.
BOW
I AM SO SORRY...
...ABOUT EVERYTHING!!
I CANNOT BELIEVE THAT STUPID GRANDSON OF MINE.
YOU COULD HAVE CALLED IN THE POLICE FOR WHAT HE DID, BUT YOU SPARED HIM...
I CAN'T TAKE THIS ANYMORE.
PLEASE DON'T BOW TO ME.
I CAME HERE TO TELL YOU SOMETHING...
I'M GOING TO END IT TODAY.

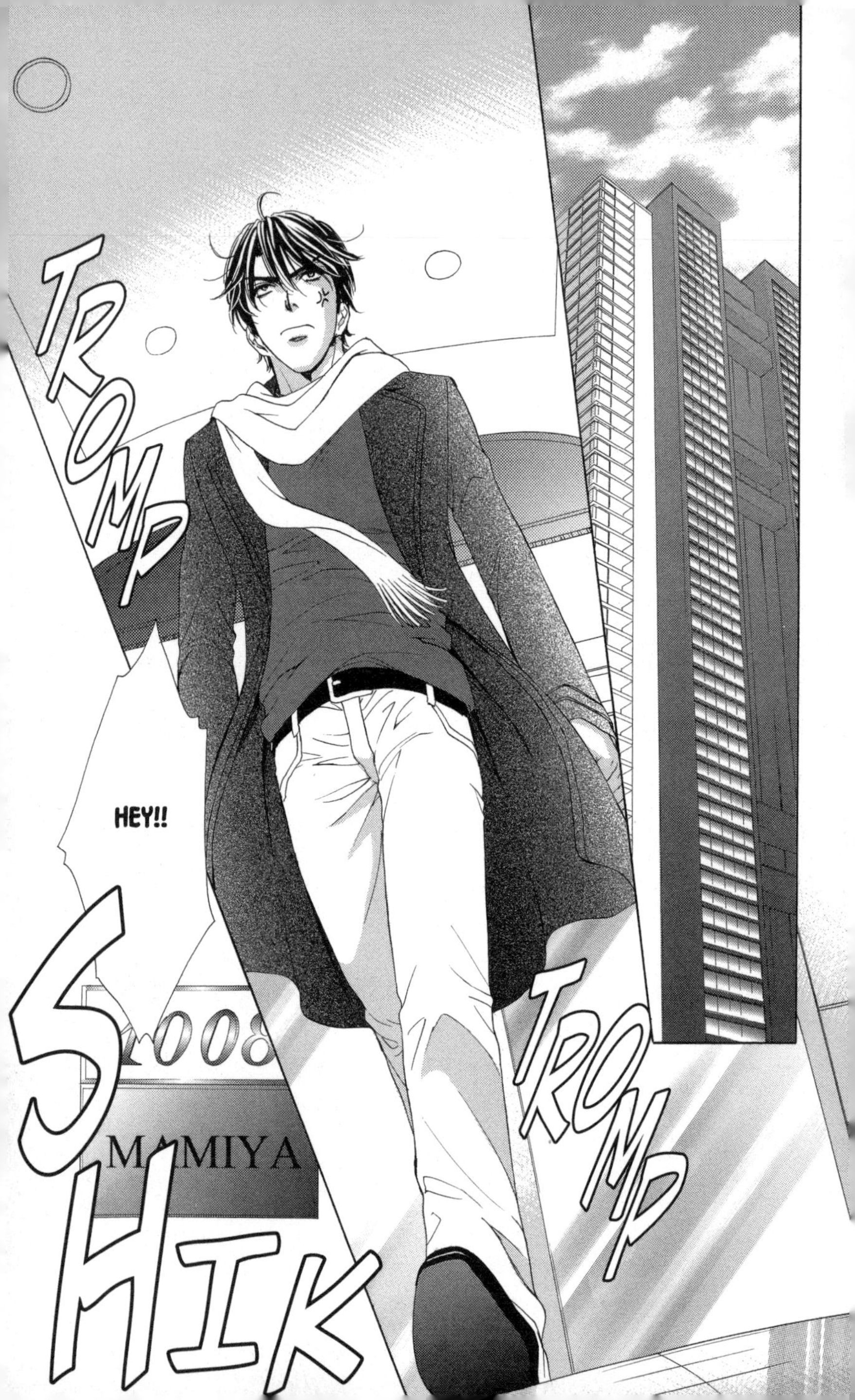
TROMP
TROMP
HEY!!
2008
MAMIYA
SHIK

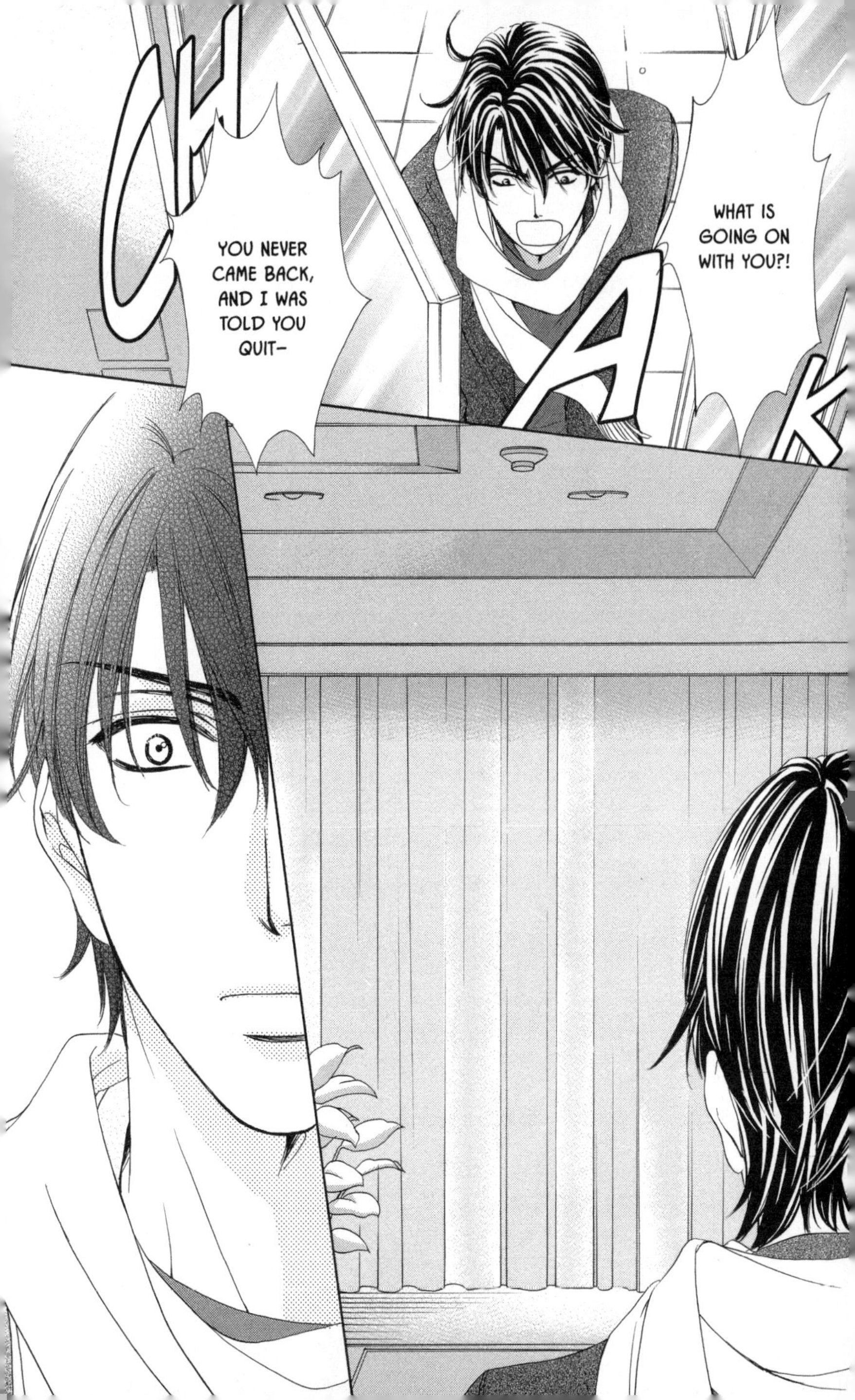
CHAK
WHAT IS GOING ON WITH YOU?!
YOU NEVER CAME BACK, AND I WAS TOLD YOU QUIT–

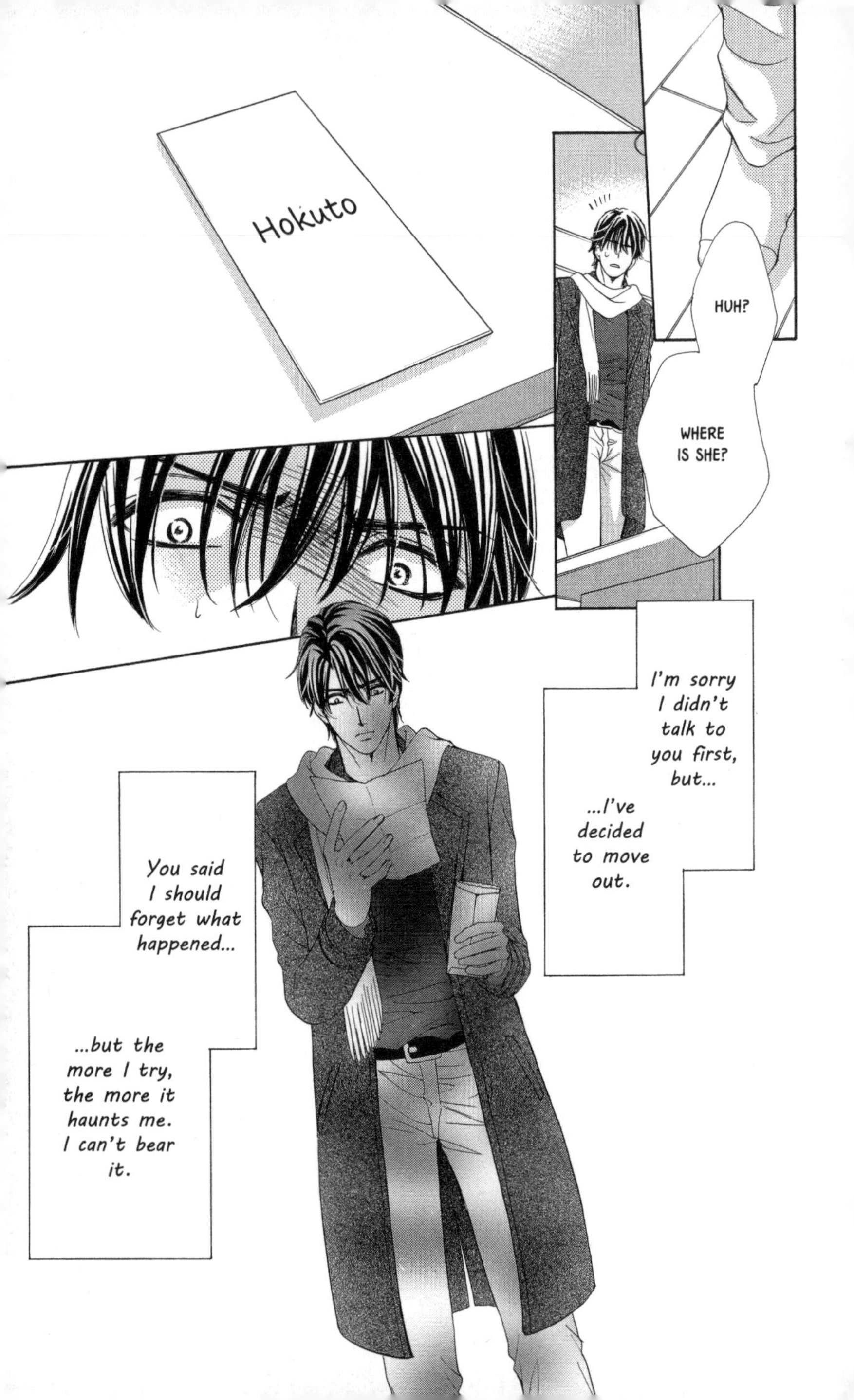
HUH?
WHERE IS SHE?
Hokuto
I'm sorry I didn't talk to you first, but...
...I've decided to move out.
You said I should forget what happened...
...but the more I try, the more it haunts me. I can't bear it.

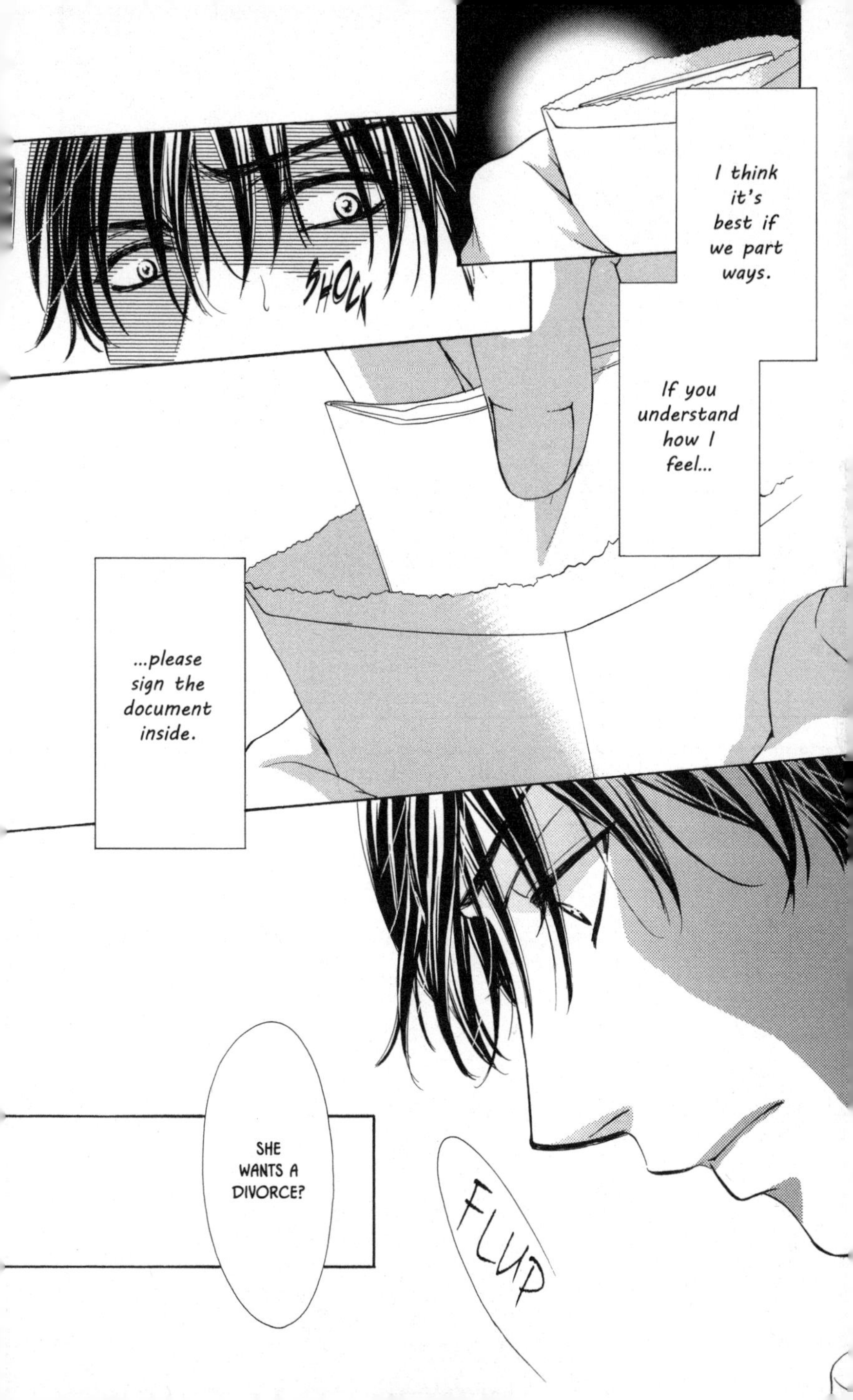
I think it's best if we part ways.
SHOCK
If you understand how I feel...
...please sign the document inside.
FLIP
SHE WANTS A DIVORCE?

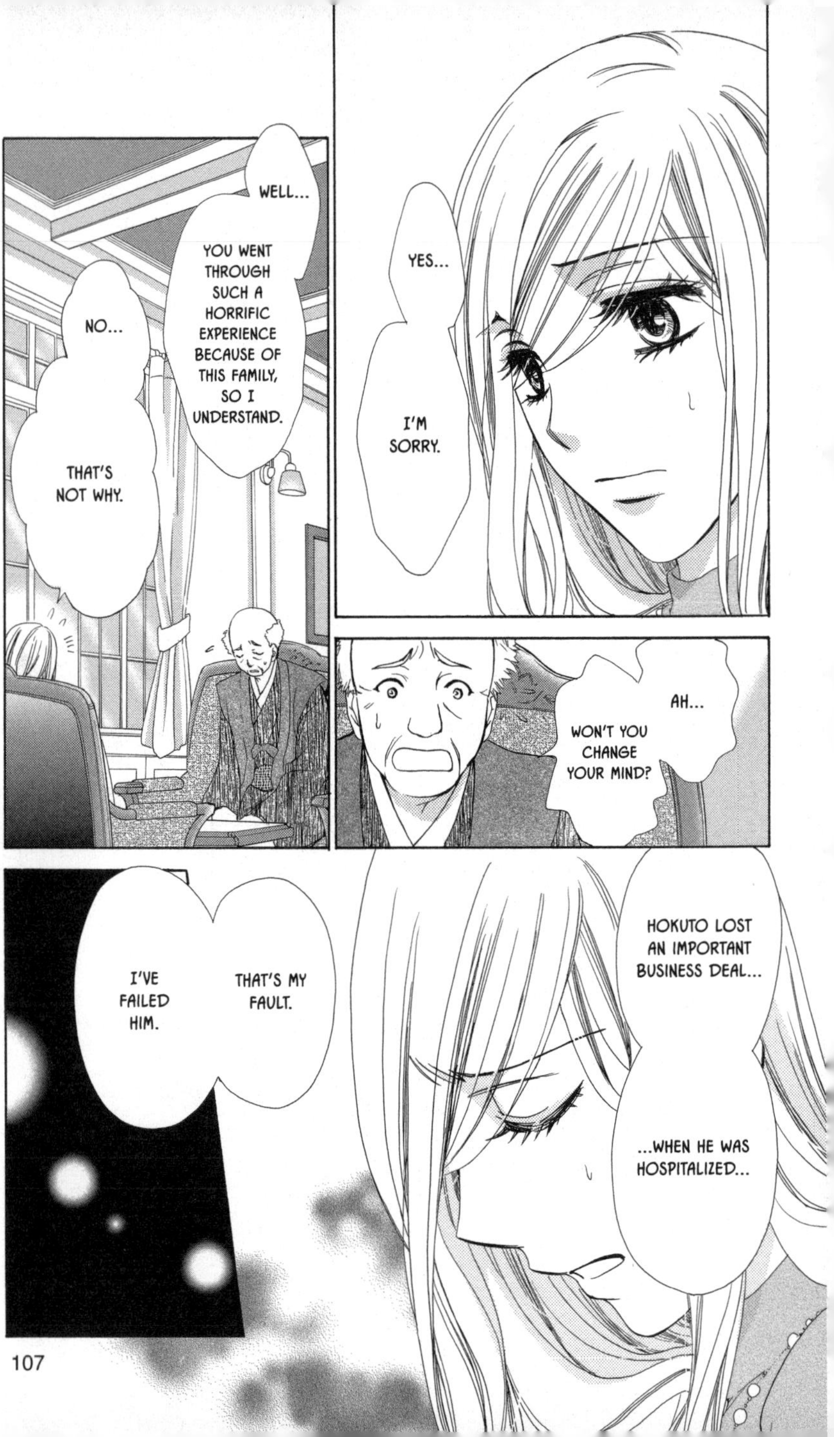
YES...
I'M SORRY.
AH...
WON'T YOU CHANGE YOUR MIND?
WELL...
YOU WENT THROUGH SUCH A HORRIFIC EXPERIENCE BECAUSE OF THIS FAMILY, SO I UNDERSTAND.
NO...
THAT'S NOT WHY.
HOKUTO LOST AN IMPORTANT BUSINESS DEAL...
...WHEN HE WAS HOSPITALIZED...
THAT'S MY FAULT.
I'VE FAILED HIM.

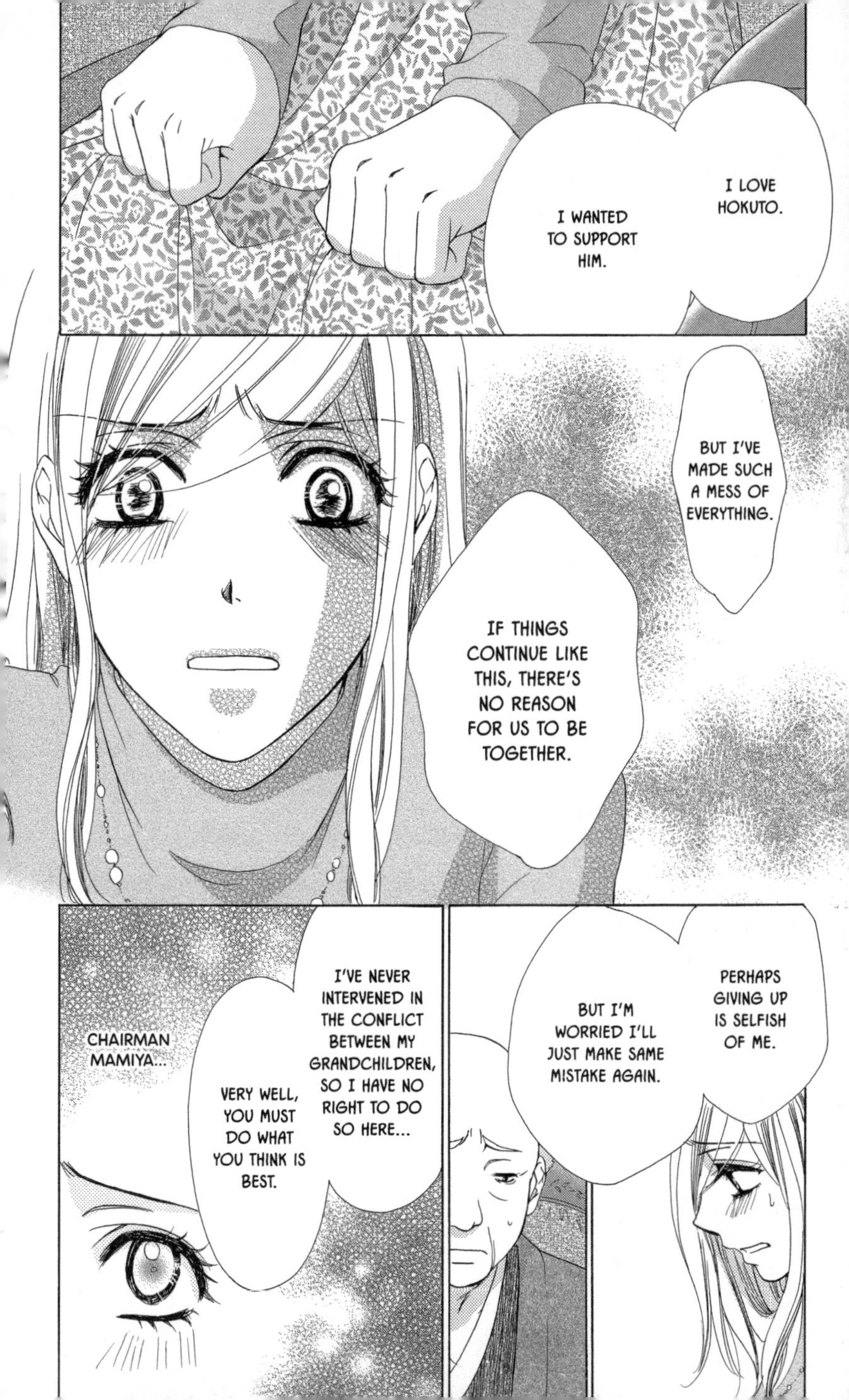
I LOVE HOKUTO.
I WANTED TO SUPPORT HIM.
BUT I'VE MADE SUCH A MESS OF EVERYTHING.
IF THINGS CONTINUE LIKE THIS, THERE'S NO REASON FOR US TO BE TOGETHER.
PERHAPS GIVING UP IS SELFISH OF ME.
BUT I'M WORRIED I'LL JUST MAKE SAME MISTAKE AGAIN.
I'VE NEVER INTERVENED IN THE CONFLICT BETWEEN MY GRANDCHILDREN, SO I HAVE NO RIGHT TO DO SO HERE...
VERY WELL, YOU MUST DO WHAT YOU THINK IS BEST.
CHAIRMAN MAMIYA...

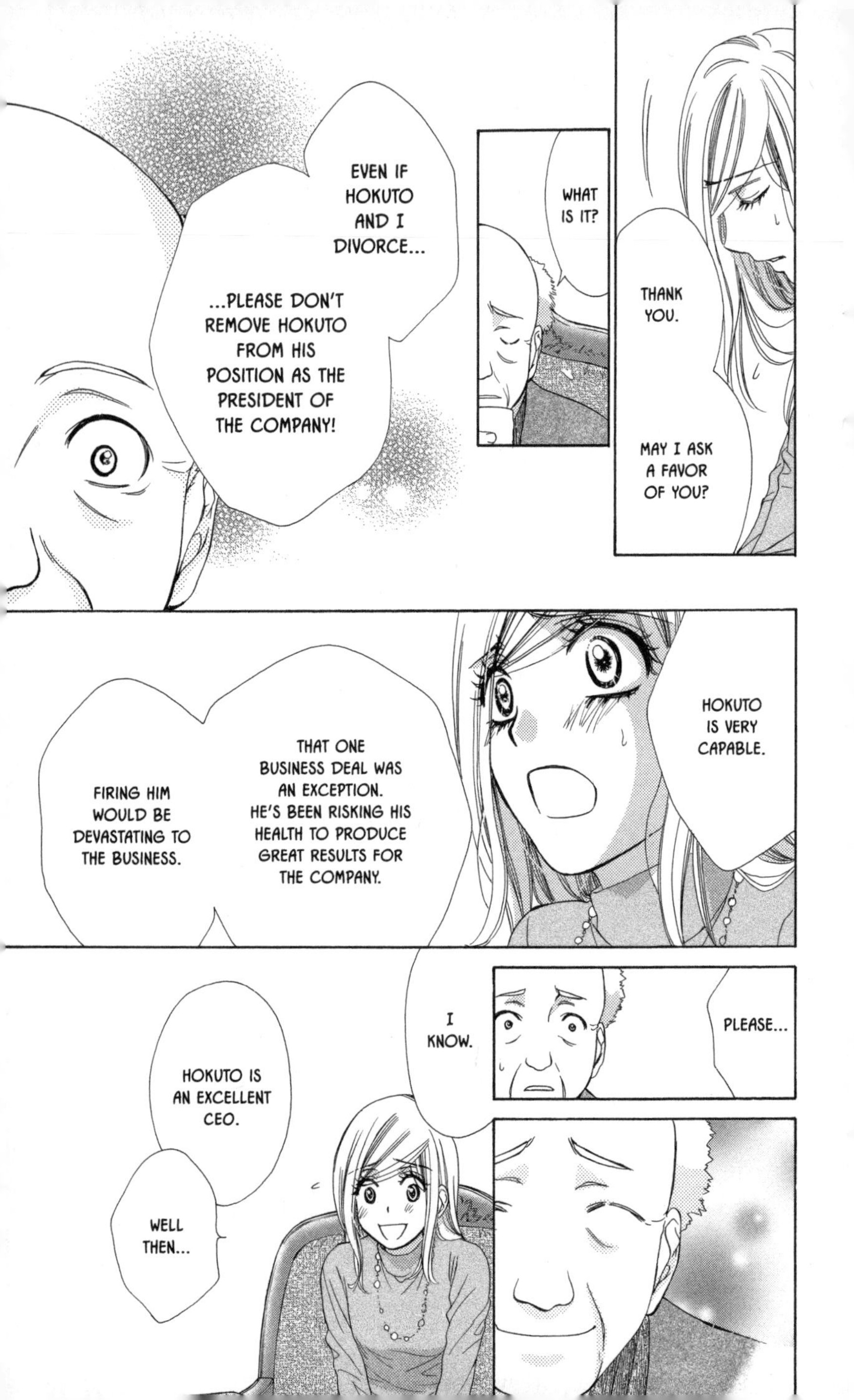
THANK YOU.
MAY I ASK A FAVOR OF YOU?
WHAT IS IT?
EVEN IF HOKUTO AND I DIVORCE...
...PLEASE DON'T REMOVE HOKUTO FROM HIS POSITION AS THE PRESIDENT OF THE COMPANY!
HOKUTO IS VERY CAPABLE.
THAT ONE BUSINESS DEAL WAS AN EXCEPTION. HE'S BEEN RISKING HIS HEALTH TO PRODUCE GREAT RESULTS FOR THE COMPANY.
FIRING HIM WOULD BE DEVASTATING TO THE BUSINESS.
PLEASE...
I KNOW.
HOKUTO IS AN EXCELLENT CEO.
WELL THEN...

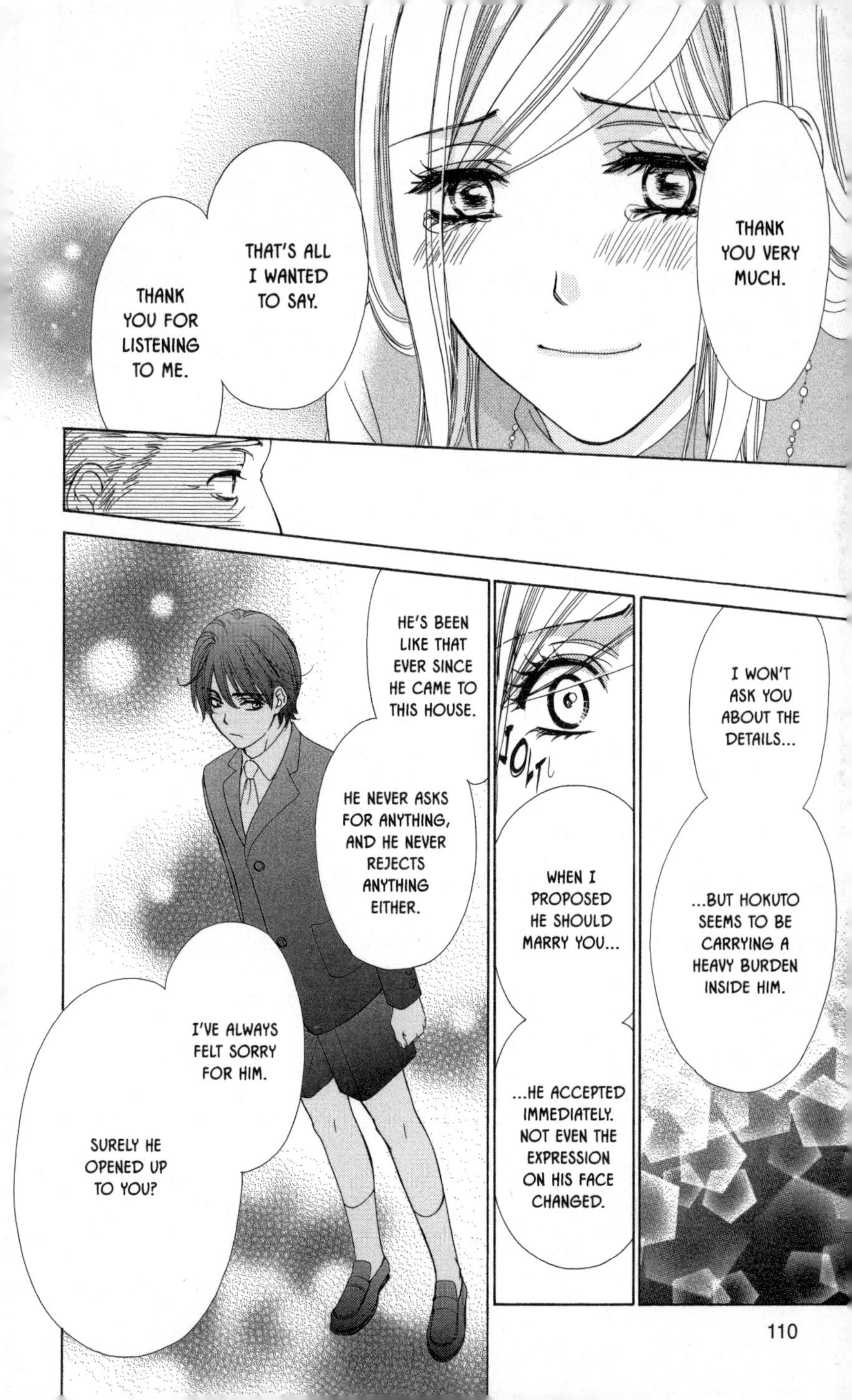
THANK YOU VERY MUCH.
THAT'S ALL I WANTED TO SAY.
THANK YOU FOR LISTENING TO ME.
I WON'T ASK YOU ABOUT THE DETAILS...
...BUT HOKUTO SEEMS TO BE CARRYING A HEAVY BURDEN INSIDE HIM.
JOLT
WHEN I PROPOSED HE SHOULD MARRY YOU...
...HE ACCEPTED IMMEDIATELY. NOT EVEN THE EXPRESSION ON HIS FACE CHANGED.
HE'S BEEN LIKE THAT EVER SINCE HE CAME TO THIS HOUSE.
HE NEVER ASKS FOR ANYTHING, AND HE NEVER REJECTS ANYTHING EITHER.
I'VE ALWAYS FELT SORRY FOR HIM.
SURELY HE OPENED UP TO YOU?

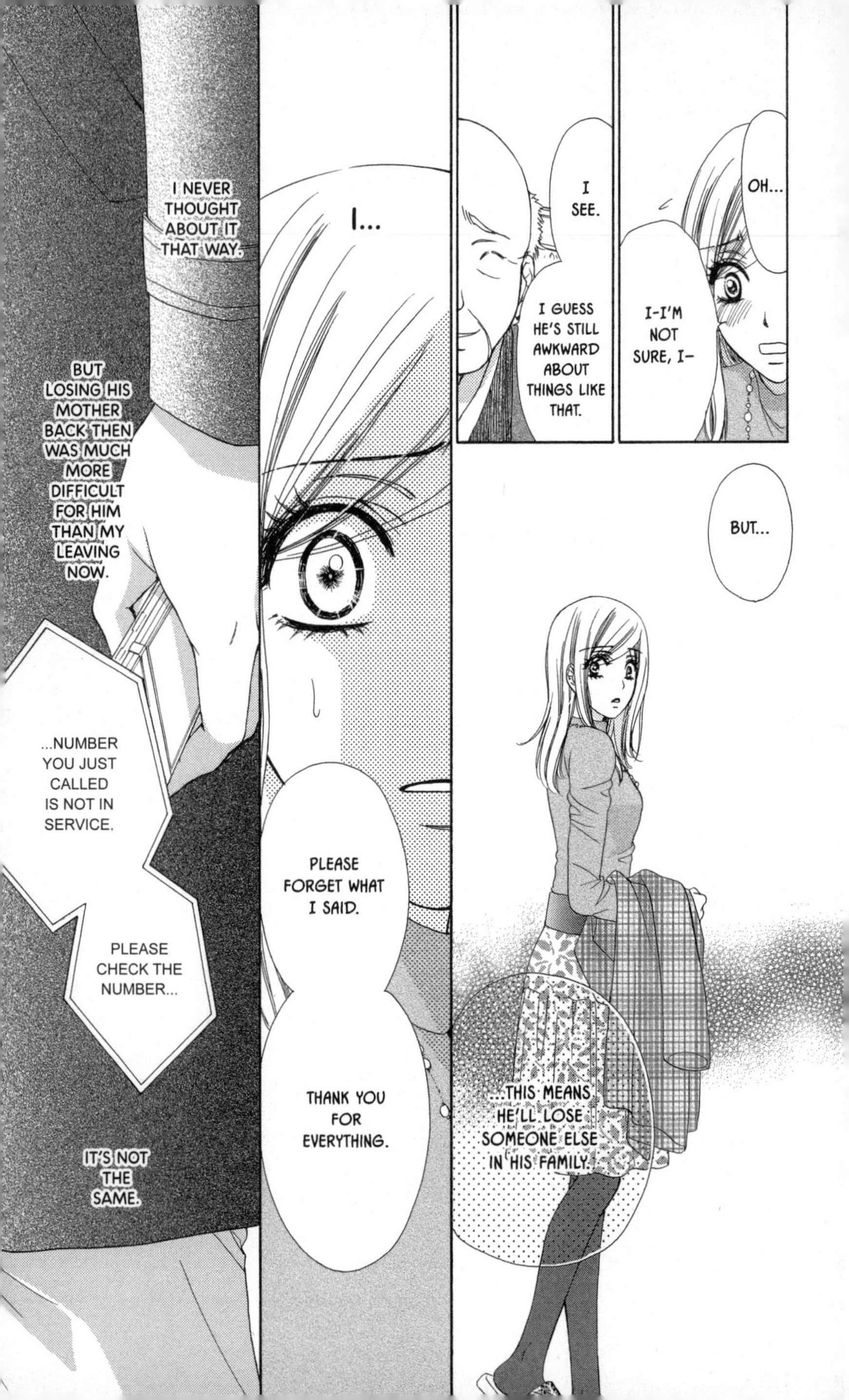
OH...
I-I'M NOT SURE, I-
I SEE.
I GUESS HE'S STILL AWKWARD ABOUT THINGS LIKE THAT.
BUT...
...THIS MEANS HE'LL LOSE SOMEONE ELSE IN HIS FAMILY.
I...
PLEASE FORGET WHAT I SAID.
THANK YOU FOR EVERYTHING.
I NEVER THOUGHT ABOUT IT THAT WAY.
BUT LOSING HIS MOTHER BACK THEN WAS MUCH MORE DIFFICULT FOR HIM THAN MY LEAVING NOW.
...NUMBER YOU JUST CALLED IS NOT IN SERVICE.
PLEASE CHECK THE NUMBER...
IT'S NOT THE SAME.

I'VE ALWAYS BEEN...
...TOO BUSY THINKING ABOUT MYSELF.
...AND CALL AGAIN.
I KEPT FORCING MY FEELINGS ON HIM...
...BECAUSE I WANTED TO KNOW HOW HE FELT ABOUT ME.
I'M SURE...
...HE NEVER...
...FELT HAPPY TO HAVE MARRIED ME.

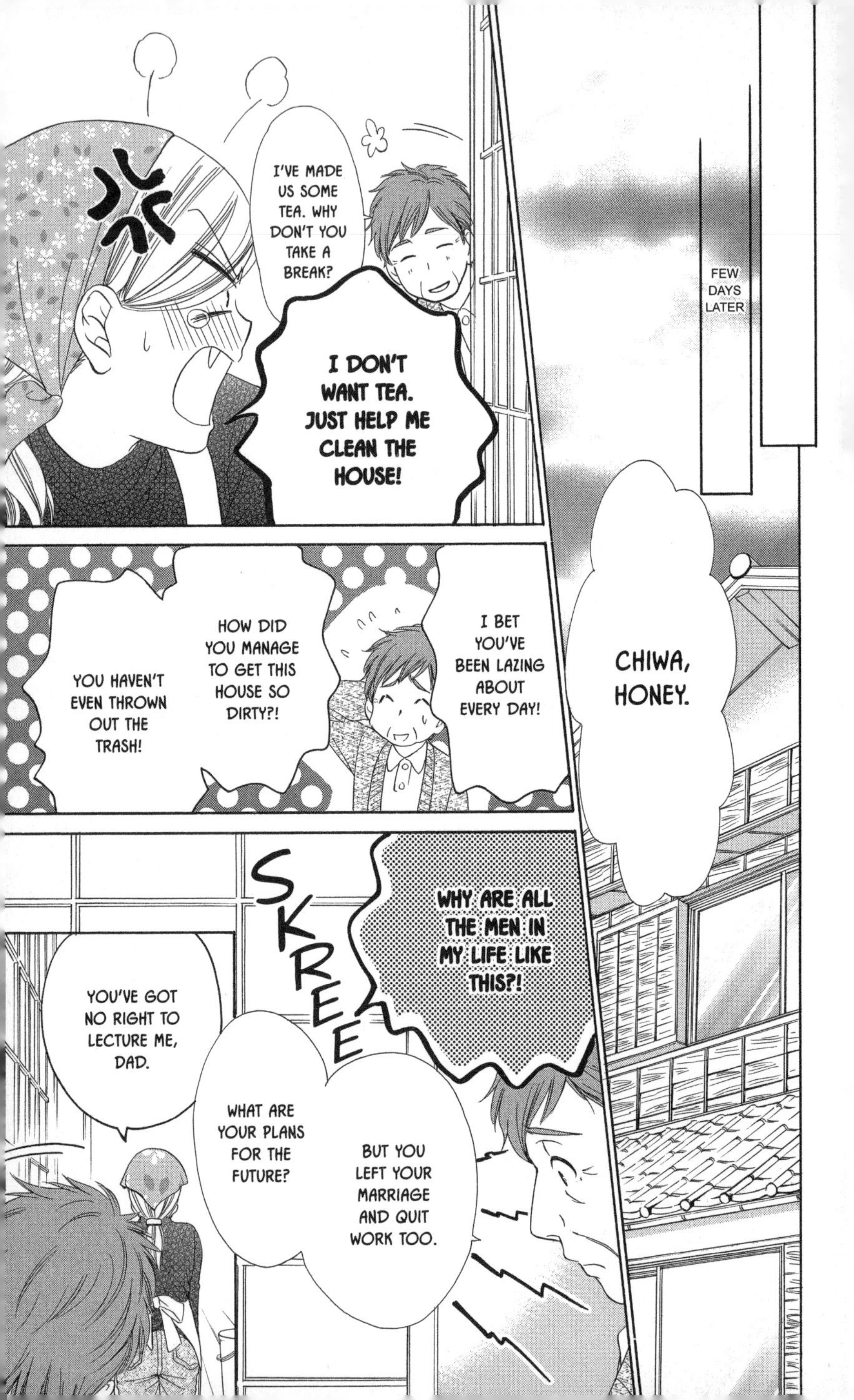

FEW DAYS LATER
CHIWA, HONEY.
I'VE MADE US SOME TEA. WHY DON'T YOU TAKE A BREAK?
I DON'T WANT TEA. JUST HELP ME CLEAN THE HOUSE!
I BET YOU'VE BEEN LAZING ABOUT EVERY DAY!
HOW DID YOU MANAGE TO GET THIS HOUSE SO DIRTY?!
YOU HAVEN'T EVEN THROWN OUT THE TRASH!
WHY ARE ALL THE MEN IN MY LIFE LIKE THIS?!
SKREE
BUT YOU LEFT YOUR MARRIAGE AND QUIT WORK TOO.
WHAT ARE YOUR PLANS FOR THE FUTURE?
YOU'VE GOT NO RIGHT TO LECTURE ME, DAD.

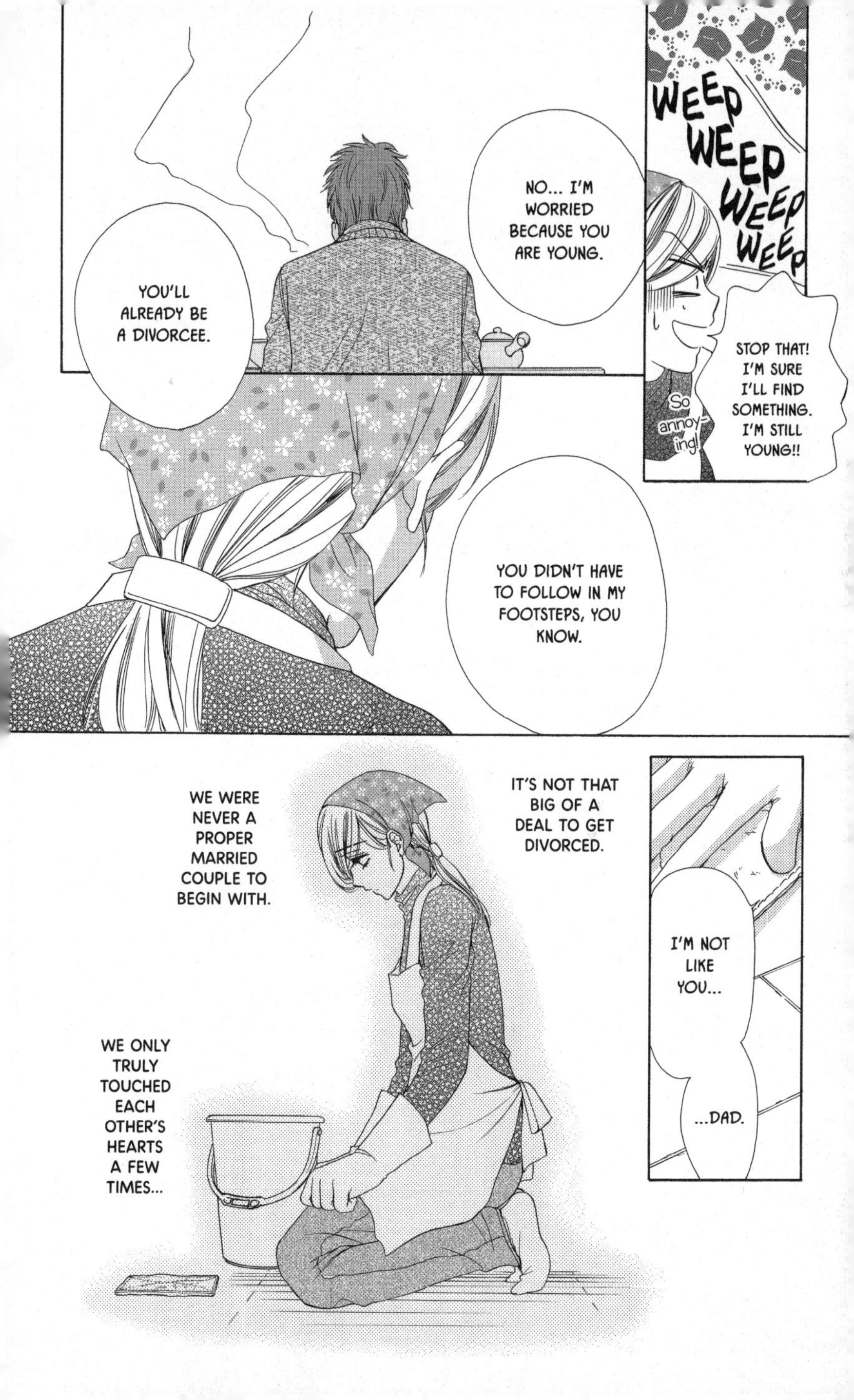
WEEP WEEP WEEP WEEP
STOP THAT! I'M SURE I'LL FIND SOMETHING. I'M STILL YOUNG!!
So annoy-ing!
NO... I'M WORRIED BECAUSE YOU ARE YOUNG.
YOU'LL ALREADY BE A DIVORCEE.
YOU DIDN'T HAVE TO FOLLOW IN MY FOOTSTEPS, YOU KNOW.
I'M NOT LIKE YOU...
...DAD.
IT'S NOT THAT BIG OF A DEAL TO GET DIVORCED.
WE WERE NEVER A PROPER MARRIED COUPLE TO BEGIN WITH.
WE ONLY TRULY TOUCHED EACH OTHER'S HEARTS A FEW TIMES...

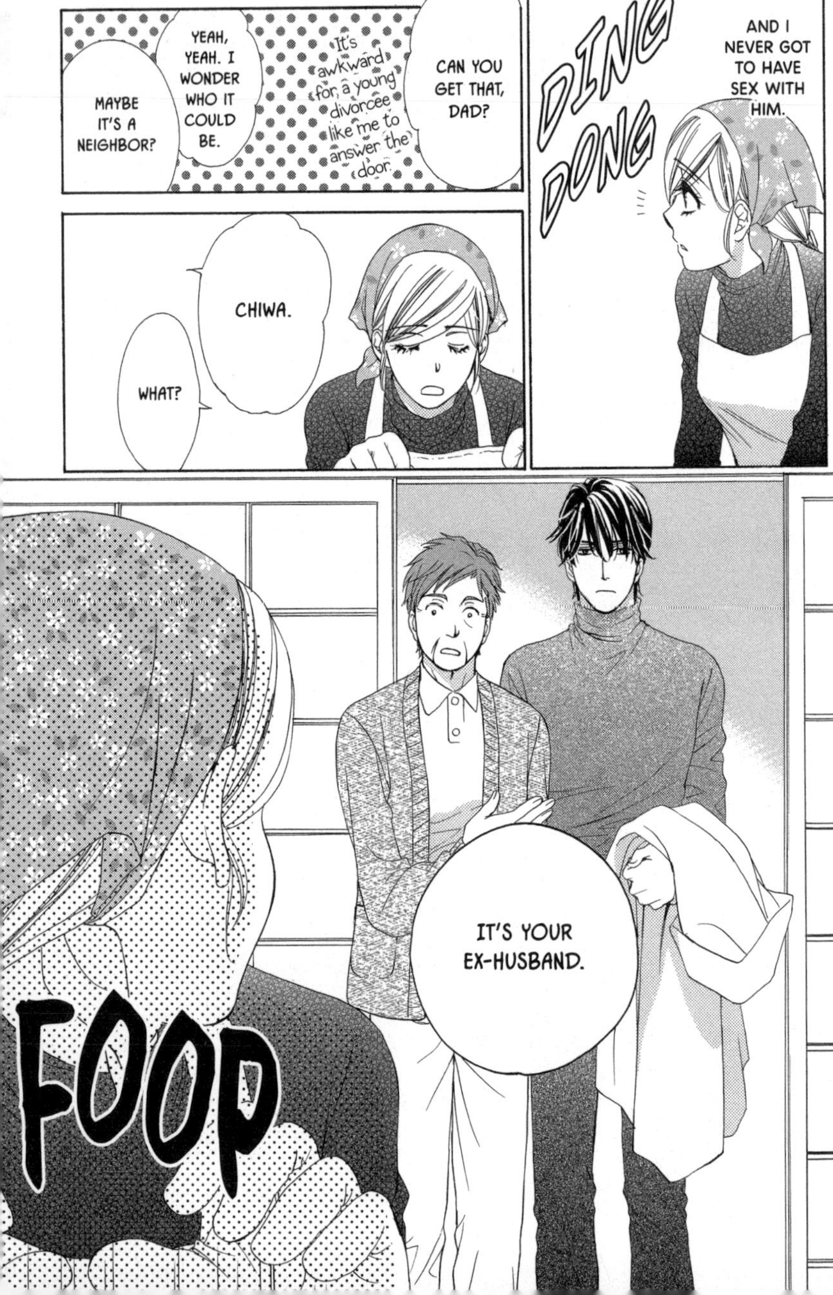
AND I NEVER GOT TO HAVE SEX WITH HIM.
DING DONG
CAN YOU GET THAT, DAD?
It's awkward for a young divorcee like me to answer the door.
YEAH, YEAH. I WONDER WHO IT COULD BE.
MAYBE IT'S A NEIGHBOR?
CHIWA.
WHAT?
IT'S YOUR EX-HUSBAND.
FOOP

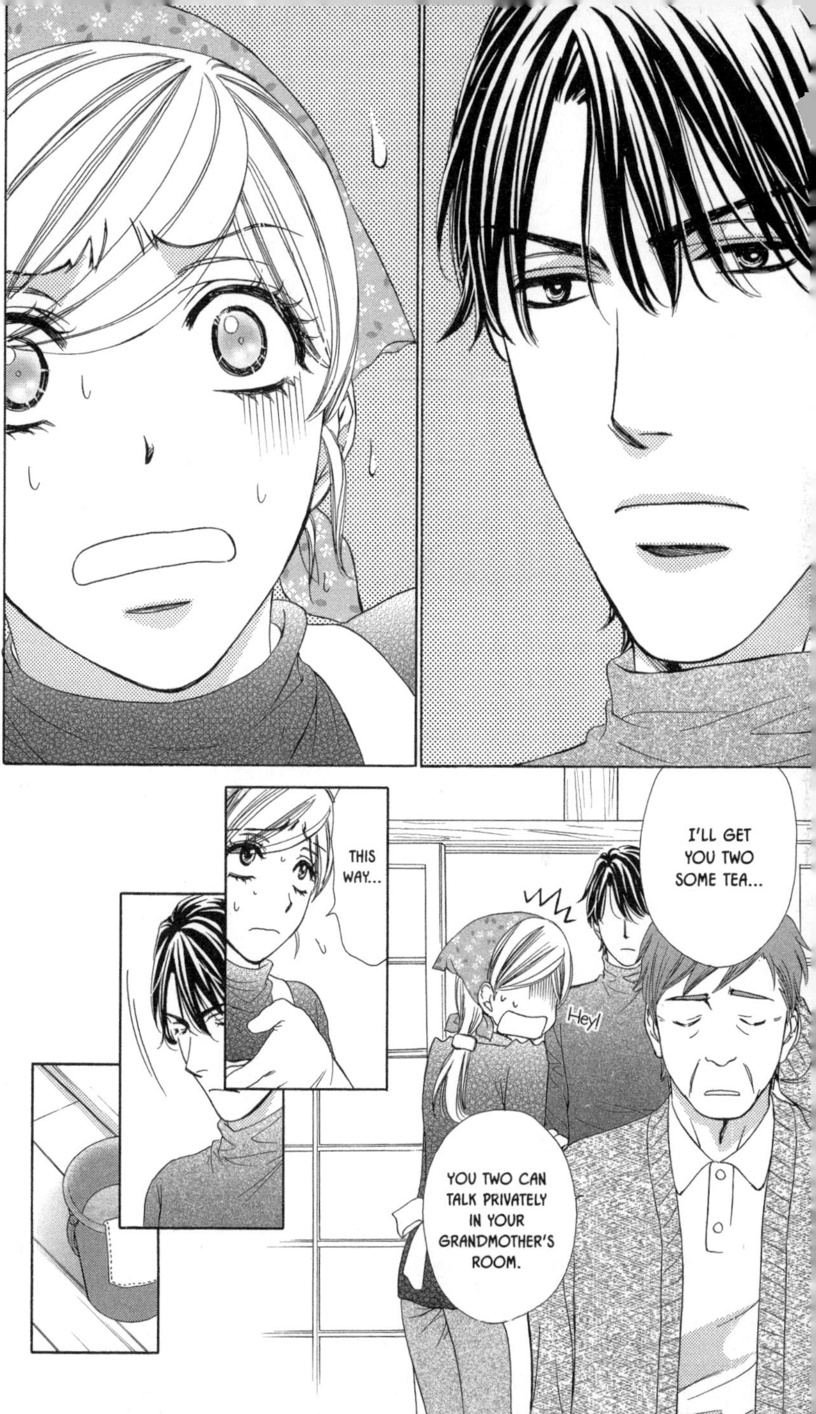
I'LL GET YOU TWO SOME TEA...
Hey!
YOU TWO CAN TALK PRIVATELY IN YOUR GRANDMOTHER'S ROOM.
THIS WAY...

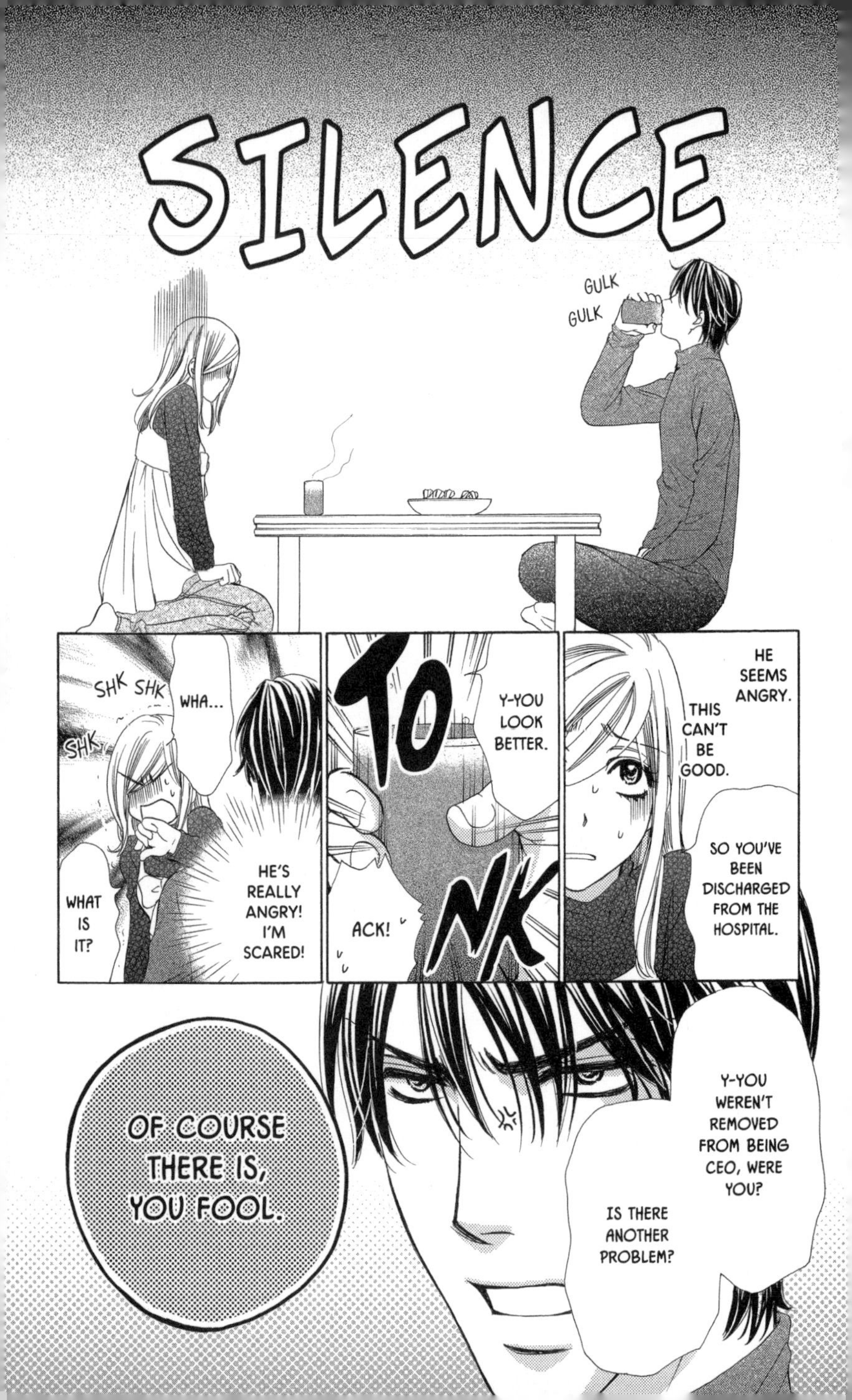
SILENCE
GULK
GULK
HE SEEMS ANGRY.
THIS CAN'T BE GOOD.
SO YOU'VE BEEN DISCHARGED FROM THE HOSPITAL.
TONK
Y-YOU LOOK BETTER.
ACK!
SHK SHK
SHK
WHA...
HE'S REALLY ANGRY! I'M SCARED!
WHAT IS IT?
Y-YOU WEREN'T REMOVED FROM BEING CEO, WERE YOU?
IS THERE ANOTHER PROBLEM?
OF COURSE THERE IS, YOU FOOL.

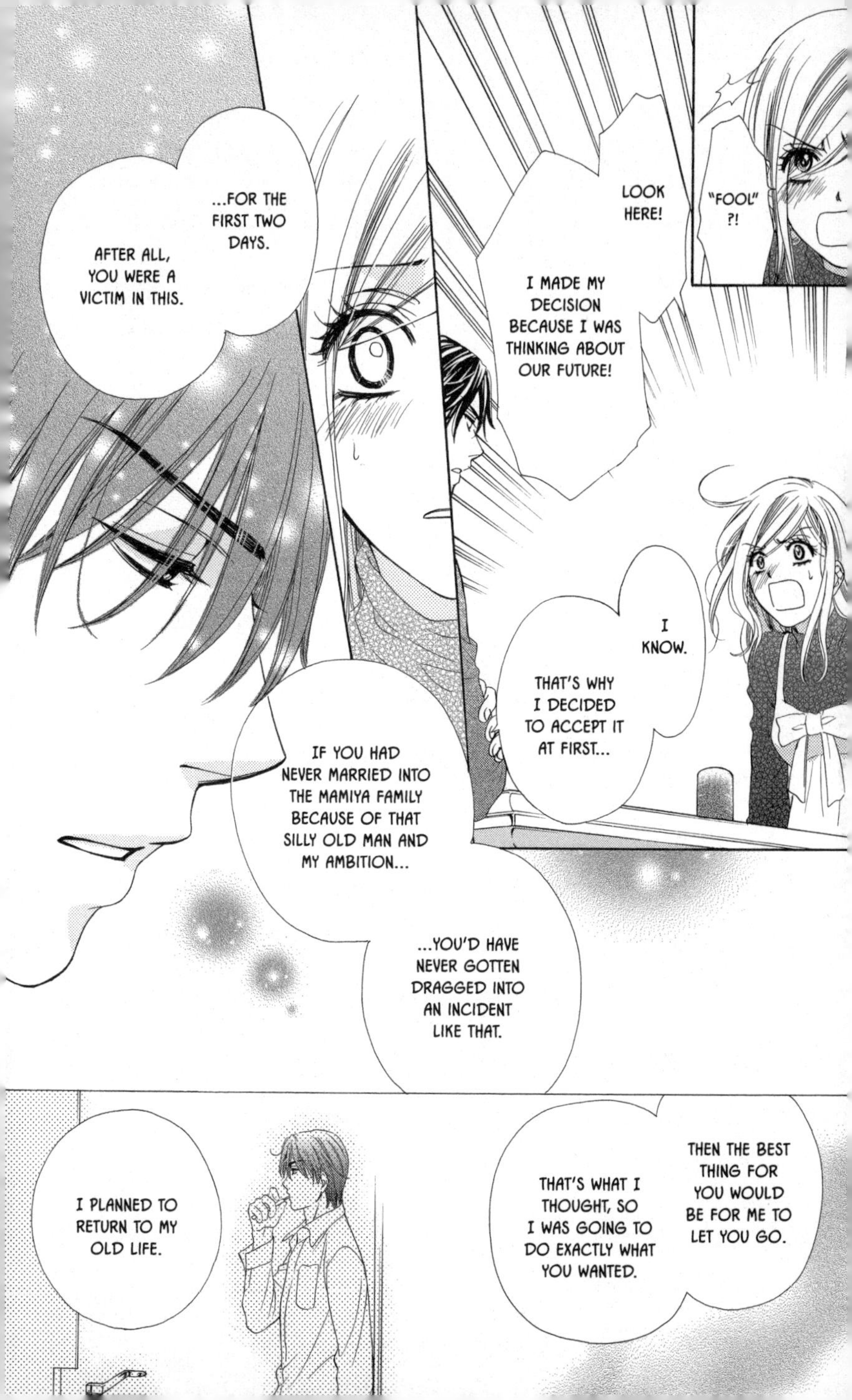
"FOOL" ?!
LOOK HERE!
I MADE MY DECISION BECAUSE I WAS THINKING ABOUT OUR FUTURE!
I KNOW.
THAT'S WHY I DECIDED TO ACCEPT IT AT FIRST...
...FOR THE FIRST TWO DAYS.
AFTER ALL, YOU WERE A VICTIM IN THIS.
IF YOU HAD NEVER MARRIED INTO THE MAMIYA FAMILY BECAUSE OF THAT SILLY OLD MAN AND MY AMBITION...
...YOU'D HAVE NEVER GOTTEN DRAGGED INTO AN INCIDENT LIKE THAT.
THEN THE BEST THING FOR YOU WOULD BE FOR ME TO LET YOU GO.
THAT'S WHAT I THOUGHT, SO I WAS GOING TO DO EXACTLY WHAT YOU WANTED.
I PLANNED TO RETURN TO MY OLD LIFE.

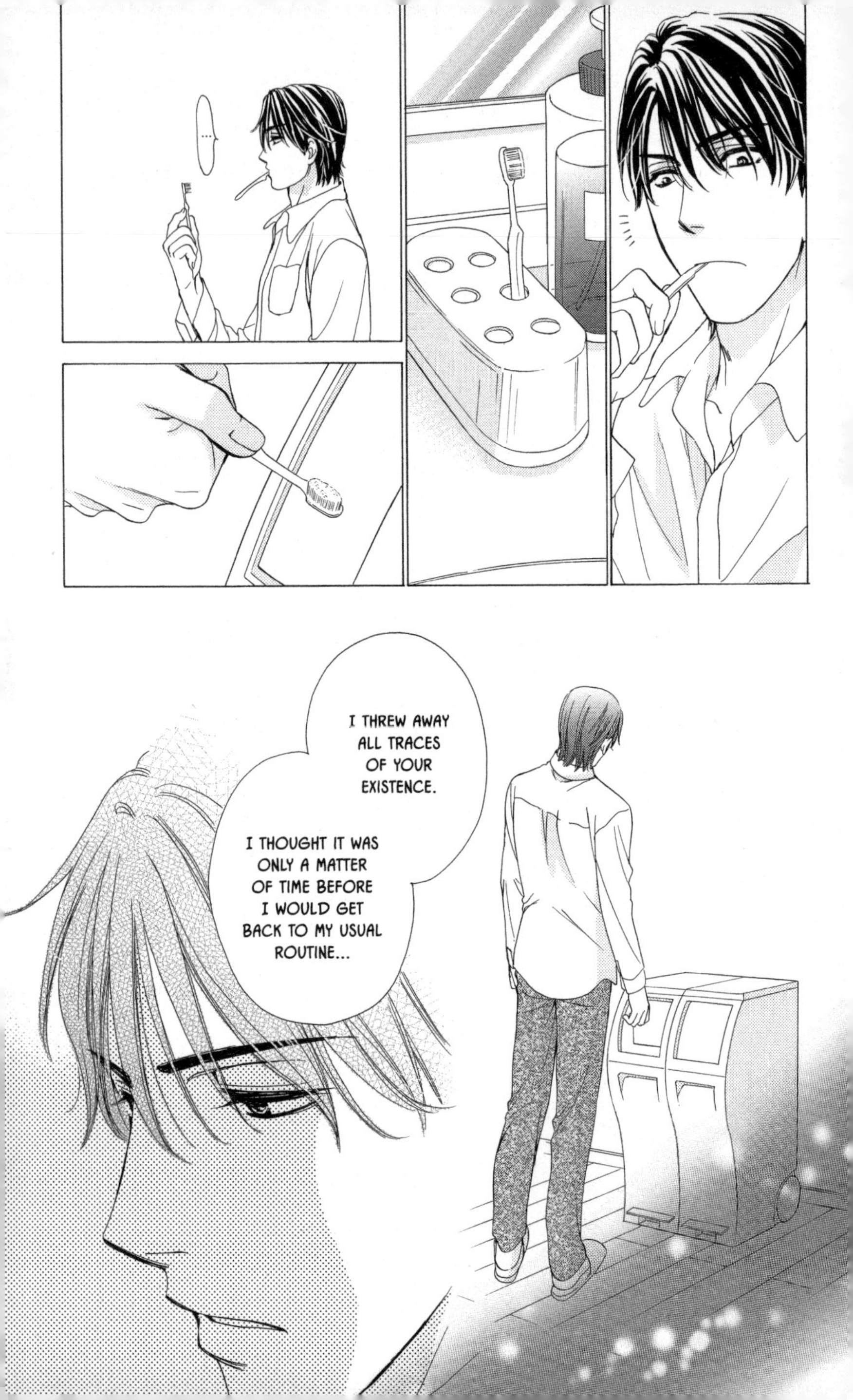
...
I THREW AWAY ALL TRACES OF YOUR EXISTENCE.
I THOUGHT IT WAS ONLY A MATTER OF TIME BEFORE I WOULD GET BACK TO MY USUAL ROUTINE...

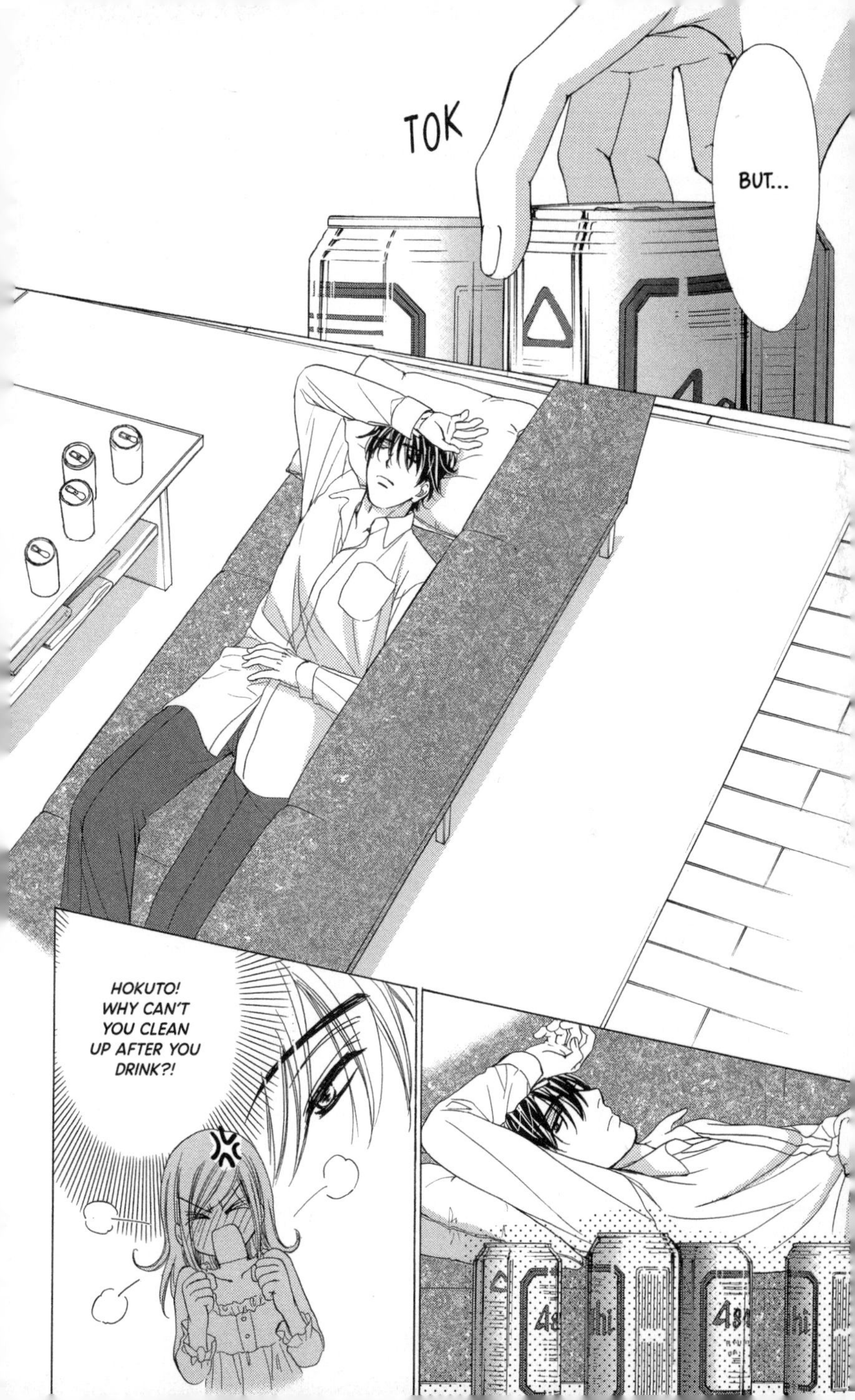
TOK
BUT...
HOKUTO! WHY CAN'T YOU CLEAN UP AFTER YOU DRINK?!

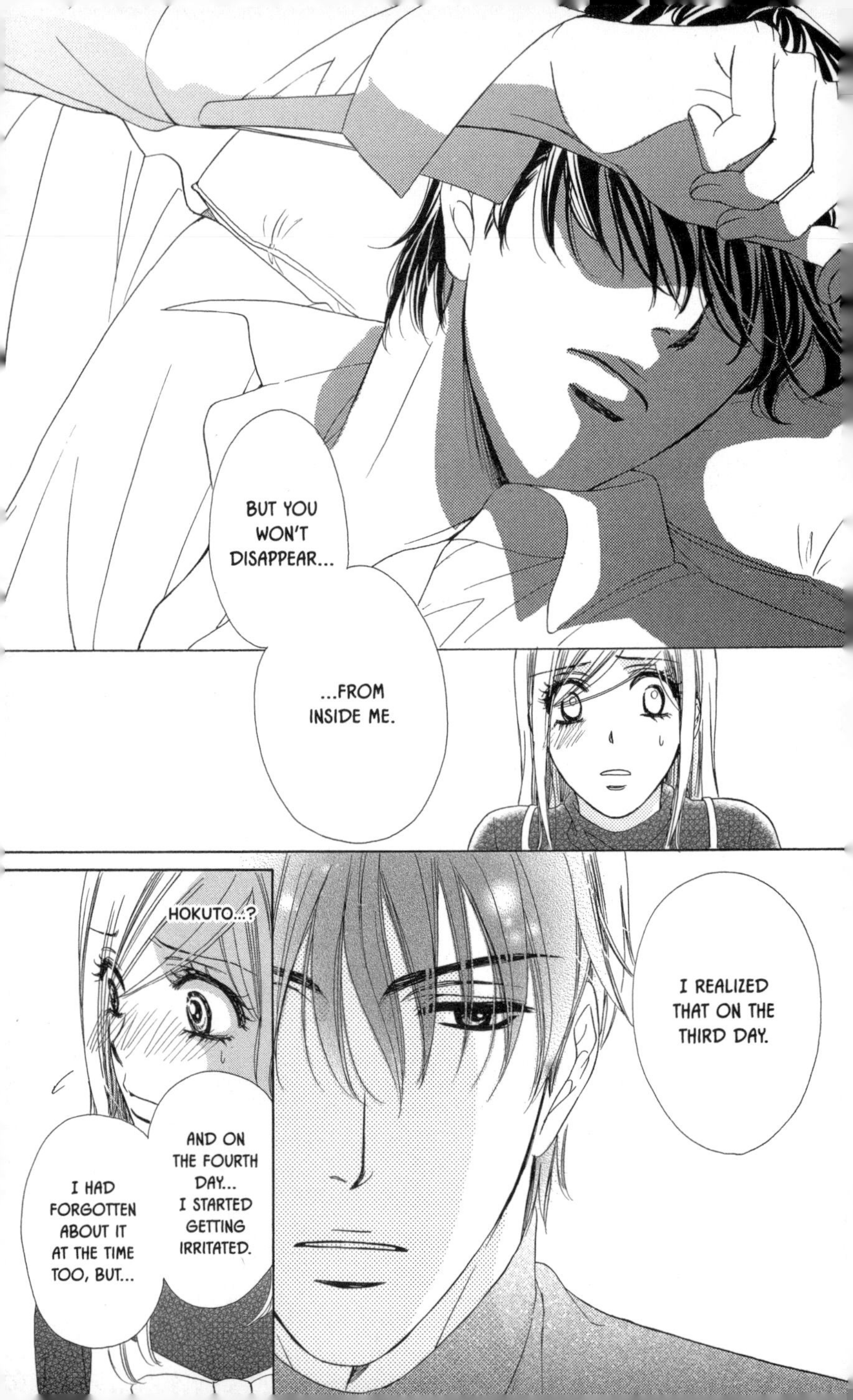
BUT YOU WON'T DISAPPEAR...
...FROM INSIDE ME.
I REALIZED THAT ON THE THIRD DAY.
HOKUTO...?
AND ON THE FOURTH DAY... I STARTED GETTING IRRITATED.
I HAD FORGOTTEN ABOUT IT AT THE TIME TOO, BUT...

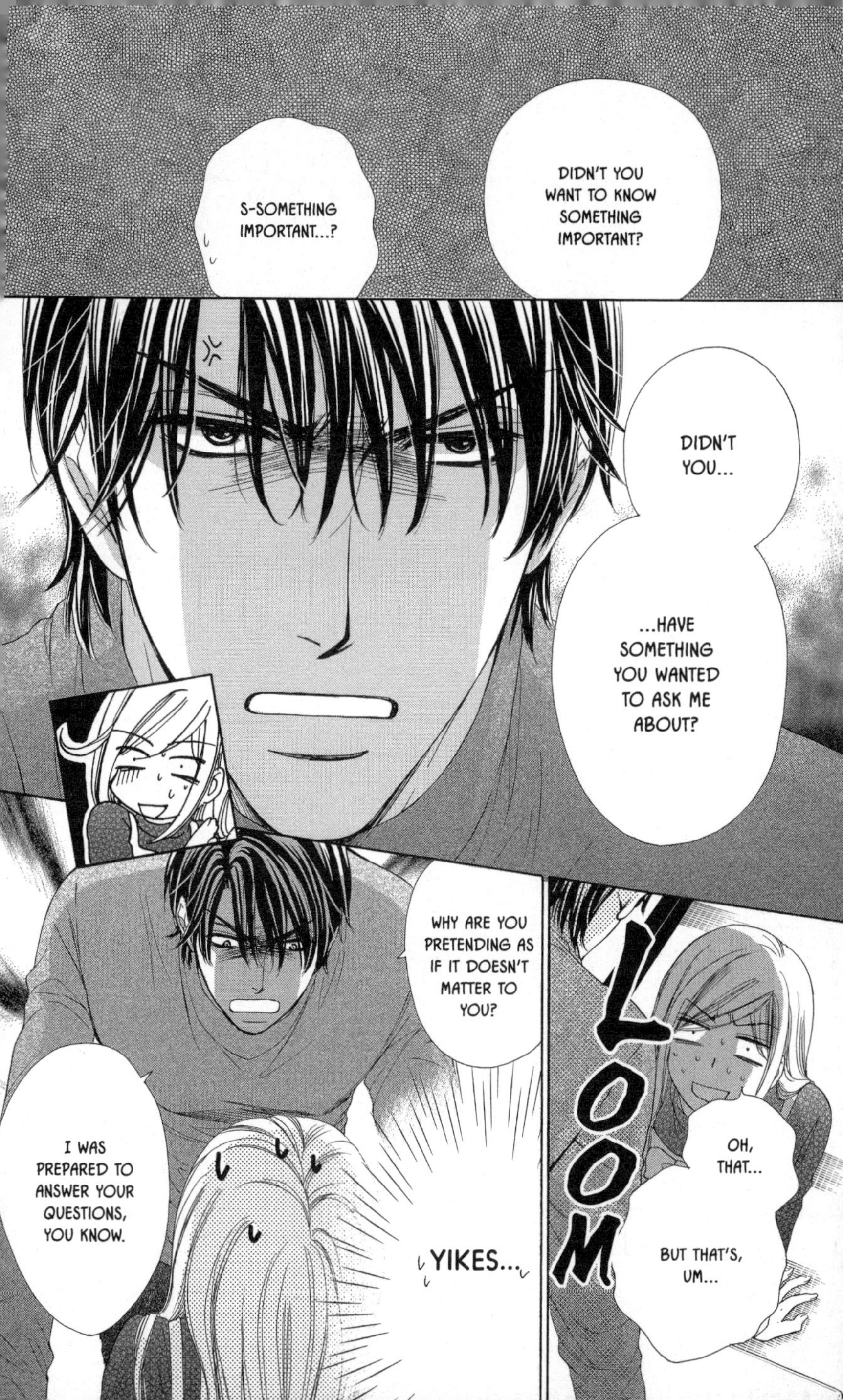
DIDN'T YOU WANT TO KNOW SOMETHING IMPORTANT?
S-SOMETHING IMPORTANT...?
DIDN'T YOU...
...HAVE SOMETHING YOU WANTED TO ASK ME ABOUT?
LOOOM
OH, THAT...
BUT THAT'S, UM...
WHY ARE YOU PRETENDING AS IF IT DOESN'T MATTER TO YOU?
I WAS PREPARED TO ANSWER YOUR QUESTIONS, YOU KNOW.
YIKES...

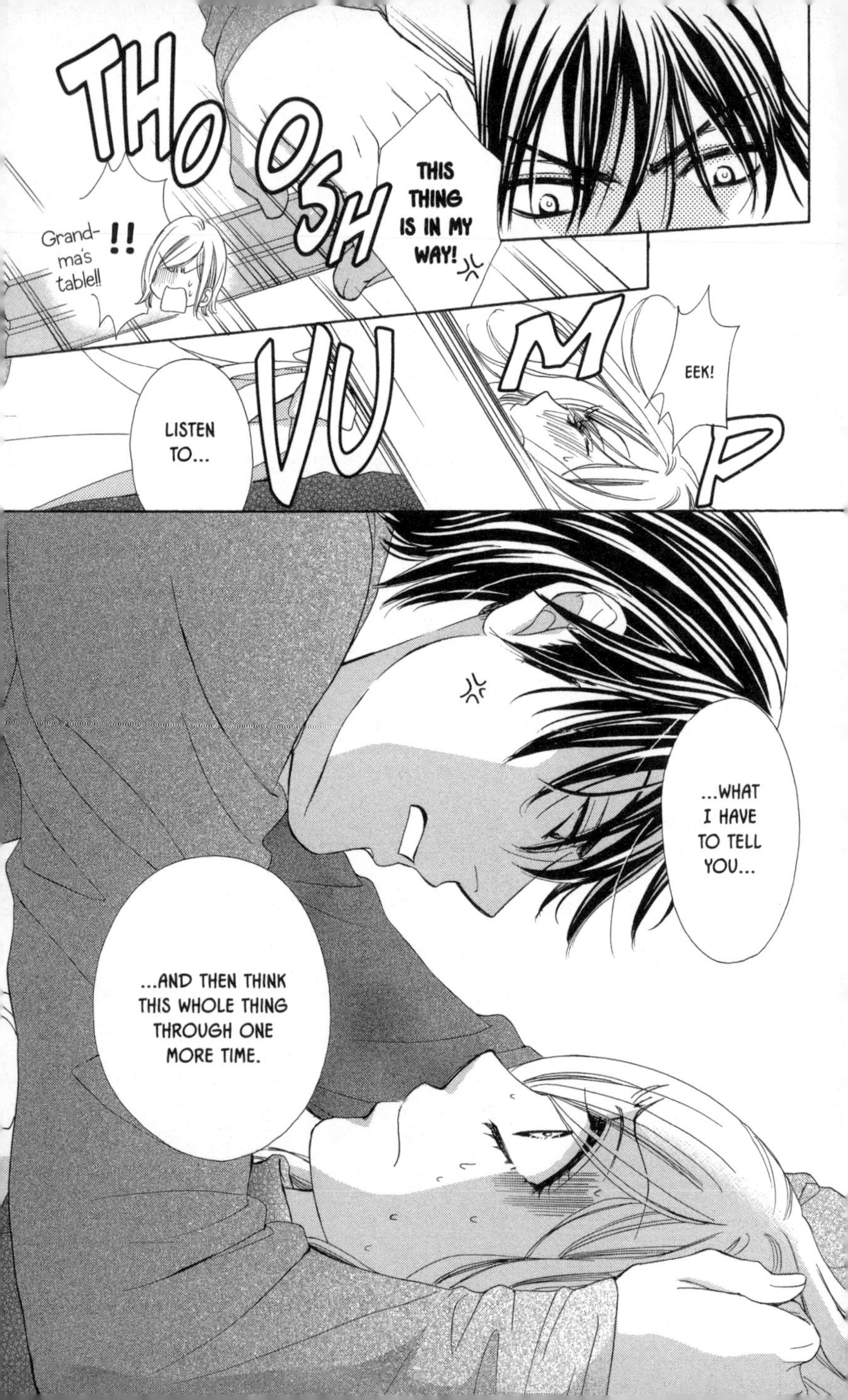
THIS THING IS IN MY WAY!
THOOSH
Grand-ma's table!! !!
EEK!
VUMP
LISTEN TO...
...WHAT I HAVE TO TELL YOU...
...AND THEN THINK THIS WHOLE THING THROUGH ONE MORE TIME.

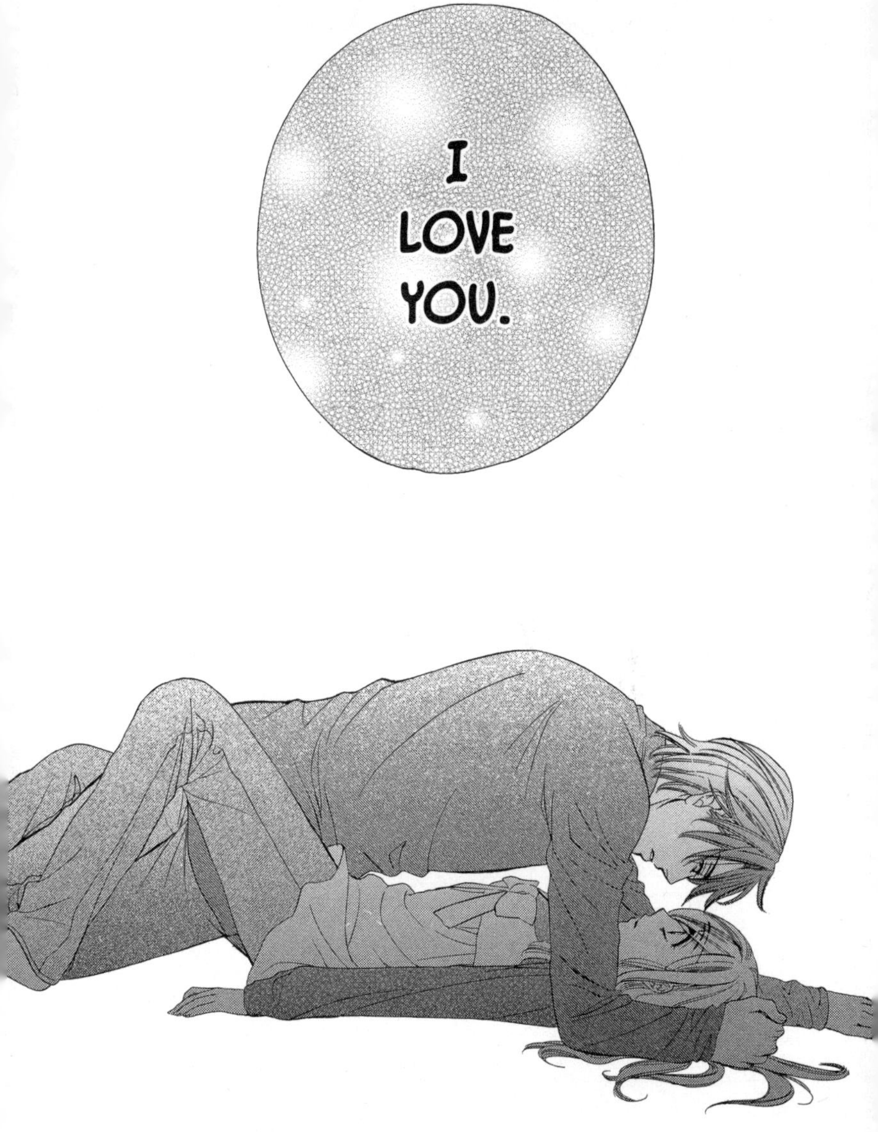
I LOVE YOU.

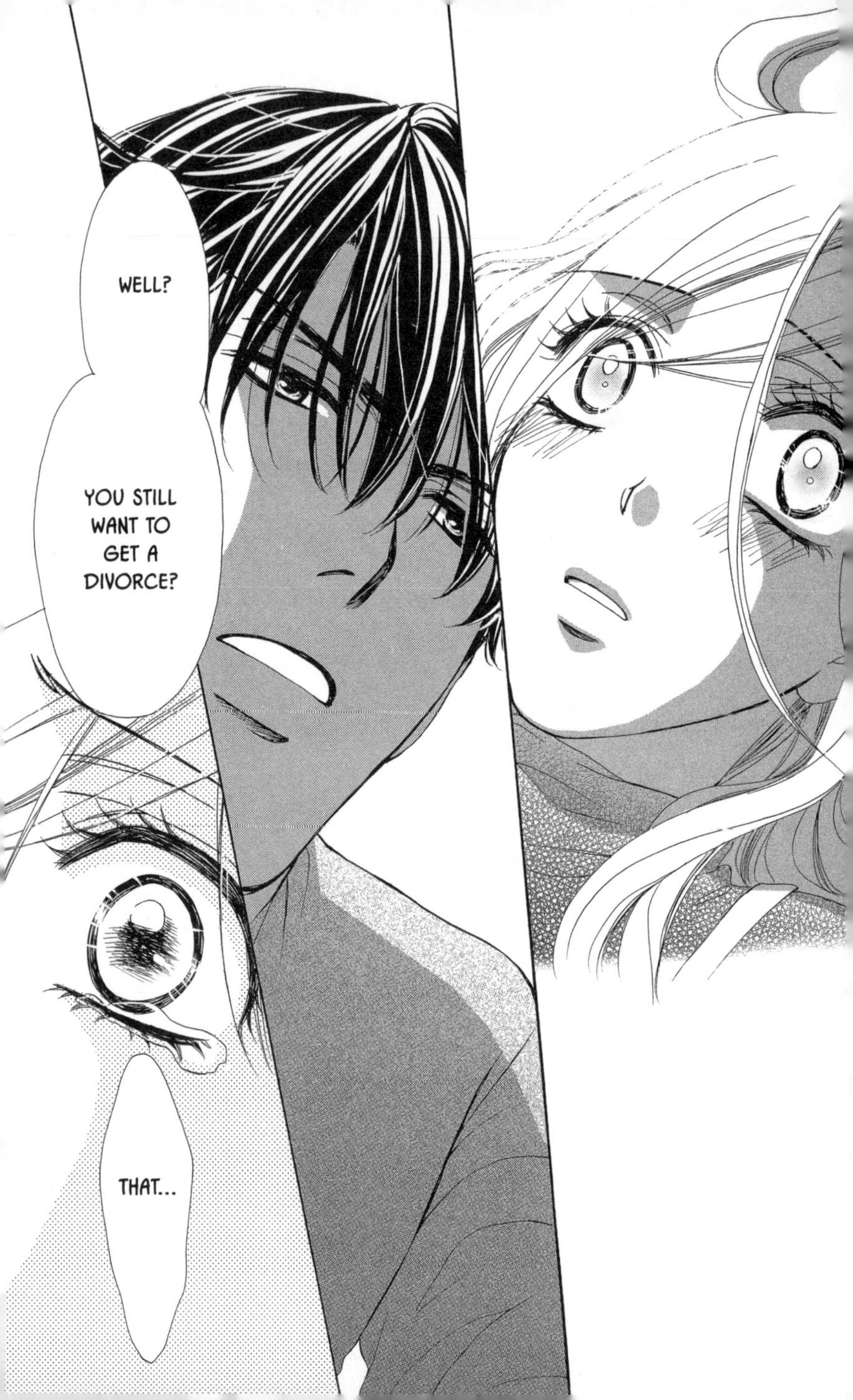
WELL?
YOU STILL WANT TO GET A DIVORCE?
THAT...

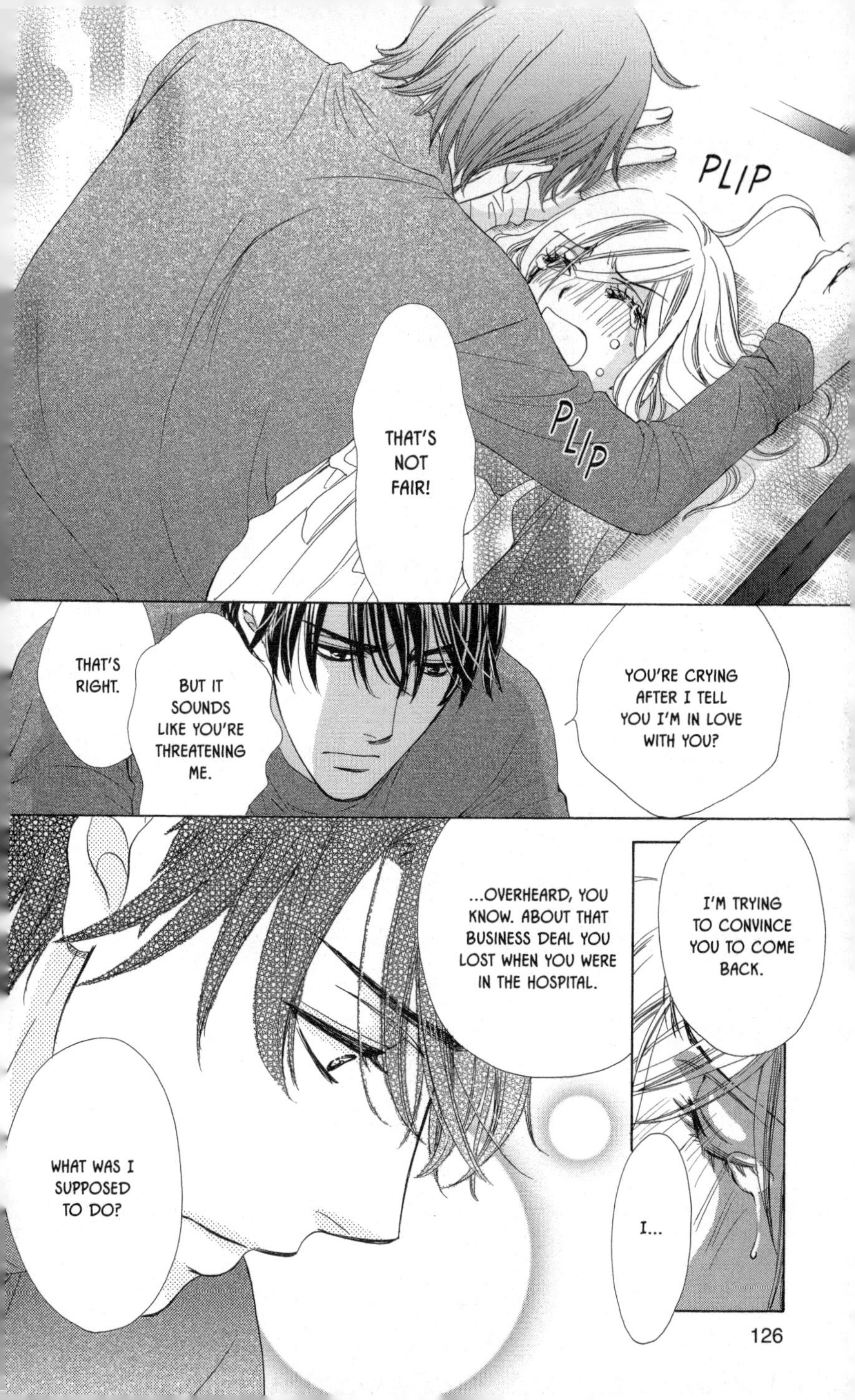
PLIP
PLIP
THAT'S NOT FAIR!
YOU'RE CRYING AFTER I TELL YOU I'M IN LOVE WITH YOU?
BUT IT SOUNDS LIKE YOU'RE THREATENING ME.
THAT'S RIGHT.
I'M TRYING TO CONVINCE YOU TO COME BACK.
I...
...OVERHEARD, YOU KNOW. ABOUT THAT BUSINESS DEAL YOU LOST WHEN YOU WERE IN THE HOSPITAL.
WHAT WAS I SUPPOSED TO DO?

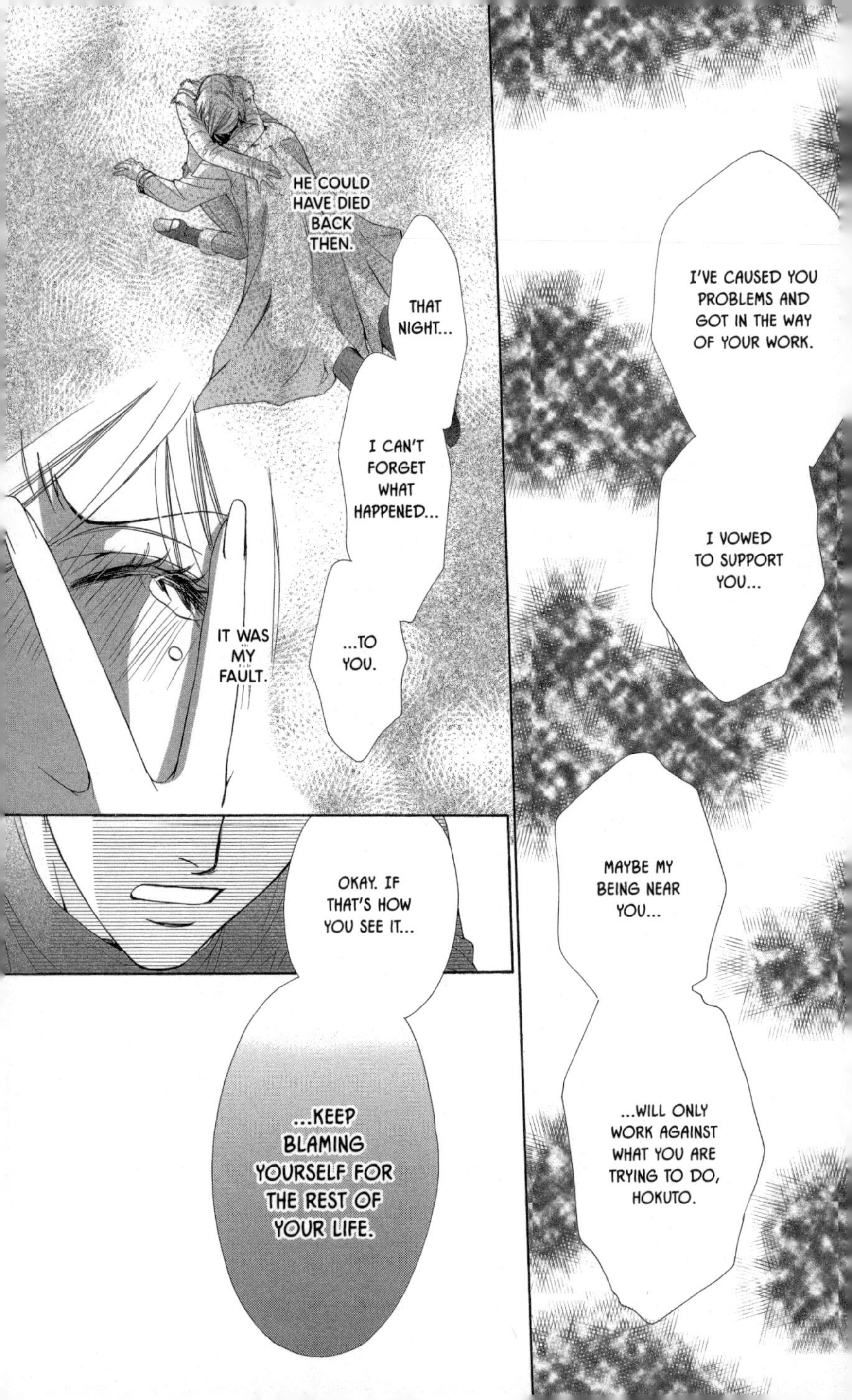
I'VE CAUSED YOU PROBLEMS AND GOT IN THE WAY OF YOUR WORK.
I VOWED TO SUPPORT YOU...
MAYBE MY BEING NEAR YOU...
...WILL ONLY WORK AGAINST WHAT YOU ARE TRYING TO DO, HOKUTO.
THAT NIGHT...
I CAN'T FORGET WHAT HAPPENED...
...TO YOU.
HE COULD HAVE DIED BACK THEN.
IT WAS MY FAULT.
OKAY. IF THAT'S HOW YOU SEE IT...
...KEEP BLAMING YOURSELF FOR THE REST OF YOUR LIFE.

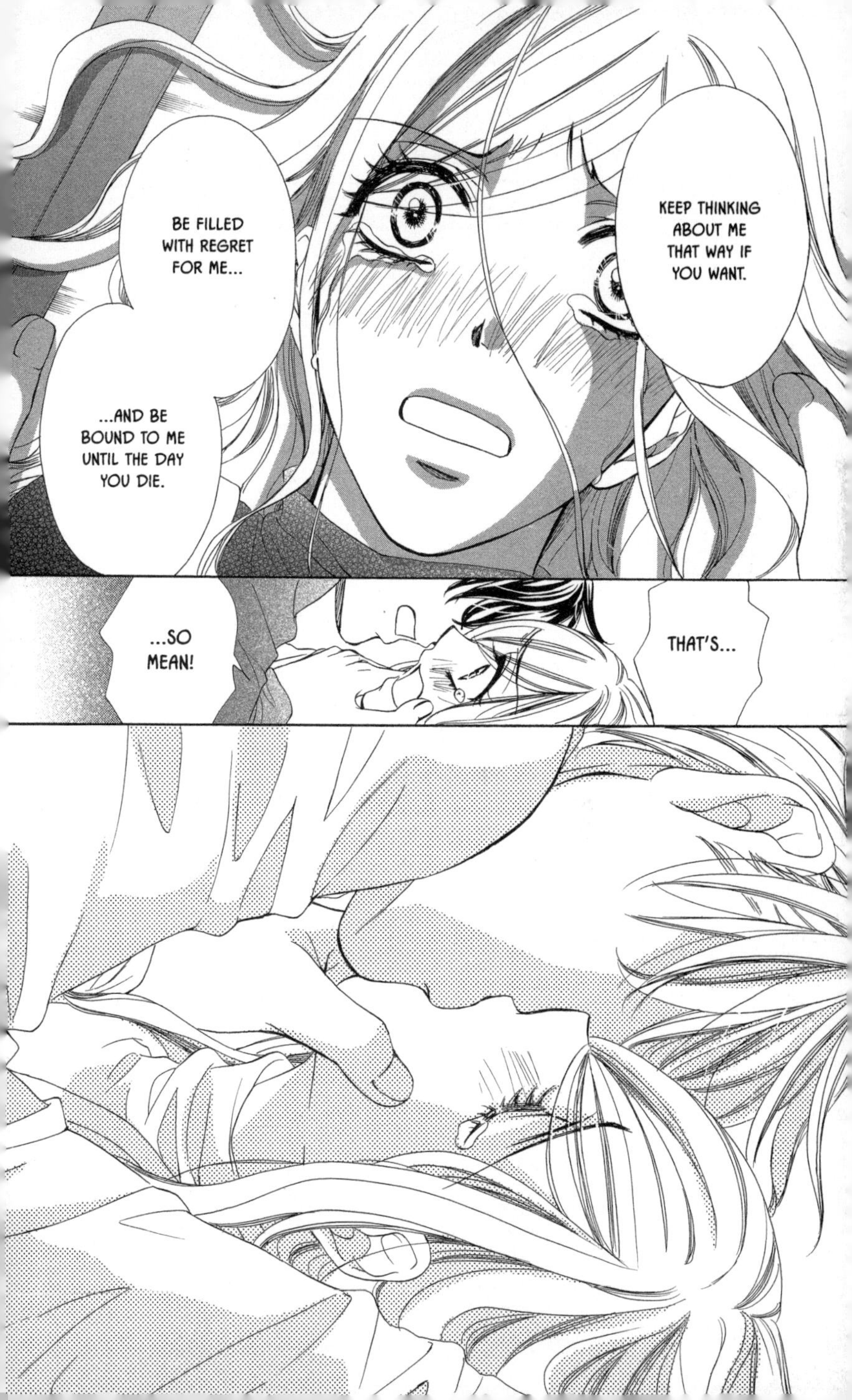
KEEP THINKING ABOUT ME THAT WAY IF YOU WANT.
BE FILLED WITH REGRET FOR ME...
...AND BE BOUND TO ME UNTIL THE DAY YOU DIE.
THAT'S...
...SO MEAN!

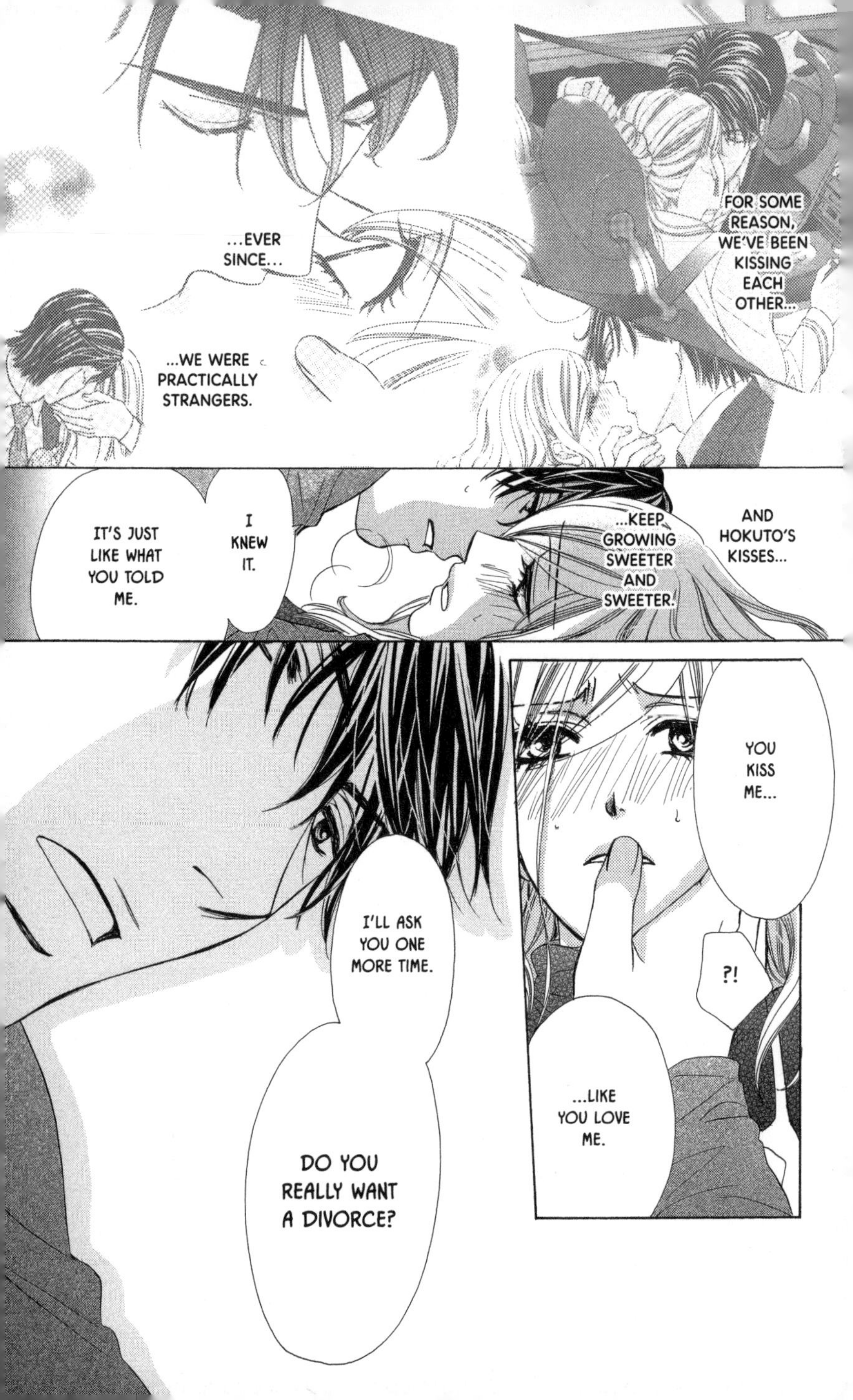
FOR SOME REASON, WE'VE BEEN KISSING EACH OTHER...
...EVER SINCE...
...WE WERE PRACTICALLY STRANGERS.
AND HOKUTO'S KISSES...
...KEEP GROWING SWEETER AND SWEETER.
I KNEW IT.
IT'S JUST LIKE WHAT YOU TOLD ME.
YOU KISS ME...
?!
...LIKE YOU LOVE ME.
I'LL ASK YOU ONE MORE TIME.
DO YOU REALLY WANT A DIVORCE?

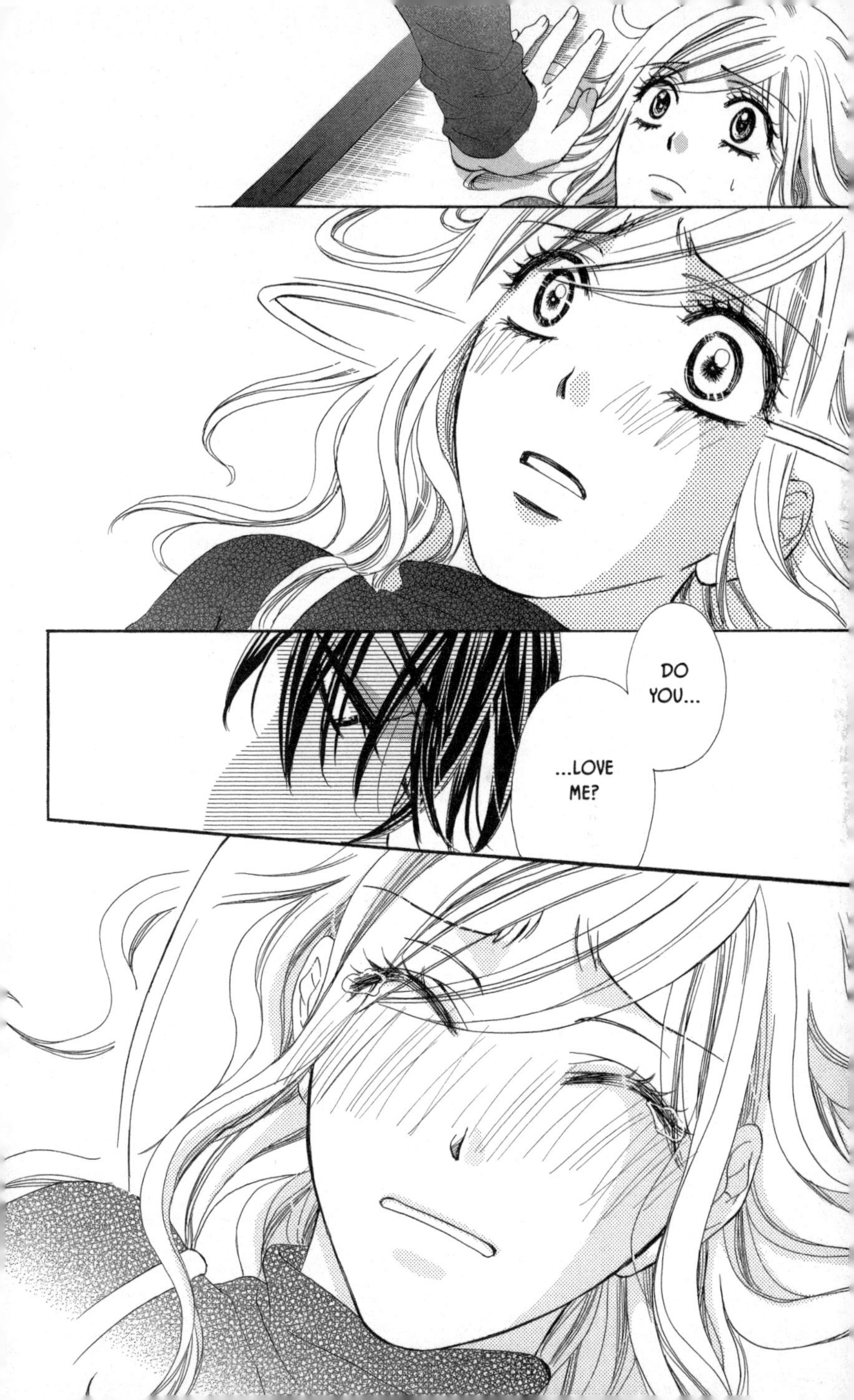
DO YOU...
...LOVE ME?

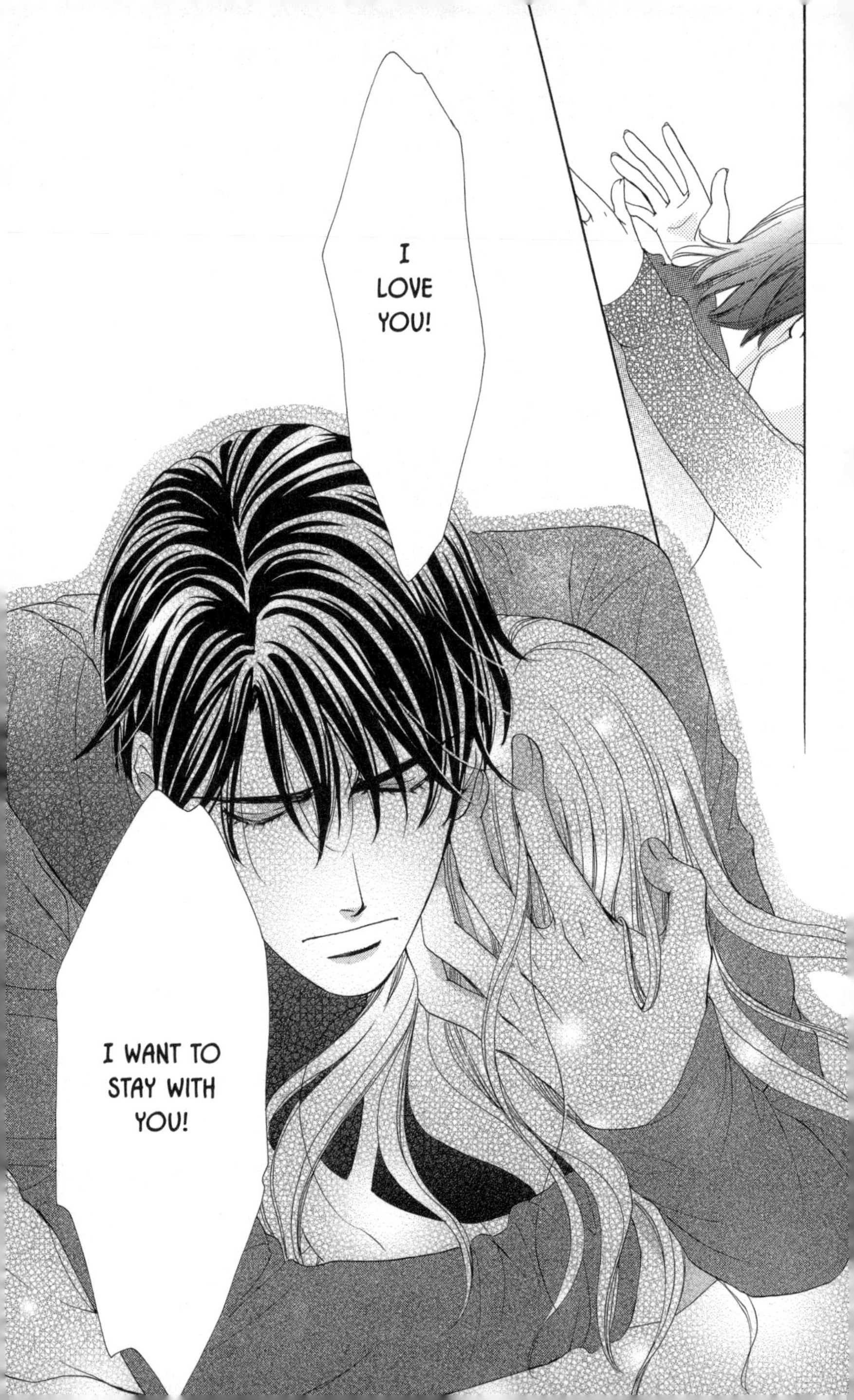
I LOVE YOU!
I WANT TO STAY WITH YOU!

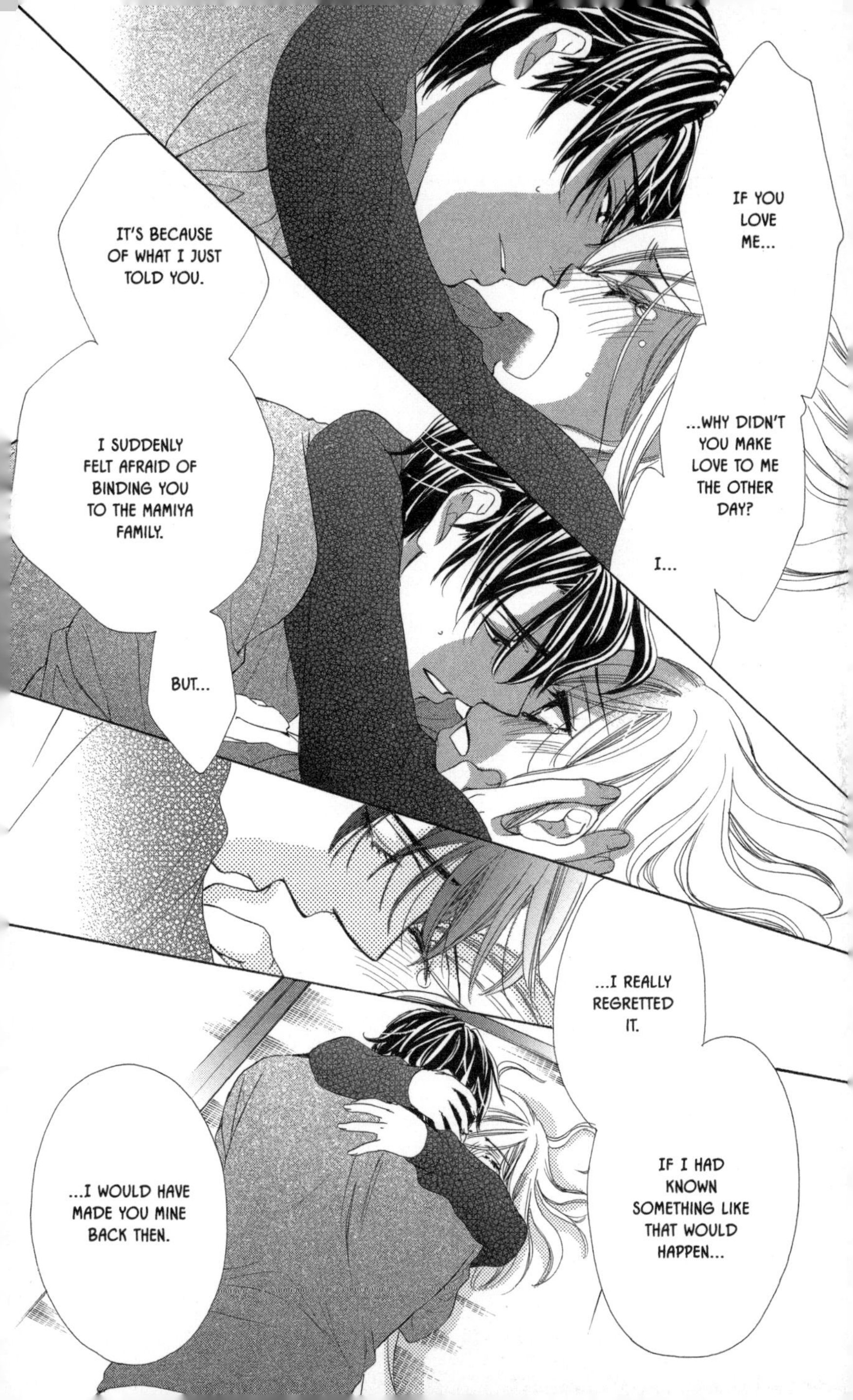
IF YOU LOVE ME...
...WHY DIDN'T YOU MAKE LOVE TO ME THE OTHER DAY?
IT'S BECAUSE OF WHAT I JUST TOLD YOU.
I SUDDENLY FELT AFRAID OF BINDING YOU TO THE MAMIYA FAMILY.
I...
BUT...
...I REALLY REGRETTED IT.
IF I HAD KNOWN SOMETHING LIKE THAT WOULD HAPPEN...
...I WOULD HAVE MADE YOU MINE BACK THEN.

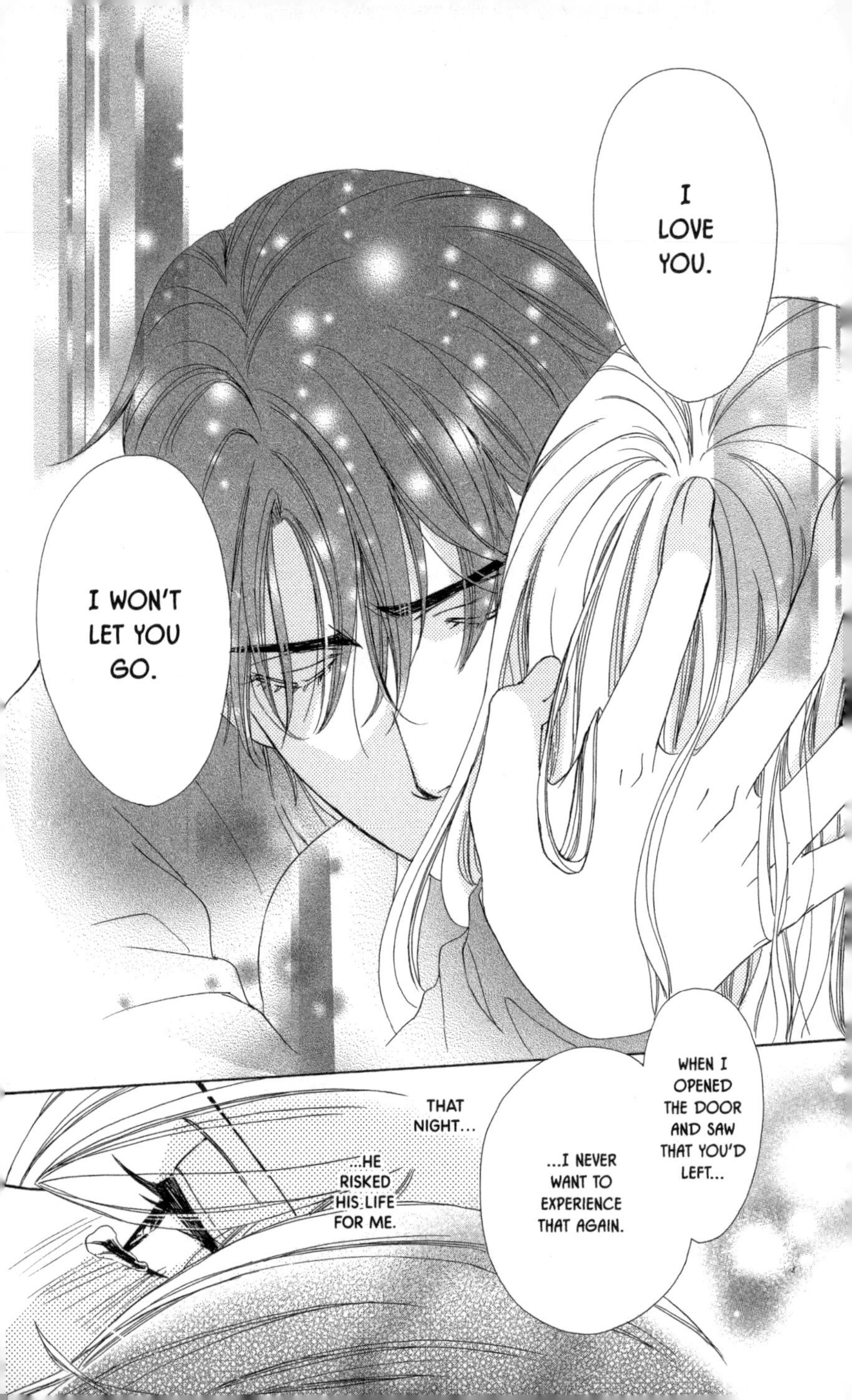
I LOVE YOU.
I WON'T LET YOU GO.
WHEN I OPENED THE DOOR AND SAW THAT YOU'D LEFT...
...I NEVER WANT TO EXPERIENCE THAT AGAIN.
THAT NIGHT...
...HE RISKED HIS LIFE FOR ME.

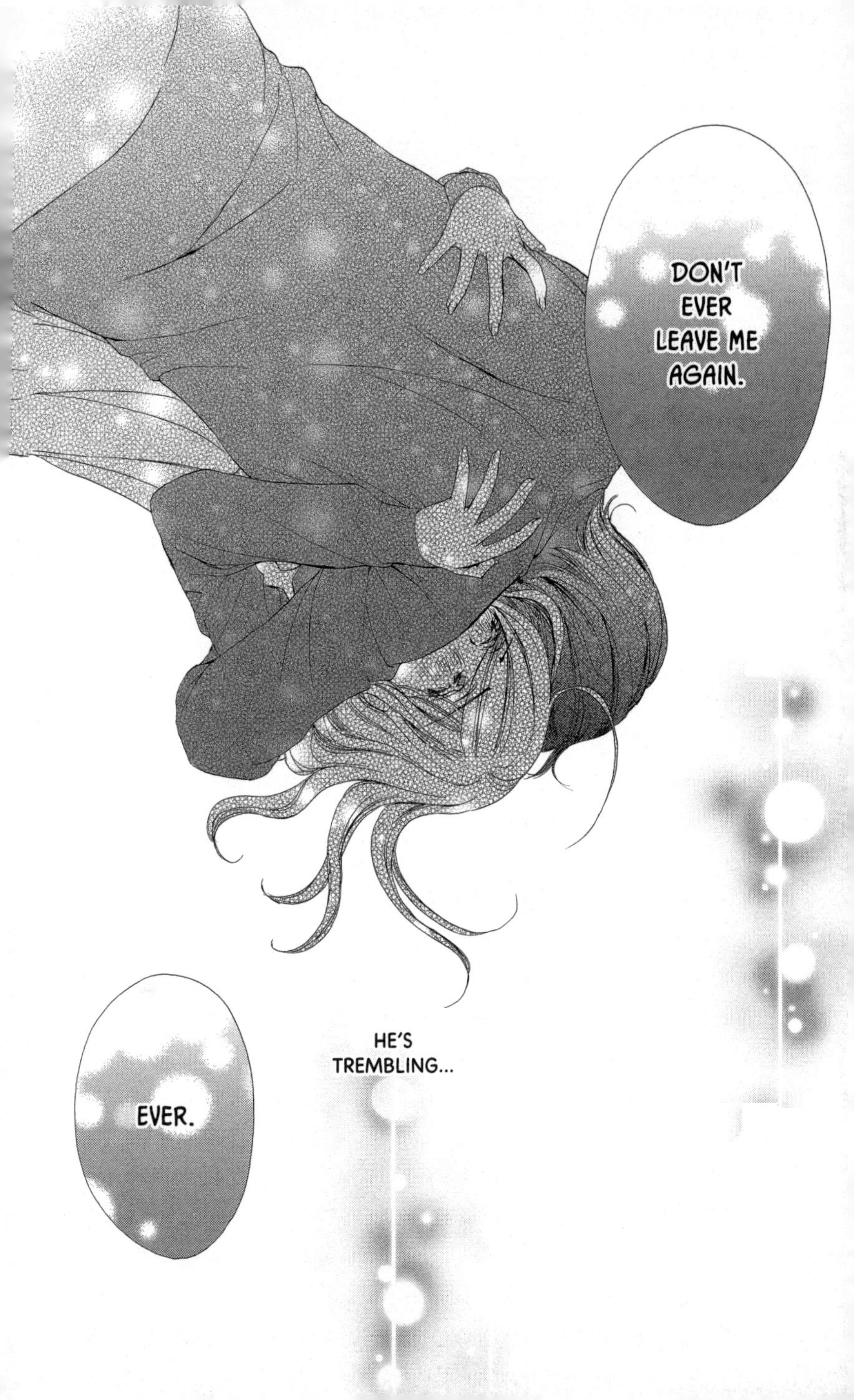
DON'T EVER LEAVE ME AGAIN.
HE'S TREMBLING...
EVER.

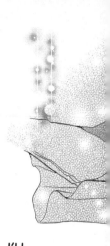

UM...

HOKUTO.

WHAT?

I'LL
CHERISH
THIS
MOMENT
FOREVER.

THIS IS MY
GRANDMA'S
ROOM...

OH...!

...

Right...

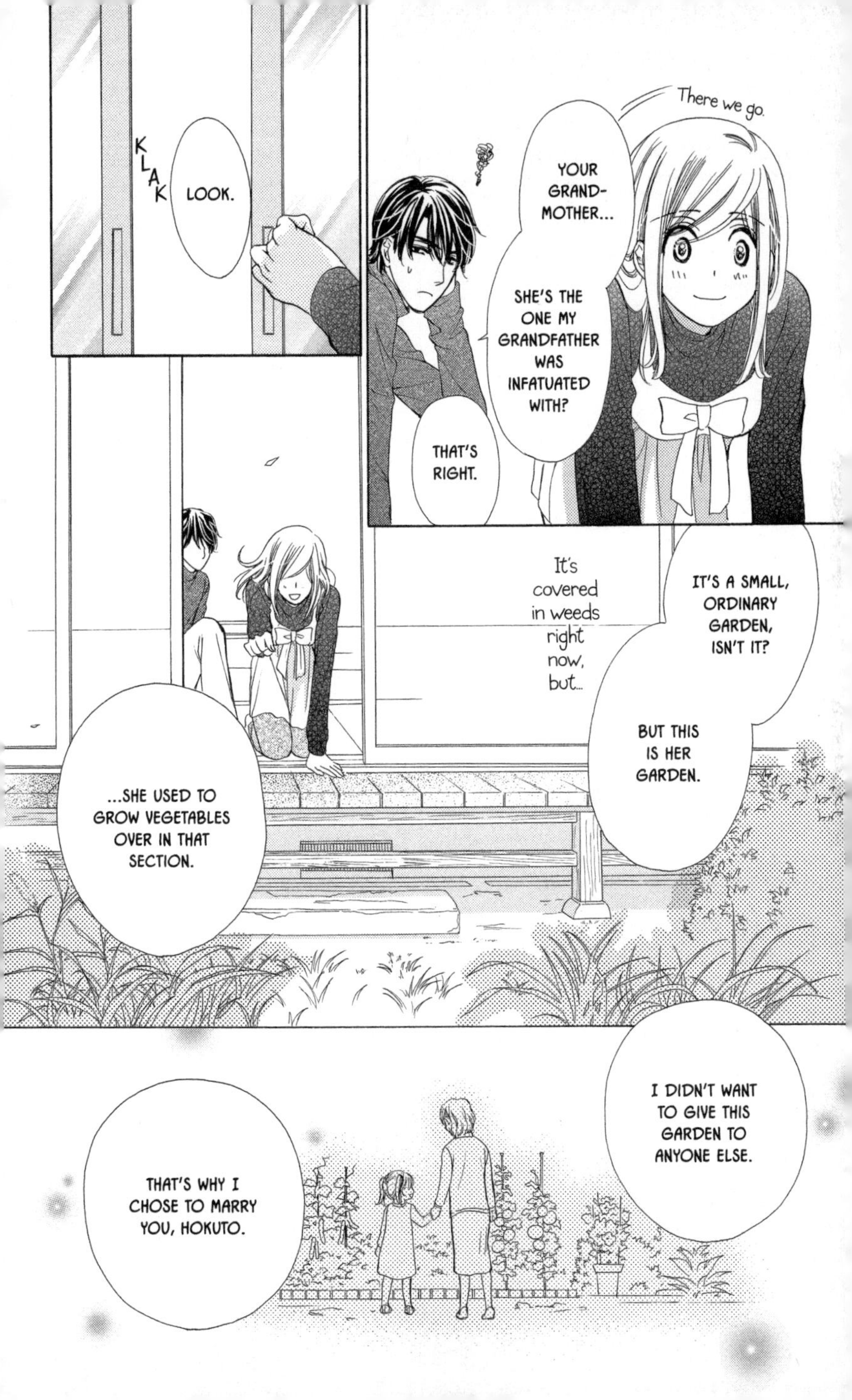
There we go.
YOUR GRAND-MOTHER...
SHE'S THE ONE MY GRANDFATHER WAS INFATUATED WITH?
THAT'S RIGHT.
KLAK
LOOK.
IT'S A SMALL, ORDINARY GARDEN, ISN'T IT?
BUT THIS IS HER GARDEN.
It's covered in weeds right now, but...
...SHE USED TO GROW VEGETABLES OVER IN THAT SECTION.
I DIDN'T WANT TO GIVE THIS GARDEN TO ANYONE ELSE.
THAT'S WHY I CHOSE TO MARRY YOU, HOKUTO.

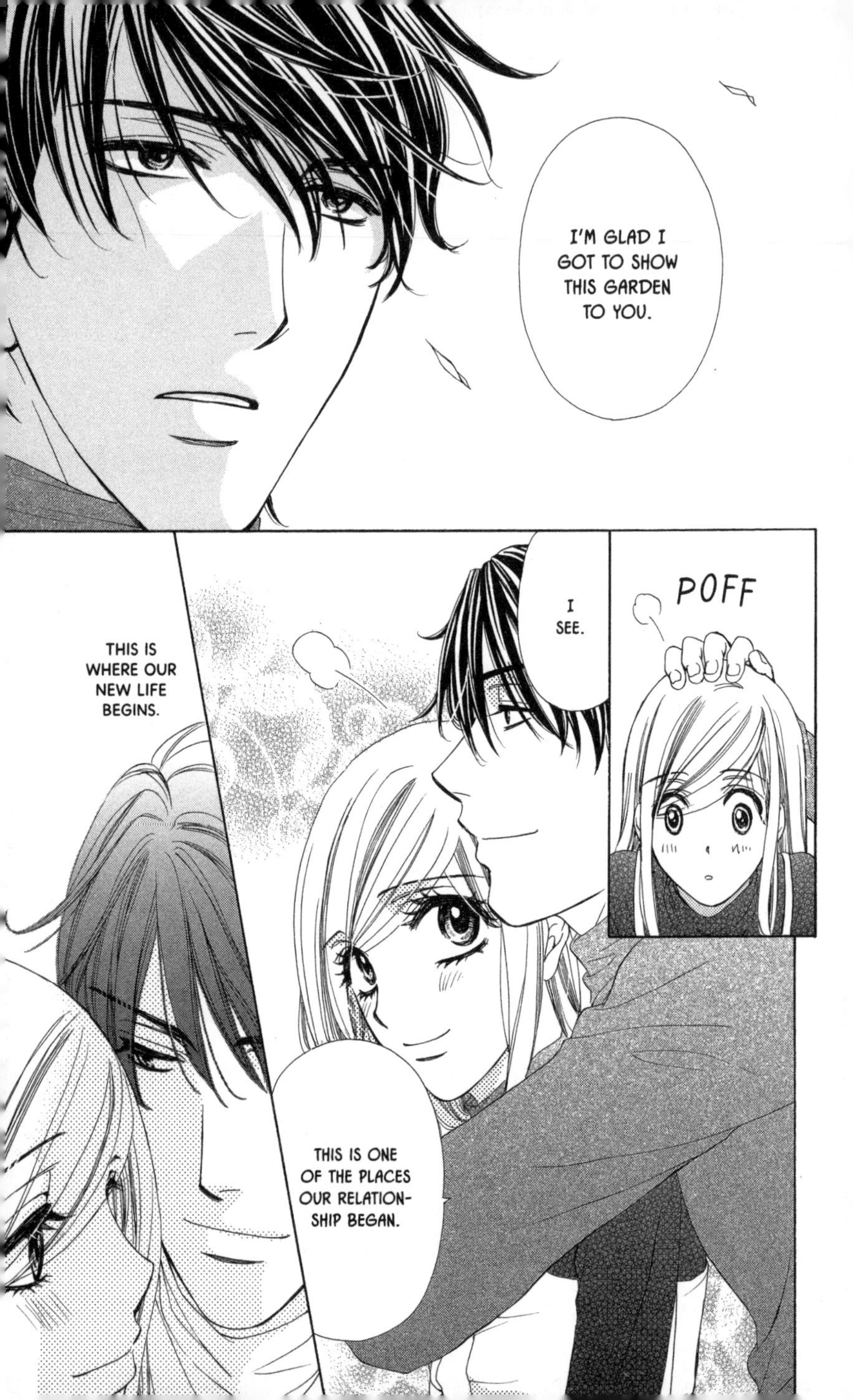
I'M GLAD I GOT TO SHOW THIS GARDEN TO YOU.
POFF
I SEE.
THIS IS ONE OF THE PLACES OUR RELATION-SHIP BEGAN.
THIS IS WHERE OUR NEW LIFE BEGINS.

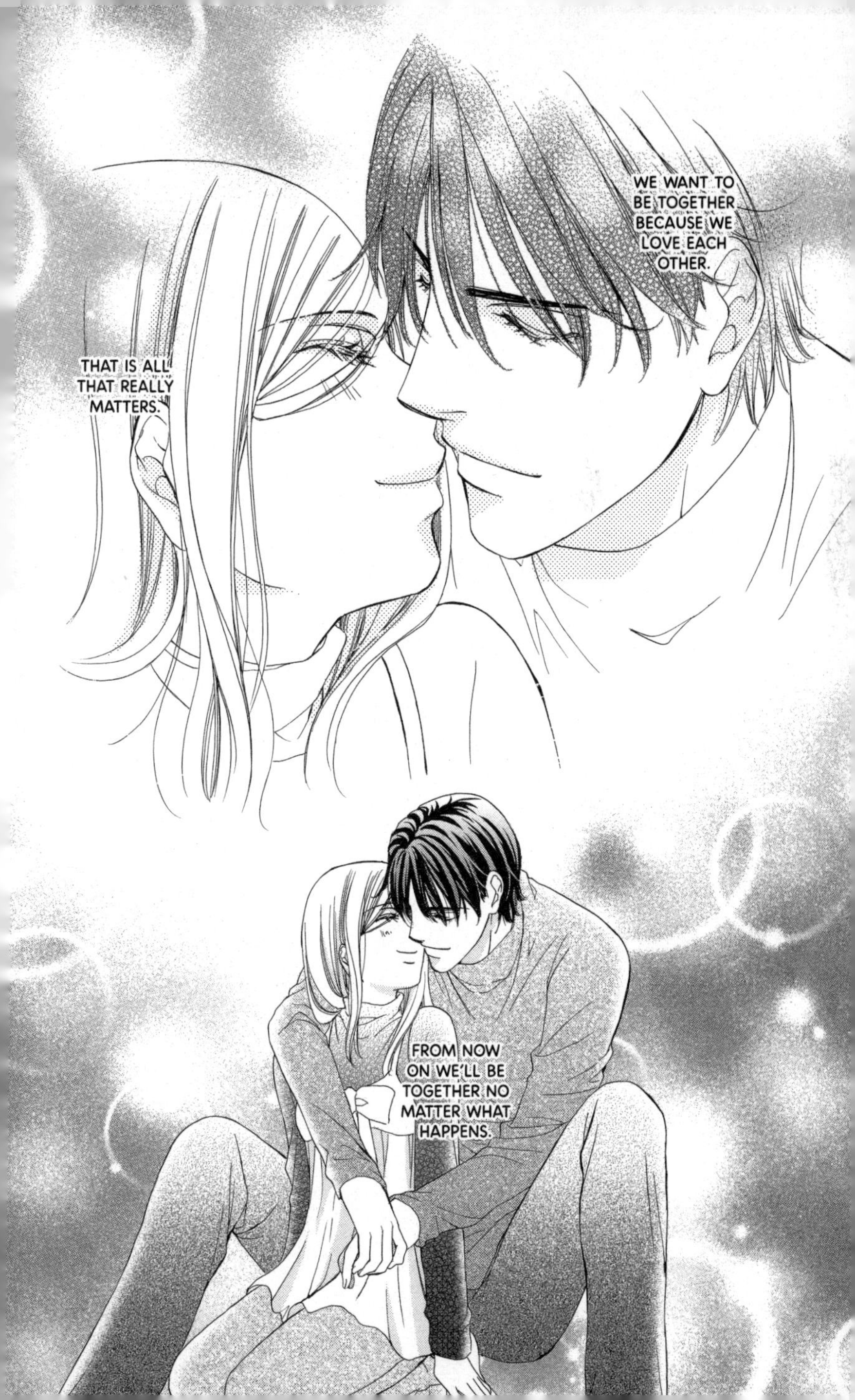
WE WANT TO BE TOGETHER BECAUSE WE LOVE EACH OTHER.
THAT IS ALL THAT REALLY MATTERS.
FROM NOW ON WE'LL BE TOGETHER NO MATTER WHAT HAPPENS.

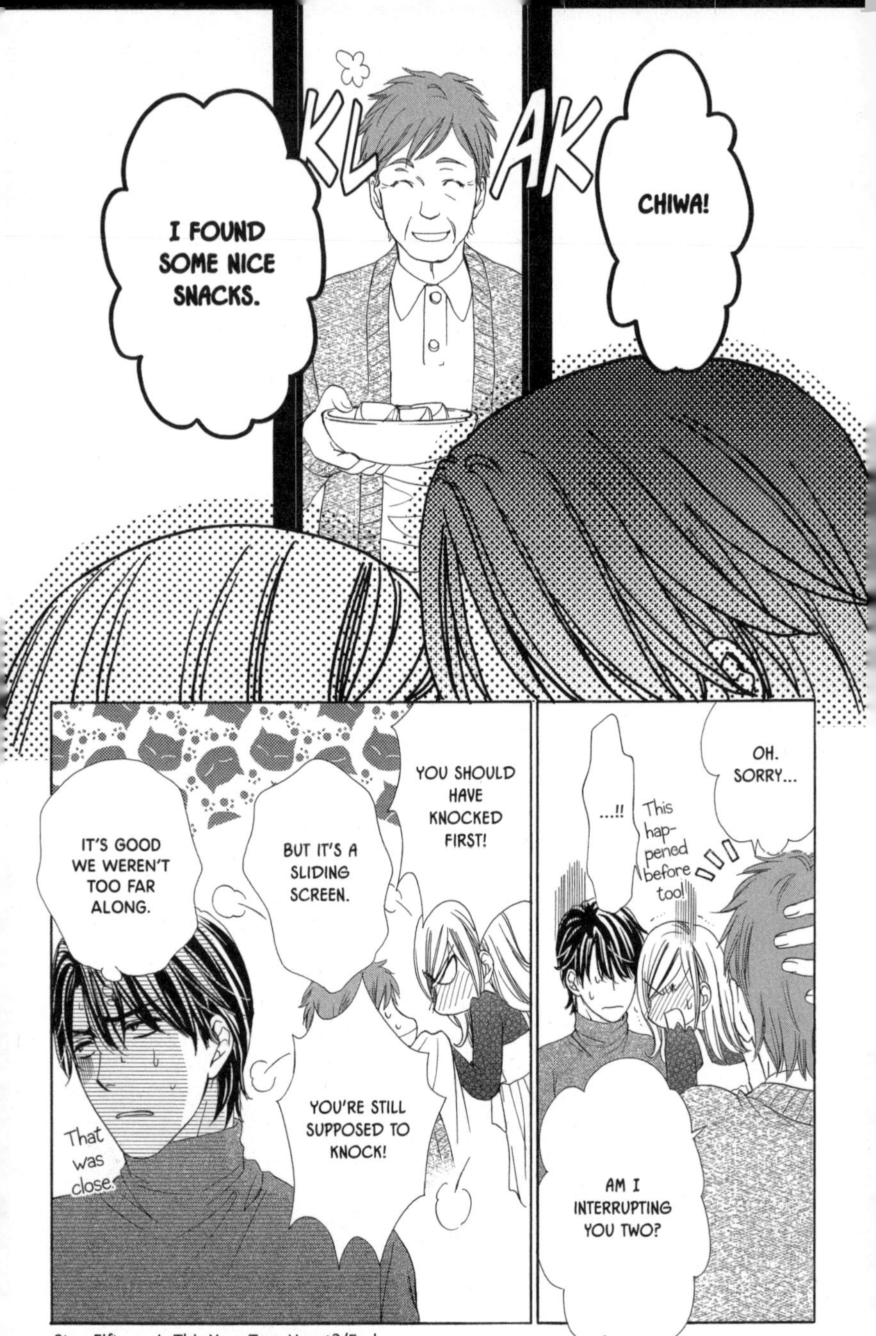
KLAK
CHIWA!
I FOUND SOME NICE SNACKS.
OH. SORRY...
This hap-pened before too!
...!!
AM I INTERRUPTING YOU TWO?
YOU SHOULD HAVE KNOCKED FIRST!
BUT IT'S A SLIDING SCREEN.
IT'S GOOD WE WEREN'T TOO FAR ALONG.
YOU'RE STILL SUPPOSED TO KNOCK!
That was close.

Step Fifteen: Is This Your True Heart?/End

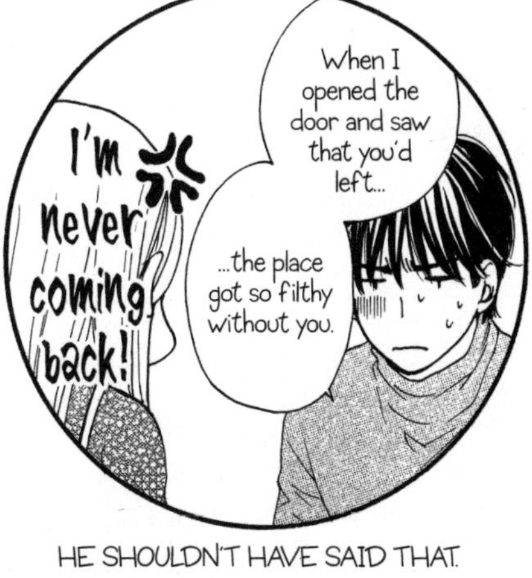
When I opened the door and saw that you'd left...
...the place got so filthy without you.
I'm never coming back!
HE SHOULDN'T HAVE SAID THAT.

Step Sixteen: Will You Make Me Yours?

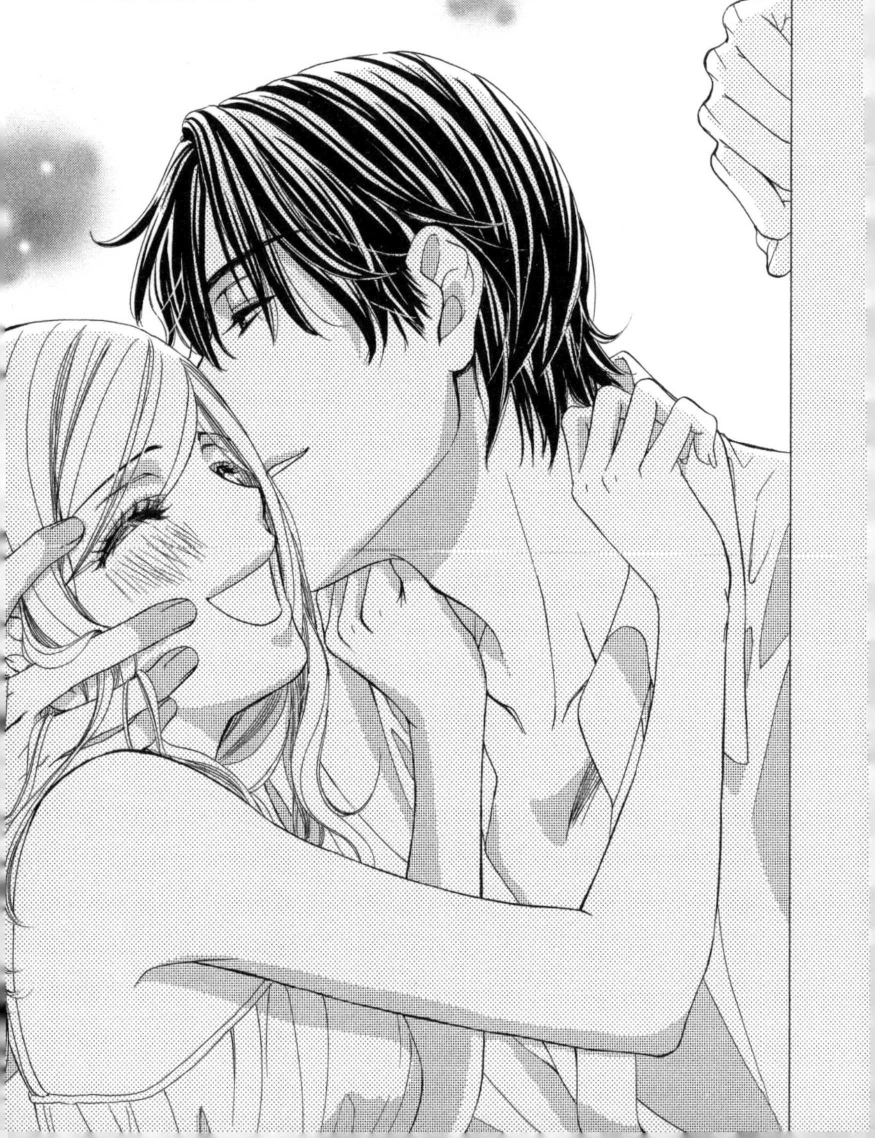

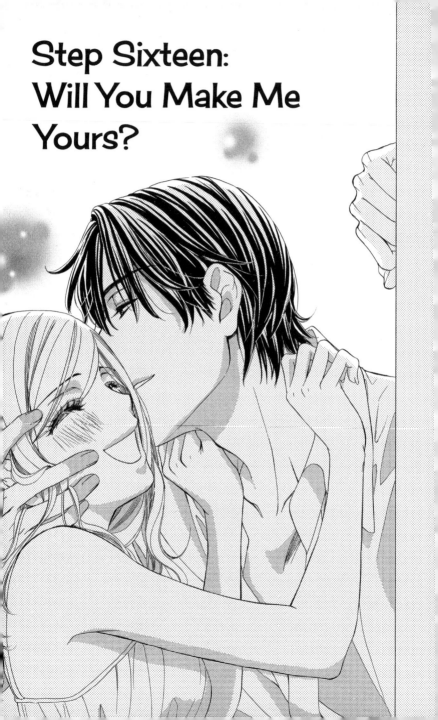

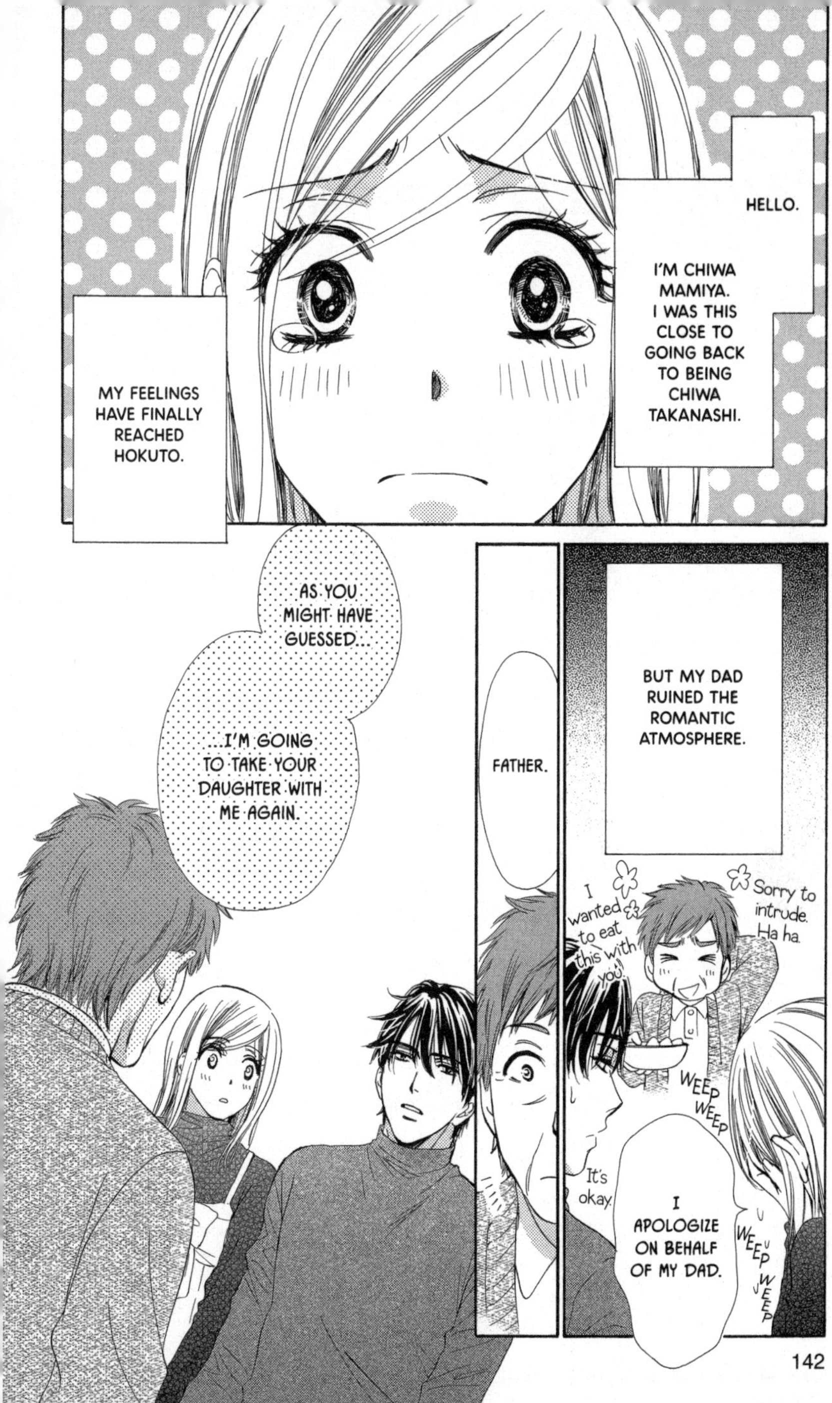
HELLO.
I'M CHIWA MAMIYA. I WAS THIS CLOSE TO GOING BACK TO BEING CHIWA TAKANASHI.
MY FEELINGS HAVE FINALLY REACHED HOKUTO.
BUT MY DAD RUINED THE ROMANTIC ATMOSPHERE.
Sorry to intrude. Ha ha.
I wanted to eat this with you!
WEEP WEEP
It's okay.
I APOLOGIZE ON BEHALF OF MY DAD.
WEEP WEEP
FATHER.
AS YOU MIGHT HAVE GUESSED...
...I'M GOING TO TAKE YOUR DAUGHTER WITH ME AGAIN.

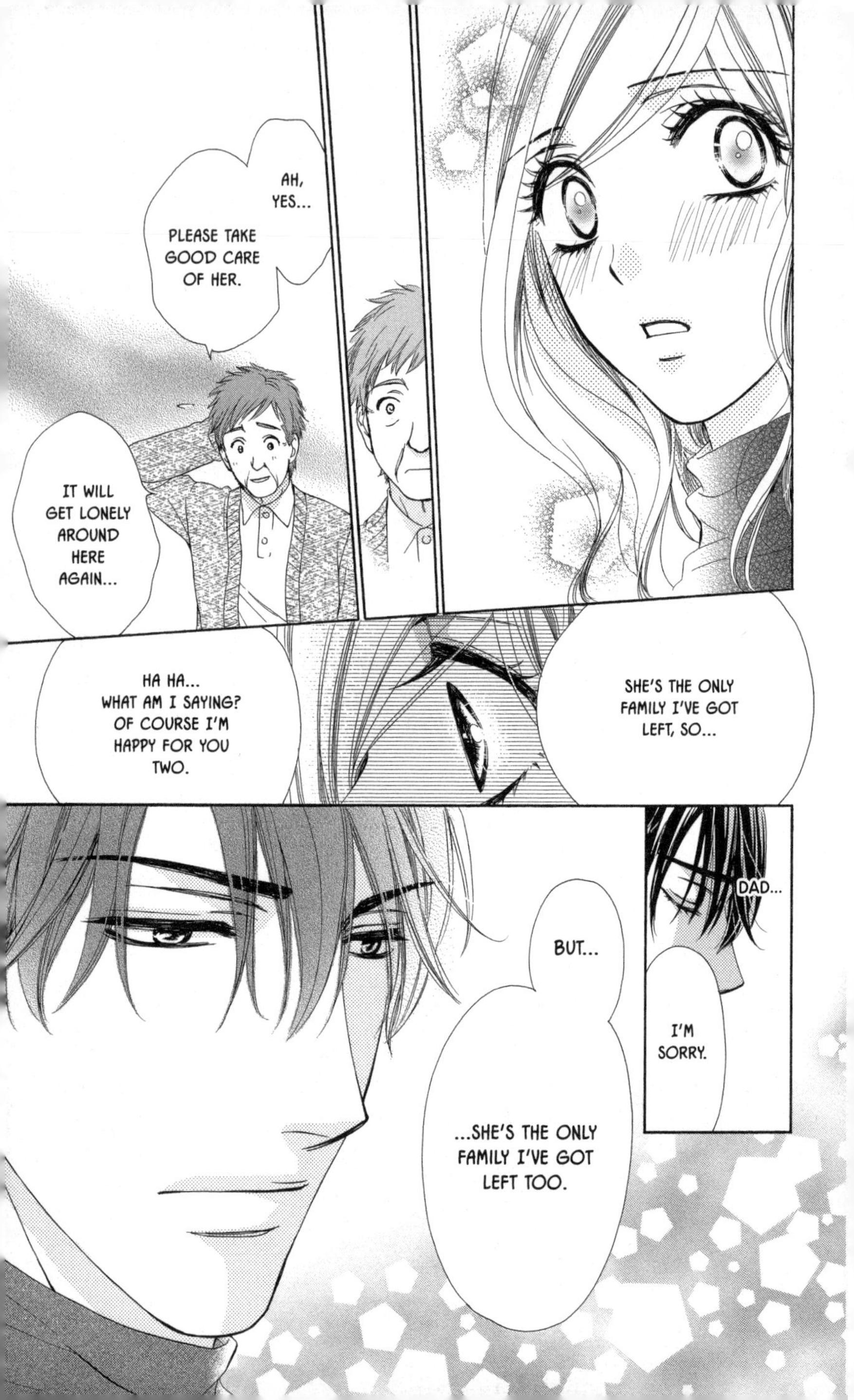
AH, YES...
PLEASE TAKE GOOD CARE OF HER.
IT WILL GET LONELY AROUND HERE AGAIN...
SHE'S THE ONLY FAMILY I'VE GOT LEFT, SO...
HA HA... WHAT AM I SAYING? OF COURSE I'M HAPPY FOR YOU TWO.
DAD...
I'M SORRY.
BUT...
...SHE'S THE ONLY FAMILY I'VE GOT LEFT TOO.

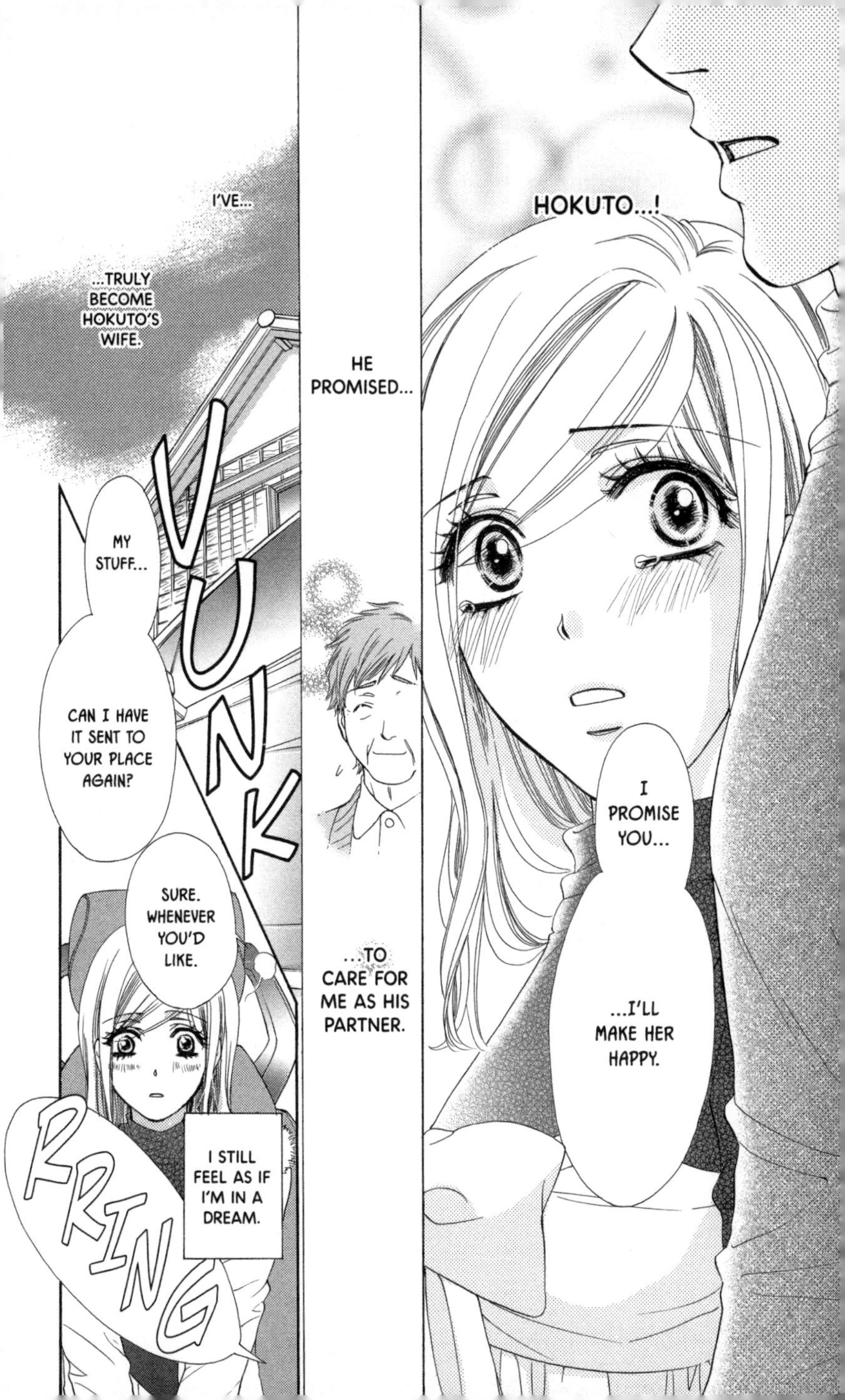
HOKUTO...!
I PROMISE YOU...
...I'LL MAKE HER HAPPY.
HE PROMISED...
...TO CARE FOR ME AS HIS PARTNER.
I'VE...
...TRULY BECOME HOKUTO'S WIFE.
VUNK
MY STUFF...
CAN I HAVE IT SENT TO YOUR PLACE AGAIN?
SURE. WHENEVER YOU'D LIKE.
I STILL FEEL AS IF I'M IN A DREAM.
RRING

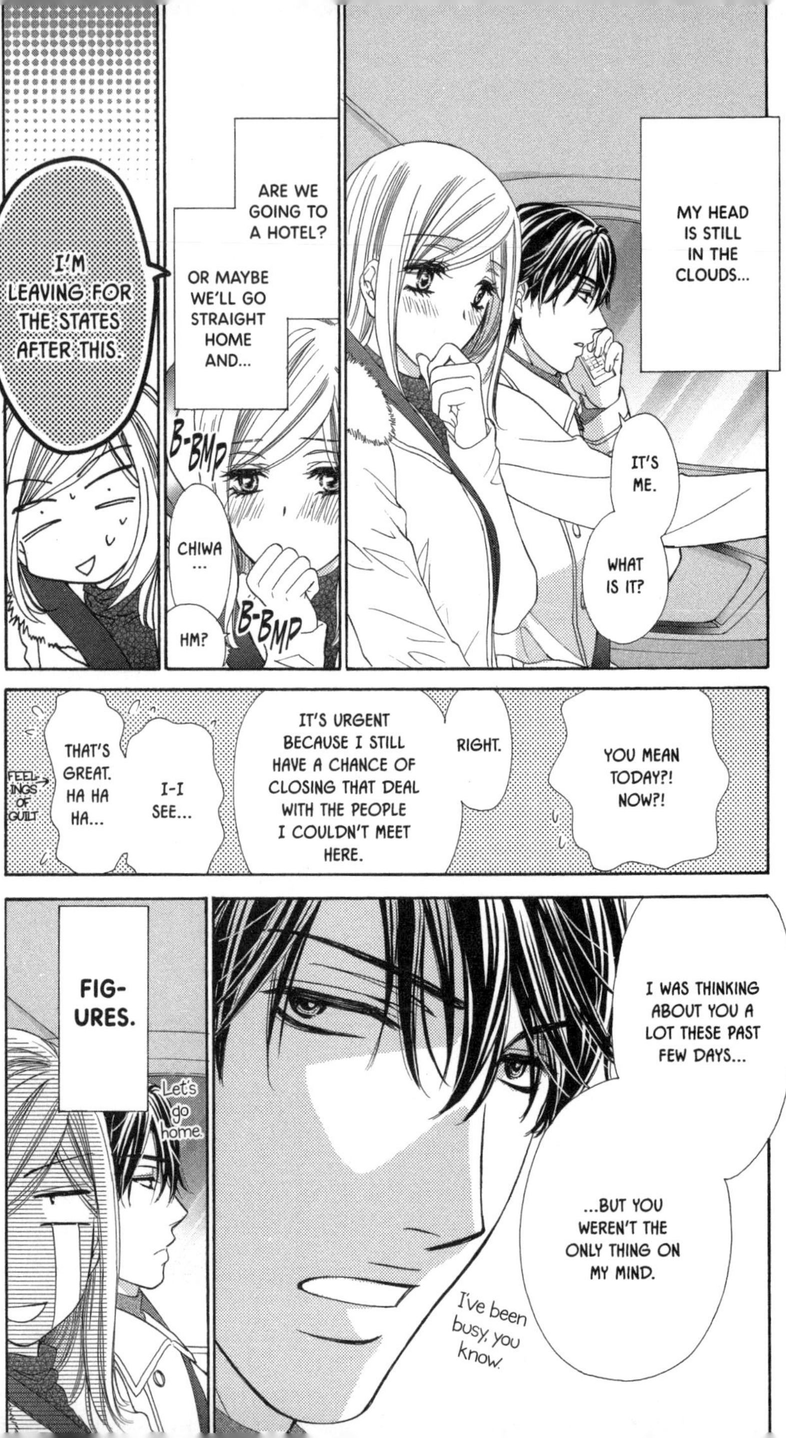
MY HEAD IS STILL IN THE CLOUDS...
IT'S ME.
WHAT IS IT?
ARE WE GOING TO A HOTEL?
OR MAYBE WE'LL GO STRAIGHT HOME AND...
B-BMP
CHIWA...
HM?
B-BMP
I'M LEAVING FOR THE STATES AFTER THIS.
YOU MEAN TODAY?! NOW?!
RIGHT.
IT'S URGENT BECAUSE I STILL HAVE A CHANCE OF CLOSING THAT DEAL WITH THE PEOPLE I COULDN'T MEET HERE.
I-I SEE...
THAT'S GREAT. HA HA HA...
FEELINGS OF GUILT
I WAS THINKING ABOUT YOU A LOT THESE PAST FEW DAYS...
...BUT YOU WEREN'T THE ONLY THING ON MY MIND.
I've been busy, you know.
FIG-URES.
Let's go home.

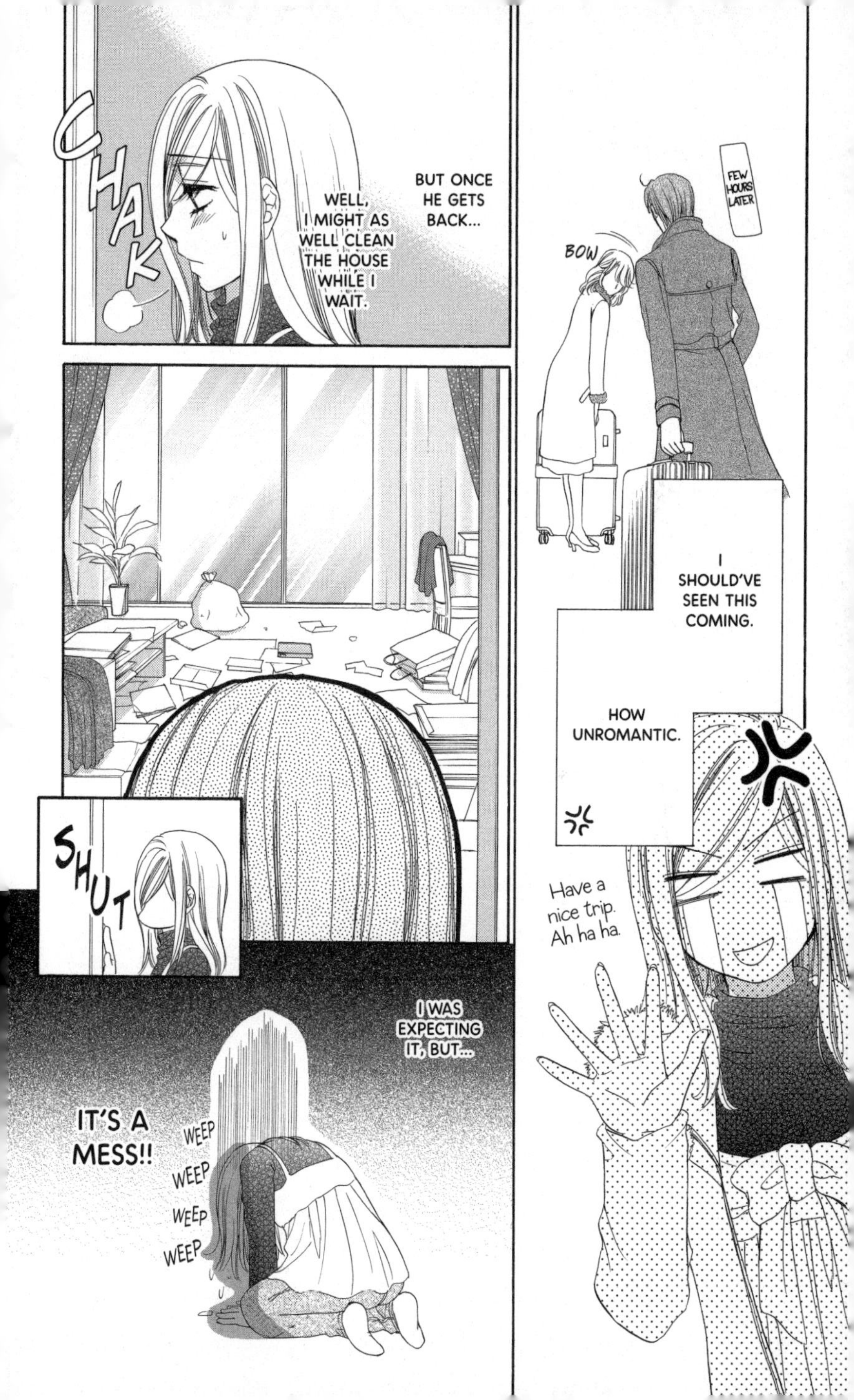
FEW HOURS LATER
BOW
I SHOULD'VE SEEN THIS COMING.
HOW UNROMANTIC.
Have a nice trip. Ah ha ha.
BUT ONCE HE GETS BACK...
WELL, I MIGHT AS WELL CLEAN THE HOUSE WHILE I WAIT.
CHAK
SHUT
I WAS EXPECTING IT, BUT...
IT'S A MESS!!
WEEP
WEEP
WEEP
WEEP

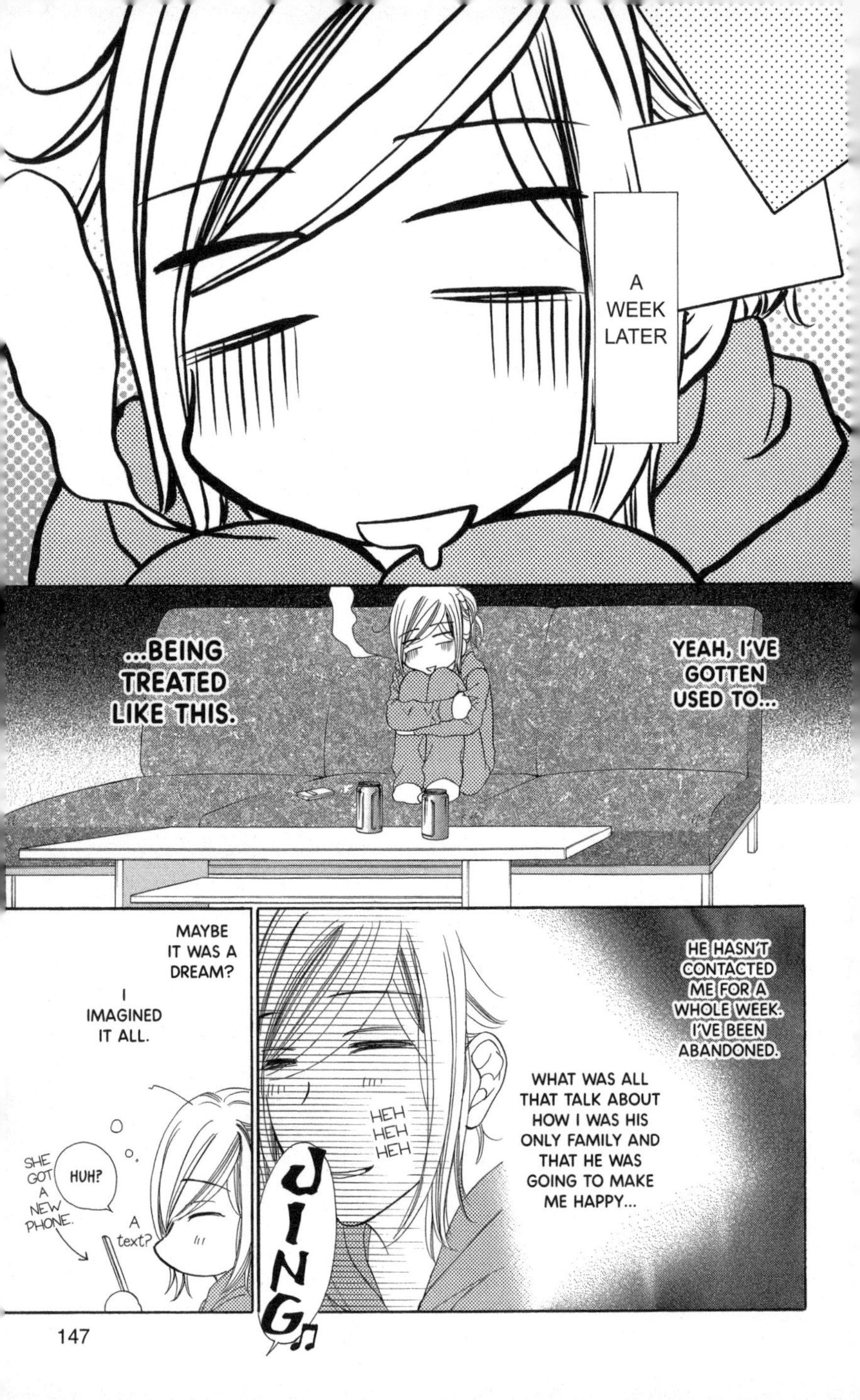
A WEEK LATER
YEAH, I'VE GOTTEN USED TO...
...BEING TREATED LIKE THIS.
HE HASN'T CONTACTED ME FOR A WHOLE WEEK. I'VE BEEN ABANDONED.
WHAT WAS ALL THAT TALK ABOUT HOW I WAS HIS ONLY FAMILY AND THAT HE WAS GOING TO MAKE ME HAPPY...
HEH HEH HEH
JING♫
MAYBE IT WAS A DREAM?
I IMAGINED IT ALL.
HUH?
A text?
SHE GOT A NEW PHONE.

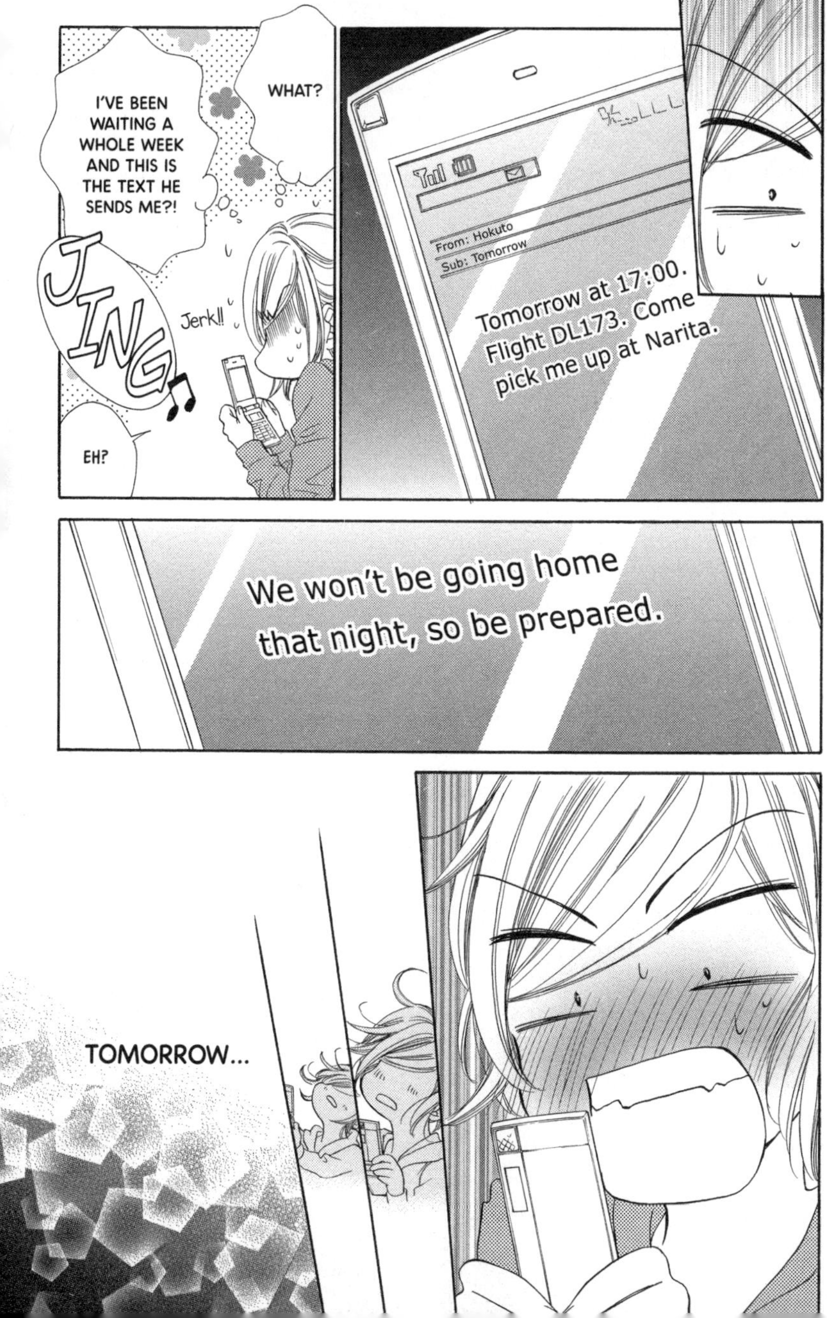

From: Hokuto
Sub: Tomorrow
Tomorrow at 17:00. Flight DL173. Come pick me up at Narita.
WHAT?
I'VE BEEN WAITING A WHOLE WEEK AND THIS IS THE TEXT HE SENDS ME?!
JING
Jerk!!
EH?
We won't be going home that night, so be prepared.
TOMORROW...

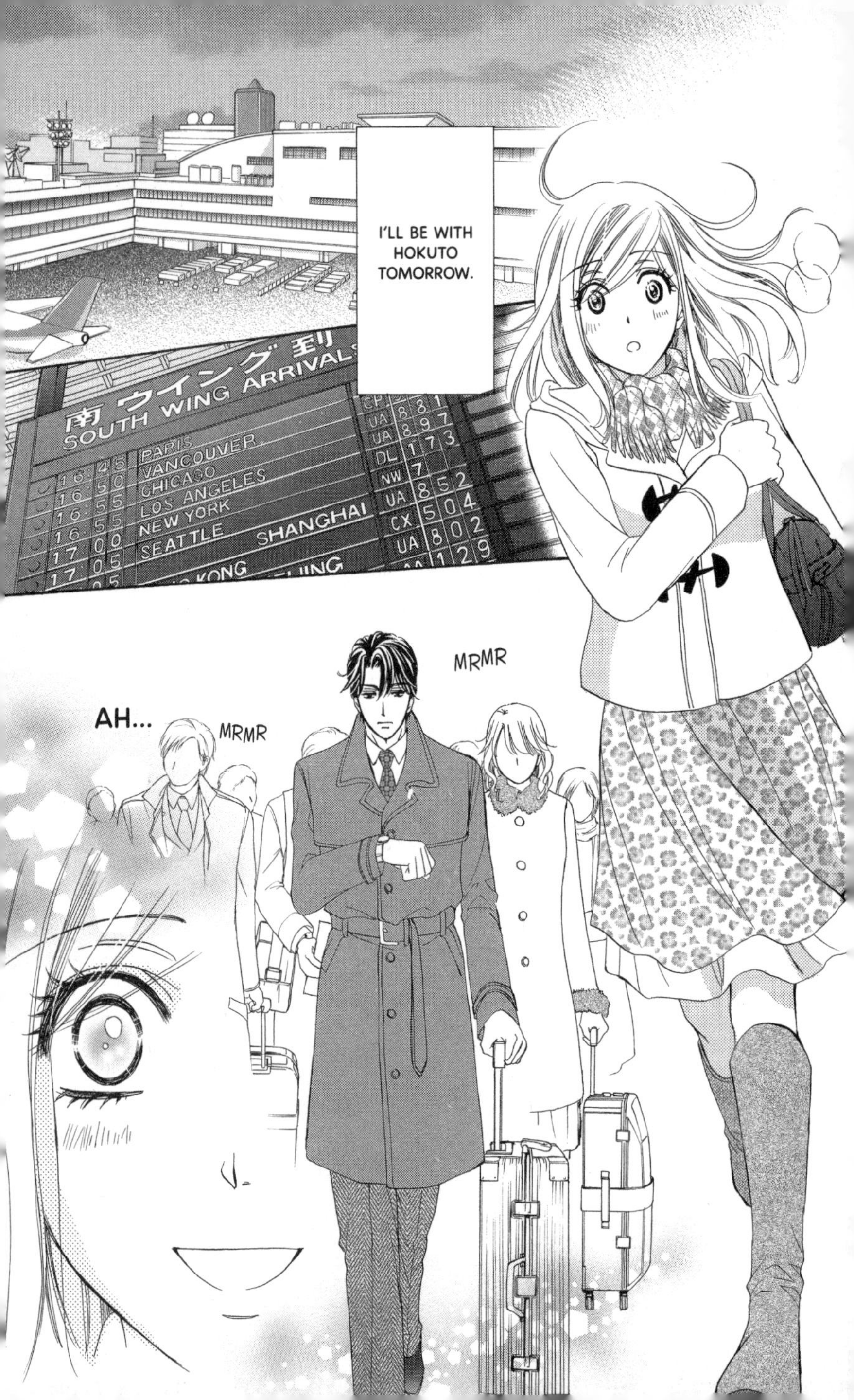
I'LL BE WITH HOKUTO TOMORROW.
南ウイング到
SOUTH WING ARRIVALS
PARIS
VANCOUVER
CHICAGO
LOS ANGELES
NEW YORK
SEATTLE
SHANGHAI
MRMR
MRMR
AH...

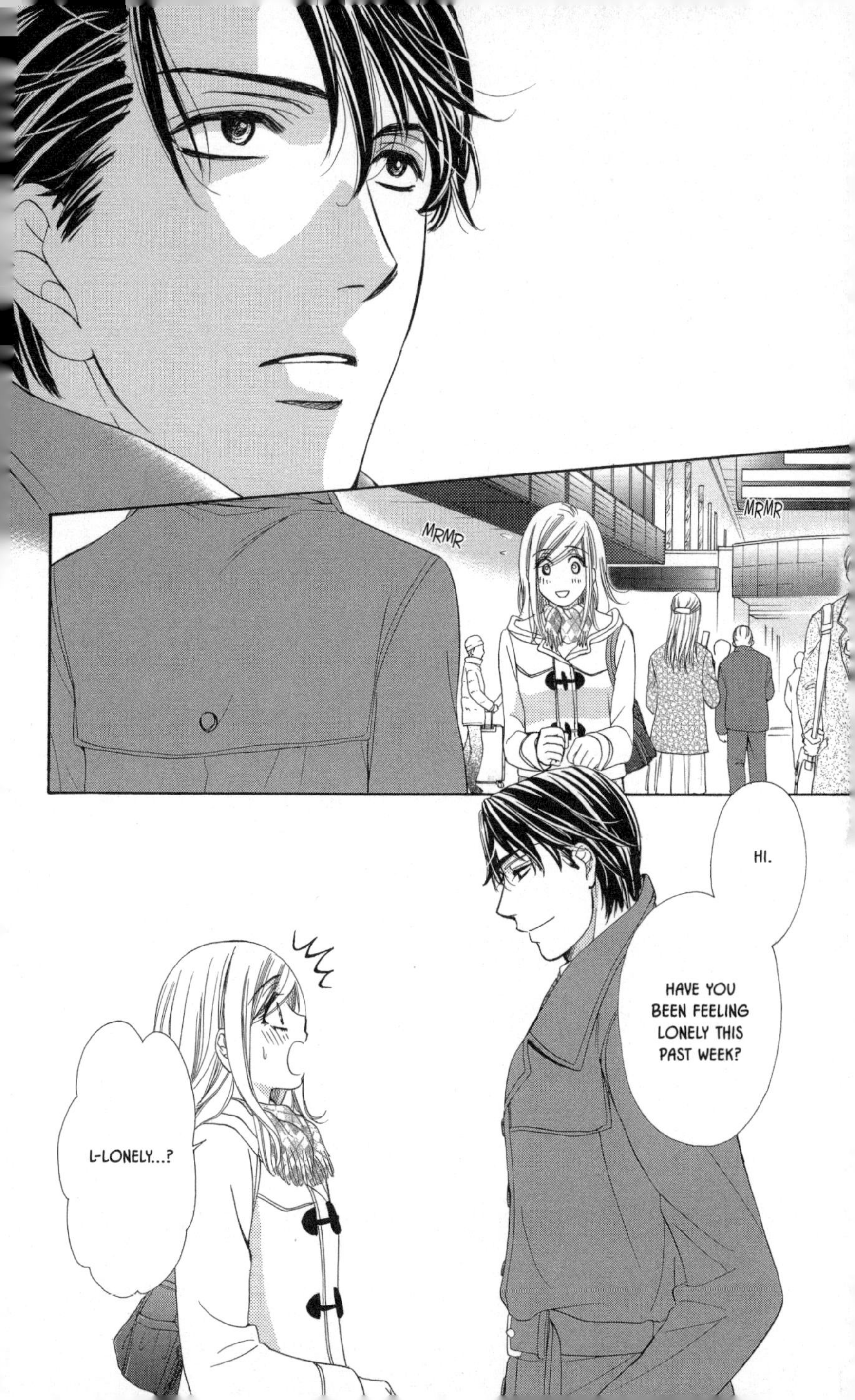
MRMR
MRMR
HI.
HAVE YOU BEEN FEELING LONELY THIS PAST WEEK?
L-LONELY...?

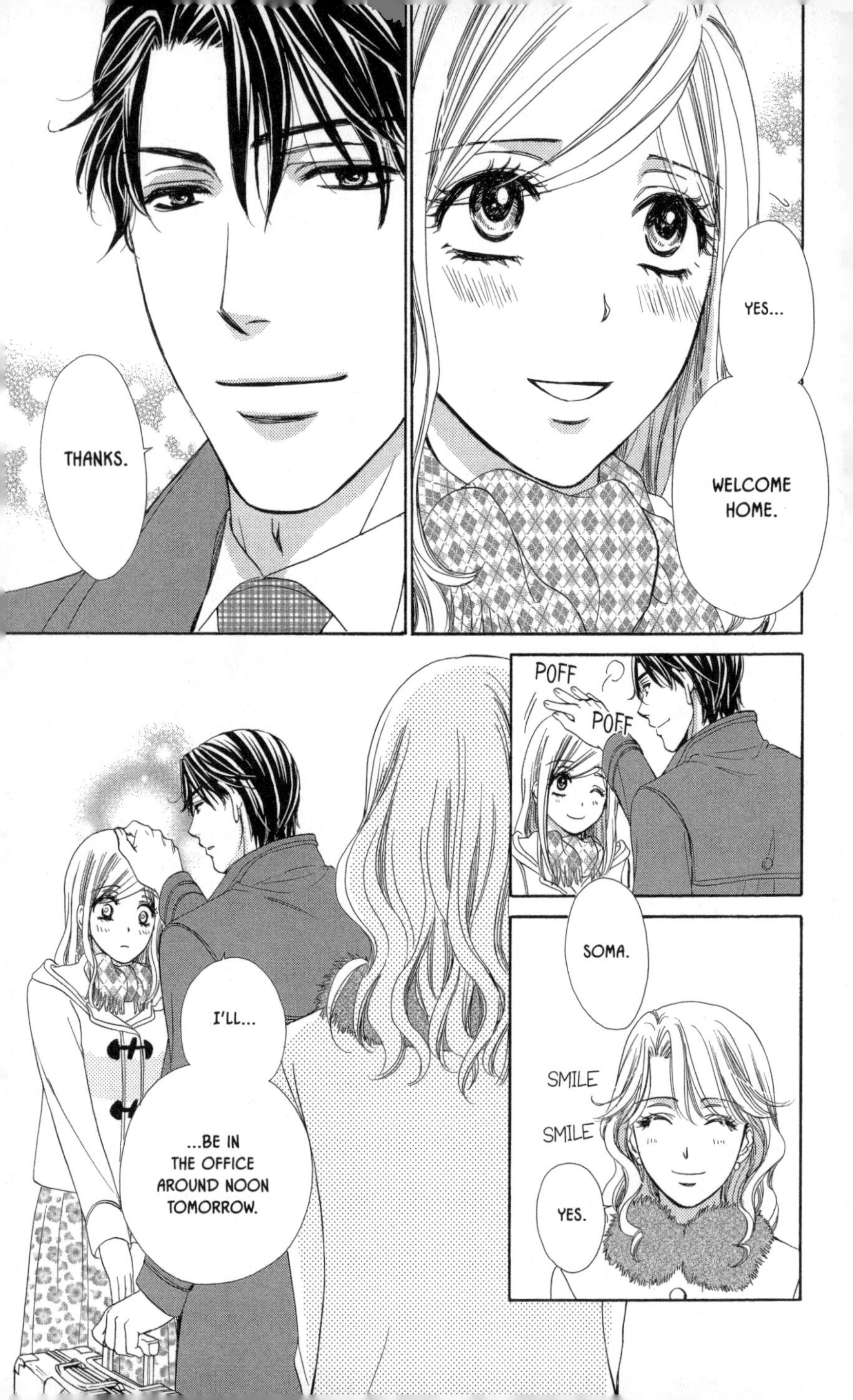
YES...
WELCOME HOME.
THANKS.
POFF
POFF
SOMA.
SMILE
SMILE
YES.
I'LL...
...BE IN THE OFFICE AROUND NOON TOMORROW.

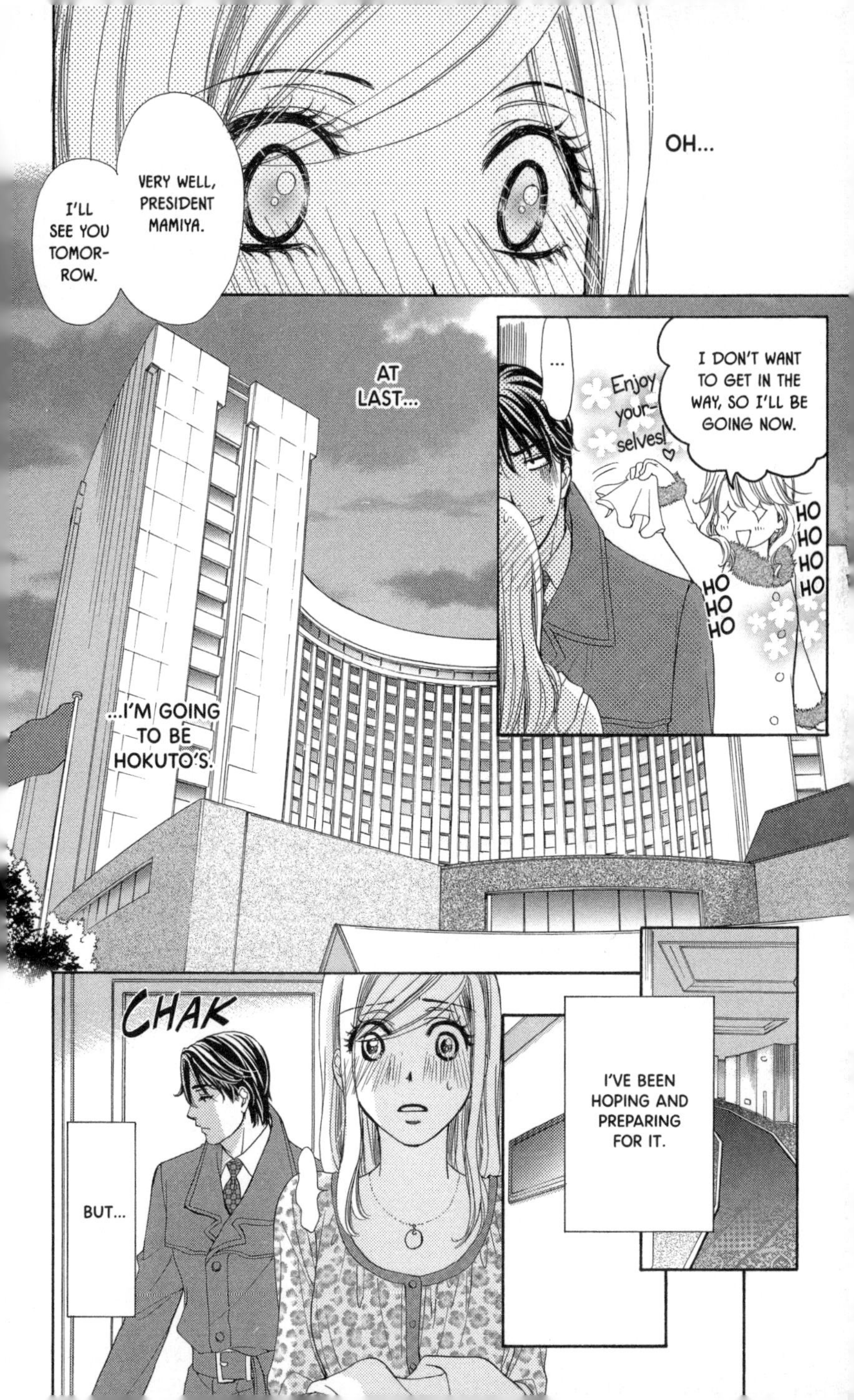
OH...
VERY WELL, PRESIDENT MAMIYA.
I'LL SEE YOU TOMOR-ROW.
I DON'T WANT TO GET IN THE WAY, SO I'LL BE GOING NOW.
Enjoy your-selves! ♡
HO HO HO HO
HO HO HO
...
AT LAST...
...I'M GOING TO BE HOKUTO'S.
I'VE BEEN HOPING AND PREPARING FOR IT.
CHAK
BUT...

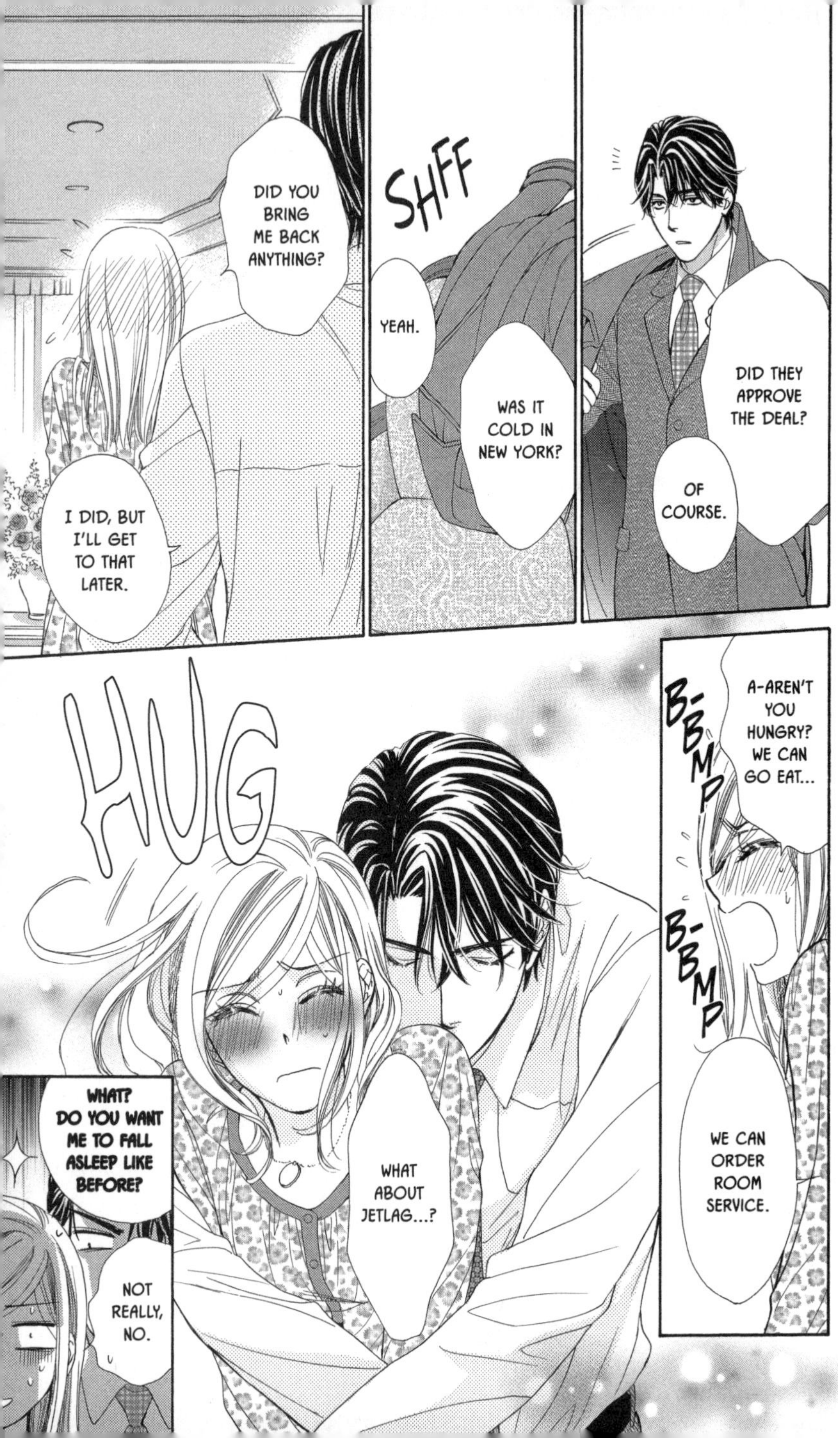
DID THEY APPROVE THE DEAL?
OF COURSE.
SHFF
WAS IT COLD IN NEW YORK?
YEAH.
DID YOU BRING ME BACK ANYTHING?
I DID, BUT I'LL GET TO THAT LATER.
A-AREN'T YOU HUNGRY? WE CAN GO EAT...
B-BMP
B-BMP
WE CAN ORDER ROOM SERVICE.
HUG
WHAT ABOUT JETLAG...?
WHAT? DO YOU WANT ME TO FALL ASLEEP LIKE BEFORE?
NOT REALLY, NO.

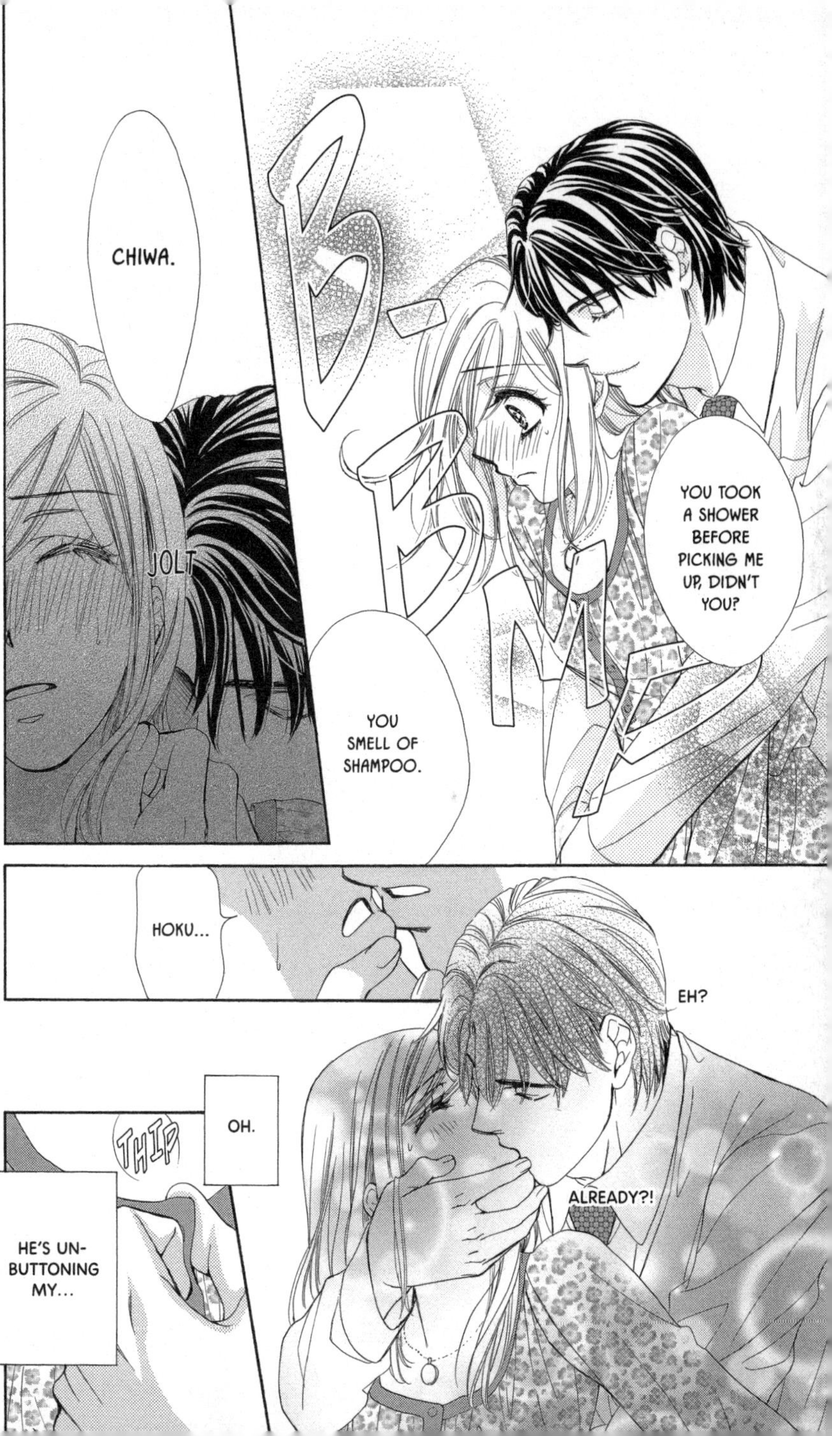
YOU TOOK A SHOWER BEFORE PICKING ME UP, DIDN'T YOU?
YOU SMELL OF SHAMPOO.
CHIWA.
JOLT
EH?
ALREADY?!
HOKU...
OH.
THIP
HE'S UN-BUTTONING MY...

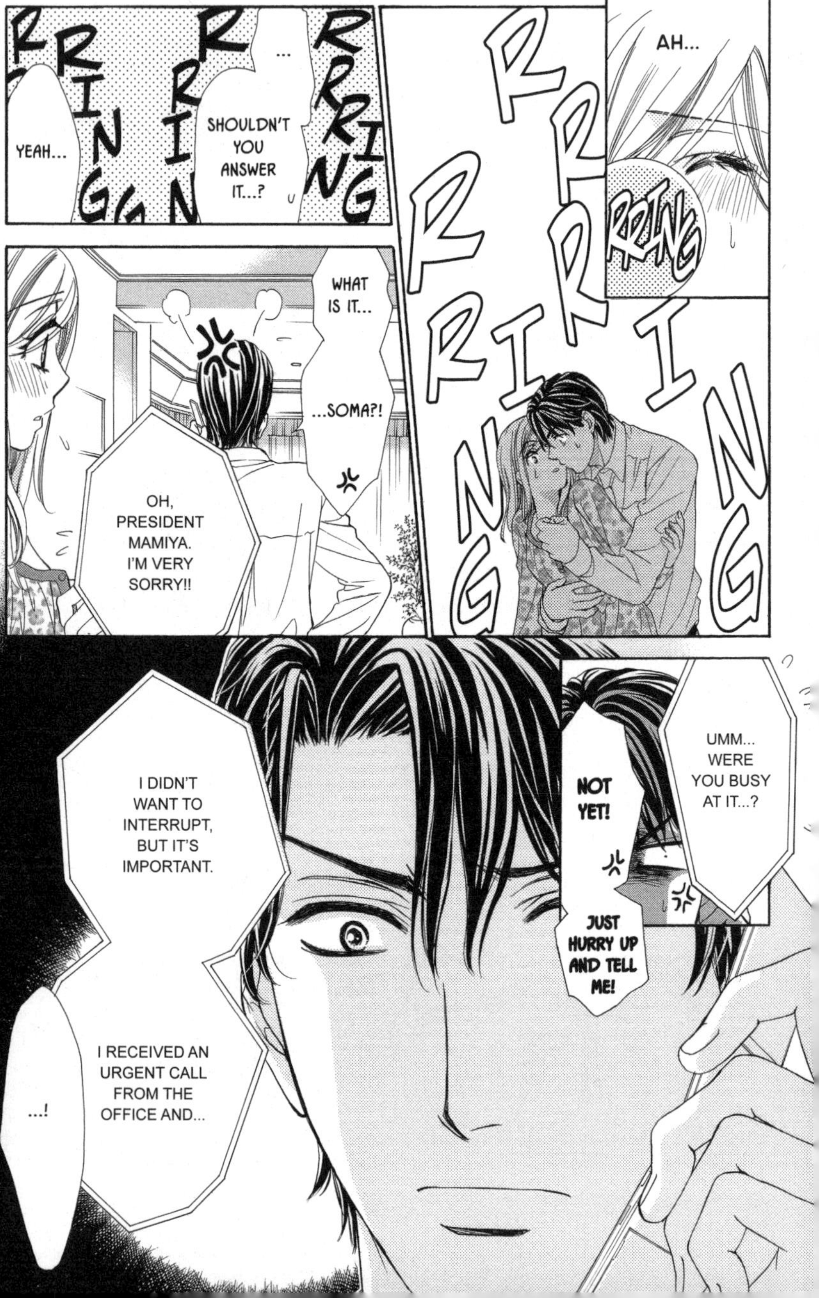

AH...
RRING
RRRING
RRRING
RRRING
...
SHOULDN'T YOU ANSWER IT...?
RRING
YEAH...
WHAT IS IT...
...SOMA?!
OH, PRESIDENT MAMIYA. I'M VERY SORRY!!
UMM... WERE YOU BUSY AT IT...?
NOT YET!
JUST HURRY UP AND TELL ME!
I DIDN'T WANT TO INTERRUPT, BUT IT'S IMPORTANT.
I RECEIVED AN URGENT CALL FROM THE OFFICE AND...
...!

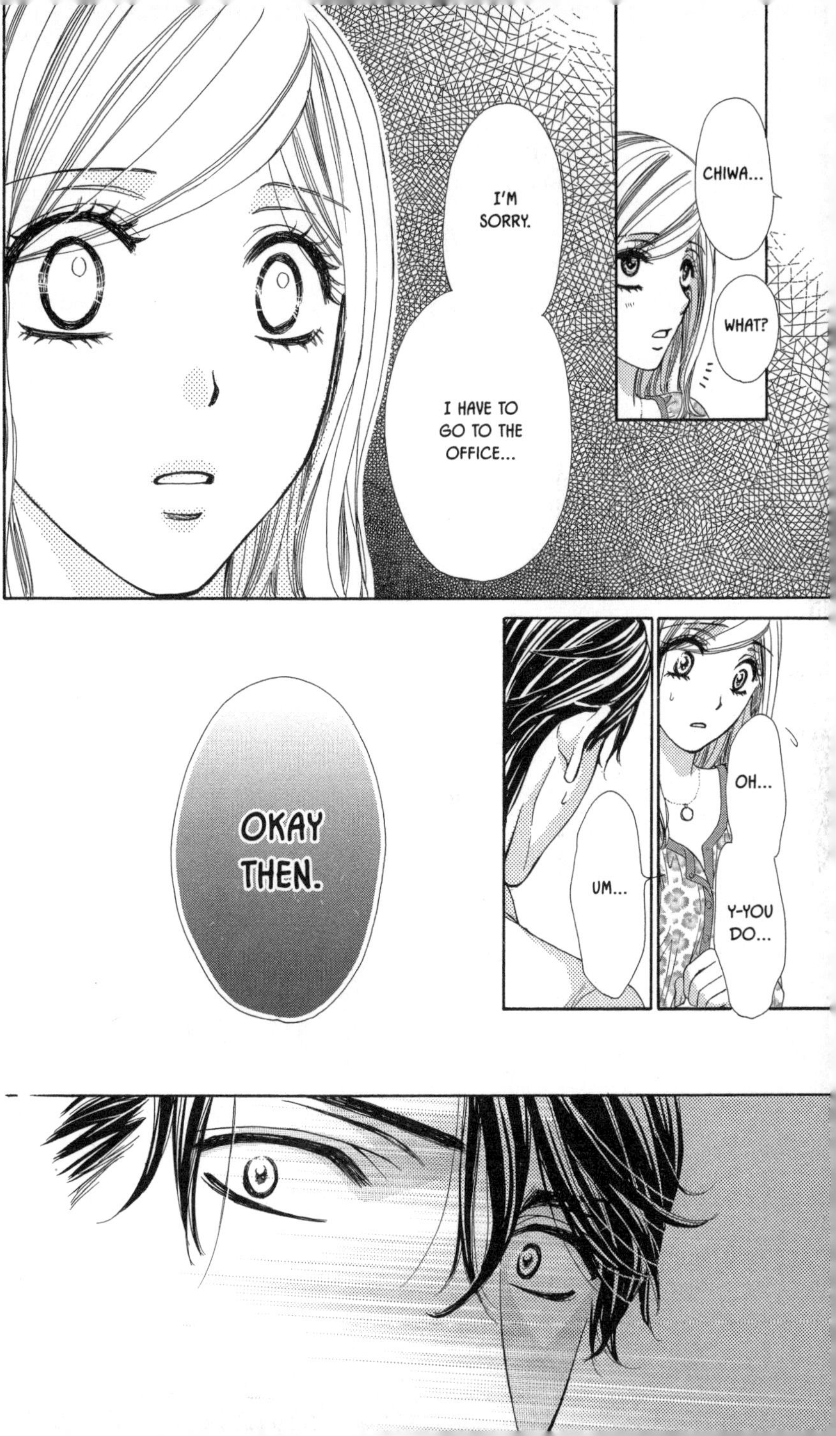
CHIWA...
WHAT?
I'M SORRY.
I HAVE TO GO TO THE OFFICE...
OH...
Y-YOU DO...
UM...
OKAY THEN.

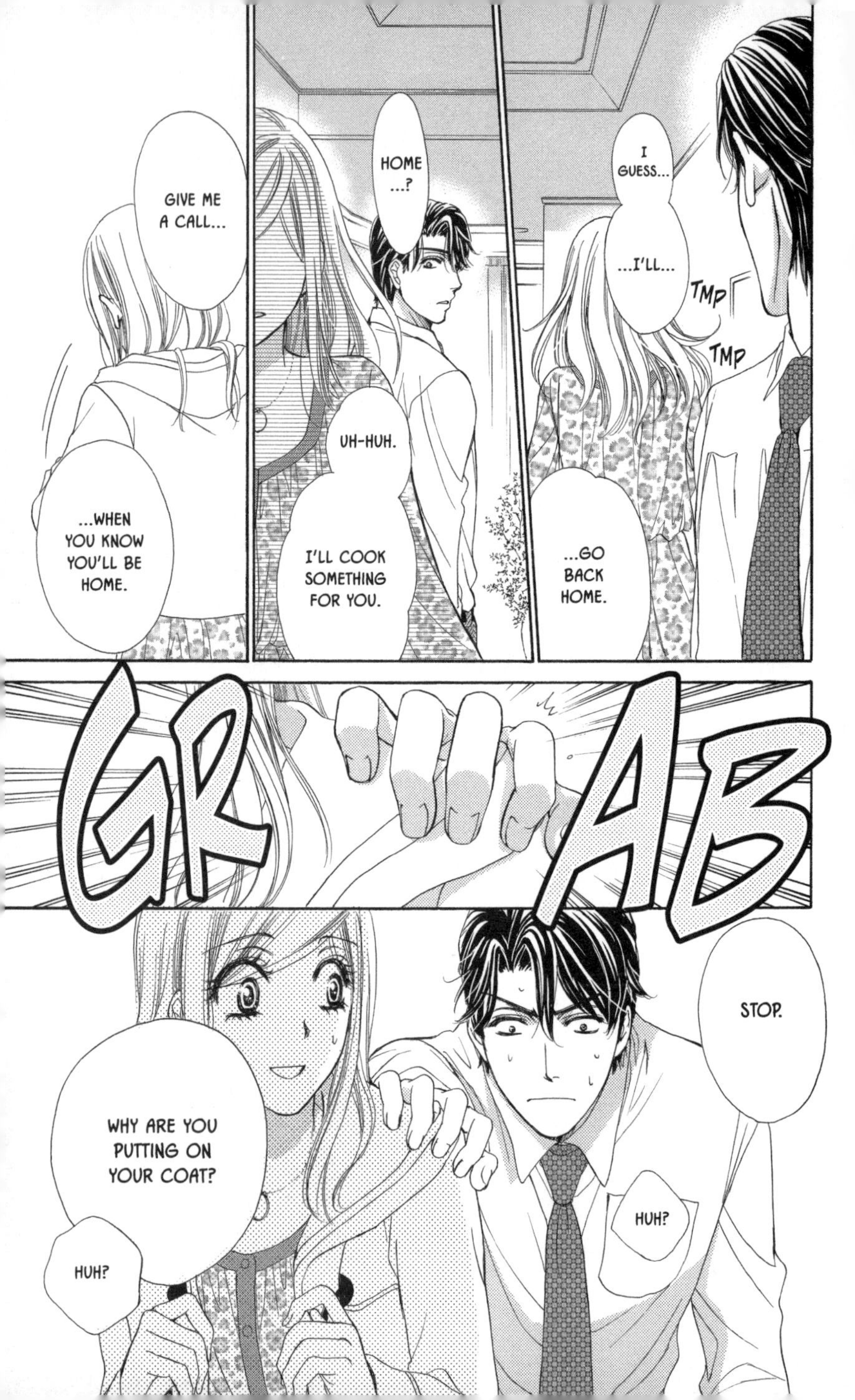
I GUESS...
...I'LL...
TMP
TMP
...GO BACK HOME.
HOME ...?
UH-HUH.
I'LL COOK SOMETHING FOR YOU.
GIVE ME A CALL...
...WHEN YOU KNOW YOU'LL BE HOME.
GRAB
STOP.
WHY ARE YOU PUTTING ON YOUR COAT?
HUH?
HUH?

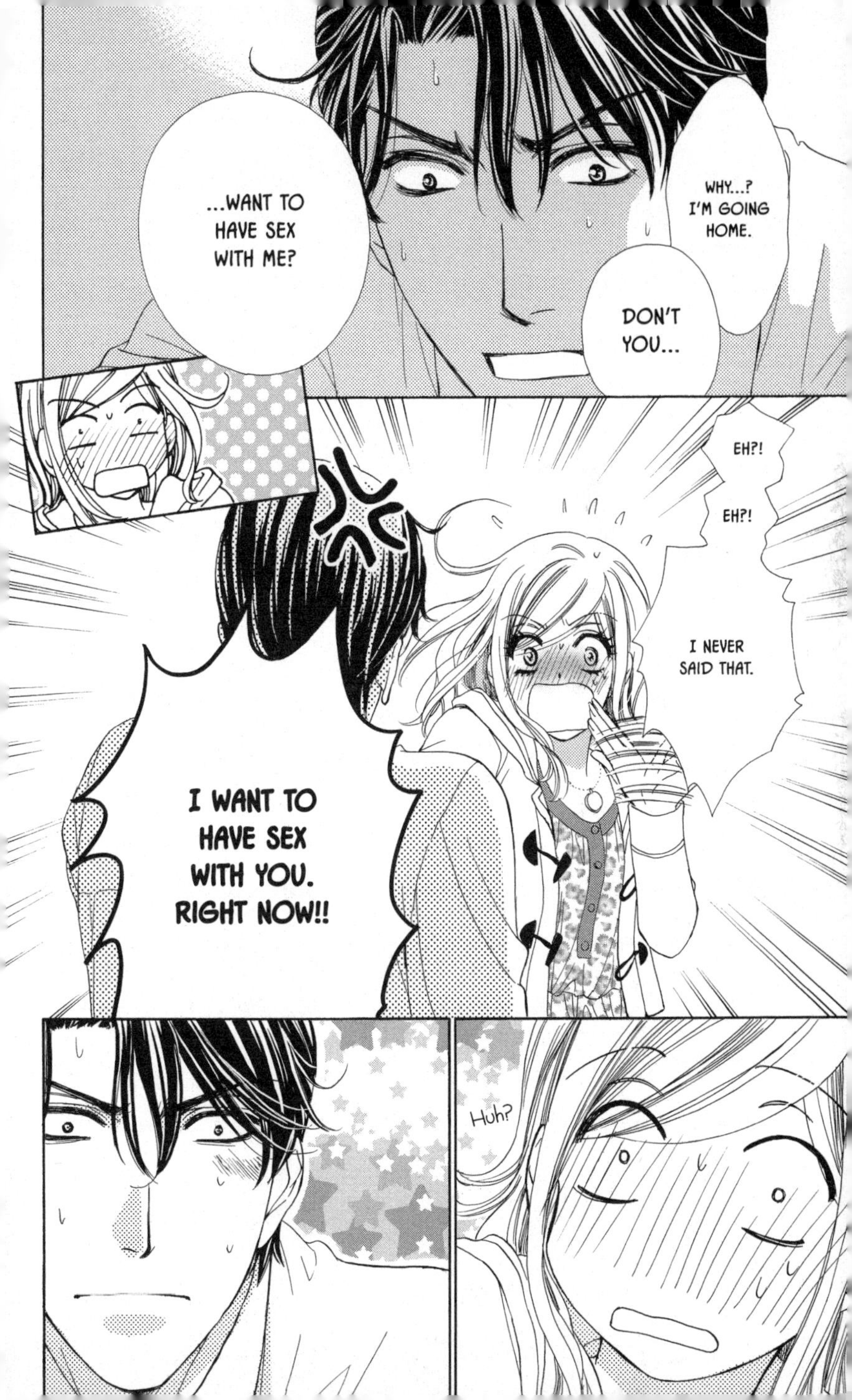
WHY...? I'M GOING HOME.
DON'T YOU...
...WANT TO HAVE SEX WITH ME?
EH?!
EH?!
I NEVER SAID THAT.
I WANT TO HAVE SEX WITH YOU. RIGHT NOW!!
Huh?

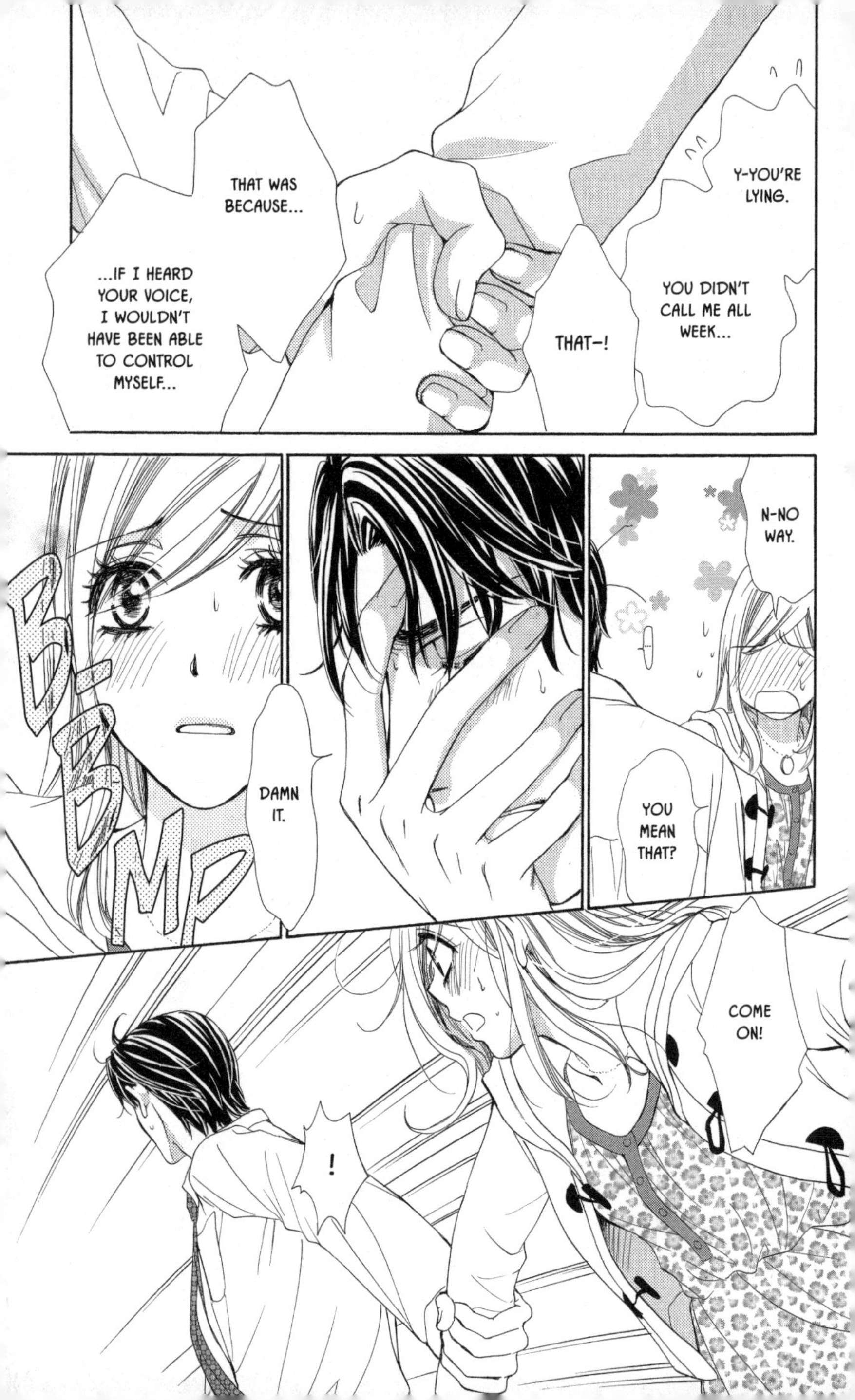
Y-YOU'RE LYING.
YOU DIDN'T CALL ME ALL WEEK...
THAT—!
THAT WAS BECAUSE...
...IF I HEARD YOUR VOICE, I WOULDN'T HAVE BEEN ABLE TO CONTROL MYSELF...
N-NO WAY.
YOU MEAN THAT?
DAMN IT.
B-BDMP
COME ON!
!

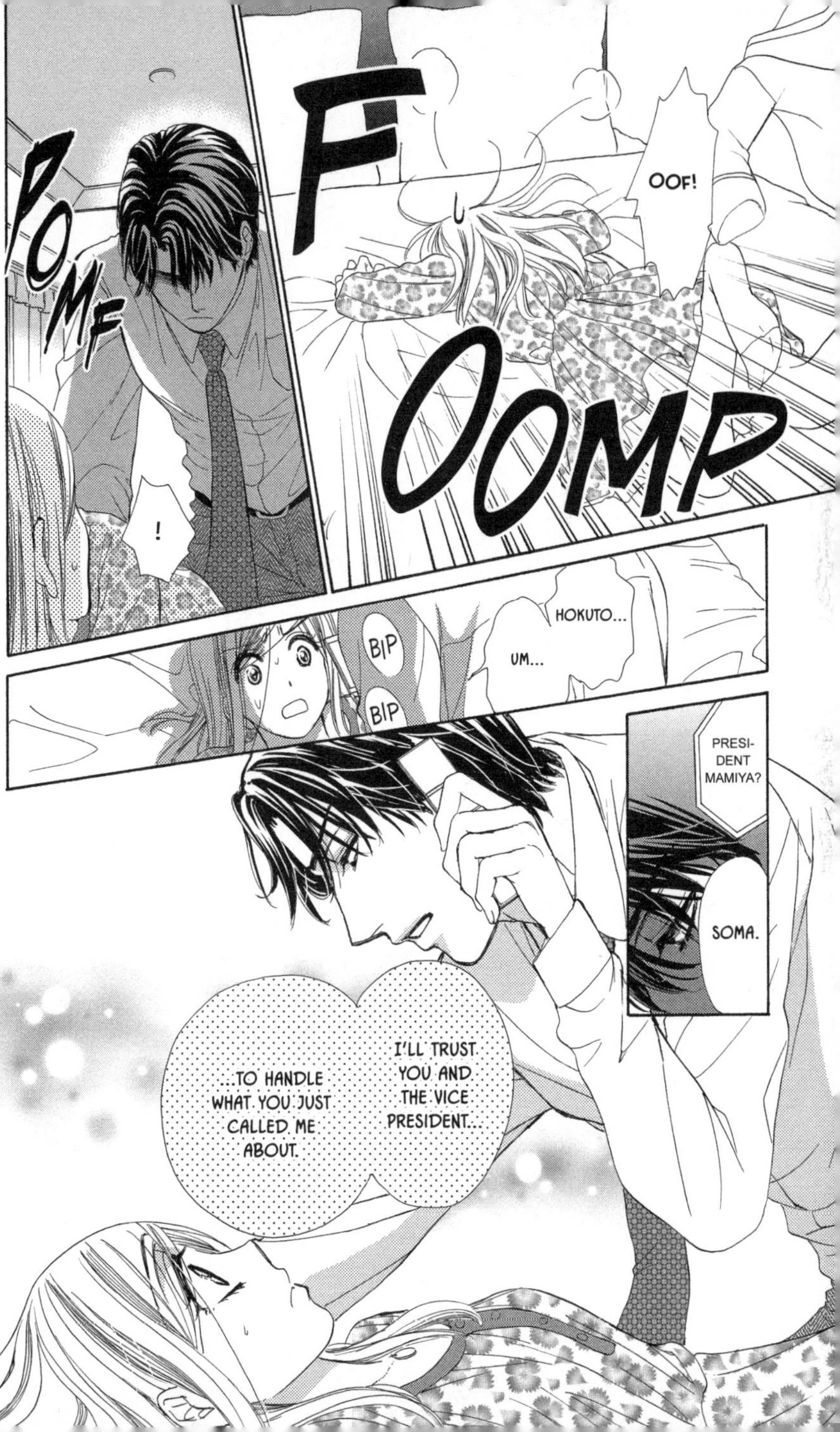
OOF!
F
OOMP
POMF
!
HOKUTO...
UM...
BIP
BIP
PRESI-
DENT
MAMIYA?
SOMA.
I'LL TRUST YOU AND THE VICE PRESIDENT...
...TO HANDLE WHAT YOU JUST CALLED ME ABOUT.

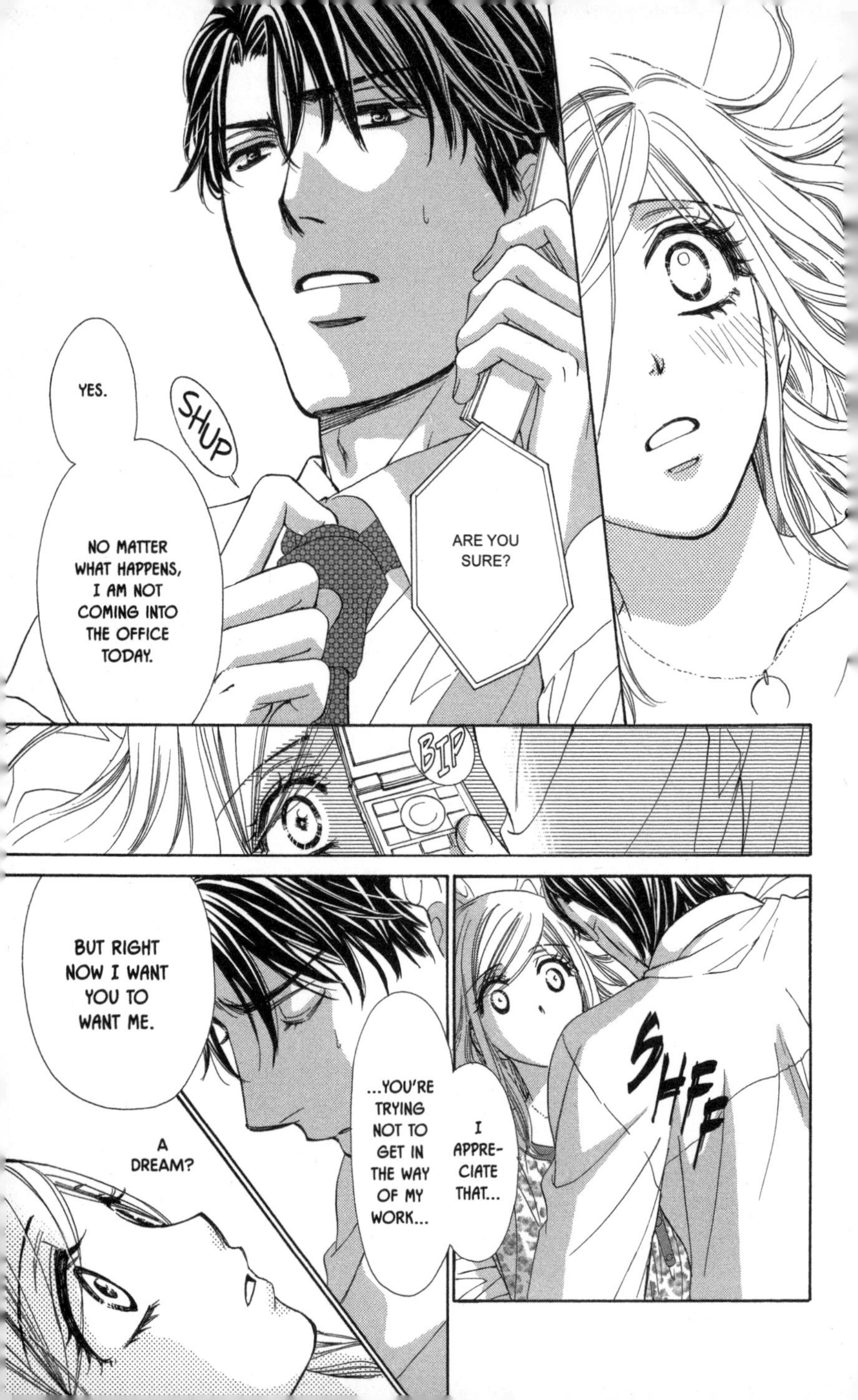
ARE YOU SURE?
SHUP
YES.
NO MATTER WHAT HAPPENS, I AM NOT COMING INTO THE OFFICE TODAY.
BIP
SHFF
I APPRECIATE THAT...
...YOU'RE TRYING NOT TO GET IN THE WAY OF MY WORK...
BUT RIGHT NOW I WANT YOU TO WANT ME.
A DREAM?

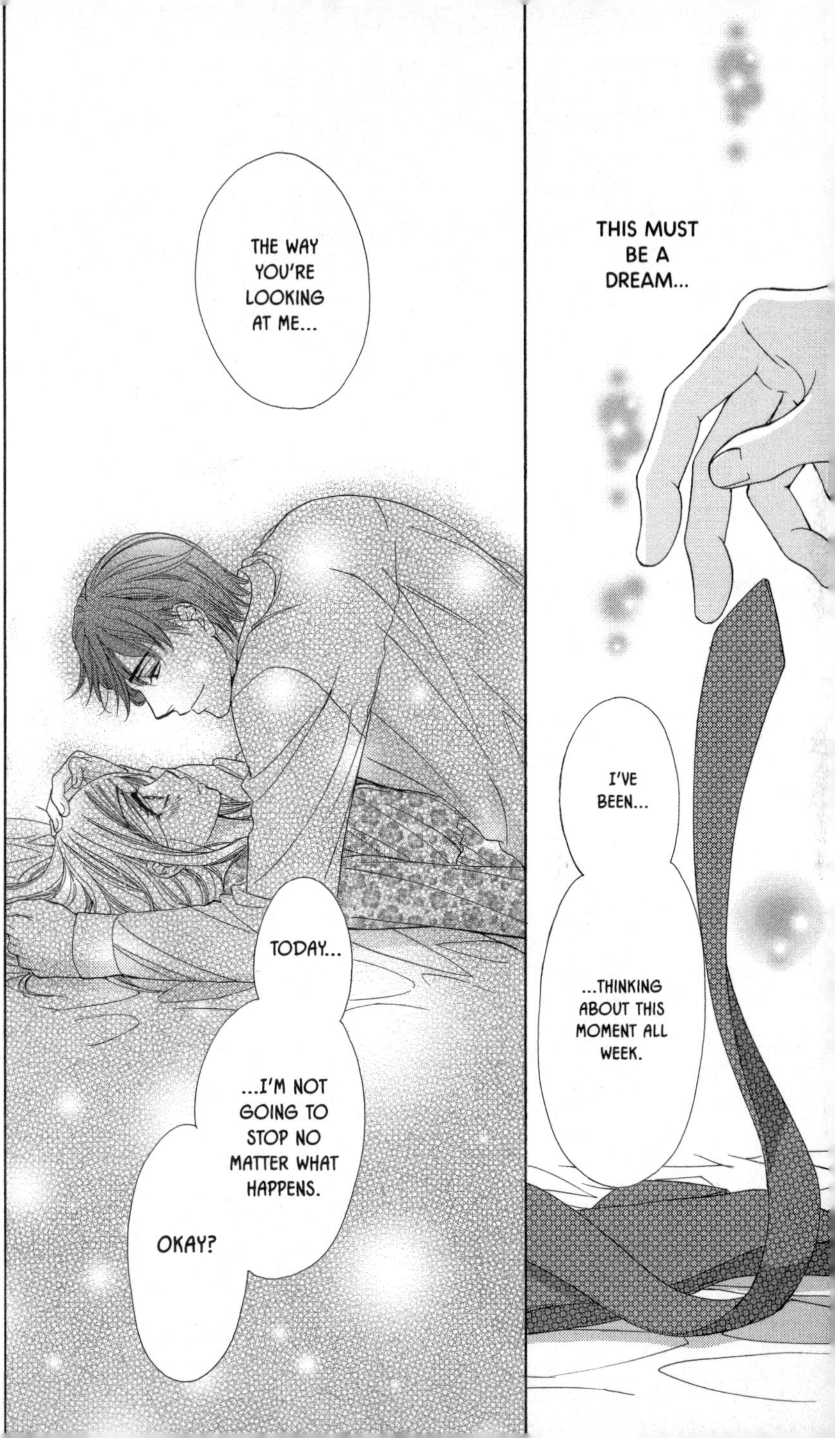
THIS MUST BE A DREAM...
I'VE BEEN...
...THINKING ABOUT THIS MOMENT ALL WEEK.
THE WAY YOU'RE LOOKING AT ME...
TODAY...
...I'M NOT GOING TO STOP NO MATTER WHAT HAPPENS.
OKAY?

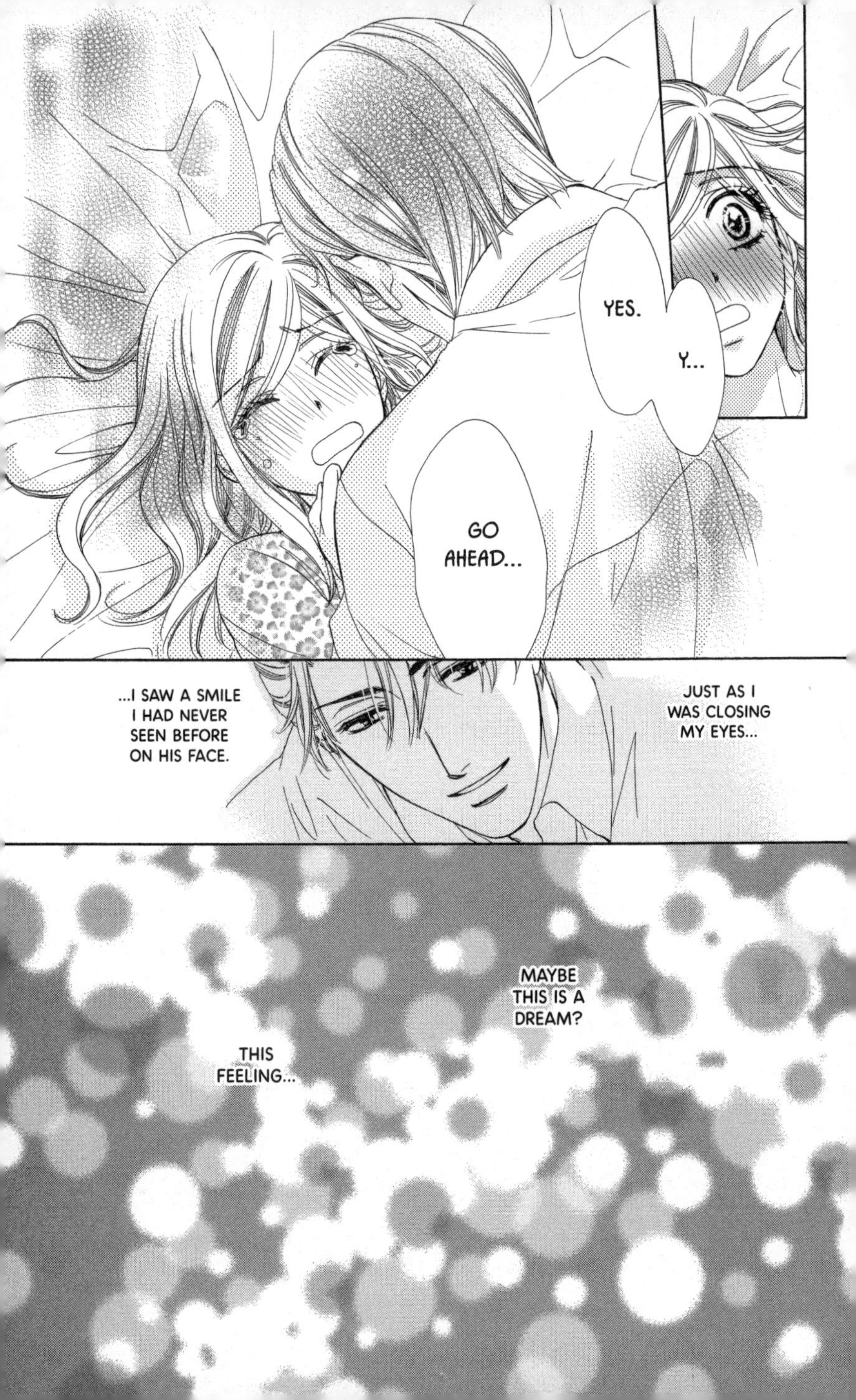
Y...
YES.
GO AHEAD...
JUST AS I WAS CLOSING MY EYES...
...I SAW A SMILE I HAD NEVER SEEN BEFORE ON HIS FACE.
MAYBE THIS IS A DREAM?
THIS FEELING...

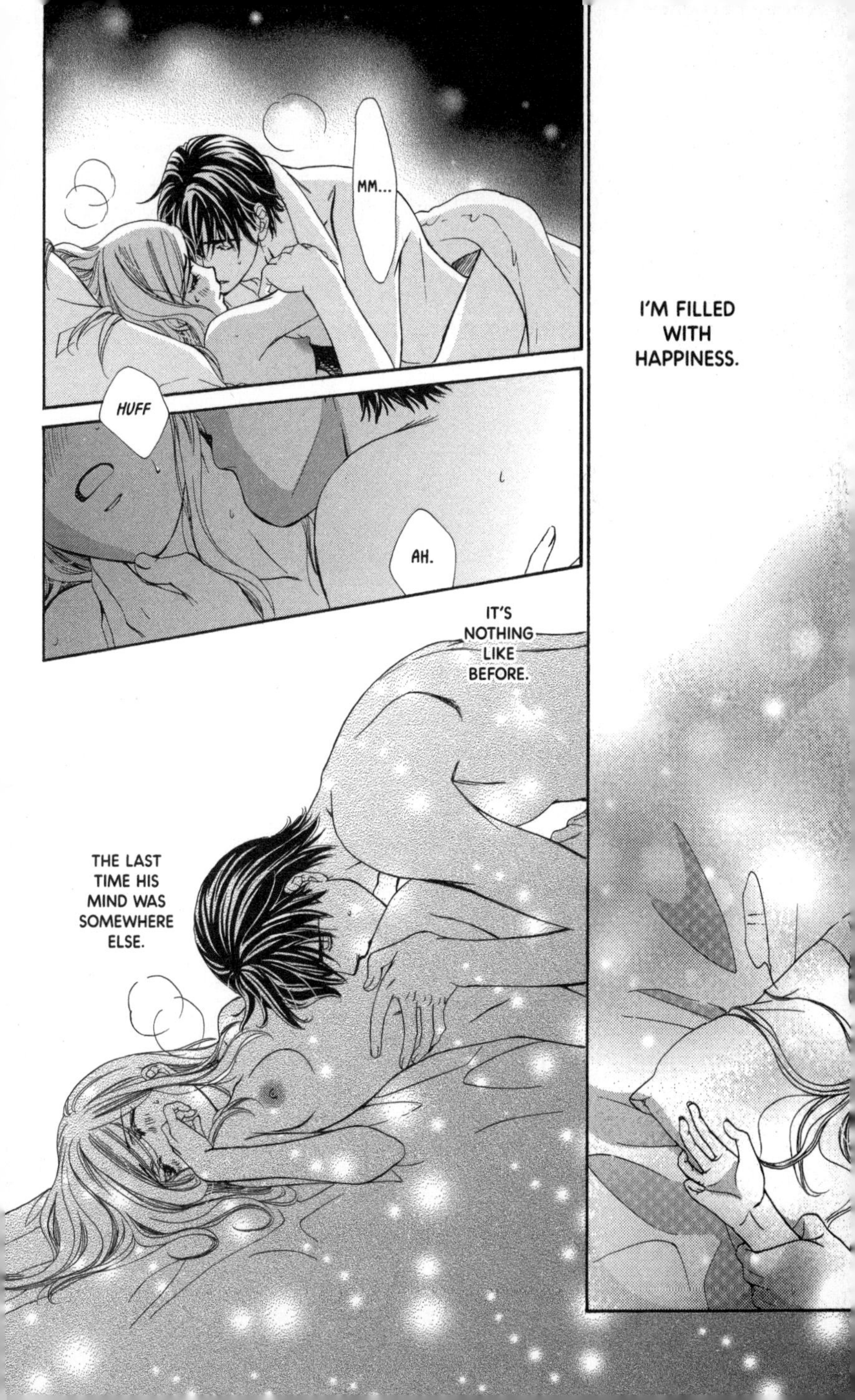
I'M FILLED WITH HAPPINESS.
MM...
HUFF
AH.
IT'S NOTHING LIKE BEFORE.
THE LAST TIME HIS MIND WAS SOMEWHERE ELSE.

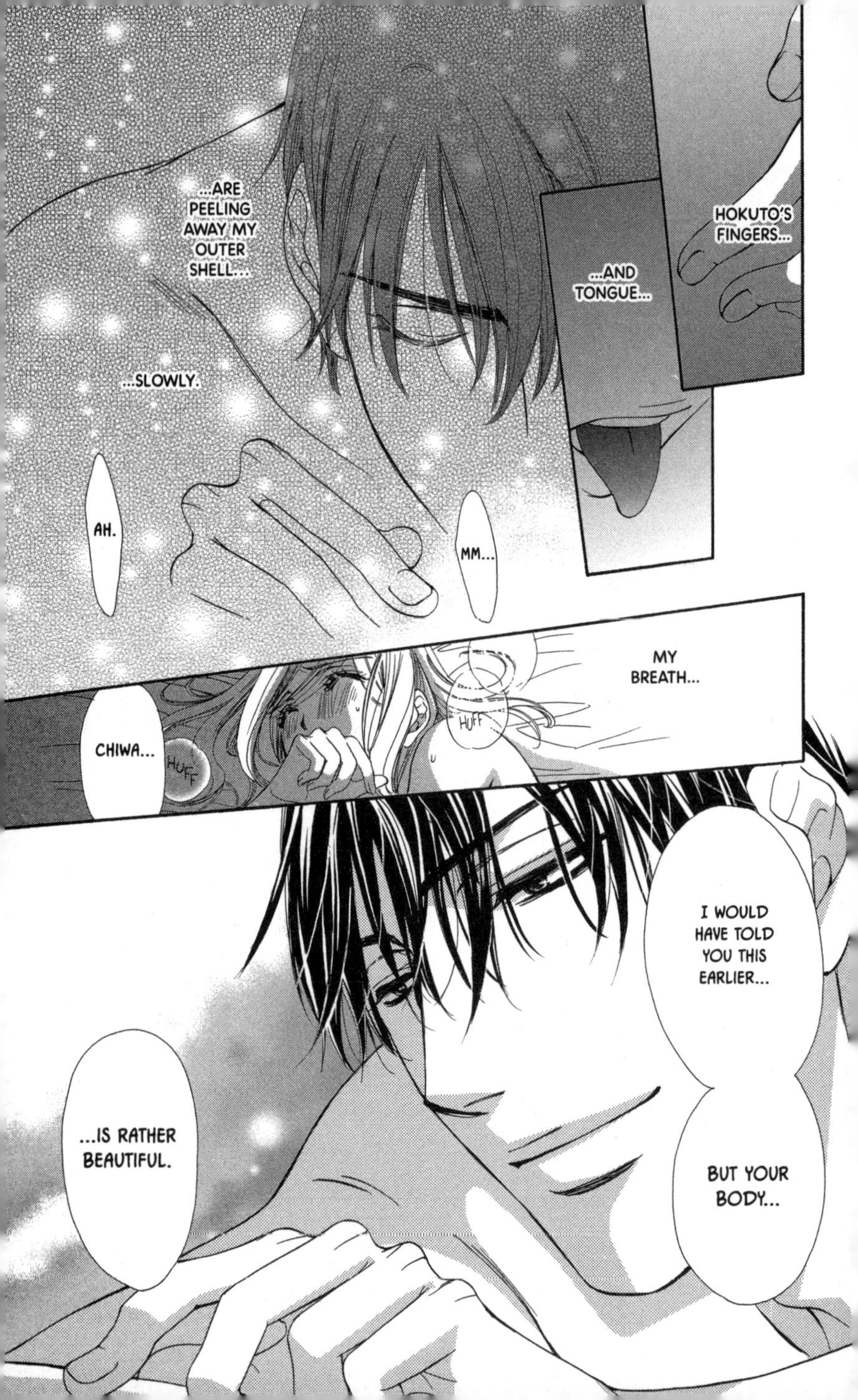
HOKUTO'S FINGERS...
...AND TONGUE...
...ARE PEELING AWAY MY OUTER SHELL...
...SLOWLY.
MM...
AH.
MY BREATH...
HUFF
HUFF
CHIWA...
I WOULD HAVE TOLD YOU THIS EARLIER...
BUT YOUR BODY...
...IS RATHER BEAUTIFUL.

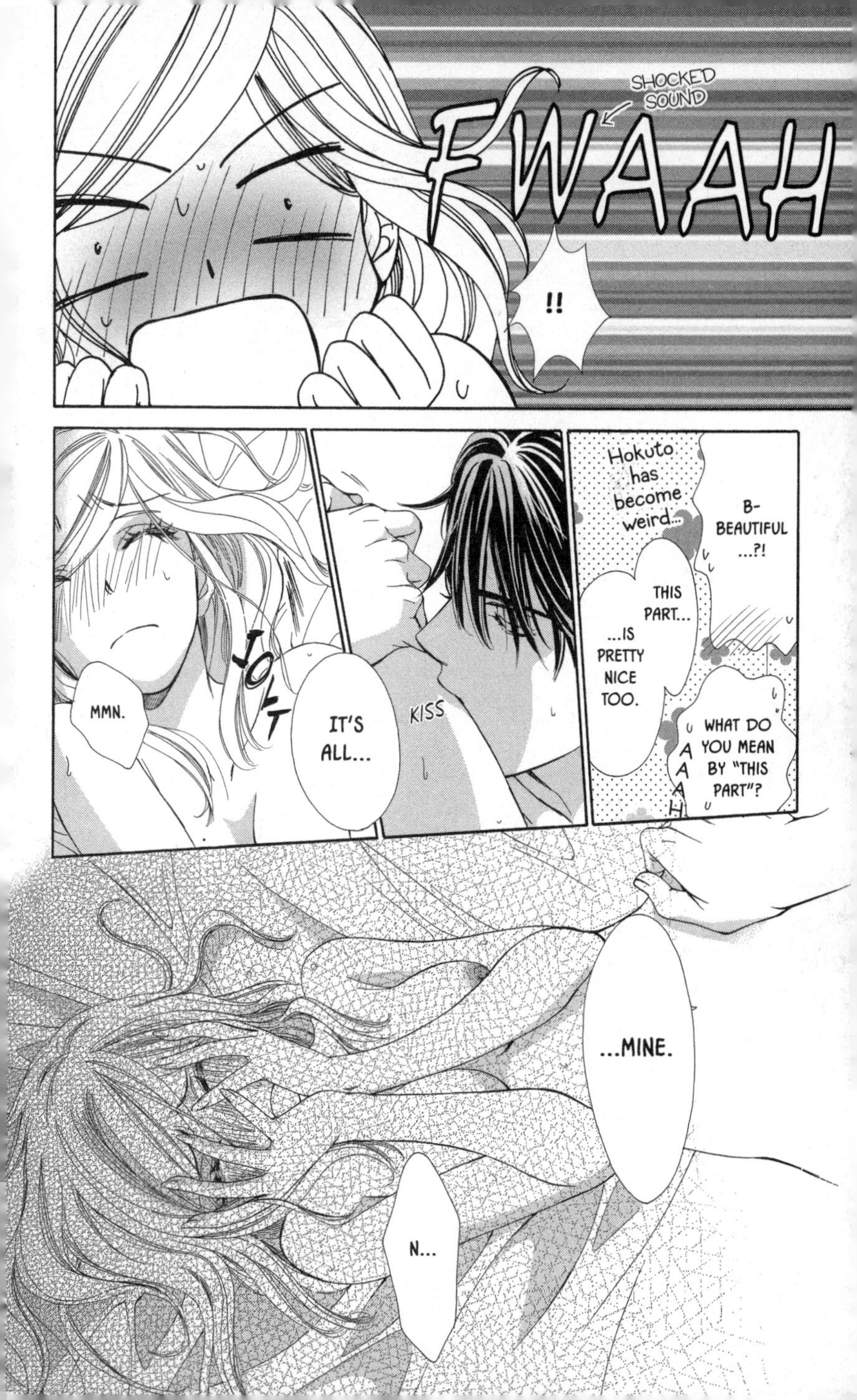
SHOCKED SOUND
FWAAH
!!
B-BEAUTIFUL ...?!
Hokuto has become weird...
THIS PART...
...IS PRETTY NICE TOO.
WHAT DO YOU MEAN BY "THIS PART"?
AAAH
KISS
IT'S ALL...
JOLT
MMN.
...MINE.
N...

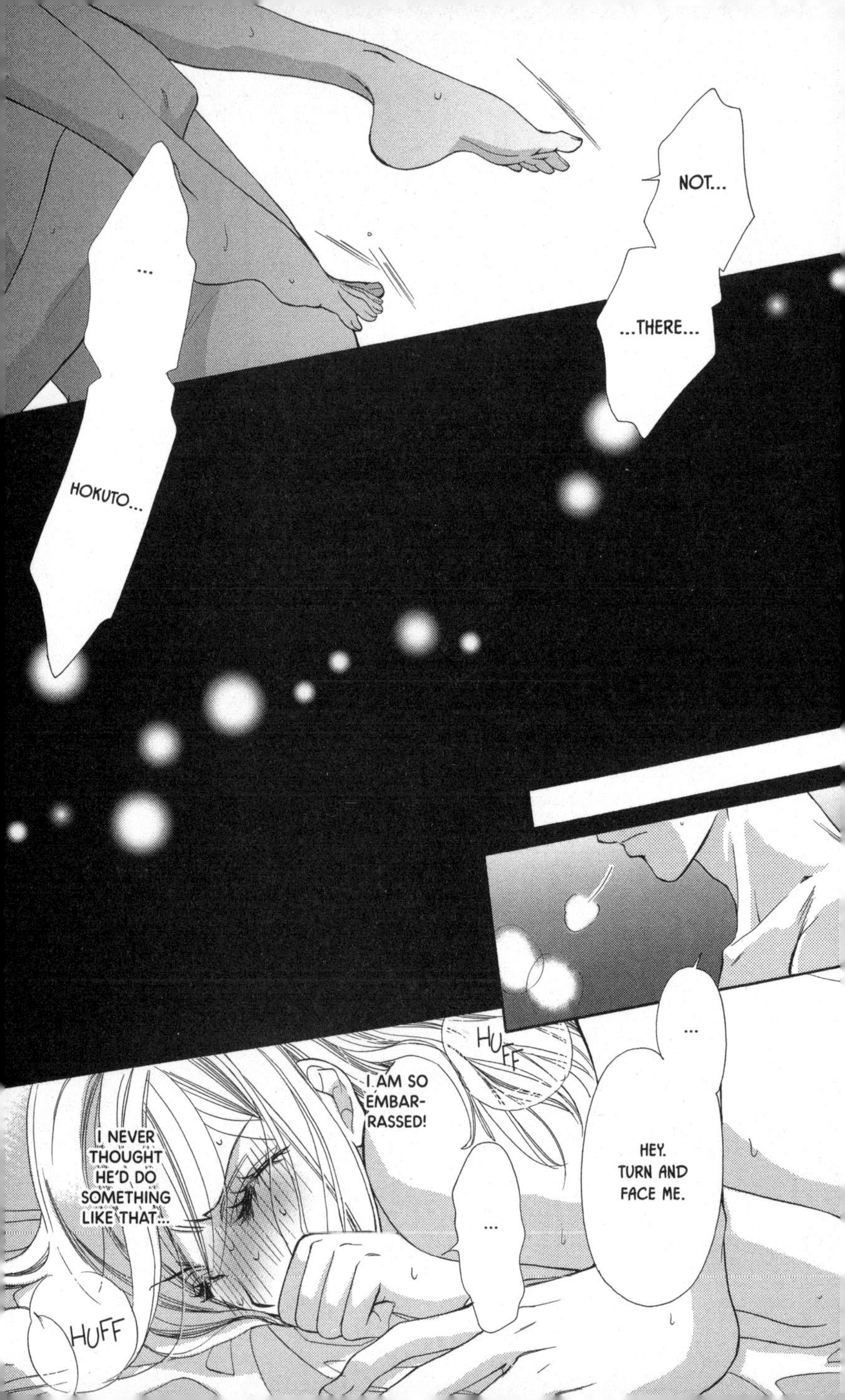

NOT...
...THERE...
...
HOKUTO...
...
HUFF
HEY. TURN AND FACE ME.
I AM SO EMBARRASSED!
...
I NEVER THOUGHT HE'D DO SOMETHING LIKE THAT...
HUFF

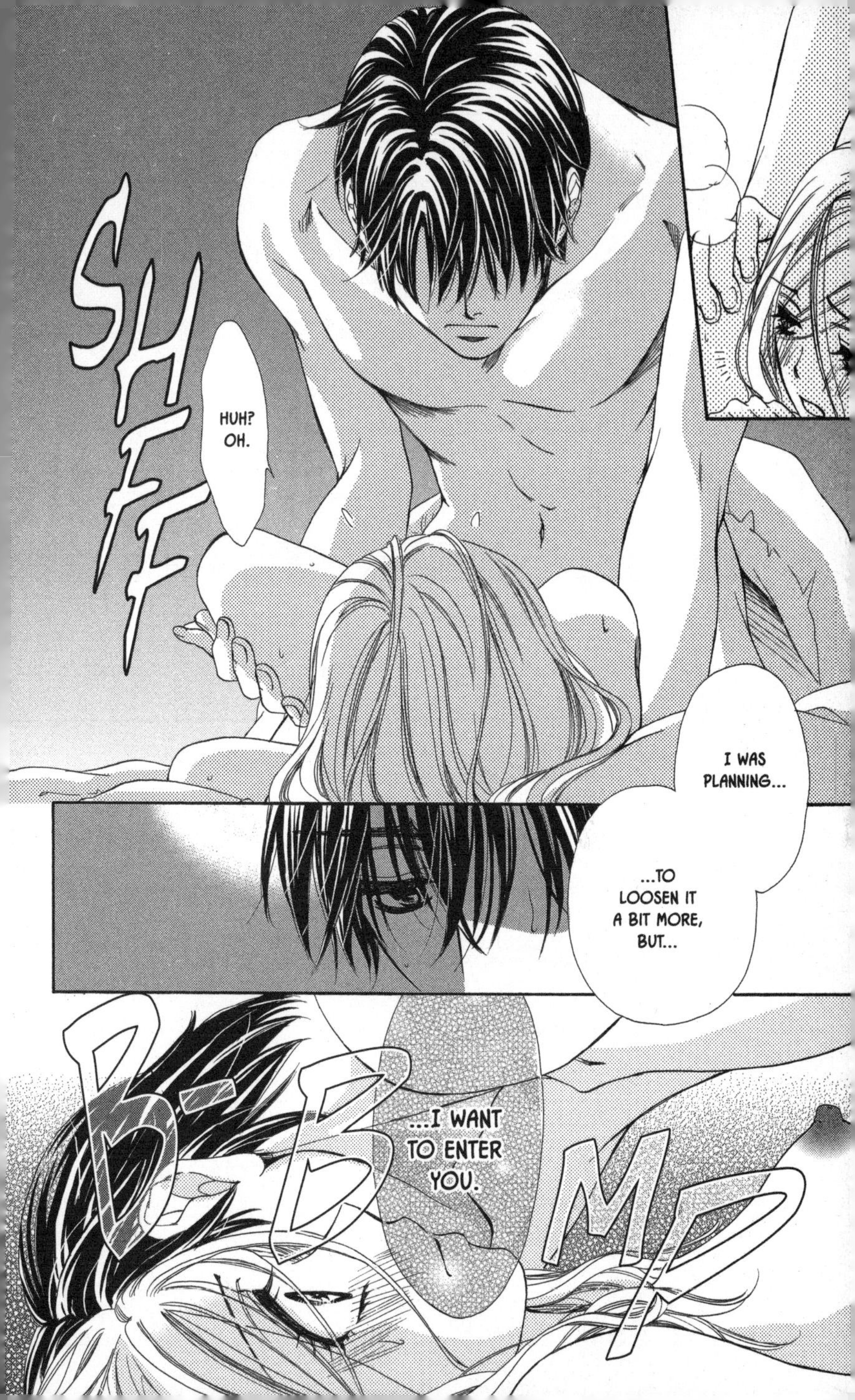
HUH? OH.
SHFF
I WAS PLANNING...
...TO LOOSEN IT A BIT MORE, BUT...
...I WANT TO ENTER YOU.
B-BMP

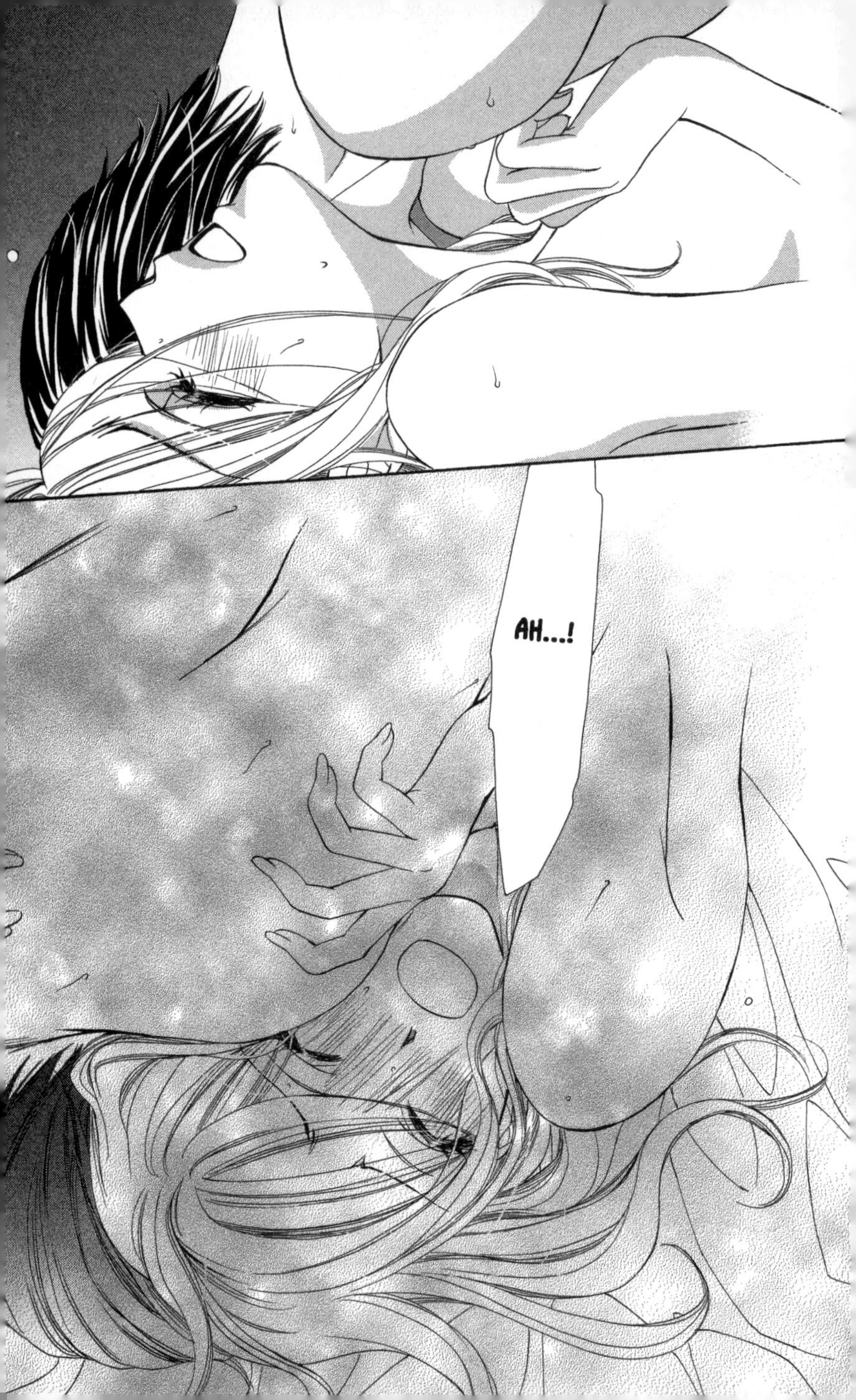
AH...!

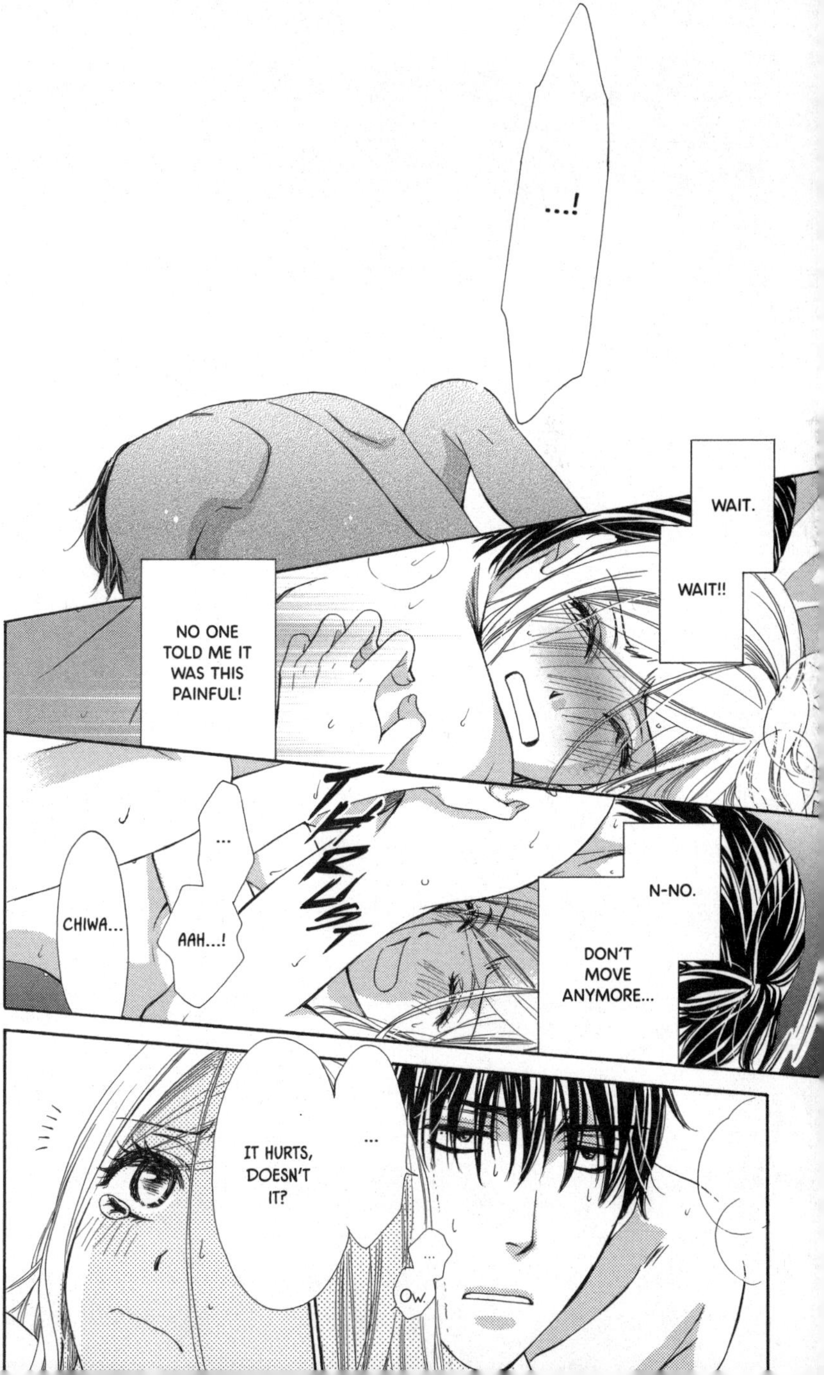
...!
WAIT.
WAIT!!
NO ONE TOLD ME IT WAS THIS PAINFUL!
N-NO.
DON'T MOVE ANYMORE...
THRUST
...
AAH...!
CHIWA...
...
Ow.
...
IT HURTS, DOESN'T IT?

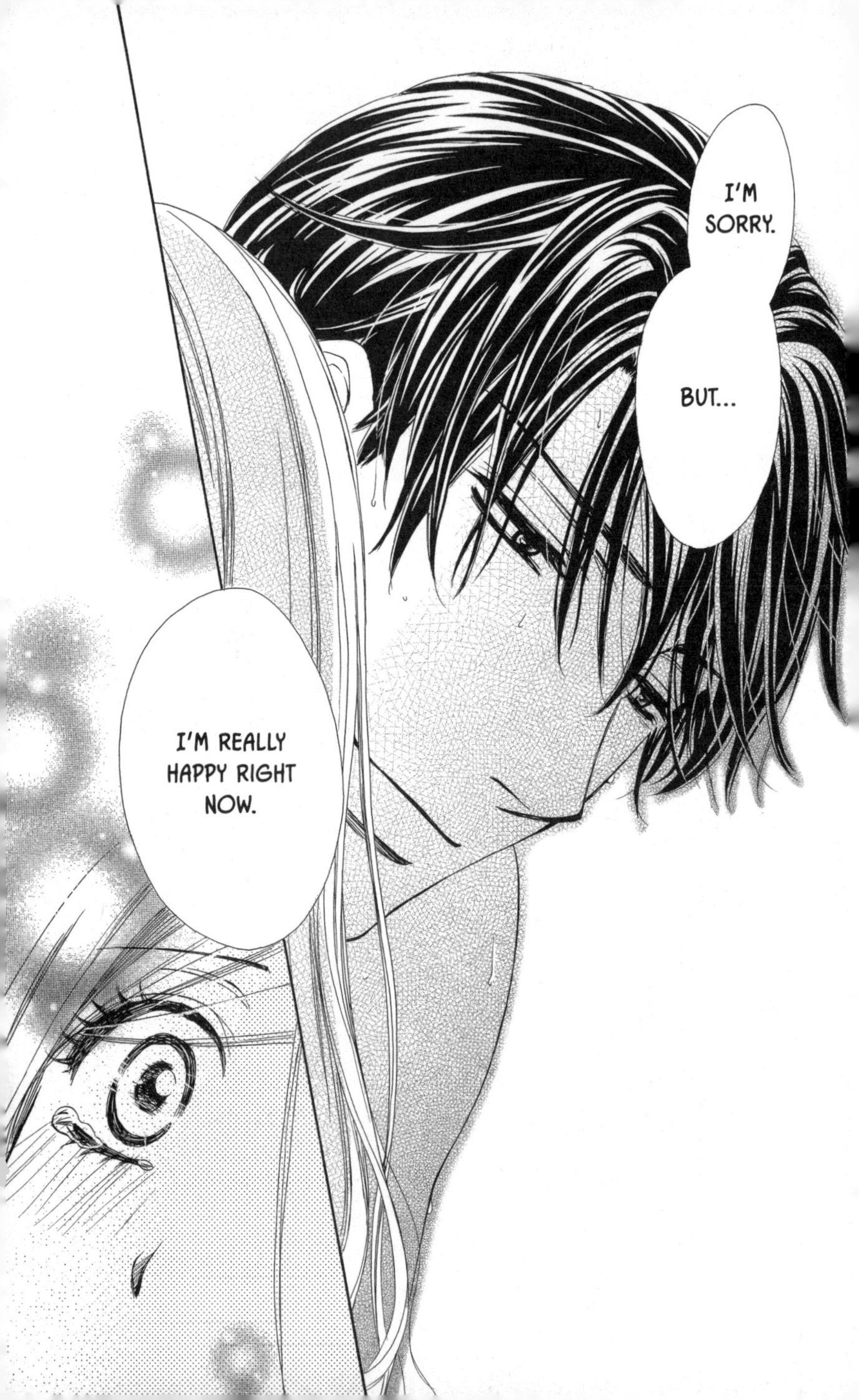
I'M SORRY.
BUT...
I'M REALLY HAPPY RIGHT NOW.

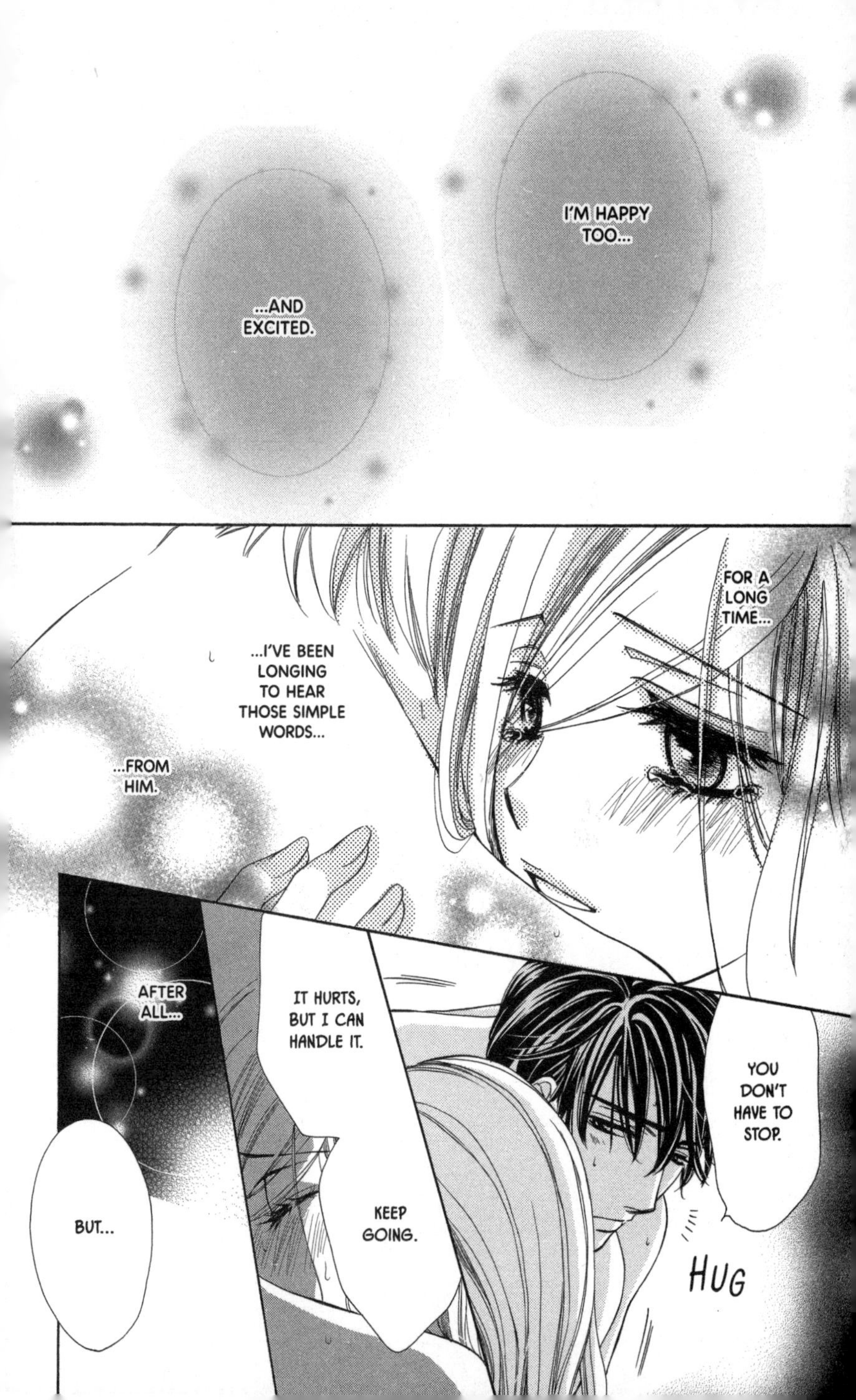
I'M HAPPY TOO...
...AND EXCITED.
FOR A LONG TIME...
...I'VE BEEN LONGING TO HEAR THOSE SIMPLE WORDS...
...FROM HIM.
YOU DON'T HAVE TO STOP.
HUG
IT HURTS, BUT I CAN HANDLE IT.
KEEP GOING.
AFTER ALL...
BUT...

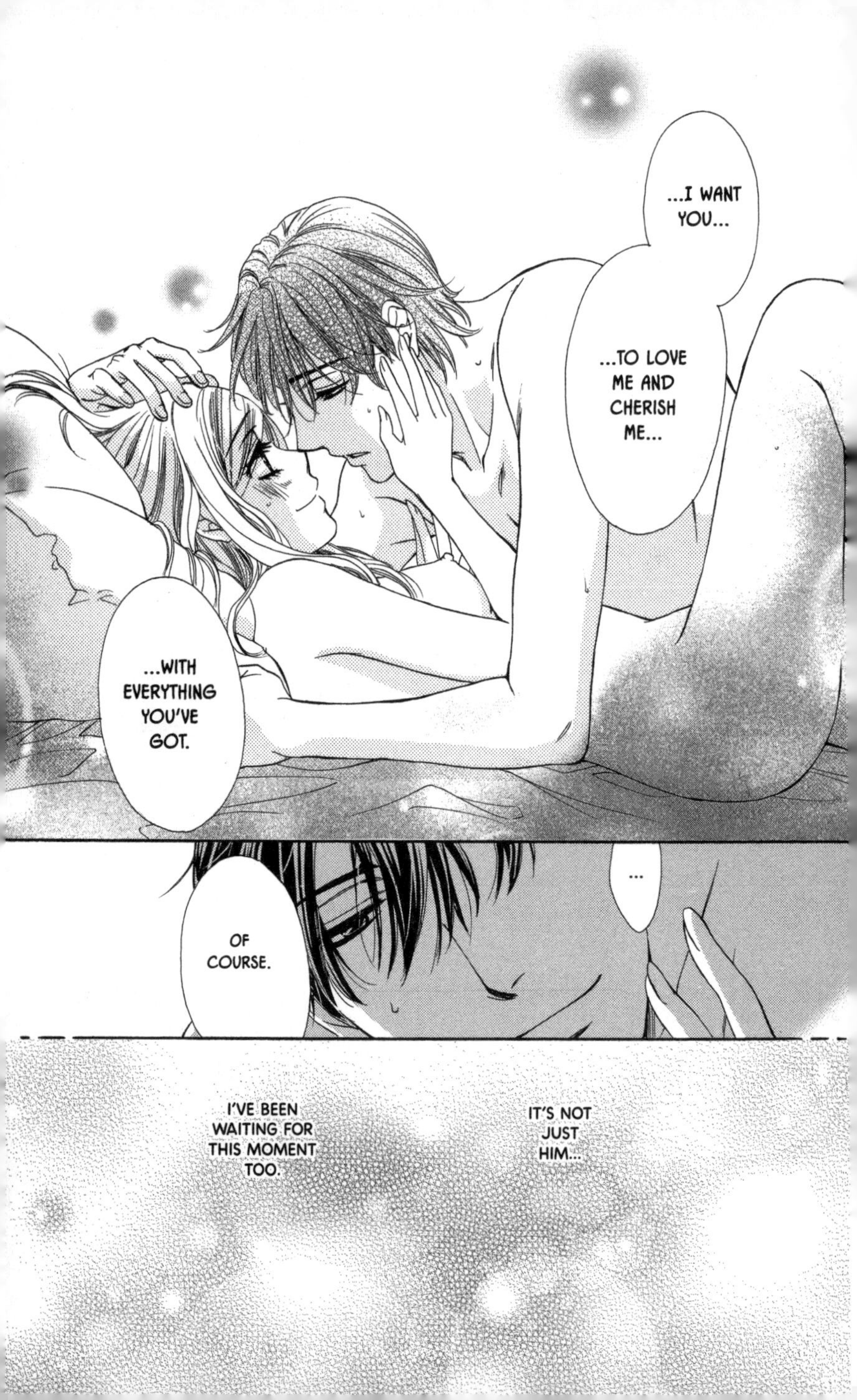
...I WANT YOU...
...TO LOVE ME AND CHERISH ME...
...WITH EVERYTHING YOU'VE GOT.
...
OF COURSE.
IT'S NOT JUST HIM...
I'VE BEEN WAITING FOR THIS MOMENT TOO.

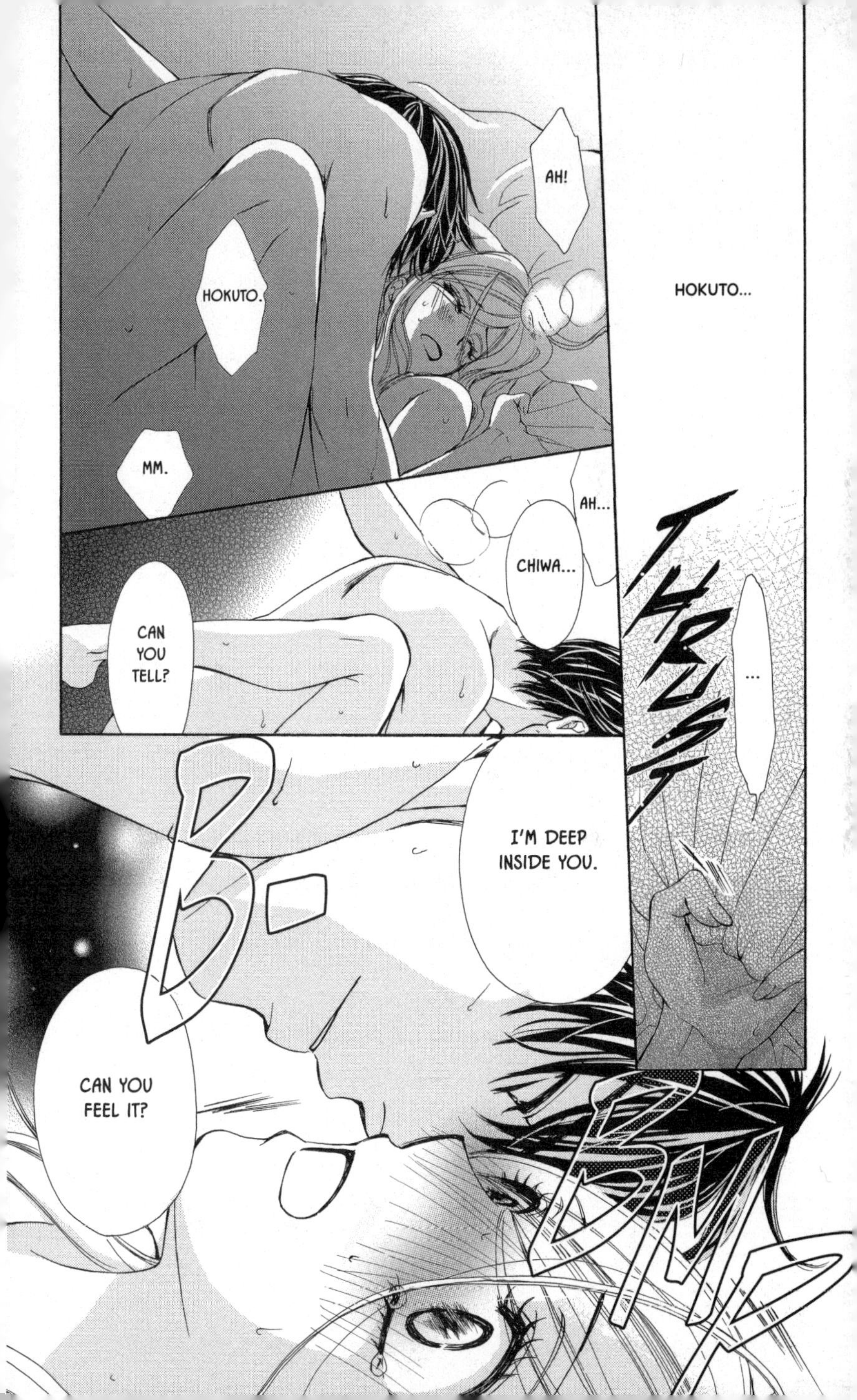
HOKUTO...
THRUST
...
AH!
HOKUTO.
MM.
AH...
CHIWA...
CAN YOU TELL?
I'M DEEP INSIDE YOU.
BMP
B-
CAN YOU FEEL IT?

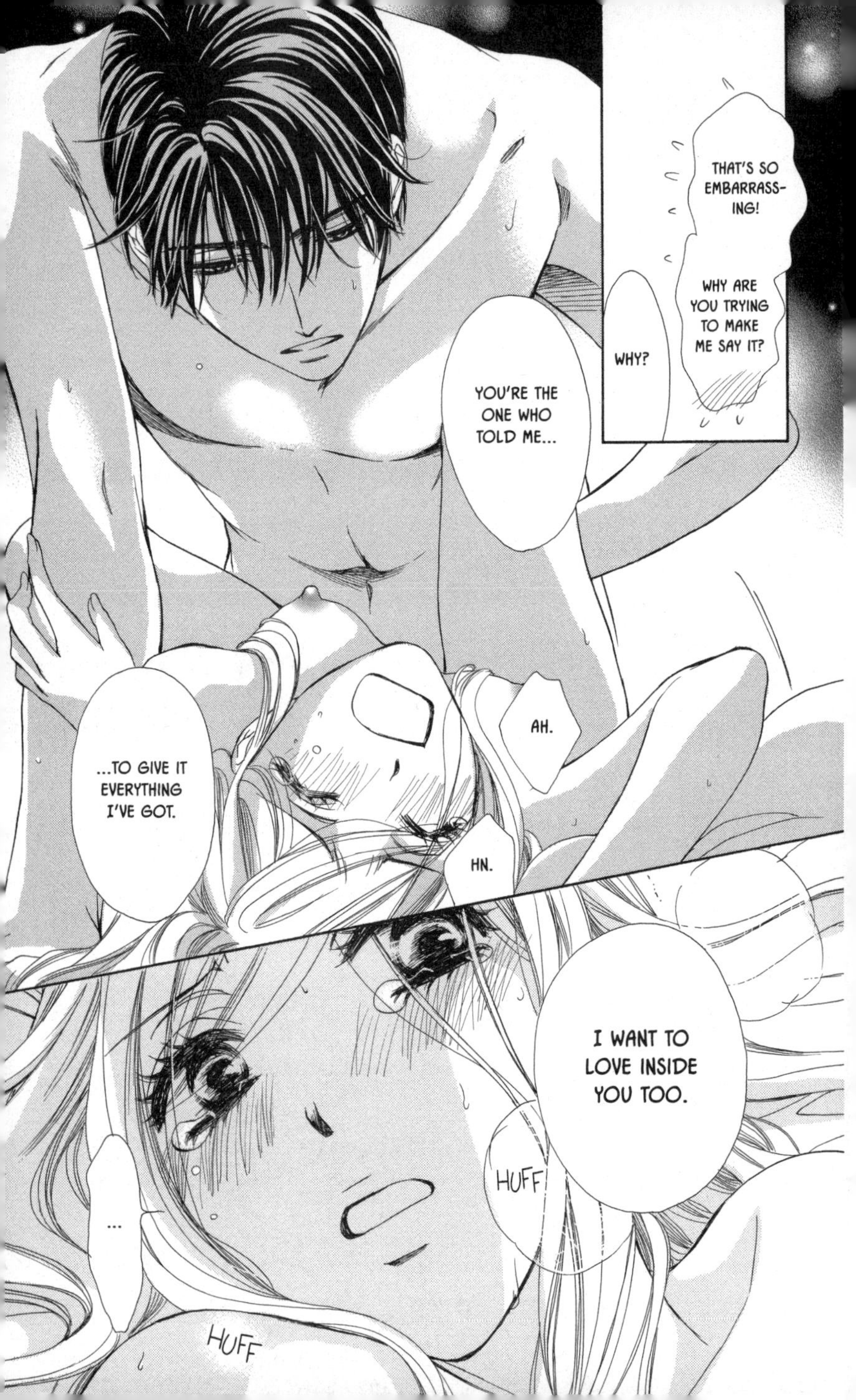
THAT'S SO EMBARRASS-ING!
WHY ARE YOU TRYING TO MAKE ME SAY IT?
WHY?
YOU'RE THE ONE WHO TOLD ME...
AH.
...TO GIVE IT EVERYTHING I'VE GOT.
HN.
I WANT TO LOVE INSIDE YOU TOO.
HUFF
...
HUFF

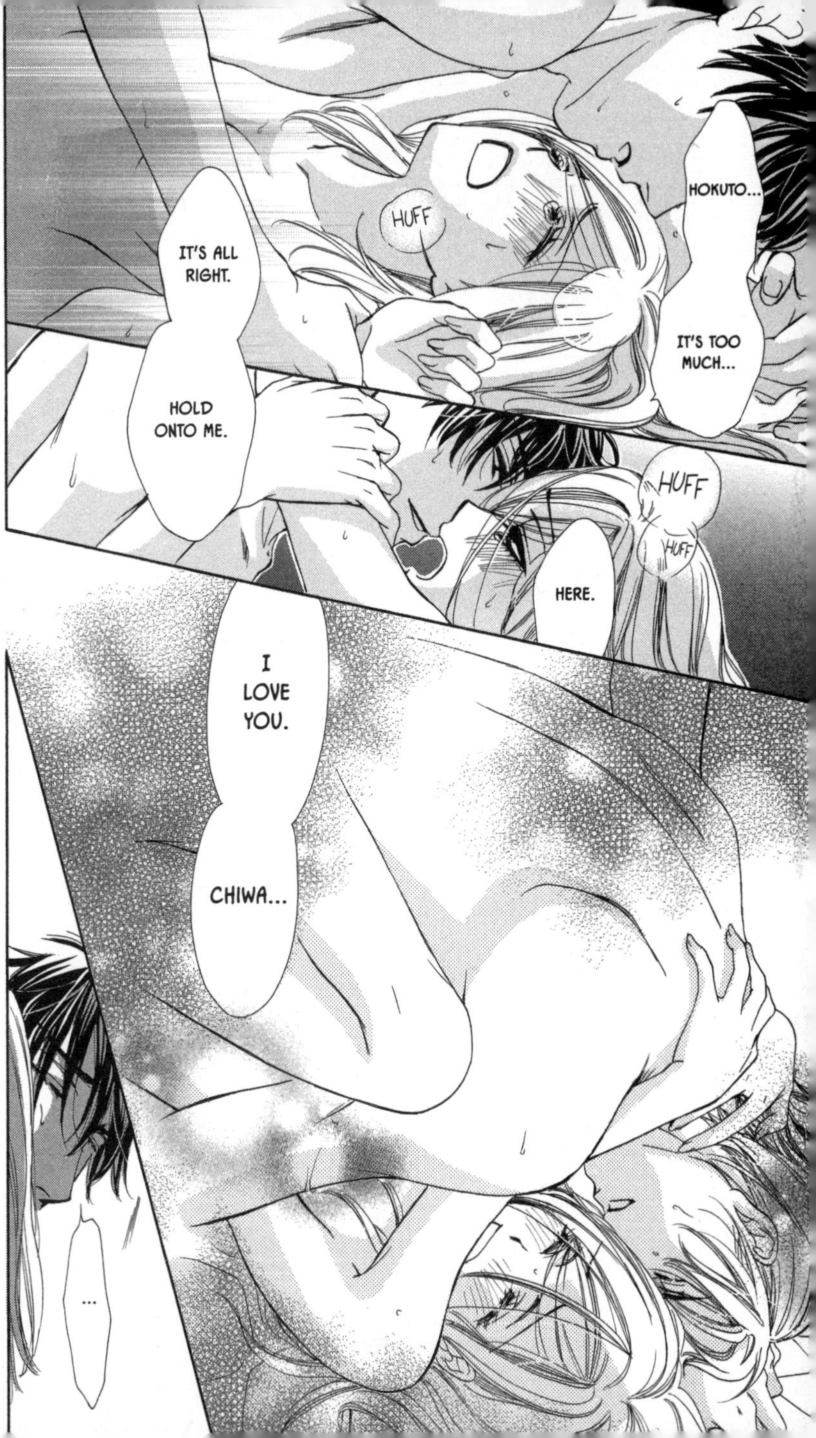
HOKUTO...
HUFF
IT'S TOO MUCH...
IT'S ALL RIGHT.
HUFF
HUFF
HOLD ONTO ME.
HERE.
I LOVE YOU.
CHIWA...
...

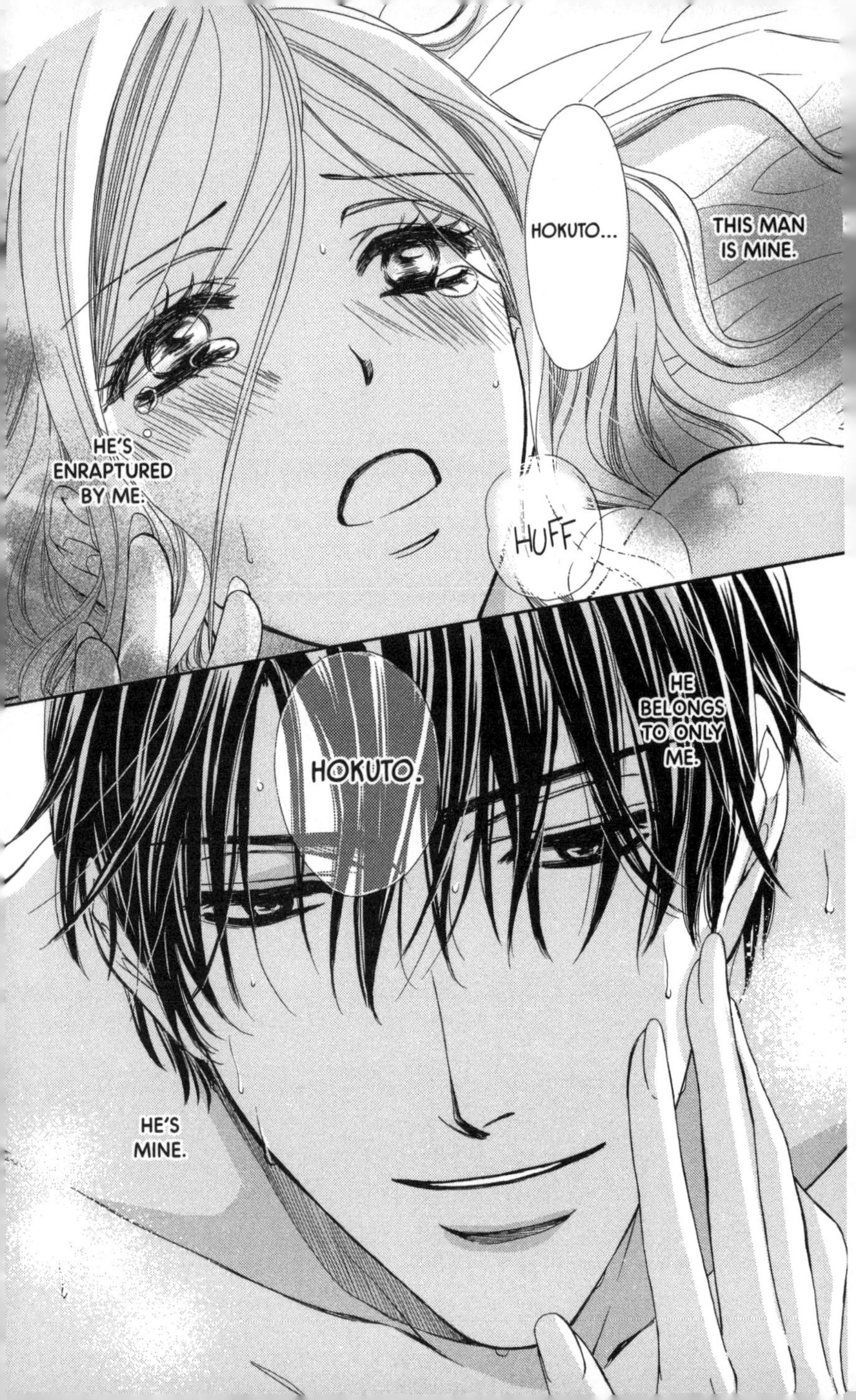
THIS MAN IS MINE.
HOKUTO...
HUFF
HE'S ENRAPTURED BY ME.
HE BELONGS TO ONLY ME.
HOKUTO.
HE'S MINE.

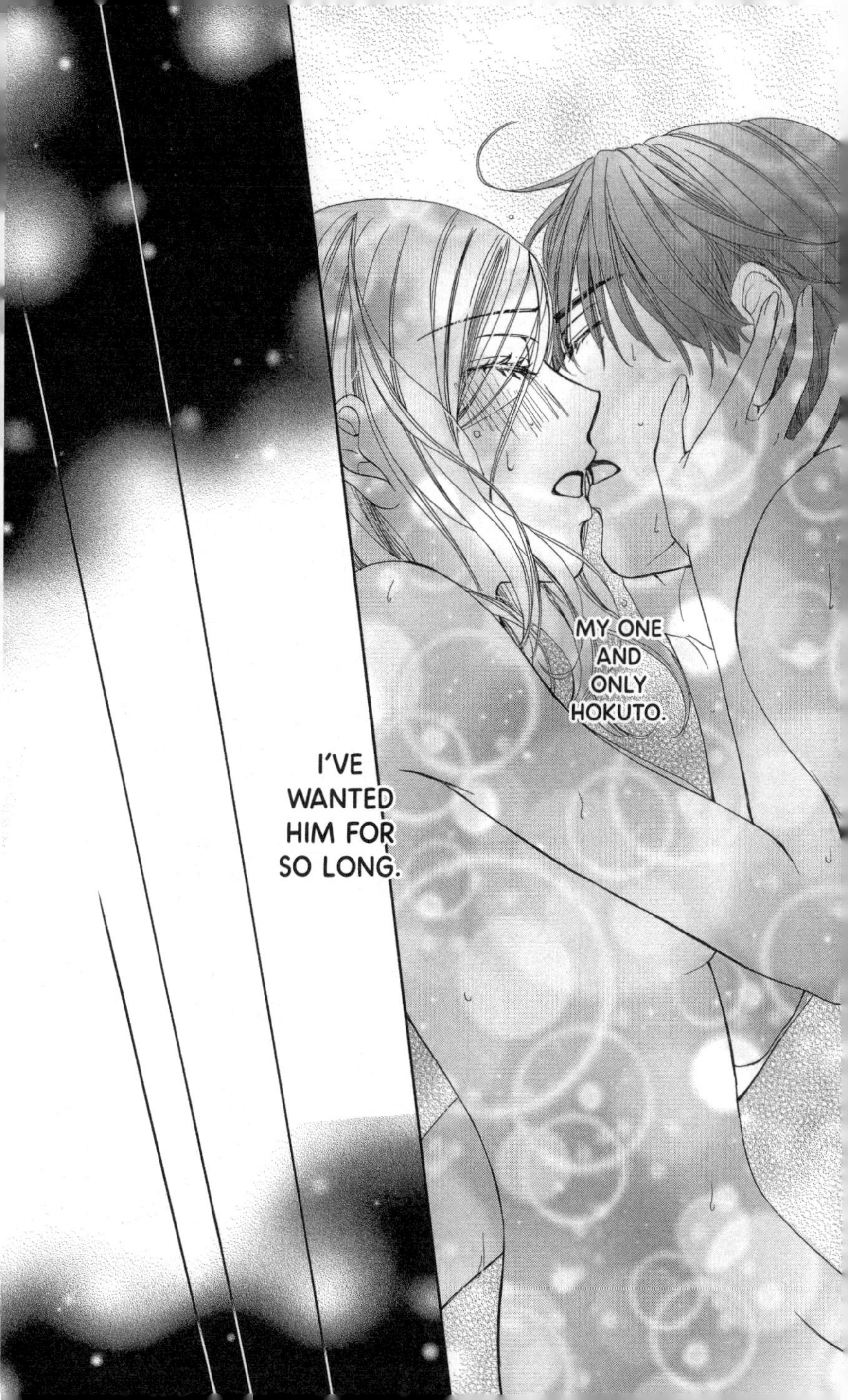
MY ONE AND ONLY HOKUTO.
I'VE WANTED HIM FOR SO LONG.

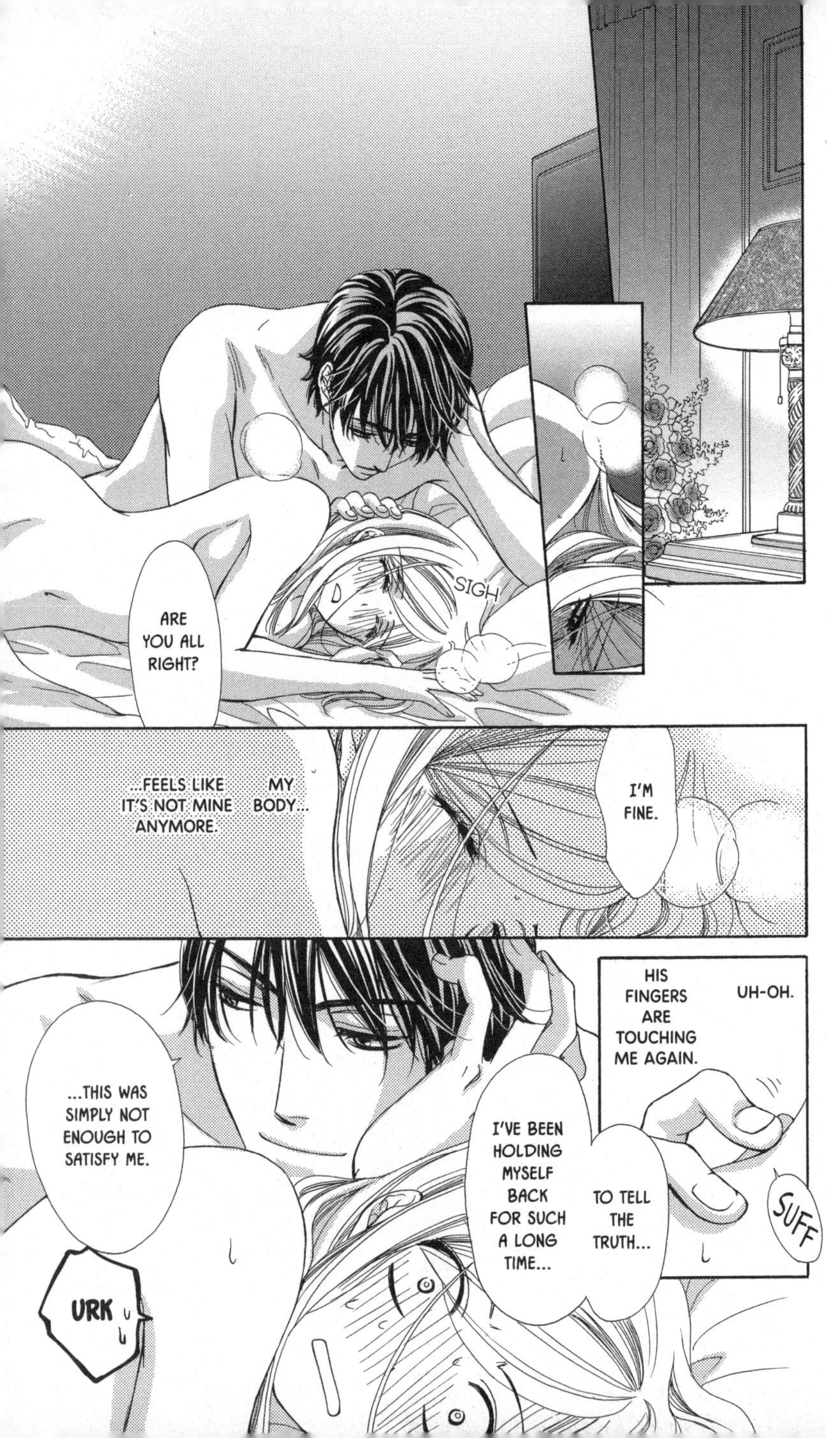
SIGH
ARE YOU ALL RIGHT?
I'M FINE.
MY BODY...
...FEELS LIKE IT'S NOT MINE ANYMORE.
UH-OH.
HIS FINGERS ARE TOUCHING ME AGAIN.
SUFF
TO TELL THE TRUTH...
I'VE BEEN HOLDING MYSELF BACK FOR SUCH A LONG TIME...
...THIS WAS SIMPLY NOT ENOUGH TO SATISFY ME.
URK

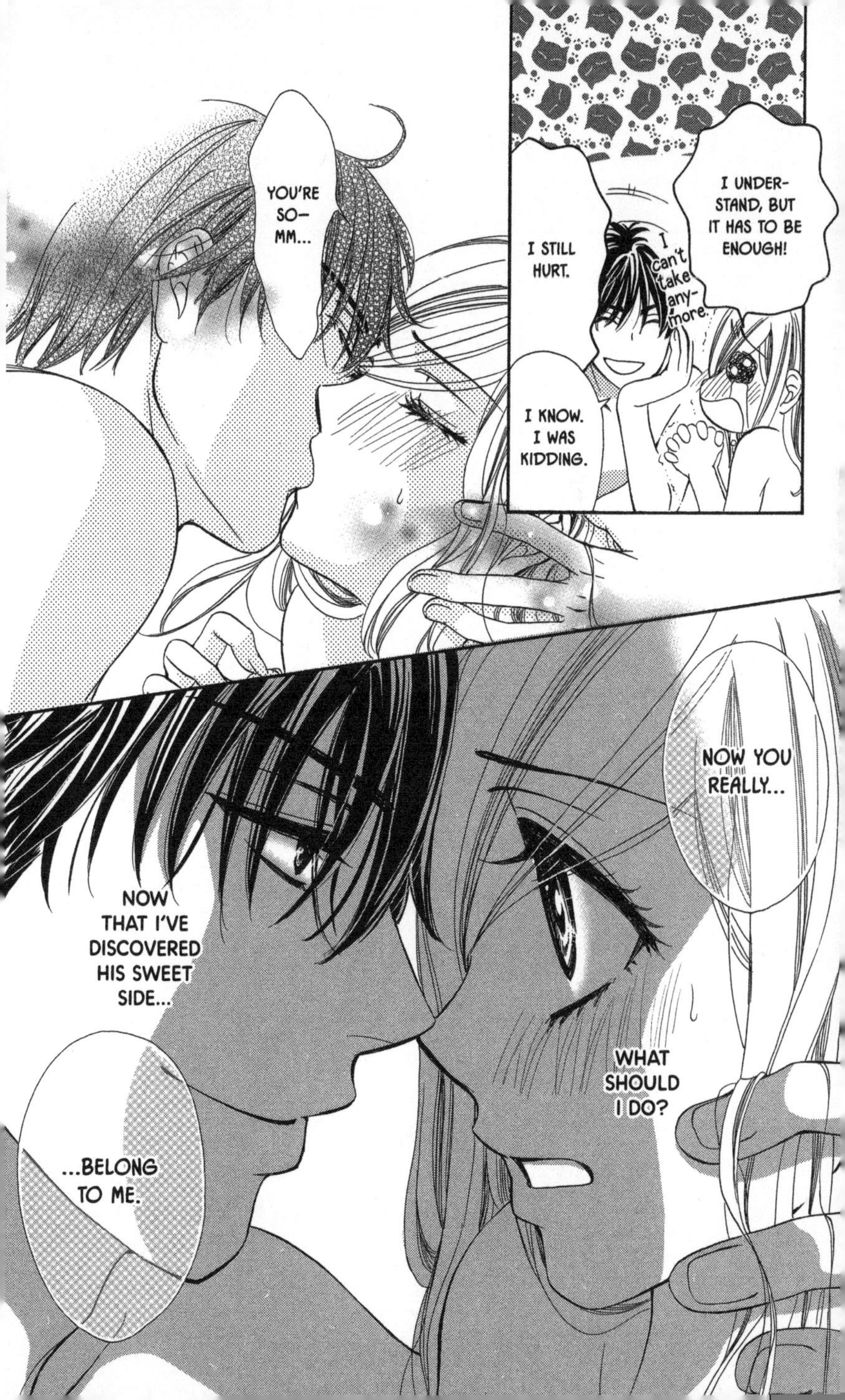
I UNDER-
STAND, BUT
IT HAS TO BE
ENOUGH!
I can't take any-more.
I STILL HURT.
I KNOW. I WAS KIDDING.
YOU'RE SO— MM...
NOW YOU REALLY...
NOW THAT I'VE DISCOVERED HIS SWEET SIDE...
WHAT SHOULD I DO?
...BELONG TO ME.

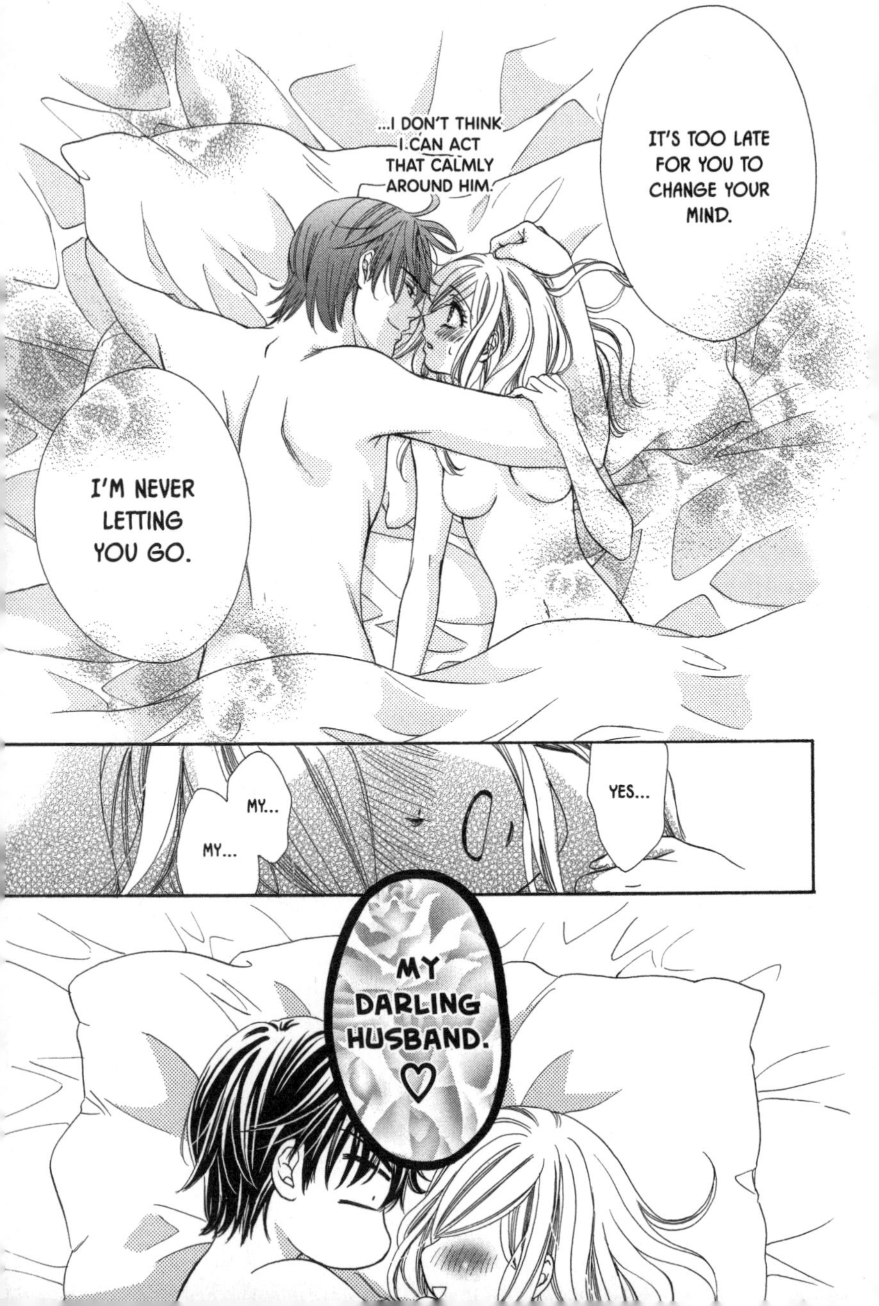
IT'S TOO LATE FOR YOU TO CHANGE YOUR MIND.
...I DON'T THINK I CAN ACT THAT CALMLY AROUND HIM.
I'M NEVER LETTING YOU GO.
YES...
MY...
MY...
MY DARLING HUSBAND. ♡

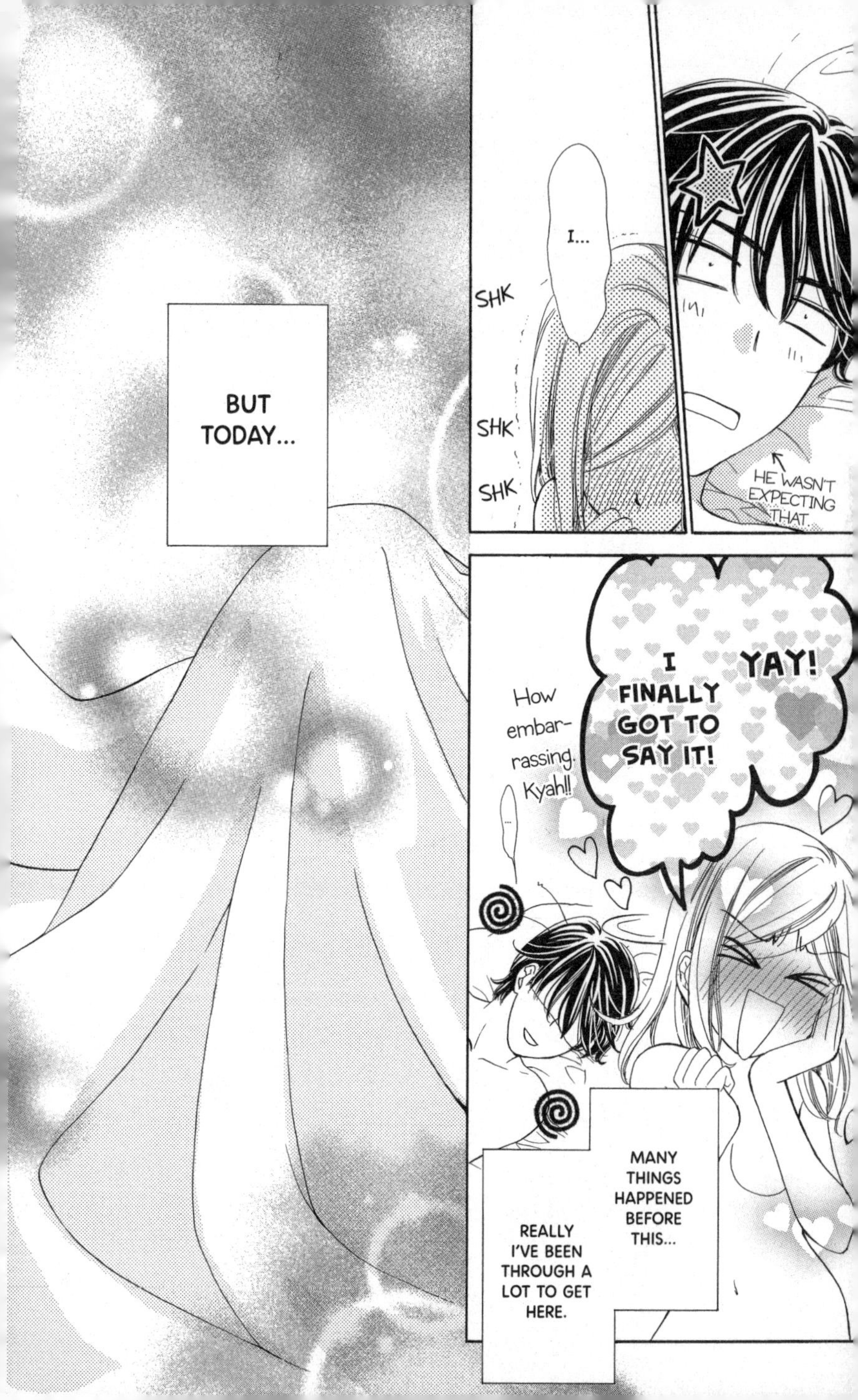
HE WASN'T EXPECTING THAT.
I...
SHK
SHK
SHK
YAY! I FINALLY GOT TO SAY IT!
How embarrassing. Kyah!!
...
MANY THINGS HAPPENED BEFORE THIS...
REALLY I'VE BEEN THROUGH A LOT TO GET HERE.
BUT TODAY...

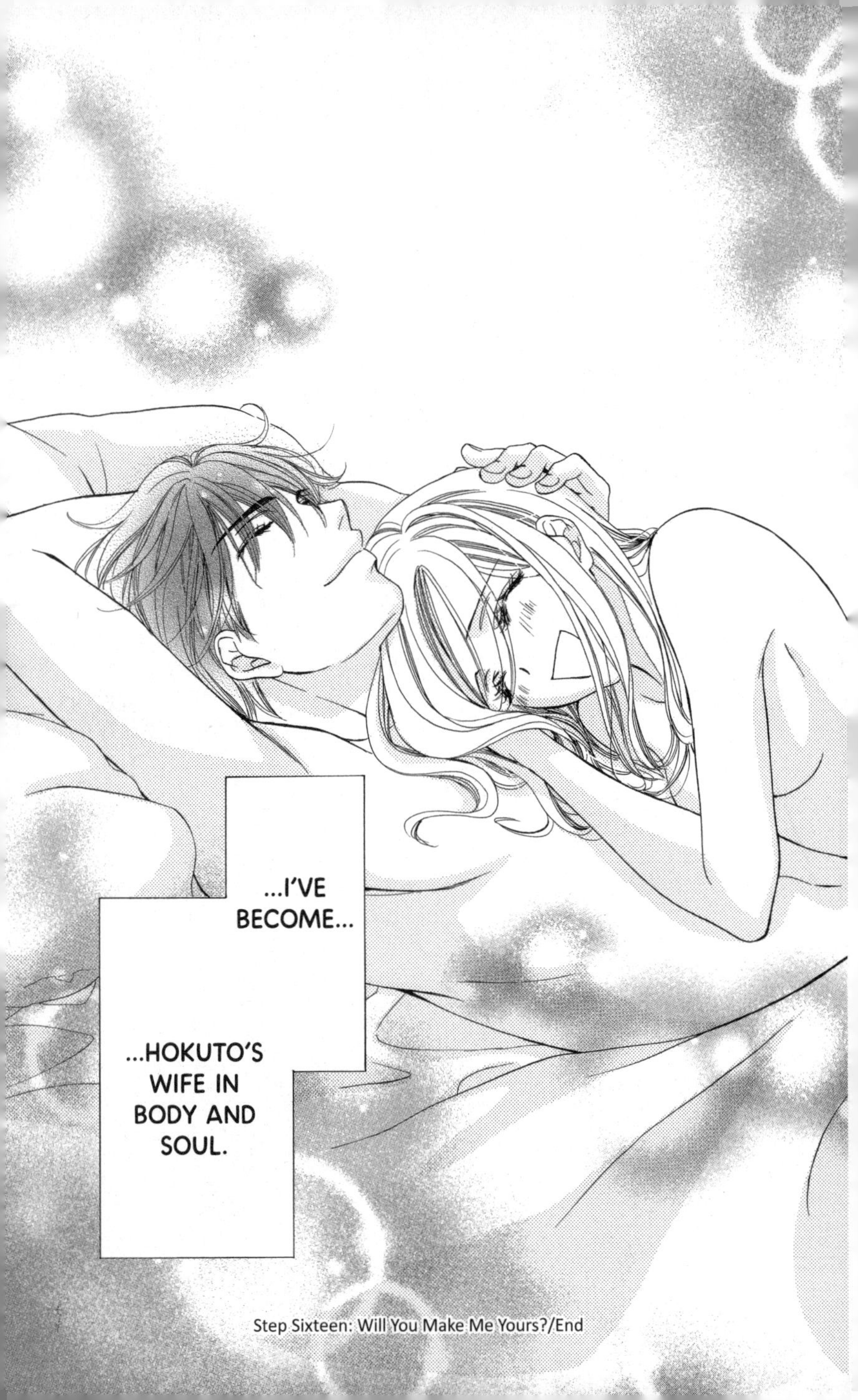
...I'VE BECOME...
...HOKUTO'S WIFE IN BODY AND SOUL.
Step Sixteen: Will You Make Me Yours?/End

Special Thanks

Assistants

K. Sano
E. Shimojo
Y. Michishita
N. Hori

Editor

M. Okada

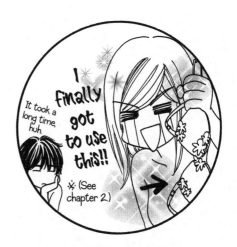

I finally got to use this!!
※ (See chapter 2.)
It took a long time, huh.

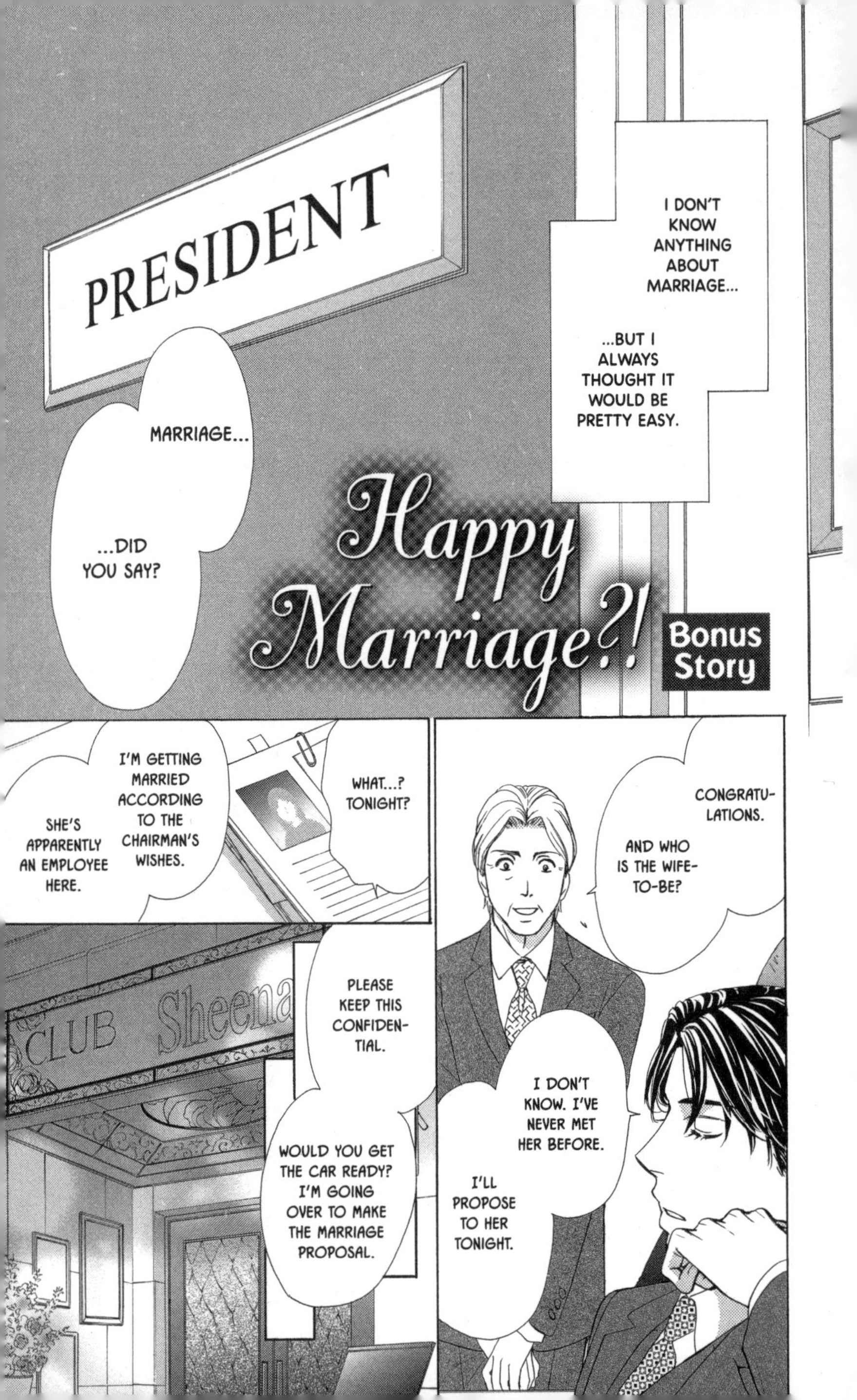
I DON'T KNOW ANYTHING ABOUT MARRIAGE...
...BUT I ALWAYS THOUGHT IT WOULD BE PRETTY EASY.
Happy Marriage?!
Bonus Story
PRESIDENT
MARRIAGE... ...DID YOU SAY?
CONGRATULATIONS.
AND WHO IS THE WIFE-TO-BE?
I DON'T KNOW. I'VE NEVER MET HER BEFORE.
I'LL PROPOSE TO HER TONIGHT.
WHAT...? TONIGHT?
I'M GETTING MARRIED ACCORDING TO THE CHAIRMAN'S WISHES.
SHE'S APPARENTLY AN EMPLOYEE HERE.
PLEASE KEEP THIS CONFIDENTIAL.
WOULD YOU GET THE CAR READY? I'M GOING OVER TO MAKE THE MARRIAGE PROPOSAL.
CLUB Sheena

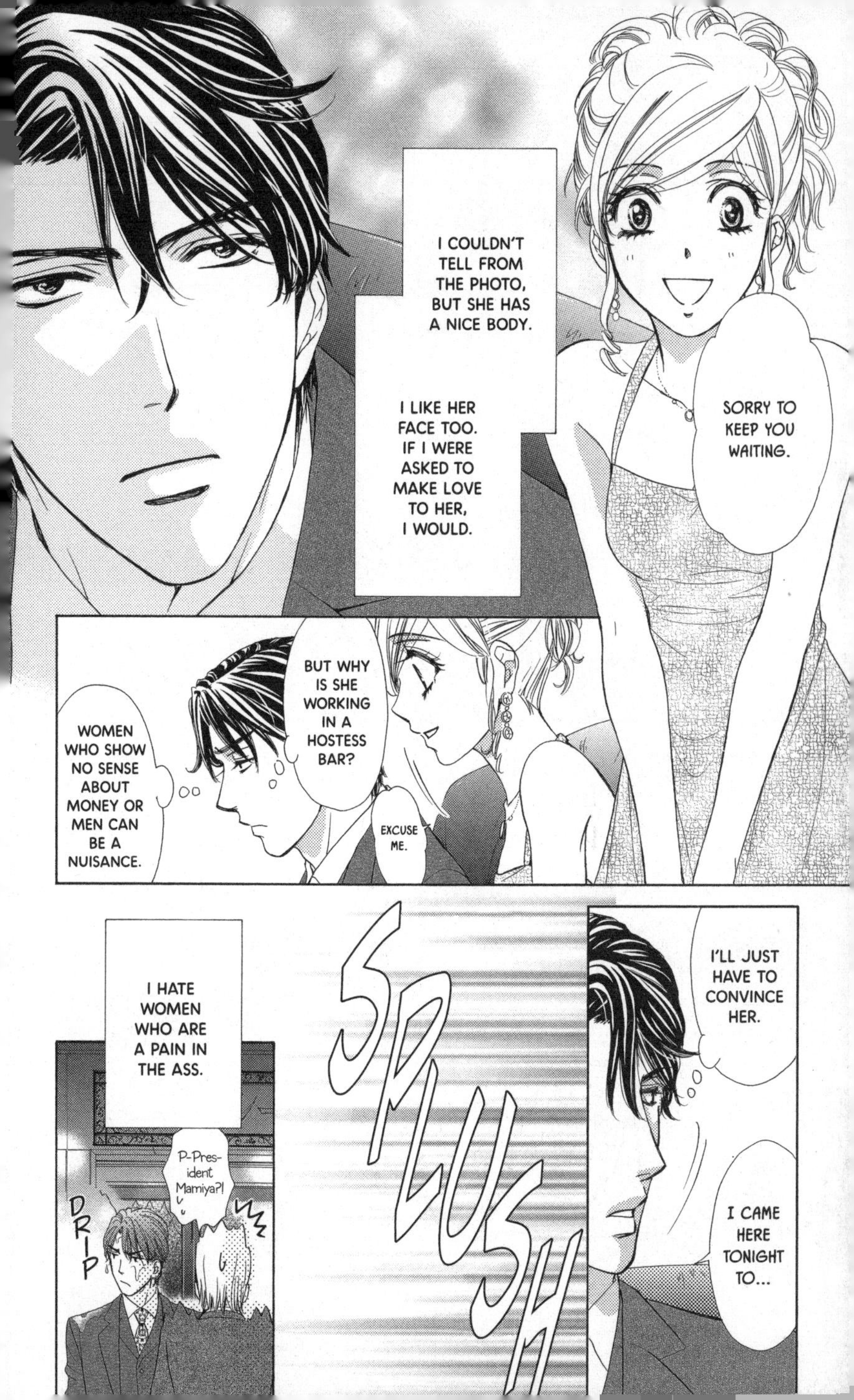
SORRY TO KEEP YOU WAITING.
I COULDN'T TELL FROM THE PHOTO, BUT SHE HAS A NICE BODY.
I LIKE HER FACE TOO. IF I WERE ASKED TO MAKE LOVE TO HER, I WOULD.
BUT WHY IS SHE WORKING IN A HOSTESS BAR?
EXCUSE ME.
WOMEN WHO SHOW NO SENSE ABOUT MONEY OR MEN CAN BE A NUISANCE.
I'LL JUST HAVE TO CONVINCE HER.
I CAME HERE TONIGHT TO...
SPLUSH
I HATE WOMEN WHO ARE A PAIN IN THE ASS.
P-President Mamiya?!
DRIP

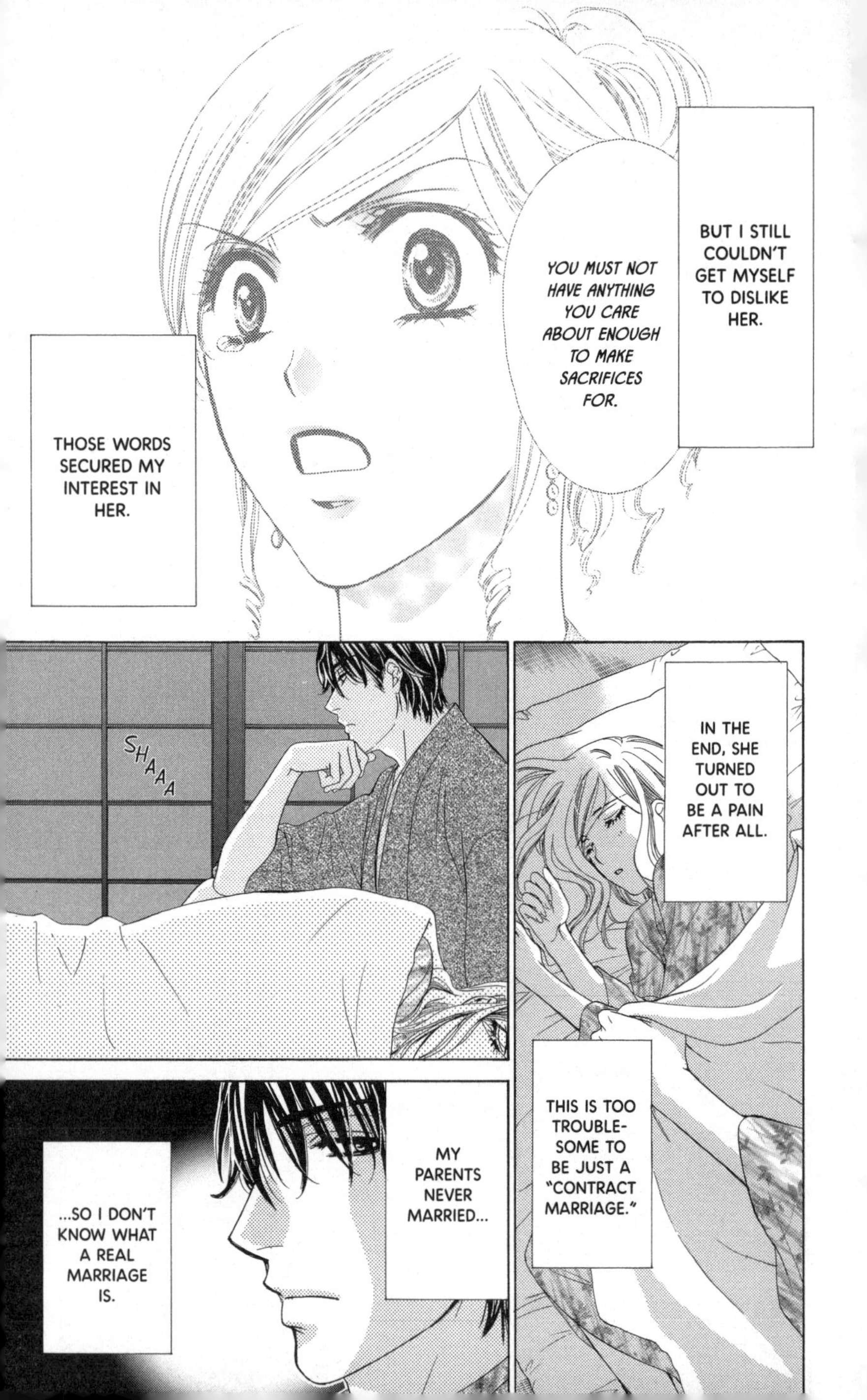
BUT I STILL COULDN'T GET MYSELF TO DISLIKE HER.
YOU MUST NOT HAVE ANYTHING YOU CARE ABOUT ENOUGH TO MAKE SACRIFICES FOR.
THOSE WORDS SECURED MY INTEREST IN HER.
IN THE END, SHE TURNED OUT TO BE A PAIN AFTER ALL.
THIS IS TOO TROUBLE-SOME TO BE JUST A "CONTRACT MARRIAGE."
SHAAA
MY PARENTS NEVER MARRIED...
...SO I DON'T KNOW WHAT A REAL MARRIAGE IS.

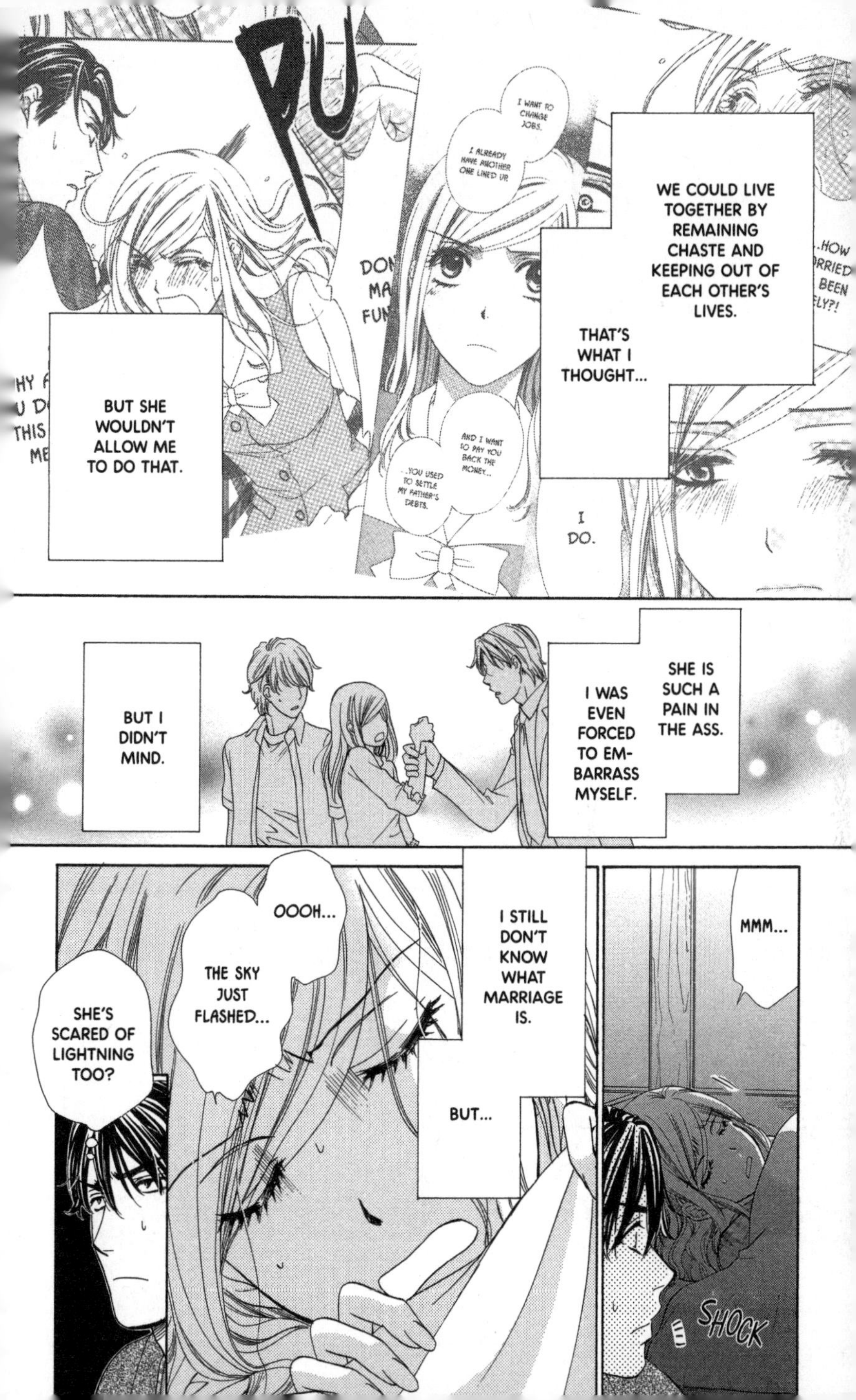

WE COULD LIVE TOGETHER BY REMAINING CHASTE AND KEEPING OUT OF EACH OTHER'S LIVES.
THAT'S WHAT I THOUGHT...
I DO.
I WANT TO CHANGE JOBS.
I ALREADY HAVE ANOTHER ONE LINED UP.
AND I WANT TO PAY YOU BACK THE MONEY...
...YOU USED TO SETTLE MY FATHER'S DEBTS.
PU
BUT SHE WOULDN'T ALLOW ME TO DO THAT.
SHE IS SUCH A PAIN IN THE ASS.
I WAS EVEN FORCED TO EM-BARRASS MYSELF.
BUT I DIDN'T MIND.
MMM...
SHOCK
I STILL DON'T KNOW WHAT MARRIAGE IS.
BUT...
OOOH...
THE SKY JUST FLASHED...
SHE'S SCARED OF LIGHTNING TOO?

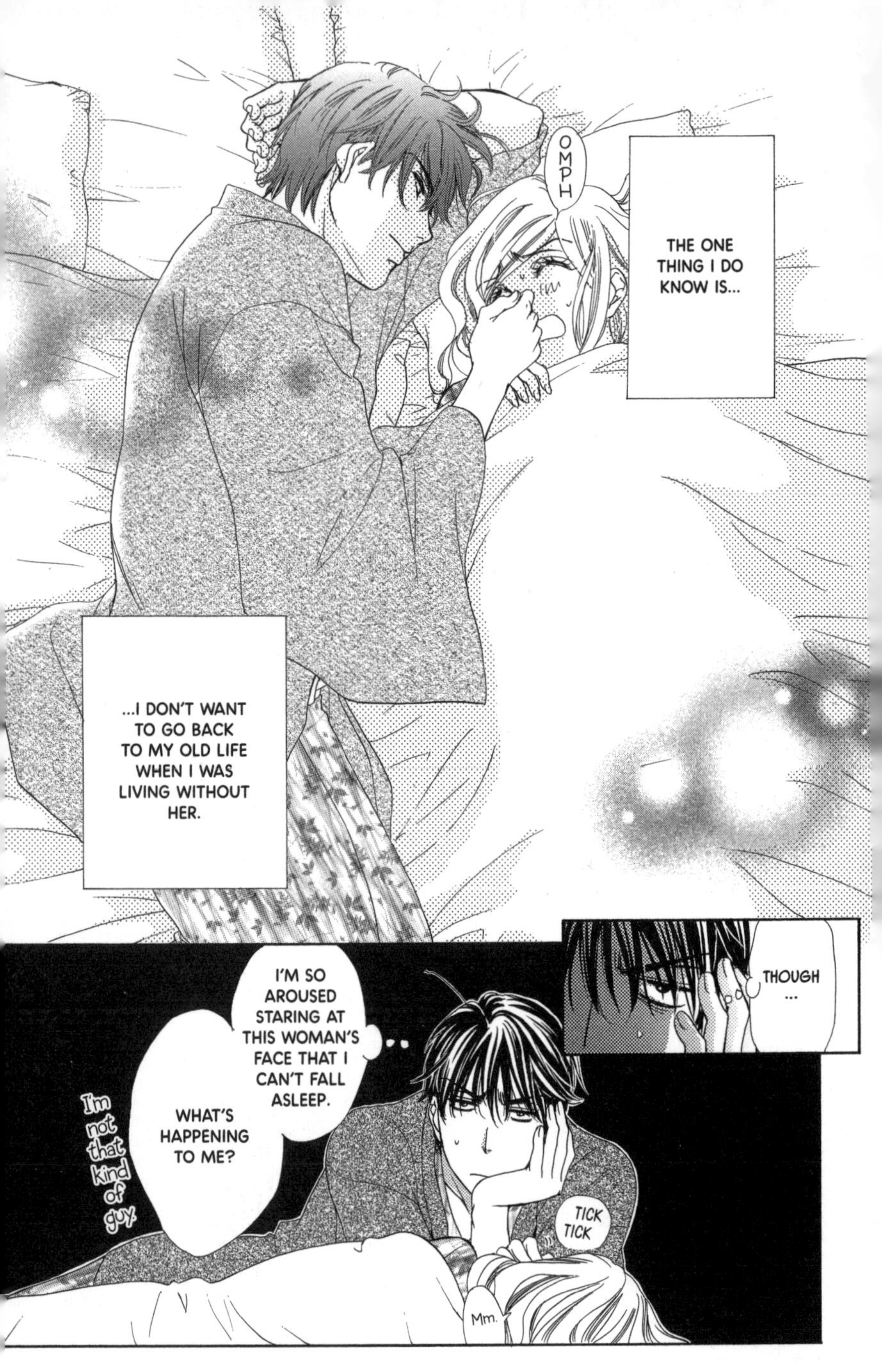
THE ONE THING I DO KNOW IS...
OMPH
...I DON'T WANT TO GO BACK TO MY OLD LIFE WHEN I WAS LIVING WITHOUT HER.
THOUGH ...
I'M SO AROUSED STARING AT THIS WOMAN'S FACE THAT I CAN'T FALL ASLEEP.
WHAT'S HAPPENING TO ME?
I'm not that kind of guy.
TICK TICK
Mm.

Bonus Story/End

A GIRL'S DREAM

A blog, an illustration blog, Twitter...
I've started all sorts of accounts, but I
don't last more than three days. (I don't
have anything to write about...). I have
kept doing that you-know-what SNS for
six years now. But recently, all I do is
plant vegetables on a farm, breed animals
and drop by other people's farms to do
mischief... Does this mean I'm socially
withdrawn even on the internet?

–Maki Enjoji

Maki Enjoji was born on December 8 in
Tokyo. She made her debut with *Fu•Junai*
(Wicked Pure Love). She currently works
with *Petit Comics*. *Happy Marriage?!* is her
fourth series.